Springer Proceedings in Business and Economics

Springer Proceedings in Business and Economics brings the most current research presented at conferences and workshops to a global readership. The series features volumes (in electronic and print formats) of selected contributions from conferences in all areas of economics, business, management, and finance. In addition to an overall evaluation by the publisher of the topical interest, scientific quality, and timeliness of each volume, each contribution is refereed to standards comparable to those of leading journals, resulting in authoritative contributions to the respective fields. Springer's production and distribution infrastructure ensures rapid publication and wide circulation of the latest developments in the most compelling and promising areas of research today.

The editorial development of volumes may be managed using Springer Nature's innovative EquinOCS, a proven online conference proceedings submission, management and review system. This system is designed to ensure an efficient timeline for your publication, making Springer Proceedings in Business and Economics the premier series to publish your workshop or conference volume.

This book series is indexed in SCOPUS.

Ilona Bartuseviciene · Buracas Antanas ·
Anastasios Karasavvoglou ·
Persefoni Polychronidou
Editors

Building Resilience Through Digital Transformation and Sustainable Innovation

Proceedings of the 16th International Conference on the Economies of the Balkan and Eastern European Countries (EBEEC) in Vilnius, Lithuania, 2024

Springer

Editors
Ilona Bartuseviciene
Mykolas Romeris University
Vilnius, Lithuania

Buracas Antanas
Mykolas Romeris University
Vilnius, Lithuania

Anastasios Karasavvoglou
Democritus University of Thrace
Kavala, Greece

Persefoni Polychronidou
Economic Sciences Department
International Hellenic University
Serres, Greece

ISSN 2198-7246 ISSN 2198-7254 (electronic)
Springer Proceedings in Business and Economics
ISBN 978-3-031-90053-2 ISBN 978-3-031-90054-9 (eBook)
https://doi.org/10.1007/978-3-031-90054-9

This Springer imprint is published by the registered company Springer Nature Switzerland AG
The registered company address is: Gewerbestrasse 11, 6330 Cham, Switzerland

Preface

This book features a collection of papers that were presented at the 16th International Conference "Economies of the Balkan and Eastern European Countries" (EBEEC), held at the University of the Mykolas Romeris University in Vilnius, Lithuania, May 17–19, 2024. This volume addresses endeavors to navigate global adversities across different sectors and geographical regions, emphasizing the importance of resilient and sustainable economic development, adaptive policy frameworks, and fortifying organizational capacities in the context of persistent adversities. Prominent presentations investigate topics that delve into the avenues of resilient and sustainable development, the potential of digital transformations, patterns of changing consumer behaviors, and the prospects of artificial intelligence. By employing a variety of analytical frameworks, this volume offers valuable insights into the cultivation of resilience within both local and global economic landscapes, thereby equipping stakeholders with the tools to maneuver through intricate and variable environments adeptly.

The book is divided into three main parts: i.e., (1) The Prospects of Economic Security and Resilience; (2) Sustainability, Circular Economy, and Innovation; (3) Digital Transformation and Consumer Behavior, and presents twenty-three scientific papers. All selected manuscripts have gone through the peer-review process, are carefully edited, and are certainly making a significant contribution to the broader field of economy.

Part I delivers eight papers that delve into academic perspectives on economic security and resilience development patterns prevalent in Eastern European and Balkan economies.

Lazaros Mitsou, who collaborates with Theodora Vainterli, Ioannis Paliokas, and Vasilis Zoumpoulidis, is the author of the first paper from the Democritus University of Thrace. This paper provides a comparative analysis of how COVID-19 impacted the economies of Greece, Spain, Italy, and Portugal, focusing on macroeconomic variables like unemployment, inflation, and GDP between 2017 and 2023. The goal is to assess each country's economic resilience and security during the pandemic, enhancing existing literature by providing new insights into Southern European economic stability.

The following paper, authored by Egis Zaimaj from the Canadian Institute of Technology in collaboration with Chrysanthi Balomenou from Epoka University, examines the insurance market dynamics in the Balkans. The study investigates factors influencing insurance consumption across eight Balkan countries, aiming to identify key determinants of insurance industry development. The research contributes to future policy reforms and offers insights that could significantly enhance the insurance sector's growth in the region.

The third paper, authored by Spyros Roukanas and Vaggelis Vitzileos from the University of Piraeus, delves into the role of the International Monetary Fund (IMF) in crisis lending, explicitly focusing on the cases of Greece and Argentina. The paper discusses how political and geopolitical factors can influence IMF lending policies, particularly in an era of de-globalization and international competition, with implications for developing and middle-income countries under stricter lending conditions.

Further, Cigdem Varol from Gazi University, in collaboration with Aydan Sat, Emrah Soylemez, Elif Varol, and Nazlı Tunar Özcan, investigates urban mobility patterns following the February 6, 2023, earthquakes in Turkey. They focus on the socio-demographic characteristics influencing behavior responses during emergencies. The study explores differences in human mobility during the earthquake and routine reactions, providing a basis for understanding how demographics and economic factors shape disaster response and preparedness to cope with adversities.

The following paper is by Dijana Čičin-Šain from the University of Zadar, along with co-authors Martina Mate and Anita Peša. The research examines the stability of Croatia's exchange rate and long-term interest rates as the country joins the Eurozone in early 2023. It highlights Croatia's efforts to meet the European Central Bank's convergence criteria through the ERM II mechanism, detailing the adjustments made in response to economic integration requirements.

Miltiadis Staboulis, who works with Antonios Kostas, Ioannis Tsoukalidis, and Anastasios Karasavvoglou, is the author of the sixth paper from the University of Macedonia. This study focuses on the skills gap in the Greek manufacturing sector amidst advances in artificial intelligence. The research proposes a strategic framework to align vocational education with industry needs, addressing challenges in workforce adaptation to technological environments, which affects Greece's manufacturing competitiveness on an international scale.

The seventh paper is authored by Goran Karanovic from the University of Rijeka, with Ana Stambuk and Persefoni Polychronidou. Based on survey data from 346 participants, the study examines Greek students' financial well-being and migration intentions. It reveals students' significant economic challenges, including limited savings capacity and high migration intentions driven by financial insecurity and aspirations for improved living standards. This highlights the need for policies to address youth migration.

The final paper is authored by Tania Pantazi from the Hellenic Open University in collaboration with Vasileios Vlachos from the International Hellenic University. This research reviews short-term rental regulations in five EU countries—France, Greece, Italy, Portugal, and Spain—and assesses the role of European law. The study underscores a fragmented regulatory approach, with local-level variances, and suggests that EU-wide regulation could better address health, safety, and professional standards in the short-term rental market.

Part II elucidates scholarly viewpoints on sustainability-driven innovations that enhance environmental responsibility across industries, including healthcare, agriculture, and education. This section contains six papers.

It starts with a paper focusing on the potential for digitalization in Ukraine. Authored by Tatiana Gorokhova from the Centre for Advanced Internet Studies and Pryazovskyi State Technical University. The research examines the role of digitalization in advancing a circular economy (CE) within Ukraine. The study identifies the potential and challenges of incorporating digitalization into CE business models, highlighting data management and collaboration issues. The paper emphasizes the role of digitalization in restoring Ukraine by analyzing qualitative data gathered from online interviews with various stakeholders. It provides strategies to overcome implementation barriers in Ukraine's business sector.

Further, Michela Bobini from SDA Bocconi School of Management and her colleagues from University of Florence and University of Ferrara investigate circular economy strategies within healthcare, focusing on the enlightening role of group purchasing organizations in Italy. This paper examines the potential for the public healthcare sector to adopt circular practices, such as equipment refurbishment and sustainable supply chain management. Using interviews with healthcare public organizations, the authors analyze the feasibility of integrating the circular economy in a government-funded healthcare setting and discuss challenges such as hazardous waste recycling and the need for clear reusable standards.

In another paper, Claudio D'Alonzo from the Catholic University Our Lady of Good Counsel explores the influence of environmental, social, and governance (ESG) factors on business structures in Italy. This study argues that integrating ESG into business operations aligns with contemporary demands for sustainability and restructures companies toward hopeful and environmentally responsible models. D'Alonzo highlights how increasing focus on ESG affects company planning, emphasizing the shift in organizational targets toward sustainable development in response to ongoing environmental and societal challenges.

Another paper by Savvas Zachariadis from the University of Macedonia and Professor Georgios Makris links sustainability challenges with the concept of entropy in the economy. This theoretical study draws parallels between economic systems and the entropy law, which suggests that resource limits impose constraints on economic growth. By aligning economic activities with thermodynamic principles, Zachariadis and Makris propose a revised perspective on sustainability, particularly within the financial sector, to curb growth-driven resource depletion.

Further, Achilleas Kontogeorgos from the International Hellenic University collaborates with George Tsiamis from the University of Patras to assess Greek farmers' motivations for adopting biopesticides as part of the European Green Deal. This study evaluates farmers' perspectives on switching from chemical pesticides to biopesticides, exploring both advantages and barriers to adoption. The authors employ a questionnaire to capture farmers' willingness to adopt environmentally friendly pest control, suggesting communication strategies to enhance adoption rates in Greece's agricultural sector.

Lastly, Chiara Barchielli from the Institute of Management at Sant'Anna School of Advanced Studies leads a study examining patient-reported experience measures (PREMs) in Tuscany's healthcare system. This research, conducted with the Azienda USL Toscana Centro, uses PREMs to assess patient satisfaction post-hospitalization. By analyzing over 12,000 qualitative responses, the study highlights patients' satisfaction with care quality but points out areas needing improvement, such as information access and coordination. This work contributes to a patient-centered approach in healthcare management.

Part III, the final part, consisting of seven articles, provides an overview of the scientific outlook on how digital technologies and artificial intelligence influence consumer preferences, business practices, consumer acceptance, and adult learning patterns.

It starts with a paper by Julia Mischin from Neapolis University Pafos, in collaboration with Georgios A. Deirmentzoglou, Sofia Daskou, and Eirini Vlassi. This research investigates the role of artificial intelligence (AI) in personalizing product recommendations within e-commerce. Through a quantitative survey of 182 German e-commerce users, the authors find that user satisfaction significantly impacts online purchase decisions when AI-driven recommendation tools are used. The paper emphasizes the effectiveness of AI in enhancing consumer satisfaction and conversion rates in digital retail environments.

Mehmet Cem Bölen, Embiya Çelik, Erol Kılıç from Ataturk University research on consumer resistance to refurbished smartphones. The study employs innovation resistance theory and uncovers key barriers such as value, tradition, and image that deter consumers from purchasing refurbished devices. By analyzing survey data from 430 individuals, the study underscores the substantial obstacles posed by value and tradition, while risk and usage barriers have minimal impact. These findings contribute significantly to our understanding of consumer behavior in the context of circular economy products.

Georgios A. Deirmentzoglou from Neapolis University Pafos and his colleagues delve into the potential of metaverse applications in the tourism and hospitality sector. Using the Technology Acceptance Model (TAM), the study assesses how perceived usefulness and ease of use influence Greek tourists' intention to use metaverse experiences. The results underscore a positive correlation between these factors and adoption intentions, highlighting the metaverse's potential to revolutionize tourism and enrich immersive experiences.

Stavros Valsamidis from Democritus University of Thrace and his co-authors explore the impact of digital marketing on product promotion and advertising. Their survey, conducted among 177 respondents across Greek cities, reveals that digital advertising, mainly through discounts and online stores, has significantly altered consumer purchasing behavior. The study concludes that digital channels, driven by the convenience and reach of online media, are pivotal for effective marketing.

Another study by Lambros Tsourgiannis and his team analyzes Greek civil servants' attitudes toward e-government applications. The authors categorize civil servants using principal component and cluster analyses based on their engagement with e-government tools. Findings reveal varying acceptance levels and demographic profiles, providing insights into factors that shape adoption within the public sector.

Finally, Lambros Tsourgiannis, in collaboration with others, also investigates Greek consumers' purchasing behavior regarding olive oil quality. The research uses principal component, cluster, and discriminant analyses to segment consumer preferences. Results indicate diverse demographic profiles and motivations for selecting different olive oil classes, contributing to consumer behavior insights within Greece's agrifood sector.

Vilnius, Lithuania	Ilona Bartuseviciene
Vilnius, Lithuania	Buracas Antanas
Kavala, Greece	Anastasios Karasavvoglou
Serres, Greece	Persefoni Polychronidou

Contents

The Prospects of Economic Security and Resilience

Economic Security and Resilience in the Era of Covid-19: A Comparative Analysis of the Economies of Greece, Spain, Italy and Portugal

Lazaros Mitsou, Theodora Vainterli, Ioannis Paliokas, and Vasilios Zoumpoulidis

Abstract At a time when the social and economic balance of the countries of Europe and the world is being shaken daily, this paper aims to investigate and present how the health crisis of Covid-19 affected specific economies of Southern European and Mediterranean countries. In particular, the variables used in this research are the values of some key macroeconomic variables during the period 2017 to 2023, such as unemployment, inflation, GDP, etc. These variables, as well as the indicators presented, are considered crucial in order to simultaneously carry out a comparative approach of the economies of the four selected countries. The aim of this paper is to capture and evidence the demonstration - or not - of resilience of the economies of Greece, Spain, Portugal and Italy during the Covid-19 pandemic. In addition, through the data and the analysis conducted, it is possible to identify the level of economic security of each country, during the period 2017–2023. In conclusion, this research is set to directly enrich the existing literature, adding conclusions and results that have so far not been clear or widely shared in the academic community.

Keywords Covid-19 · Economic security · Resilience · Comparative analysis · European economies

JEL Classification Coads G01 · P51

Present Address:
L. Mitsou (✉) · T. Vainterli · I. Paliokas · V. Zoumpoulidis
Department of Accounting & Finance, Democritus University of Thrace, Kavala, Greece
e mail: mitsou_lazaros@hotmail.com

T. Vainterli
e-mail: dorabainterle@gmail.com

I. Paliokas
e-mail: ipaliokas@af.ihu.gr

V. Zoumpoulidis
e-mail: vzumpu@af.ihu.gr

I. Bartuseviciene et al. (eds.), *Building Resilience Through Digital Transformation and Sustainable Innovation*, Springer Proceedings in Business and Economics,
https://doi.org/10.1007/978-3-031-90054-9_1

1 Introduction

The COVID-19 pandemic was an unprecedented event for global economies, highlighting the need for economic security and resilience in emergency situations. Effective management of financial resources and strengthening of economic protection mechanisms became more urgent as countries such as Greece, Italy, Portugal, and Spain experienced adverse impacts on their national economies. In this general context, examining the strategies developed to deal with the crisis becomes essential to understanding how these particular countries attempted to preserve their economic security and strengthen their resilience in the face of turbulence.

However, economic security during the pandemic is primarily focused on the ability of states to maintain economic stability and protect citizens' incomes despite any external pressures. Resilience, on the other hand, is expressed as the ability of recovery and resilience of economic systems to adapt and rebuild after such crises. This research therefore builds on the measures and policies adopted by these countries, also examining how the various policies have helped to enhance economic security and resilience in an environment of high uncertainty and change.

2 Literature Review

The Coronavirus Disease 2019 (COVID-19) pandemic was an unprecedented event for global economies, highlighting the need for economic security and resilience in emergency situations. Greece, Spain, Italy and Portugal had already been dealing with the lingering repercussions of the financial crisis of 2008, yet the COVID-19 pandemic led to severe economic disruptions for them (Kapitsinis et al., 2021; Sane Schepisi et al., 2021). Also, except from their financial crisis before the pandemic and their reliance on tourism, these countries had some commonalities during it such as the severe lockdowns and the high percentage of COVID-19 cases. This comparative analysis explores and discusses how these countries overcame such financial obstacles, for their economic security and resilience as well.

First and foremost, it should be stated that the economic conditions of these countries before the pandemic were somewhat weak; for example, Greece had a fragile economy since the country was recovering from a long debt crisis, and its Gross Domestic Product (GDP) was trying to recover again, but public debt and still high unemployment were evident (Nikiforos, 2021). Furthermore, the pre-pandemic financial situation in Spain was somewhat better with its unemployment to be decreasing and GDP to show a consistent growth, but again it was weak to manage the COVID-19 economic shock as it was relying on tourism and other services (Morales & Devesa, 2017). Moreover, Portugal, like Spain, has again a low GDP and it was relying on tourism thus it was susceptible to the financial collapse due to COVID-19, despite its economic growth and public deficit reduction –its debt was lower than the Greek debt

(Fund, 2022). Finally, Italy, the third-largest Eurozone economy was again susceptible to COVID-19 financial fallout because of its increased public debt, important inefficiencies and the aging population (Praussello, 2015).

Undeniably, COVID-19 had a significant impact on the economies of these countries. In our country, Greece, the strict lockdown policies resulted into a sharp financial contraction which exacerbated the already existed vulnerabilities, the Greek tourism sector -a critical portion of its GDP- suffered a critical fallout, whereas the still increased public debt and the high unemployment reached far too critically high levels (Markantonatou, 2021). Secondly, COVID-19 hit Spain so hardly both in terms of infected cases and deaths and at a financial level as well, as -like in Greece- the austerity and the lockdowns -that included travel restrictions- had a negative impact on the tourism sector with the GDP contraction to be significant, and the economy faced a severe strain despite the fact that the Spanish government responded immediately with stimulus packages trying to support workers as well as businesses (Moreno-Luna et al., 2021). In addition, the pandemic led Portugal to face a decrease in tourism as well as exports, and despite the government's immediate implementation of fiscal stimulus measures and social safety nets for households and businesses, only few financial obstacles were overcome (McTeigue et al., 2021). Finally, concerning Italy, COVID-19 triggered a dual crisis, meaning the harsh health crisis and the critical financial downturn, since the pandemic outbreak there was early and critical and led to stringent lockdowns with profound economic impact, not to mention that the manufacturing sector was also hit hard and the public debt increased as a result of the government policies to mitigate the crisis (Falavigna & Ippoliti, 2022).

For their recovery, Greece, Spain, Portugal and Italy adopted significant fiscal measures so as to support their economies, and these national responses included wage subsidies, loans, grants to businesses and elevated spending on healthcare and other social services as well. Besides, some national structural reforms were seen, including the improvisation of the Greek investment climate, the Spanish labor market reforms, the reduction in Italian bureaucracy and the enhancement of the Portuguese social welfare system (Urbanovics & Teleki, 2021). In addition, the European Union (EU) supported the economics of these four countries via initiatives such as the Next Generation EU fund, which provided crucial economic resources to help them recover and invest in long-term resilience, especially in fields of digitalization as well as green energy and some others (Jones, 2021).

Actually, the Mediterranean countries were particularly vulnerable due to their high dependence in tourism, and their economic resilience was tested through the travel restrictions' prolonged impact; one could argue that recovery in this sector still remains a key challenge for Greece, Spain and Portugal as well. Several European countries like Greece and Italy in particular –as they have the highest levels of public debt- had to overcome important obstacles so as to maintain fiscal stability while supporting their economies, but EU support gave a crucial buffer which allowed these two countries to recover and not destabilize their national economies to further extents (Mitsi, 2023). What's more, compared to Greece and Portugal which implemented more flexible labor policies, Spain and Italy, which were characterized by relative rigidity in labor markets, had higher unemployment and lower recovery (Asensio & Ferreira, 2024).

At a first glance, the long-term implication of such events is the economic diversification away from sectors like tourism, but in favor of sectors like the technology, the renewable energy and manufacturing as well. Secondly, the economic consequences of the pandemic to vulnerable populaces can be managed through maintaining social cohesion via strong social safety nets and targeted support –since countries who focused on that showed more successful recovery efforts. Besides, the pandemic crisis reinforced the significance of EU integration and solidarity and the recovery funds and related EU strategies were of vital importance and beneficial for deeper financial coordination (Wolff & Ladi, 2020).

Yet, a significant implication were also the inflationary pressures resulting from the Ukranian war which are deeply attributed to the economic vulnerabilities during the pandemic, which weakened the fiscal and financial resilience of Greece, Spain, Italy and Portugal, leaving them extremely exposed to war shocks; pandemic recovery challenges, energy price surges, supply chain disruptions and increasing public debt were all attributed to a complexity in which financial security and resilience are critically tested, and such countries now have to manage inflation while recovering from COVID-19 –all within a context of both fiscal and monetary policy choices (Pereira & Gaspar, 2022). Yet, the war between Ukraine and Russia affected several other fields that were common for these European countries, including the increased energy prices as all four countries are heavily dependent on energy imports, the prices of essential goods and the cost of living, the supply chain and especially the agriculture sector, the public finances as well as the social and political stability, since the combined pressures of rising living costs, unemployment and economic uncertainty have increased social tensions in them and governments face protests and strikes as citizens demand more effective measures so as to protect their livelihoods (Bluszcz & Valente, 2019; Shubalyi & Gordiichuk, 2022).

To conclude with, Greece, Spain, Italy, and Portugal faced severe financial obstacles during the pandemic, exposing vulnerabilities in tourism, high public debt, and the necessity for reforms. EU support and national efforts were critical, but continuous adaptation and novelty are pivotal for future resilience.

3 Comparative Analysis

The primary objective of this research is to study to what extent the covid-19 pandemic affected specific economies of Southern European and Mediterranean countries. Also, a secondary objective is to test whether the economies of certain countries demonstrated economic security and resilience during the pandemic period. For this purpose, a survey was conducted with secondary data, covering the period 2017 to 2023. The survey variables were various macroeconomic variables (e.g. Unemployment, GDP, Debt, etc.) and indicators, which were deemed useful to meet

Table 1 Unemployment rate (%) per country (2017–2023)

Year	Greece (%)	Spain (%)	Italy (%)	Portugal (%)
2017	21.4	17.2	11.2	8.9
2018	19.2	15.3	10.6	7.0
2019	17.3	14.1	10.0	6.5
2020	16.4	15.5	9.2	7.2
2021	15.2	15.6	9.8	6.7
2022	12.2	12.9	8.1	5.8
2023	11.0	12.1	7.6	6.5

Source The World Bank

the above objectives. In addition, the survey also covers the countries of Greece, Spain, Italy and Portugal and a comparative analysis of these is provided below.

3.1 Unemployment Rate

Regarding the unemployment rate of each country for the years 2017 to 2023, it appears that each country shows a distinct trend, except for the period 2017–2019 when all countries have a downward trend in unemployment. To begin with, Greece shows a continuous decrease in the unemployment rate, starting in 2017 with a rate of 21.4% and ending in 2023 with a rate of 11%, without showing any impact of the Covid-19 pandemic. Subsequently, Spain and Portugal show a similar trend over this period, with unemployment increasing in 2020 due to the influence of the pandemic, and then gradually decreasing until 2023. In Portugal, however, the rate increases for the year 2023. Finally, Italy manages to reduce the unemployment rate from 2019 to 2020 (the year of the pandemic), then it increases in 2021 and decreases again, reaching a value of 7.6% in 2023. In comparison, Greece and Spain show the highest unemployment rates during the period under study, followed by Italy and finally Portugal which has the lowest (Table 1 and Graph 1).

3.2 Inflation Rate

According to the World Bank's inflation data, the countries under study seem to follow an identical trend. In particular, all 4 countries show an inflation rate of around 1.5% in the year 2017, then this rate decreases until 2020, in the years 2021–2022 there is a huge increase in inflation, while in 2023 it decreases again. Notable inflation rates are Greece's, which in 2020 shows a negative value (−1.2%) and in 2022 where the highest value since 1995 to date is found (+9.6%). Comparing the four countries, it appears that Greece is the country with the most pronounced

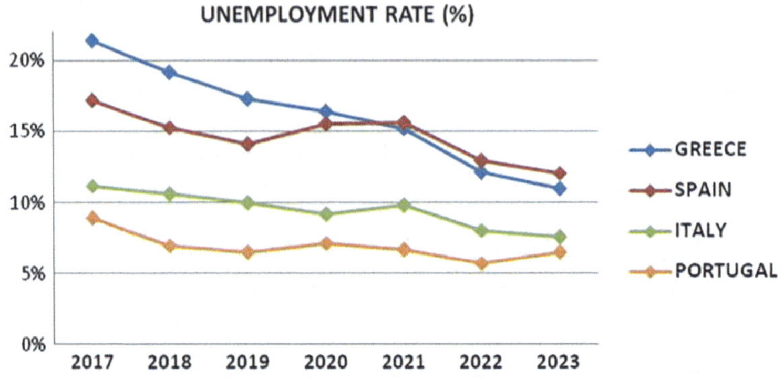

Graph 1 Unemployment rate (%) per country (2017–2023)

Table 2 Inflation rate (%) per country (2017–2023)

Year	Greece (%)	Spain (%)	Italy (%)	Portugal (%)
2017	1.1	2.0	1.2	1.4
2018	0.6	1.7	1.1	1.0
2019	0.3	0.7	0.6	0.3
2020	−1.2	−0.3	−0.1	0.0
2021	1.2	3.1	1.9	1.3
2022	9.6	8.4	8.2	7.8
2023	4.2	3.4	5.9	5.3

Source The World Bank

extremes, in contrast to Portugal which has the mildest. Spain and Italy follow a similar pattern of fluctuations. The common denominator for all four countries is the fairly low inflation rates in 2020, due to the pandemic, but also the jump in these rates after the pandemic (Table 2 and Graph 2).

3.3 Imports (% of GDP)

By studying imports as an indicator to GDP, the aim is to capture how much imports affect GDP, since they are part of a country's economic activity. Specifically, it is observed that all countries have a steady import share path from 2017 to 2019, decreased their imports during the covid-19 period (2019 to 2020) and then gradually increased them until 2022. However, 2023 is a year of import rate decline for the study countries. The countries with the highest import share in terms of their GDP are Greece and Portugal. This is followed by Spain with rates between 30 and 40% and finally Italy, which has the least imports as a percentage of its GDP for the

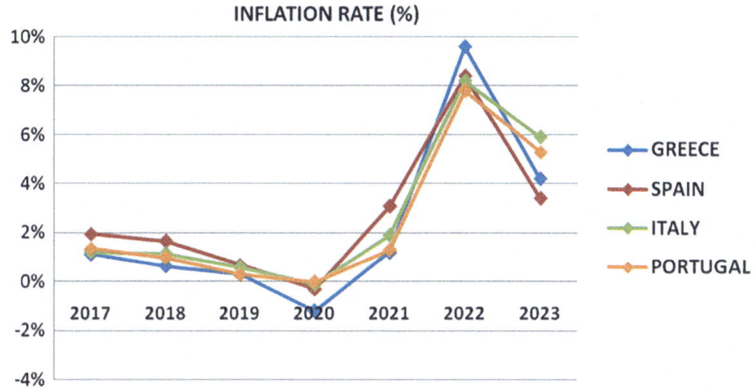

Graph 2 Inflation rate (%) per country (2017–2023)

Table 3 Imports-to-GDP ratio by country (2017–2023)

Year	Greece (%)	Spain (%)	Italy (%)	Portugal (%)
2017	36.5	31.5	27.9	41.7
2018	41.2	32.4	28.9	43.0
2019	41.8	32.0	28.3	43.1
2020	39.8	29.3	25.8	39.2
2021	48.7	33.2	29.8	44.2
2022	58.9	39.7	38.1	52.0
2023	49.8	34.8	33.7	46.6

Source Trading Economics

period 2017–2023. Common to all the countries under study is that the majority of their imports are fossil fuels, oils, distillation products, followed by machinery and vehicles (Table 3 and Graph 3).

3.4 Exports (% of GDP)

As far as each country's exports are concerned, it was preferred to analyse them as a percentage of GDP, because it is easier to measure the economic performance of a country. For the years 2017–2019 there is a stable trend in exports, with no particular fluctuations, followed by a decrease from 2019 to 2020, due to the Covid-19 phenomenon. This decline in the export-to-GDP ratio is, however, followed by an increase until 2022, reaching rates of 36% to 50%, and ending in 2023 with a further decline. As for the imports of each country, analysed previously, it appears

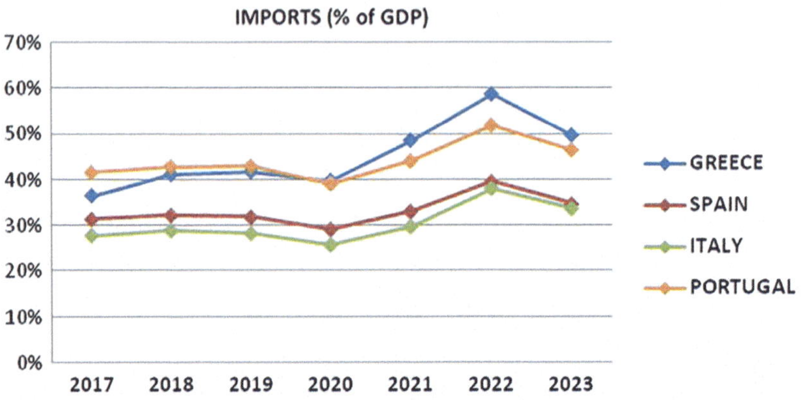

Graph 3 Imports-to-GDP ratio by country (2017–2023)

Table 4 Exports-to-GDP ratio by country (2017–2023)

Year	Greece (%)	Spain (%)	Italy (%)	Portugal (%)
2017	35.0	35.1	30.7	42.7
2018	39.0	35.1	31.4	43.4
2019	40.1	34.9	31.6	43.5
2020	32.1	30.8	29.4	37.0
2021	40.9	34.2	32.1	41.4
2022	49.1	40.9	36.6	49.6
2023	44.9	39.0	35.1	47.4

Source Trading Economics

that Portugal has the highest export rates, followed by Greece with small deviations, then Spain and finally Italy, which has the lowest export rates. In contrast to imports, each study country seems to export something different from the others. In particular, Spain exports vehicles, Greece exports fossil fuels, oils and distillation products, Portugal exports electronic equipment and vehicles, and finally Italy exports machinery, nuclear reactors and boilers. Exports are an important part of any economy, since they are linked to a country's productivity and boost its competitiveness, but also because they contribute to the recovery of the economy after major crises, such as the example of the coronavirus pandemic (Table 4 and Graph 4).

3.5 Real GDP Per Capita

The study of Real GDP per capita is also quite important, as it is an indicator of the social welfare of an economy or a country and is used to measure the performance of

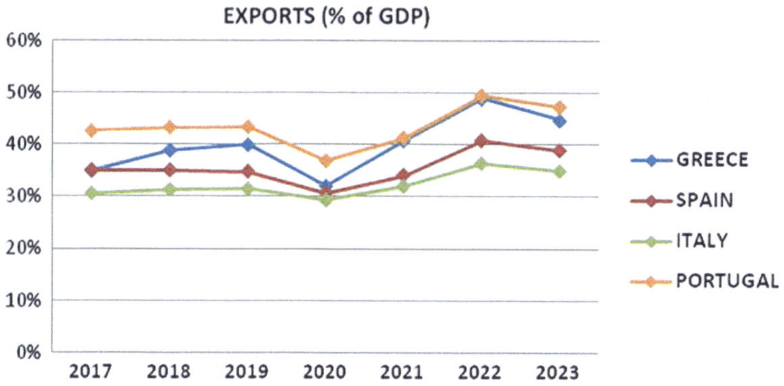

Graph 4 Exports-to-GDP ratio by country (2017–2023)

economies over time. Therefore, by studying Real GDP per capita, there seems to be a clearer picture between the countries under study because the population factor is introduced. More specifically, in all the countries under study there are small increases in GDP from 2017 to 2019, a decrease in it during the Covid-19 pandemic, while in the following years (2021–2023) it increases significantly, reaching pre-pandemic levels. Comparing the data for each country, Italy appears as the country with the highest GDP per capita (26,000€–29,000€), then Spain is identified with 22,000€–25,000€, followed by Portugal with 17,000€-20,000€ and finally Greece with the lowest GDP per capita values (from 15,000€ to 18,000€). Therefore, one can say that Italians and Spaniards show more social well-being, compared to Portuguese and Greeks (Table 5 and Graph 5).

Table 5 Real GDP per capita by country (2017–2023)

Year	Greece	Spain	Italy	Portugal
2017	16,498 €	24,551 €	28,160 €	18,424 €
2018	16,807 €	25,002 €	28,475 €	18,979 €
2019	17,141 €	25,316 €	28,945 €	19,484 €
2020	15,577 €	22,379 €	26,476 €	17,848 €
2021	17,089 €	23,787 €	28,825 €	18,754 €
2022	18,285 €	24,968 €	29,996 €	19,942 €
2023	18,771 €	25,279 €	30,440 €	20,169 €

Source The World Bank

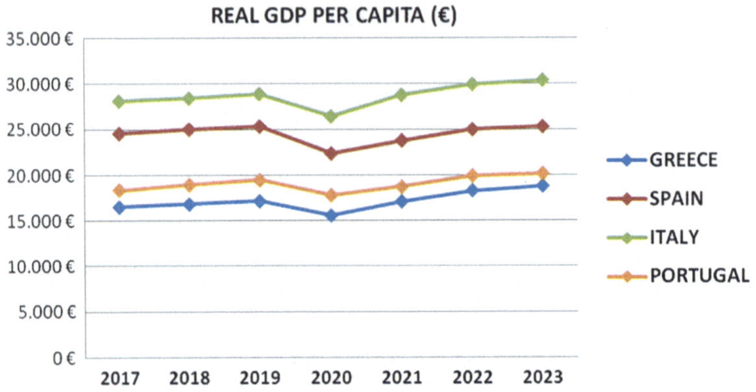

Graph 5 Real GDP per capita by country (2017–2023)

3.6 *Public Debt (% of GDP)*

To conclude the analysis of the macroeconomic variables and their evolution, the public debt-to-GDP ratio is presented for each country. The four countries have the same path of the ratio over the study period. Initially, from 2017 to 2019 a mild debt reduction is detected, then the debt ratio increases due to the onset of the Covid-19 pandemic, while from 2020 to 2022 it gradually decreases, and no data are available for 2023. In this case, Greece appears as the country with the highest rate, and in particular a rate that has never been seen before in any country in the European Union. Next comes Italy with debt-to-GDP ratios ranging between 130% and 150.5%, Portugal from 118.8% to 138.8% and finally Spain with ratios between 88 and 108%. However, a different picture emerges when studying the amount of debt of countries in absolute terms, as countries with high GDP tend to have large but sustainable debts, respectively. For example, Spain had the second highest amount of public debt, in absolute terms, while if you study its debt to GDP ratio, you will find that it is the country with the lowest rates. The opposite of the above is true in Greece (Table 6 and Graph 6).

Table 6 Public debt-to-GDP ratio by country (2017–2022)

Year	Greece (%)	Spain (%)	Italy (%)	Portugal (%)
2017	185.8	90.3	129.6	128.8
2018	199.9	89.9	130.1	124.6
2019	194.2	88.0	130.0	119.5
2020	226.1	107.9	150.5	138.8
2021	213.8	106.1	145.6	129.8
2022	192.4	102.3	140.6	118.8

Source International Monetary Fund

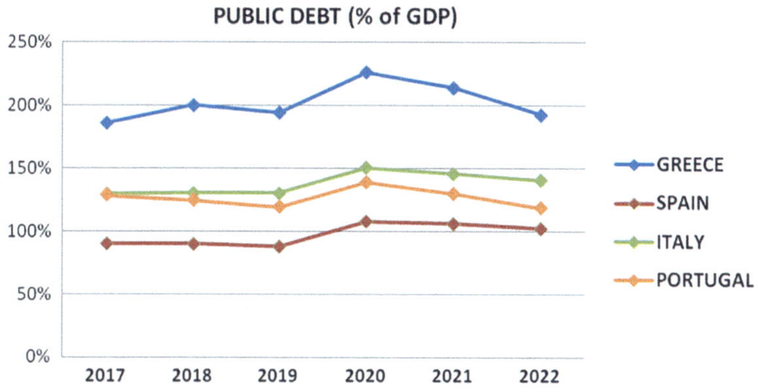

Graph 6 Public debt-to-GDP ratio by country (2017–2022)

3.7 Economic Resilience Index (ERI)

According to the ZOE, Institute for Future-Fit Economies report, published in early 2023, the Economic Resilience Index, which measures and assesses the level of economic resilience in 25 different countries of the European Union for the years 2020–2021, is presented below. The importance of this index focuses on showing and capturing the readiness of economies to possible future crises. It is also an important tool for the governments of the countries concerned, as it is crucial for taking the most appropriate measures and decisions aimed at ensuring economic resilience. The ERI contains six (6) main subcategories of indicators, which cover Financial Resilience, Social Progress and Cohesion, Governance, Economic Independence, Productive Capacity, and Education & Skills. The final index value is determined as an average of the values from the 6 subcategories. The ERI indicator usually takes values from 0 to 1. A country with a score close to zero indicates a worse performance in the country's economic resilience, while a score close to one indicates a better performance. In the 2023 report, countries' values range from 0.78 to 0.25.

Table 7 presents the scores of the four countries studied in this survey. However, it is worth mentioning that the overall ranking is dominated by the Scandinavian countries (Sweden, Denmark), while the last positions are occupied by the Balkan countries (Bulgaria, Greece, Romania). Spain ranks 18th, Italy 19th, Portugal 21st and Greece 24th out of 25 countries. Spain and Italy have an overall score of 0.39, followed by Portugal with a score of 0.35 and finally Greece with 0.28.

At the same time, because, as mentioned above, the value of the ERI is derived from the average of the six subcategories, it appears that each country is lagging behind in some area and is lowering its average. Greece has the lowest value (0.09) in the area of financial resilience and the highest value (0.47) in financial independence. Spain, like Italy, shows strong financial independence but weakness in the area of productive capacity. In contrast to the other countries, Portugal lags behind in the area of financial independence (0.17) and ahead in education and skills (0.55).

Table 7 Economic Resilience Index by country

Country	Economic independence	Education & skills	Financial resilience	Governance	Production capacity	Social progress & cohesion	ERI's score
Greece	0.47	0.20	0.09	0.35	0.25	0.28	**0.28**
Spain	0.53	0.45	0.34	0.44	0.16	0.40	**0.39**
Italy	0.67	0.34	0.30	0.38	0.28	0.34	**0.39**
Portugal	0.17	0.55	0.24	0.37	0.37	0.39	**0.35**

Source ZOE Institute for Future-fit Economies

In conclusion, the presentation of the ERI (Economic Resilience Index) values for the years 2020–2021 shows that the countries under study are lagging behind in economic security and resilience during the pandemic period of the coronavirus pandemic. This is confirmed by the previous comparative analysis of macroeconomic indicators, which indicated a deterioration in these indicators in the same years.

4 Conclusion

Firstly, it is found that Greece and Portugal, from 2020 (the year of the beginning of the pandemic) until today, have seen a continuous decrease in the unemployment rate, year after year. In contrast, Spain and Italy show a slight increase in 2021 and since then until today they have been decreasing this rate. In addition, a rapid increase in inflation, for all countries, from 2021 to 2022, suggesting a rebound from the pandemic of 2020 (due to negative values becoming positive), but inflation has very high values which is directly related to the war between Ukraine and Russia. In terms of the ratios of exports and imports to GDP, there is a similar pattern for the entire 2017–2023 period in all countries (decreasing in 2020 and then increasing to date), i.e. countries seem to export as much as they import with small deviations. It is surprising that Portugal and Italy, despite having lower GDP than the other countries, have the highest export and import ratios for the period 2017–2023. All countries had a decline in GDP in the year 2020 due to the covid-19 pandemic. First Italy and then Spain appear to have higher levels of social welfare, in contrast to Portugal and Greece which have the lowest amounts of Real GDP per capita. Spain has the second highest debt and at the same time shows the lowest debt-to-GDP ratio, a conclusion that suggests better and sustainable debt management on its part. On the other hand, Greece has the second lowest debt, while showing extremely high debt-to-GDP ratios, at levels never seen before in a Eurozone country. In conclusion, it seems that the covid-19 pandemic has made its impact and effects evident in the majority of the Eurozone countries, as well as in the countries studied, as confirmed by the macroeconomic aggregates and indicators analysed above.

5 Discussion

This study has potential limitations. First of all, there are exogenous factors that cannot be controlled, such as political changes or global economic conditions, that may affect the results. Also, limitations to drawing conclusions are defined as conditions vary from country to country, which may lead to generalisation of results. At the same time, the data used in the survey refers to a specific time period (2017–2023), but the analysis of this period may not be sufficient to detect long-term trends. Finally, there may be more relevant indicators that were not included in the above analysis, or other European countries may not have been considered, which may have shown notable results.

A future perspective of this study is to extend the time horizon of the survey to include more years before and after a pandemic. Furthermore, a possible addition is the inclusion of more countries, and corresponding economies, in the above comparative analysis. In addition, it would be useful to assess the policy implications of the pandemic in the countries under study in order to take a holistic approach. Finally, the application of new analytical methods or technological tools could contribute to a more detailed understanding of the data and predict future trends.

References

Asensio, M., & Ferreira, C. (2024). Labor-market reforms in southern europe: From protection to flexibility. *IntechOpen*. https://doi.org/10.5772/intechopen.1004623

Bluszcz, J., & Valente, M. (2019). *The war in europe: Economic costs of the Ukrainian conflict* (SSRN Scholarly Paper 3392199). https://doi.org/10.2139/ssrn.3392199

Falavigna, G., & Ippoliti, R. (2022). Relief policy and the sustainability of covid-19 pandemic: Empirical evidence from the Italian manufacturing industry. *Sustainability, 14*(22), 15437. https://doi.org/10.3390/su142215437

Fund., I. M. (2022). *Portugal: 2022 article iv consultation-press release; staff report; and statement by the executive director for Portugal*. International Monetary Fund 2022.

Jones, E. (2021). Next generation EU: Solidarity, opportunity, and confidence. https://cadmus.eui.eu/handle/1814/74052

Kapitsinis, N., Saroukou, A., Sykas, G., & Psarologos, D. (2021, Ιούνιος 28). *An overview of the covid-19 effects on employment during 2020. Evidence from Cyprus, France, Spain, Greece, Italy, Malta, Croatia and Portugal* [Monograph]. http://www.youthshare-project.org/wp-content/uploads/2021/07/Annual-report.pdf

Markantonatou, M. (2021). From austerity to the pandemic and back again? Lockdown politics in Greece. *Historical Social Research/Historische Sozialforschung, 46*(4), 143–162. https://www.jstor.org/stable/27081878

McTeigue, C., Sanchez, C., Santos, E., Walter, C. E., & Au-Yong-Oliveira, M. (2021). A strategy for tourism growth, rebound, and revival: Promoting Portugal as a destination post-covid-19. *Sustainability, 13*(22), 12588. https://doi.org/10.3390/su132212588

Mitsi, D. (2023). Public debt and economic growth after Covid-19 in Europe: Challenges and policy implications. *Review of European Studies, 15*(4), p31. https://doi.org/10.5539/res.v15n4p31

Morales, J. M. L., & Devesa, M. J. S. (2017). Business cycle and external dependence on tourism: Evidence for Spain. *Tourism Economics, 23*(1), 187–199. https://doi.org/10.5367/te.2015.0506

Moreno-Luna, L., Robina-Ramírez, R., Sánchez, M.S.-O., & Castro-Serrano, J. (2021). Tourism and sustainability in times of covid-19: The case of Spain. *International Journal of Environmental Research and Public Health, 18*(4), 1859. https://doi.org/10.3390/ijerph18041859

Nikiforos, M. (2021). Crisis, austerity, and fiscal expenditure in Greece: Recent experience and future prospects in the post-COVID-19 era. *European Journal of Economics and Economic Policies, 19*(2), 186–203. https://doi.org/10.4337/ejeep.2021.0076

Pereira, J. A. M., & Gaspar, F. (2022). *Impact of pandemics and war in EU's cohesion policy: Problematics and challenges*. Third Joint EU Cohesion Policy Conference. https://repositorio.ipsantarem.pt/handle/10400.15/4119

Praussello, F. (2015). The impact of the Eurozone crisis on a periphery country: The case of Italy. Στο S. Katsikides & P. I. Koktsidis (Επιμ.), Societies in Transition: Economic, Political and Security Transformations in Contemporary Europe (σσ. 57–86). Springer International Publishing. https://doi.org/10.1007/978-3-319-13814-5_4

Sane Schepisi, M., Di Napoli, A., Asciutto, R., Vecchi, S., Mirisola, C., & Petrelli, A. (2021). The 2008 financial crisis and changes in lifestyle-related behaviors in italy, greece, spain, and portugal: A systematic review. *International Journal of Environmental Research and Public Health, 18*(16), 8734. https://doi.org/10.3390/ijerph18168734

Shubalyi, O., & Gordiichuk, A. (2022). The socio-economic consequences of the war in ukraine: The national, regional, and global dimensions. *Regional Barometer. Analyses & Prognoses, 18*(1), 19–37. https://doi.org/10.56583/br.721

Urbanovics, A. & Teleki, B. (2021). The economic context of the COVID-19 pandemic in the Mediterranean countries. *Intersections. East European Journal of Society and Politics, 7*(3), 157–177. https://www.ceeol.com/search/article-detail?id=1012060

Wolff, S., & Ladi, S. (2020). European union responses to the COVID-19 pandemic: Adaptability in times of permanent emergency. *Journal of European Integration, 42*(8), 1025–1040. https://doi.org/10.1080/07036337.2020.1853120

ZOE Institute for Future-fit Economies. (2023). *Economic Resilience Index: Final Report*. ZOE Institute for Future-fit Economies. https://zoe-institut.de/wp-content/uploads/2023/09/Economic_Resilience_Index_Final-1.pdf

Reliance on Insurance: An Investigation into the Current Dynamics in the Balkans

Egis Zaimaj and Chrysanthi Balomenou

Abstract This paper aims to analyze the drivers behind insurance market development in a highly dynamic region such as the Balkans. The majority of the Balkan countries are working to progress with the integration process, provide the enabling conditions for accession, conduct reforms, fight corruption, and promote stable economic growth. In this regard, it becomes important to understand where one important pillar of the financial system stands: the insurance industry. In this study, we focus on the reliance of the people of the Balkans on insurance, as captured by the insurance consumption. The empirical analysis builds on annual data obtained for 8 Balkan countries, namely Albania, Kosovo, Croatia, Greece, North Macedonia, Romania, Montenegro, and Bulgaria for the years 2010–2022. These countries are characterized by numerous similarities with respect to the context of insurance sector development, structural factors, and the historic past. The very inception of the modern, private insurance markets for the sample countries occurred relatively late, in the 90s. This is the first cause explaining why such a group of countries is lagging in terms of insurance market development. To understand other reasons as to why the insurance consumption in the region is low and the sector is generally falling behind, three regression models are estimated explaining respectively premium volume, insurance density and penetration. Four groups of factors: financial, demographic, regulatory and economic were employed across three regressions, thus allowing to check the marginal impact and statistical significance of each variable. Data for the independent variables is taken from the World Bank: inflation rate, financial development, trade, income, population, regulatory quality and corruption. Given the numerous functions that the insurance industry serves, such as protection and security, risk transfer, investments, and contribution to economic growth, it becomes necessary to carefully analyze its significant drivers, supporters and impediments. The in-depth panel data regression analysis allows us to achieve the main aim

E. Zaimaj (✉)
Canadian Institute of Technology, Tirana, Albania
e-mail: egis.zaimaj@cit.edu.al

C. Balomenou
Epoka University, Tirana, Albania
e-mail: cbalomenou@epoka.edu.al

I. Bartuseviciene et al. (eds.), *Building Resilience Through Digital Transformation and Sustainable Innovation*, Springer Proceedings in Business and Economics,
https://doi.org/10.1007/978-3-031-90054-9_2

of this paper, hence being able to point out the main factors which can be incorporated in future reforms and policies to trigger further development and expansion of the industry. This research will certainly serve the policymakers in their day-to-day decisions, as well as firms, practitioners, and academicians.

Keywords Insurance industry · GWP · Balkans · Panel data · Regression analysis

JEL Classification Codes C23 · G22 · O52.

1 Introduction

The insurance industry contributes to individuals, business entities and the economy as a whole in various aspects. Through its functions of risk sharing and indemnity, insurance paves the way to higher investments, enhanced competition, innovation, and increased awareness on various forms of dangerous behavior. The application of risk-based pricing produces financial benefits and more for the careful policyholders and society at large. Furthermore, insurance provides support to other sectors of the financial system. Banking for instance capitalizes on a variety of insurance products such as: life insurance, property insurance, car insurance and alike to generate a higher efficiency rate (Feyen et al., 2013). At a macro level, it is seen that the development of financial industry, insurance included, lays the foundations for economic growth and development (Kalaj et al., 2017; Sharku & Bajrami, 2021). The fact that insurance can serve as a complementary engine toward better living standards is especially important in the case of developing countries such are those in Balkans. Balkan economies are each too small, hence extremely vulnerable to internal and external shocks. The financial system together with insurance can generate positive spillover effects that are gradually translated to a better economic climate. However, it is important to underline that for this to happen, companies need to think strategically as on how to increase the demand and consumption of voluntary insurance products, hence triggering an increase in insurance penetration rates (Berisha, 2019).

During recent years, the insurance industry faced major challenges which put its resilience to the test. Covid 19 pandemic affected premiums earned on many lines of non-life business, with border insurance, green card, cargo insurance and alike suffering most. In the meantime, life insurers had to cope with ever increasing claims and liquidity pressures. Nonetheless, it is to be underlined that this difficult period was characterized by the proliferation of new products, some of which came as a result of distance working such was cybercrime insurance (Koçi et al., 2021). Not long before, the repercussions of geopolitical tensions peaking with the war between Ukraine and Russia presented another threat to the industry. Insurers in the Balkans and beyond had to provide for smooth continuity of business while battling uncontrolled inflation, increasing unemployment, supply chain disruptions and massive uncertainty. Yet even the small Balkan economies did successfully overcome all these challenges. Insurance companies showed that they were proactive in responding to major external shocks, while being also fast in adapting with a dynamic landscape that is frequently facing legal changes, further alignment with EU laws and directives, fast-paced technological advances, and rapid climate change.

Given the wide scope of implications that insurance brings in many different areas of life, there is a plethora of theoretical and empirical research focused on this industry. Many authors have examined and analyzed how this segment of the financial system can be led to development and expansion. Internal and external factors appear to be responsible. Let us focus on internal factors first. Economies of scale hypothesis states that as production expands, the average cost per product drops as fixed costs are shared amongst many more units. On the other hand, there is the economies of scope hypothesis which also has its proponents and opponents. One line of thought states that portfolio diversification is translated in efficiency gains (Conglomeration Hypothesis), while the other states that benefits do arise once the firm specializes. This is also known as the Strategic focus hypothesis. Apart from specialization and size, there is a plethora of demand side, or external factors, that shape the insurance development. External factors are generally categorized into 4 groups: demographic, economic, regulatory, and financial. These are the factors that would be at the center of this study.

In this paper, we will examine the demand-side factors which determine insurance consumption across a randomly selected sample of Balkan countries (Greece, Albania, Croatia, Kosovo, Republic of North Macedonia, Montenegro, and Bulgaria). The very inception of the modern, private insurance markets for the sample countries have occurred within a very similar, if not the same historic context. The development of the industry would start gradually in the 90 s with the proliferation of private companies as opposed to state-ownership which dominated throughout the totalitarian regimes. The markets would evolve from monopolistic structures and state ownership to a state with no barriers to entry neither for domestic nor for international insurance companies. Yet, the late establishment of a modern, private insurance market structure, and the subsequent paths that the countries followed in terms of the economic, political, and social progress resulted in low levels of penetration of insurance, a dominance of non-life vs. life business, a prevalence of compulsory insurance products and a heavy reliance on banking as opposed to other sectors of the financial industry. The underdevelopment of the insurance market in Balkans gives rise to this study which attempts to dig deeper and identify additional forces, besides the historic context, that deter and underpin industry's progress. This study takes a comprehensive empirical approach rarely found in pertinent, regional literature to discover such factors of relevance for the future of the industry.

A thorough examination of the existing literature, regional and international, with a focus on demand side factors is presented next. In Sect. 3, the secondary data on which the study builds are discussed alongside the methodology. The main empirical findings derived from the regression analysis are presented in Sect. 4. Section 5 summarizes the findings of this paper and puts forward some useful recommendations.

2 Literature Review

There is a plethora of research studying the wide range of determinants that can be used to boost insurance sales, hence expanding the industry. In the case of the Balkan region, and its comprising economies, literature is more limited given the late proliferation of insurance markets and the low contribution of industry to economic growth. Yet, given the intense dynamics that such countries are undergoing as well as attempts made to increase the financial sector development, it becomes necessary to identify the factors that can help policymakers navigate through such a dynamic landscape with maximum effectiveness. In the following paragraphs the existing literature on demand-side determinants of insurance development is presented in this order: financial, demographic, regulatory and lastly economic determinants.

High inflationary environments affect the confidence of economic agents by making them think twice before making any investment decisions on new financial or real assets. Given that inflation not only spreads massive uncertainty, but it also erodes the value of insurance policies, it is expected that high levels of inflation are associated with lower demand for insurance. The importance of inflation in shaping insurance-related demand decisions is proved by many researchers: Yavorska et al. (2022), Kolapo et al. (2022), Brokešová and Vachálková (2016), Feyen et al. (2013), Sen and Madheswaran (2013) and many more. Hussels et al. (2005) provided a synopsis of the existing research on insurance demand and concluded that inflation appears to be inversely related to insurance demand. Along the same lines goes Kjosevski (2012). The author used panel data analysis to examine the pool of factors that drive insurance demand in the case of Central and South-Eastern Europe. Results from a fixed effects model showed that inflation exerts a negative, statistically significant impact on insurance consumption regardless of the proxy used to capture it (density or penetration). Yet, there is another group of authors who find the opposite result. In their study of 90 developed and developing countries, Feyen et al. (2013) concluded that contrary to the expectations inflation has a positive effect on insurance consumption. It appears that especially in those economies that have frequent struggles with inflation, people tend to shift from financial to real assets. In the same vein go: Sharku et al. (2021), Abbas and Ning (2016), and Zerriaa and Noubbigh (2016). On the other hand, there are very few studies which advocate the lack of inflation relevance for insurance demand: Zerriaa et al. (2017) and Hwang and Gao (2003). In these last two studies, inflation was found to be insignificant statistics-wise.

The financial sector depth and degree of development are also critical to the expansion of insurance markets. Many studies and applied cases stress the complementarities that exist between other sectors of the financial system development and insurance on the other hand. With the progressive evolution of modern banking, increases in scope and size of banking operations, it seems that insurance and banking products have become more and more inextricably intertwined. A recent study underlined the long-term relationship that exists between financial development and insurance demand (Kolapo et al., 2022). Along the same line goes Cavalcante et al. (2018). In their cointegration analysis, on the case of Brazilian insurance markets, authors highlight the long-term positive relation that exists between financial system and insurance development. The list of proponents of such a complimentary relationship goes on with: Zerriaa et al. (2017), Zerriaa and Noubbigh (2016), Sen and Madheswaran (2013), Feyen et al. (2013), Hussels et al. (2005), and Sen (2008).

Demographic factors are also studied in the literature to investigate the impact they have on life and non-life insurance business. Population is a key variable in this category, examined by many authors. It is expected that population has a positive impact on insurance demand given that it equates with a larger, potential client base and the possibility to capitalize on economies of scale (Feyen et al., 2013; Hussels et al., 2005; Kolapo et al., 2022; Zhang & Zhu, 2005). As economic realities change, especially in the small developing countries, the phenomenon of internal migration intensifies. That said, some authors have also studied a specific fraction of the population i.e., urban population. As collectivism fades, people become more self-centered, hence their support circle gets smaller. With such a social phenomenon also comes a heavy reliance on formal, private contracts to protect one's future. Grabova and Sharku (2021) carried out a study for Western Balkan economies over 2006–2019 time period. Their findings suggest that urban population has a positive, significant impact on insurance consumption. Similar results are also derived by Zyka and Myftaraj (2014).

Regulatory variables present another category of demand-side factors shaping insurance consumption. Various proxies are employed by researchers to capture governance effectiveness and regulatory environment with the most popular indices being rule of law index, control of corruption index and index of regulatory quality. Literature converges on the crucial relevance that this category of factors has in stimulating insurance demand. The importance of law enforceability, higher transparency, and low corruption is stated in a wealth of scientific papers: Yavorska et al. (2022), Grabova and Sharku (2021), Feyen et al. (2013), Kjosevski (2012), and Hussels et al. (2005). Rule of law, regulatory quality and control of corruption are expected to directly influence trust levels of the general public on the proper functioning of the insurance industry. This is especially relevant to developing countries. The majority of these countries face serios problems with law enforcement and legal rights, hence the dominance of regulatory variables in shaping insurance demand. While in developed countries macroeconomic factors steer consumption of insurance, in transition economies there is the legal and regulatory environment which determines to a considerable extent insurance demand (Chang & Lee, 2012).

The last category of factors to be considered consists of economic indicators. Income is the main economic variable whose positive impact is supported by a plethora of researchers. Higher income, as captured by per capita GDP, is translated into higher affordability for insurance products and services, hence justifying its direct and significant impact (Burić et al., 2017; Feyen et al., 2013; Hussels et al., 2005; Hwang & Greenford, 2005; Kalaj et al., 2017; Zaimaj, 2023; Zhang & Zhu, 2005). On the other hand, there are very few studies that hint at the negative impact of income on insurance demand. In their paper which focused on South Asian insurance markets, Sanjeewa et al. (2019) concluded that as income increases, people start to treat insurance as an inferior good, hence decreasing the demand for it. Along similar

Table 1 Expected impact of the variables

Variable	Expected Sign	Authors
Income	+	Zaimaj (2023), Burić et al. (2017), Kalaj et al. (2017), Feyen et al. (2013), and Zhang and Zhu (2005)
Inflation	Ambiguous	(−) Kjosevski (2012), Hussels et al (2005)
		(*No impact*) Zerriaa et al. (2017) and Hwang and Gao (2003)
		(+) Feyen et al. (2013), Sharku et al. (2021), Abbas and Ning (2016), and Zerriaa and Noubbigh (2016)
Population	+	Kolapo et al. (2022), Feyen et al. (2013), Hussels et al. (2005), and Zhang and Zhu (2005)
Trade	+	Kolapo et al. (2022) and Feyen et al. (2013)
Financial Development	+	Kolapo et al (2022), Cavalcante et al. (2018), Zerriaa et al. (2017), Zerriaa and Noubbigh (2016), Sen and Madheswaran (2013), Feyen et al. (2013), Hussels et al. (2005), and Sen (2008)
Legal/Regulatory Environment	+	Yavorska et al. (2022), Grabova and Sharku (2021), Chang and Lee (2012), Feyen et al. (2013), Kjosevski (2012), and Hussels et al. (2005)

lines goes Enz (2000). The author states that at higher levels of income per capita, insurance consumption becomes less sensitive to income growth as insurance product saturation is reached.

Another economic factor which cannot be neglected is the volume of trade. Increasing exports, imports, and other trade-related transactions trigger higher need for insurance, especially in the following product lines: automobile, liability, property, and employment. Such an argument corresponds to the findings of Kolapo et al. (2022) and Feyen et al. (2013).

With reference to the foregoing, we summarize in Table 1 authors' findings about the direction of impact that each of the considered independent variables is found to have on insurance consumption and demand.

3 Data & Methodology

In this study, secondary annual data collected for the period 2010–2022 (inclusive) are employed in a panel regression analysis investigating the main factors that can be used to trigger insurance market development. The sample data is retrieved for the following, randomly selected, Balkan countries: Greece, Albania, Croatia, Kosovo, Republic of North Macedonia, Montenegro, and Bulgaria. These countries are characterized by numerous similarities with respect to the context of insurance sector development, structural factors, and the historic past. At present, these economies are also employing similar reforms to increase financial depth, expand the insurance markets, and establish a higher competitiveness of the region in the international arena.

Three indicators are used to capture the insurance demand: premium volume (per annum); insurance density and insurance penetration. Data on the total premium volume is retrieved from the official websites of the respective supervisory authorities of each country, while insurance density and insurance penetration are computed by the authors. All these three metrics appear in the literature to be reliable indicators of the insurance market development, thus allowing not only to examine drivers of insurance demand and consumption, but simultaneously the drivers behind industry's development. Gross written premium volume captures the total revenues that insurers have received, during each particular reporting period (year), from their customers in exchange for the insurance services provided. Insurance density is calculated by dividing the gross written premiums by the population of that country, while insurance penetration is computed by dividing the gross written premiums by the gross domestic product of each country.

In addition, the analysis accounts for a wide range of demand-side factors, organized into four large categories: financial, demographic, regulatory and economic. As shown in Table 1, data for the seven independent variables is obtained from the World Bank. The first category, which is that of financial variables, includes inflation rate and domestic credit to private sector by banks (as % of GDP). Inflation, as captured by consumer price index (CPI), measures the annual change in the cost of household's basket of goods and services. Literature hints at an ambiguous impact of inflation on insurance consumption. Findings regarding the effect of high inflationary pressures vary among authors, across samples and methodologies. On the other hand, the existing knowledge generally supports the complementarities that exist between financial system development and insurance consumption. In this regard, domestic credit provided by banks to the private sector is used as a proxy to capture the degree of financial development. The World Bank reports this indicator as a percentage of gross domestic product.

Secondly, literature recognizes the importance of accounting for demographic factors. The total population is found to be a crucial determinant of insurance demand as it affects the potential client base. According to the official definition provided by the World Bank, total population includes all residents regardless of legal status or citizenship.

In the third place, the study examines the potential impact of regulatory environment. Two indicators are considered in this regard: control of corruption and regulatory quality. These two indexes vary from 2.5 (best) to negative 2.5 (worst) and are published by the World Bank.[1] They allow us to investigate the potentially

[1] Regulatory quality and control of corruption are two of the six worldwide governance indicators (WGI) published by the World Bank. Regulatory quality is used to show the effectiveness of the government with respect to the formulation and implementation of policies that permit and promote private sector development. Data values closer to 2.5 demonstrate better levels of regulatory quality. Control of corruption measures government effectiveness as it relates to the extent that public officials use their power for private gain or not. Higher control of corruption levels can be found in countries with index values near 2.5.

crucial impact that regulatory factors have on insurance development, especially in the case of developing countries.

Lastly, economic determinants are investigated. Two indicators are considered from this category: per capita income and trade. The former is proxied by per capita GDP while the latter by the sum of exports and imports measured as a percentage of total GDP. Per capita income is used throughout the literature to measure the standard of living, hence also capturing the affordability of consumers for insurance products and services. On the other hand, trade volume is thought to have a direct impact on particular lines of non-life business.

Table 2 below shows the definitions and sources of data. Table 3 summarizes the descriptive statistics (mean, standard deviation, minimum and maximum values).

The empirical analysis, that is presented in Section IV, is based on three different regression equations, explaining respectively: GWP, insurance density and insurance penetration. Given the exogeneity of the explanatory variables, ordinary least squares' regressions are estimated to identify the direction of impact, size of impact and statistical significance of each variable. To decide between a random effects model or a fixed effects model, it was run the Hausman test. It allowed to test the null hypothesis in favor of no systematic differences between the two models' coefficients. Regarding the software package, E-Views 10 is employed in conducting all preliminary checks, tests, and the final empirical analysis. The specification of the regressions is provided below: subscript i denotes the country, the subscript t represents years, α_i are the cross-sectional intercept terms, β's are the slope parameters and ε stands for the error term.

$$\begin{aligned} \mathrm{LGWP_{it}} = \alpha_i &+ \beta_1 * \mathrm{CCOR_{it}} + \beta_2 * \mathrm{REG\_Q_{it}} + \beta_3 * \mathrm{GPOP_{it}} \\ &+ \beta_4 * \mathrm{LGDP\_CAP_{it}} + \beta_5 * \mathrm{TRADE_{it}} \\ &+ \beta_6 * \mathrm{INF_{it}} + \mathrm{T}\beta_7 * \mathrm{DCR\_BANK_{it}} + \varepsilon_{it} \end{aligned} \tag{1}$$

$$\begin{aligned} \mathrm{I\_DENS_{it}} = \alpha_i &+ \beta_1 * \mathrm{CCOR_{it}} + \beta_2 * \mathrm{REG\_Q_{it}} + \beta_3 * \mathrm{GPOP_{it}} \\ &+ \beta_4 * \mathrm{LGDP\_CAP_{it}} + \beta_5 * \mathrm{TRADE_{it}} \\ &+ \beta_6 * \mathrm{INF_{it}} + \beta_7 * \mathrm{DCR\_BANK_{it}} + \varepsilon_{it} \end{aligned} \tag{2}$$

$$\begin{aligned} \mathrm{I\_PEN_{it}} = \alpha_i &+ \beta_1 * \mathrm{CCOR_{it}} + \beta_2 * \mathrm{REG\_Q_{it}} + \beta_3 * \mathrm{GPOP_{it}} \\ &+ \beta_4 * \mathrm{LGDP\_CAP_{it}} + \beta_5 * \mathrm{TRADE_{it}} \\ &+ \beta_6 * \mathrm{INF_{it}} + \beta_7 * \mathrm{DCR\_BANK_{it}} + \varepsilon_{it} \end{aligned} \tag{3}$$

Table 2 Variable sources and definitions

Variables	Description	Sources
DEPENDENT:		
GWP	Total gross written premiums for the market in a year	Supervisory Authorities
Insurance Density	GWP / Population	Authors' Computations
Insurance Penetration	GWP / GDP	Authors' Computations
INDEPENDENT:		
Financial Variables:		
Inflation Rate	Inflation as measured by the consumer price index reflects the annual percentage change in the cost to the average consumer of acquiring a basket of goods and services	World Bank
Financial Development	Domestic credit to private sector by banks	World Bank
Economic Variables:		
Trade Volume	Trade is the sum of exports and imports of goods and services measured as a share of gross domestic product	World Bank
GDP per Capita	GDP per capita (current US$)	World Bank
Demographic Variables:		
Population Growth	Annual change of total population; with population counting all residents regardless of legal status or citizenship	World Bank
Regulatory Variables:		
Regulatory Quality	Regulatory Quality captures perceptions of the ability of the government to formulate and implement sound policies and regulations that permit and promote private sector development	World Bank
Control of Corruption Index	Control of Corruption captures perceptions of the extent to which public power is exercised for private gain, including both petty and grand forms of corruption, as well as "capture" of the state by elites and private interests	World Bank

Table 3 Summary of descriptive statistics

	MEAN	STD.DEV	MIN	MAX
GDP per Capita (USD/per capita)	9,708.479	5,583.785	3,009.523	26,716.650
Financial Development	52.336	22.033	24.623	119.108
Inflation Rate (%)	2.480	3.319	−1.736	15.325
Trade Volume (%)	94.808	22.542	51.197	170.818
Population Growth Rate (%)	−0.439	0.819	−5.980	0.899
Regulatory Quality (−2.5 to 2.5)	0.315	0.260	−0.389	0.701
Control of corruption Index (−2.5 to 2.5)	−0.236	0.235	−0.779	0.201
GWP (thousand EUR)	1,160,000	1,420,000	58,526	5,420,000
Insurance Penetration (%)	1.707	0.593	0.620	2.900
Insurance Density (EUR/per capita)	159.076	127.084	20.145	487.729

4 Empirical Analysis

4.1 Preliminary Tests and Hypotheses

One important consideration with panel data analysis concerns non-stationarity. The presence of a unit root in any of the variables gives rise to spurious regression problem, hence rendering the estimation results distorted and unreliable. Therefore, Philips Perron Test (Chi-Square) was run to check the following hypotheses:

H_0: The variable has a unit root.

H_a: The variable has no unit root.

Refer to Table 4 for the detailed results. As depicted below, in first differences all variables appear stationary. The null hypothesis was rejected with 95% confidence level.

Using E-Views 10, the correlation matrix was built which presents the direction (positive or negative) and strength of relationships between each pair of the explanatory variables. To avoid multicollinearity, the literature suggests that the threshold of 80% should not be exceeded. As Table 5 below suggests, there is no perfect collinearity between the regression variables.

The following hypotheses are tested for each of the models (1, 2 and 3):

H_a: The impact of control of corruption on the explained variable is significant statistics-wise.

H_a: The impact of financial development on the explained variable is significant statistics-wise.

H_a: The impact of per capita income on the explained variable is significant statistics-wise.

H_a: The impact of rule of law on the explained variable is significant statistics-wise.

H_a: The impact of regulatory quality on the explained variable is significant statistics-wise.

H_a: The impact of trade on the explained variable is significant statistics-wise.

H_a: The impact of population on the explained variable is significant statistics-wise.

Table 4 Unit root test

Variable	Symbol	Level	First Difference
Control of Corruption	CCOR	0.7081	0.0000
Domestic Credit to Private Sector	FDEV	0.2089	0.0000
GDP per capita (logged)	LGDP_CAP	0.8654	0.0000
Regulatory Quality	REG_Q	0.8976	0.0000
Trade Volume	TRADE	0.4066	0.0165
Inflation Rate	INF	0.9083	0.0312
Population Growth	GPOP	0.7823	0.0000
Insurance density	I_DENS	1.0000	0.0006
GWP (logged)	LGWP	0.9998	0.0000
Insurance Penetration	I_PEN	0.2169	0.0000

Note Numbers on this table are P-values obtained by Philips Perron Test

Table 5 Correlation table

	CCOR	REG_Q	GPOP_	LGDP_ CAP	TRADE	INF	FDEV
CCOR	1.0000						
REG_Q	−0.0006	1.0000					
GPOP_	−0.0372	0.1306	1.0000				
LGDP_ CAP	0.0916	0.0952	−0.1838	1.0000			
TRADE	0.1146	0.0697	−0.2716	0.4413	1.0000		
INF	0.0874	−0.0460	−0.3831	0.3303	0.5234	1.0000	
FDEV	−0.1306	−0.1040	0.2327	−0.2663	−0.4293	−0.2854	1.0000

4.2 FEM Model Findings

The discussion that follows is based on the final estimation results of the three fixed effects models, explaining respectively the variability in gross written premiums, insurance density and insurance penetration. For the findings, refer to Table 6.

Model one aims to investigate the main drivers behind insurance market development by analyzing the variability in gross written premium volume. According to the estimation results, it is shown that gross premium volume is explained by control of corruption and financial development. Any change in control of corruption index, increases total GWP by 19.13% ceteris paribus. The positive association between higher control of corruption as a phenomenon and insurance market development is also stated in the literature. Chang and Lee (2012) underline the critical role that regulatory and institutional variables, corruption included, play in promoting insurance specifically in developing economies. Along the same lines go Yavorska et al. (2022).

Table 6 Estimation results

	1	2	3
CCOR	0.1913* (0.1051) [1.8207]	0.0118 (0.1688) [0.0698]	0.3866** (0.1749) [2.2107]
REG_Q	0.1135 (0.0794) [1.4286]	0.2726** (0.1304) [2.0900]	0.4009** (0.1897) [2.1135]
GPOP	−0.6910 (1.0881) [−0.6351]	−6.0734*** (2.0538) [−2.9571]	2.0188 (1.2741) [1.5845]
LGDP_CAP	0.0166 (0.1632) [0.1017]	0.2499 (0.1521) [1.6434]	0.6040*** (0.1980) [3.0498]
TRADE	−0.0002 (0.0016) [−0.1140]	−0.0020 (0.0020) [−1.0000]	−0.0047 (0.0033) [−1.4558]
INF	0.0055 (0.0043) [1.2666]	0.0098* (0.0055) [1.7753]	−0.0112 (0.0079) [−1.4122]
FDEV	−0.0041* (0.0024) [−1.7428]	−0.0146*** (0.0042) [−3.4410]	0.0120** (0.0050) [2.3868]
R-Squared	0.2480	0.5112	0.2342
Prob (F-stat)	0.0439	0.0000	0.0667

Note White's heteroskedasticity-consistent t-values are given in brackets. In parentheses, there are presented the standard errors. ***, ** and * represent significance at 1, 5 and 10% level respectively

Authors underline that state, and supervisory authorities have to pay close attention to and control corruption, as it is a direct driver of insurance market development. As far as financial development is concerned, its impact appears to be negligible (−0.41%) and significant only with 90% confidence level. The other explanatory variables appear to be statistically insignificant. The overall explanatory power of the model is 24.80% as captured by the coefficient of determination (R-squared).

To explain insurance market development, Model 2 uses as a dependent variable the insurance consumption per person as proxied by insurance density. In this model, it appears that regulatory quality, population, inflation, and financial development are significant in explaining the dependent variable. In line with other researchers, it is found that regulatory quality supports insurance consumption (Feyen et al., 2013). The marginal impact of the index of regulatory quality is 0.2726. Further, population growth is seen to hinder insurance density in the case of Balkan countries. One potential reason can be the lower pace of growth in the demand for insurance, as compared to growth in population. Similarly, financial development seems to repress insurance density; the coefficient is small (−0.0146) but significant. Lastly, in the case of Balkan countries, higher inflationary pressures seem to be associated with higher insurance density. This goes in line with the findings from a plethora of researchers: Feyen et al. (2013), Sharku et al. (2021), Abbas and Ning (2016), and Zerriaa and Noubbigh (2016). The reason for this might be traced to the inherent uncertainties that citizens of this region face. In response to frequent periods of economic downturn, external and internal shocks, people of the Balkans seem to attempt to secure their future by relying on insurance. This comes as no surprise, knowing that in the region the investment opportunities are limited compared to European counterparts; mainly deposits, real estate or insurance products. Specifically, the coefficient of inflation is 0.0098 (small, yet significant). Overall, the model explains 51.12% of the variability in insurance density.

Model 3 sheds light on the main determinants of insurance penetration. According to the estimation results, population growth, trade and inflation have no significant impact on insurance penetration. Yet, the other four explanatory variables result to be significant with 95% confidence level. All four significant regressors appear to support higher insurance penetration rates, which goes in line with the examined literature. For any change in control of corruption levels, insurance penetration is expected to rise by 0.3866 percentage points ceteris paribus. This is not the only regulatory variable which seems to drive insurance penetration. Results show that an increase in regulatory quality translates to 0.4009 percentage points increase in penetration rates. Affordability plays a critical role in shaping buyers' decisions. It seems that improvements in per capita income by 1% are associated with a 0.006 percentage points increase in the dependent variable. This is expected, as it goes in line with the findings of: Zaimaj (2023), Burić et al. (2017), Kalaj et al. (2017), Feyen et al. (2013), and Zhang and Zhu (2005). Lastly, financial development appears to contribute to higher penetration rates. Such complementarities do exist between the banking and insurance industry. The majority of products provided by banks require lenders to have life or property insurance, hence explaining how the banking industry and other financial institutions can push further the development of insurance market. In line with what previous researchers suggest, it is found a positive, significant impact of financial development on Y. For any percentage point increase in domestic credit provided by banks to the private sector tends to increase the insurance penetration by 0.0120 percentage points ceteris paribus. Overall, the model has an explanatory power of 23.42%.

5 Conclusion

This paper aims to analyze the insurance market development in a highly dynamic region such as the Balkans. These countries are characterized by strong structural similarities, yet differences do exist. Besides all factors that they have in common, one important consideration has to be given to current efforts to increase economic and financial development. In this regard, it becomes important to understand where one important pillar of the financial system stands: the insurance industry. The financial system, insurance included, is found to be critical to long-term growth; however, these countries seem to fall behind when considering the development of this sector compared to their counterparts. Reasons behind this fact can be traced back to the historic context as well as market conditions, and local reality. History-wise, the very inception of the modern, private insurance markets for the sample countries have occurred relatively late, in the 90 s with the proliferation of private companies as opposed to state-ownership which dominated throughout the totalitarian regimes. The markets would evolve from monopolistic structures and state ownership to a state with no barriers to entry neither for domestic nor for international insurance companies. Yet, the late establishment of a modern, private insurance market structure, and the subsequent paths that the countries followed in terms of the economic, political, and social progress resulted in low levels of penetration of insurance, a dominance of non-life vs. life business, a prevalence of compulsory insurance products and a heavy reliance on banking as opposed to other sectors of the financial industry. This study attempts to identify additional forces, besides the historic context, that deter and underpin industry's progress. Given the numerous functions that insurance industry serves, such as protection and security, risk transfer, investments, and contribution to economic growth, it becomes necessary to understand on which factors should the reforms focus most.

In this study, we analyze insurance consumption across eight randomly-selected Balkan countries, namely Albania, Kosovo, Croatia, Greece, North Macedonia, Romania, Montenegro, and Bulgaria for the years 2010–2022. Four groups of factors were used to identify the main drivers of insurance consumption in the region: financial, demographic, regulatory and economic. To examine insurance consumption and its main determinants, three regressions were estimated explaining respectively: Gross written premiums, insurance penetration and insurance density. The in-depth panel data analysis showed that insurance density was substantially explained by regulatory quality, financial development, population, and inflation. When insurance penetration was considered, estimation results appeared significant only in the case of per capita income, financial development, control of corruption and regulatory quality. Lastly, the total premium volume was shown to be driven by financial development and control of corruption. Knowing the inherent obstacles of these countries as well as the overall institutional quality and economic state, such results prove not only meaningful, but also strongly useful. It seems that reforms have to target especially the regulatory factors. People have to firstly believe in the proper implementation of the law, contract enforcement, market regulation, transparency, and fairness of the system. For this to happen, the role of the state has to be strengthened, thus providing proper monitoring, supervision and implementation of the legal framework. If concrete steps are taken, the perspective on insurance would likely change substantially. Even the literature stresses the predominance and increased relevance that legal environment has in shaping insurance demand in the case of developing countries. Further, the economic climate has to be on focus. Improvements in the standard of living translate to higher affordability, hence triggering insurance demand and consumption. Such countries suffer from low wages, hence reforms affecting both the public and private sector are necessary to ensure better purchasing power for individuals in the region which, as shown by the empirical results, would translate to higher insurance consumption.

This research adds to the scarce regional literature by providing a thorough empirical analysis which brings to light the main drivers behind insurance consumption and development. It points out key factors which have to be considered in current and future reforms, both of a legal and economic nature. This research serves policy makers for their day-to-day decisions and reforms, as well as firms, practitioners, and academicians.

References

Abbas, A. O., & Ning, L. (2016). Factors that drive the development of insurance industry in Tanzania. *World Journal of Finance and Investment Research, 1*(1), 1–12.

Beenstock, M., Dickinson, G., & Khajuria, S. (1986). The determination of life premiums: An international cross-section analysis 1970–1981. *Insurance: Mathematics and Economics, 5*(4), 261–270.

Berisha, S. (2019). Analysis of the premium trend in the insurance industry in Kosovo 2013–2017. *Knowledge-International Journal, 31*(1), 113–122.

Brokešová, Z., & Vachálková, I. (2016). *Macroeconomic environment and insurance industry development: The case of Visegrad group countries.*

Burić, M. N., Smolović, J. C., Božović, M. L., & Filipović, A. L. (2017). Impact of economic factors on life insurance development in Western Balkan Countries. *Zbornik Radova Ekonomskog Fakulteta u Rijeci: Časopis Za Ekonomsku Teoriju i Praksu, 35*(2), 331–352.

Cavalcante, R. T., Sobreiro, V. A., & Kimura, H. (2018). Determinants of the non-life insurance market in Brazil. *Review of Development Finance, 8*(2), 89–95.

Chang, C. H., & Lee, C. C. (2012). Non-linearity between life insurance and economic development: A revisited approach. *The Geneva Risk and Insurance Review, 37*, 223–257.

Enz, R. (2000). The S-curve relation between per-capita income and insurance penetration. *The Geneva Papers on Risk and Insurance-Issues and Practice, 25*, 396–406.

Feyen, E., Lester, R. R., & Rocha, R. D. R. (2013). What drives the development of the insurance sector? An empirical analysis based on a panel of developed and developing countries. *Journal of Financial Perspectives, 1*(1).

Grabova, P., & Sharku, G. (2021). Drivers of life insurance consumption-an empirical analysis of Western Balkan countries. *Economic Annals, 66*(231), 33–58.

Hussels, S., Ward, D., & Zurbruegg, R. (2005). Stimulating the demand for insurance. *Risk Management and Insurance Review, 8*(2), 257–278.

Hwang, T., & Gao, S. (2003). The determinants of the demand for life insurance in an emerging economy–the case of China. *Managerial Finance, 29*(5/6), 82–96.

Hwang, T., & Greenford, B. (2005). A cross-section analysis of the determinants of life insurance consumption in Mainland China, Hong Kong, and Taiwan. *Risk Management and Insurance Review, 8*(1), 103–125.

Kalaj, E., Merko, F., & Zisi, A. (2017). Evaluating the insurance development-economic growth nexus in Albania. *Eastern European Business and Economics Journal, 3*(4), 350–359.

Kjosevski, J. (2012). The determinants of life insurance demand in central and southeastern Europe. *International Journal of Economics and Finance, 4*(3), 237–247.

Koçi, E., Hoxha, V., Bombaj, F., & Haderi, S. (2021). Economic and financial impact of the Covid-19 pandemic on the insurance market in Albania, Serbia and Northern Macedonia. *Acta Universitatis Danubius. Œconomica, 17*(5).

Kolapo, F. T., Oluwaleye, T. O., & Osasona, A. V. (2022). Determinants of insurance sector development in Nigeria. *Account and Financial Management Journal, 7*(03), 2672–2685.

Li, D., Moshirian, F., Nguyen, P., & Wee, T. (2007). The demand for life insurance in OECD countries. *Journal of Risk and Insurance, 74*(3), 637–652.

Sanjeewa, W. S., Hongbing, O., & Hashmi, S. H. (2019). Determinants of life insurance consumption in emerging insurance markets of South-Asia. *International Journal of Information, Business and Management, 11*(4), 109–129.

Sen, S., & Madheswaran, S. (2013). Regional determinants of life insurance consumption: Evidence from selected Asian economies. *Asian-Pacific Economic Literature, 27*(2), 86–103.

Sen, S., 2008. An analysis of life insurance demand determinants for selected Asian Economies and India. *Chennai, India: Madras School of Economics.*

Sharku, G., & Bajrami, E. (2021). Insurance-economic growth nexus–evidence from selected Western Balkan's Countries. *Regional Science Inquiry, 13*(2), 53–68.

Sharku, G., & Kumi, E. (2021). Does insurance market impact the economic growth? Evidence from Albania. *The European Journal of Comparative Economics, 18*(2), 267–289.

Sharku, G., Grabova, P., & Vullnetari, D. (2021). Impact of economic factors on life and non-life insurance development in Albania–A VECM analysis. *Universal Journal of Accounting and Finance, 9*, 1280.

Yavorska, T., Lyudmyla, V., & Dmytro, V. (2022). *The impact of macroeconomic factors on the development of the insurance system in Ukraine.*

Zaimaj, E. (2023). Insurance demand in Albania—An investigation of main supporters and impediments. *Challenges of the Society facing Digital Transformation*, pp. 77–91.

Zerriaa, M., & Noubbigh, H. (2016). Determinants of life insurance demand in the MENA region. *The Geneva Papers on Risk and Insurance-Issues and Practice, 41*, 491–511.

Zerriaa, M., Amiri, M. M., Noubbigh, H., & Naoui, K. (2017). Determinants of life insurance demand in Tunisia. *African Development Review, 29*(1), 69–80.

Zhang, C., & Zhu, N. (2005). *Determinants of the development of insurance in China under the globalization.*

Zyka, E., & Myftaraj, E. (2014). Factors affecting the insurance sector development: Evidence from Albania. *The Romanian Economic Journal, 51*, 171–188.

Politics of IMF Lending in Times of Crisis: Greece and Argentina

Spyros A. Roukanas and Vaggelis Vitzileos

Abstract The global economy has been subject to severe shocks due to successive crises in recent years (global financial crisis, COVID-19, war in Ukraine, etc.). In the context of crises of this scale, the role of International Financial Institutions (IFIs), such as the International Monetary Fund (IMF), is to ensure the proper functioning of the global economy by providing financial support to countries facing difficulties due to the impact of the crisis, while strengthening cooperation at the international and regional levels. One of the IMF's fundamental missions is to provide loans that are tailored to the countries' different needs and specific circumstances, following the terms and rules of its Articles of Agreement. However, this study shows that recent cases, such as the euro zone and Argentina crisis, indicate that the Fund's lending policies are vulnerable to political and geopolitical influence. In addition, the review shows that lending with more lenient conditionality criteria is associated with the Fund's strongest shareholder countries, while more strict conditions are associated with developing and low- and middle-income countries. The study also attempts to demonstrate policies and arrangements within the Bretton Woods institution to limit its vulnerability to that influence in an era of de-globalisation, geo-economic fragmentation, and increasing international competition.

Keywords International Monetary Fund · Economic policy · Geopolitics

JEL Classification Codes F00 · F33 · F53

S. A. Roukanas · V. Vitzileos (✉)
Department of International and European Studies, University of Piraeus, Piraeus, Greece
e-mail: v.vitzileos@unipi.gr

S. A. Roukanas
e-mail: sroukana@unipi.gr

I. Bartusevičiene et al. (eds.), *Building Resilience Through Digital Transformation and Sustainable Innovation*, Springer Proceedings in Business and Economics,
https://doi.org/10.1007/978-3-031-90054-9_3

1 Introduction

The International Monetary Fund was established on 22 July 1944, at the Bretton Woods Conference in New Hampshire, USA, taking on the role of the guardian of the world economy, with the dual objective of promoting the normalisation of balance of payments and maintaining global financial stability Boughton, 2014: 35). According to Article 1 of its Articles of Agreement (fifth point), one of the Fund's main objectives is to make its resources available, under certain safeguards, to its member countries to correct balance of payments malfunctions without resorting to measures that are destructive to national or international welfare (IMF, 2022a). In particular, it provides financing to countries in crisis—due to internal or external factors—to provide them with the necessary room for manoeuvre in order to implement policies that will restore economic stability and growth (IMF, 2022b). During crises, although it does not perform the role of a central bank, the Fund operates as an international lender of last resort for countries that have lost access to bond markets (Fischer, 1999).

In this context, the IMF's Articles of Agreement stipulate that the organisation -whose member states are also its shareholders- should follow a doctrine of economic neutrality based only on economic criteria (Swedberg, 1986: 377). However, one of the main criticisms against the Fund is, according to the literature, that its policy- and decision-making is influenced by its most powerful shareholders, and especially by the most powerful of them, the United States.

During the political fermentation for the creation of the IMF and the World Bank, the United States, disagreeing with Keynes, imposed a series of mechanisms and processes that "politicised" the Bretton Woods institutions through member country quotas in the voting system (Swedberg, 1986: 378). Votes in the IMF are determined by the size of each member country (and shareholder of the Fund) and thus the larger countries have a greater say in the Fund's decisions, while their ally countries receive preferential treatment, with large loan amounts for example, even if they do not strictly adhere to the conditions imposed (Vreeland, 2006: 2).

The purpose of this study is to highlight the influence of geopolitical and political factors on the IMF's lending policy in crisis situations. By studying the cases of Greece and Argentina, it attempts to answer several questions: Do the interests and aspirations of the Fund's more powerful member states influence its lending? Does this politicisation have an exogenous origin or does it also come from within the internal processes and bureaucracy of this international organisation? How is this influence reflected on the procedures for granting loans, their conditionality, and their effectiveness?

In terms of methodology, this study is a literature review, which attempts to compare IMF policies, assessing the effectiveness of the Fund's economic policy. In this context, the choice of the two case studies, Greece and Argentina, was made in view of the differences between the two countries, which offers a favourable field for comparison, but also to highlight the broadness of the aforementioned policy factors in the IMF's lending policy, offering useful lessons for the future. The politicisation of IMF lending is a constantly evolving issue in the literature, especially as it is shaped by geopolitical correlations. Studies such as Vreeland (2006) on the IMF's conditional lending policy, Dreher and Jensen (2007) on the impact of US interests on the Fund's conditionality, and Thacker (1999) on the high politics of the international financial institution's lending reveal the multiple dimensions of this politicisation.

The comparative analysis between the Greek and Argentinean cases attempts to draw lessons for the IMF, as both cases are examples of the Fund's failure as a crisis manager. Thus, the conclusions of this comparative analysis can provide a new perspective for similar cases in the future, at different stages of IMF lending policy, using the following criteria: the conditions for programme approval, the conditionality of programmes, the conditions for continuation or interruption of the funding, and the criteria for concluding new lending agreements.

The first section is a literature review linking political factors to IMF lending policies. The second section examines the case of Greece, focusing on its recourse to the support mechanism in spring 2010, which marked the beginning of the IMF's involvement in addressing the euro zone crisis. The third section analyses the case of Argentina, with a focus on its bankruptcy in 2001 and the 2018 loan. The fourth section includes the conclusions of the study and offers suggestions for discussion on how to limit the "politicisation" of the international organisation's lending policy.

1.1 IMF Lending Policy and (Geo)political Influence

Political influence on lending processes derives from both the structure and processes within the IMF, while the means, by which such influence can be promoted through lending policy, vary.

The Fund currently comprises 191 member countries. The Board of Governors, which is the highest decision-making body in the organisation, comprises one Governor from each member state (and one alternate), who are appointed by each country (IMF, 2021). The US holds 16.5% of the votes in the Board of Governors, with the right to veto decisions, Japan 6.14%, China 6.08%, Germany 5.31%, the UK and France 4.03% each, Italy 3.02%, Russia 2.59%, and India 2.63% of the votes. The quota system is instrumental to the source of financial resources of the organisation, with the IMF's decision-making system being based on it (Naskou-Perraki et al., 2019: 244).

Methodologically, capturing and mapping the political influence on the Fund's lending policy is quite difficult since it cannot be quantified. However, research results and specific data, linking political influences to IMF lending decisions, can be found in the literature and will be presented below.

Conditionality, i.e. the conditions attached to loans in exchange for financial support, plays an important role in the lending policy and its characteristics. According to the IMF, conditionality refers to the agreement to adjust the economic policies of a country entering into a loan agreement with the Fund in order to "overcome the problems that led to the request for support." It also points out that these policies are conditions of the loans to ensure that the country "adopts strong and effective policies" (IMF, 2023). Conditionality, in essence, is the prevention/treatment of "moral hazard" to limit the risk that governments receiving financial support will avoid policies that would prevent new financial crises (Vreeland, 2006: 2). In this context, it should not be overlooked that the excessive size of a programme, in terms of the number of policy implementation conditions, can also lead to its failure (Krahnke, 2023), so it can easily be understood that conditionality can be used as leverage by the agency and its shareholders.

The inclusion of a country among the developed or developing countries of the world, especially the allies of the United States, is an important criterion for potential reliance on IMF funds. This distinction appears in the literature, with developed economies not being directly dependent on the funds and associated conditions of the international financial institutions, while developing economies, on the contrary, are necessarily turning to this option (Stasinopoulos, 2023: 169). Dreher and Jensen found in their study that the Fund's strongest shareholder country, the US, was an influential factor in programme conditionality, since countries aligned with the US in UN General Council voting positions received loans with fewer conditions (2007: 107). Indeed, the conditions were fewer when the lending support was provided before elections in the requesting countries, which were political allies of Washington. Ray et al. (2022) also found that countries closer to the US and Western countries—the strongest shareholders of the Fund—were in a more favourable position in terms of the conditions of the structural adjustment programmes they signed, while, in contrast, countries with closer diplomatic relations with China faced more onerous conditions and greater austerity. The latter element is particularly important at a time of intensifying international competition, especially after the outbreak of the war in Ukraine. At this point, it is useful to highlight the connection between US interests and IMF lending, with Oatley and Yackee (2004: 41) noting (i) the link between the interests of US commercial banks and the Fund's lending decisions, (ii) the association of these interests with privileged positions within the international organization, and (iii) the influence of US foreign policy on the Fund's lending policy making. The role of banks in IMF policy is important on multiple levels, as it is also linked to the approval of Fund financing through the US Congress (Broz & Hawes, 2006: 392). Furthermore, an aspect related to the very perspective of some borrowing countries, which contributes to the failure of IMF structural adjustment programmes, should be noted. A number of countries acknowledge that its access to financial support depends on its relations with powerful donor countries that act as their 'protectors', thus transforming conditionality from economic to political (Stone, 2004: 577).

There are of course various ways for accelerated lending from the Fund—including possible preferential treatment of countries—as has been documented. Vaubel (1996: 196) has referred to "hurry-up lending" by the IMF when the international financial institution comes close to revising the quotas of its member countries from which the Fund draws its resources. Since the review takes place at least every five years, once three years have elapsed the rate of lending from the Fund is accelerated (Vreeland, 2006: 40).

Thaker, in summary, lists three reasons why politics plays an important role within the IMF (1999: 40–41): (i) Despite countries' non-compliance with programme conditionality, the Fund continues to provide financing, not on economic but on political terms, and more specifically, according to the interests of the powerful industrialised countries; (ii) Country representatives are appointees of member governments, subsequently expressing the respective aspirations of the countries' leaders; and (iii) the weighted voting and decision-making procedures leave room for political wheeling and dealing. Lipscy and Lee (2018: 25) described the IMF as a "biased global insurance mechanism" because of the fact that decision-making in the Bretton Woods institution is deeply politicised and biased towards the interests of a small number of highly influential countries. This bias, they explain, creates a moral hazard asymmetry, encouraging some countries to pursue risky economic policies, while countries without influence necessarily opt, through the accumulation of international reserves, for "aggressive self-insurance." Furthermore, their research finds that the Fund's support on favourable terms is more likely to be granted to Western financial institutions, which thus enjoy comparative advantages in the context of international lending. However, political interventions can also have indirect consequences. Sturm and Lee Andresen (2022: 306) found that the influence of geopolitical factors on a country receiving an IMF programme creates a negative market reaction, increasing the likelihood of limiting the effectiveness of the programme itself.

In any case, as highlighted by the literature, the United States, being the strongest shareholder of the Fund, with the dollar as a key instrument, was and is de facto the main force behind the IMF system (Mundell, 1968: 142) with the international financial institution being used as a useful tool by US international policy (Mandelbaum, 2016: 46). The Washington Consensus, moreover, the policy mix of liberalisation, deregulation and privatisation (Kaya & Reay, 2019), was directly linked to the political aspirations of the United States through the Bretton Woods institutions. According to Lutz (2015: 86), the core of the Consensus was an embodied application of IMF conditionality, with conditions imposed on governments to provide loans.

Copelovitch (2010) highlights another aspect of things: in attempting to answer the question "who controls the IMF?" he concludes that, according to the usual criticisms, the Fund does indeed act to serve the interests of its most powerful shareholder countries. That said, it also acts as a broadly autonomous bureaucracy in other cases, which, he argues, reveals the above claim to be one-dimensional and simplistic.

In light of all of the above, the IMF's lending policy displays a vulnerability to political and geopolitical pressures, particularly when crisis conditions prevail. The cases of Greece and Argentina, which are discussed below, display different characteristics and objectives of the agents of political pressures.

1.2 Greece: The Systemic Risk and the Fund's Involvement in the Euro Zone

The IMF's involvement in the euro zone and in the 2010 Greek bailout has a number of particularities. The urgency of supporting the country and the Fund's involvement in the rescue of a euro area country in cooperation with the European authorities favoured conditions conducive to the influence of political pressures both in the adoption of the first structural adjustment programme, and in particular the Fund's participation in it, and in the course of this support.

In the spring of 2010, the Obama administration assessed that the crisis in the euro zone was a systemic risk capable of transmitting this crisis to the United States (Tooze, 2018: 256), two years after the outbreak of the global financial crisis, while the US economy was recovering from its consequences. Greece, moreover, was the first country in the Eurozone to face the effects of this global crisis, without the existence of any European mechanism for managing similar situations (Marangos, 2023: 2). While the ECB had no prior experience, the European Commission had only limited financial aid experience (Pisani-Ferry et al., 2013: 18–19).

The bailout of Greece was considered imperative by both the US and Europe. Thus, pressure from the US administration, combined with that from German Chancellor Angela Merkel, led to the IMF's participation in the support mechanism for Greece, a decision that was ratified at the EU Summit on 25 March 2010, overriding the objections of France and the European Central Bank, which considered the Fund's involvement in European affairs to be "humiliating" (Tooze, 2018: 266). European concerns about the reliability of the European Commission to be an effective overseer of crisis management was also one of the main reasons for the call of the IMF technocrats (Hodson 2015: 592). At the same time, countries of the European North wanted the IMF to join the support mechanism because it would take a tougher stance than the European Commission and the European Central Bank (James, 2024: 107–287).

At this point, it is important to mention that the political aspirations of the IMF itself and its leadership also played a significant role at this particular juncture. The Fund, with Dominique Strauss-Kahn as its Managing Director—who was, in fact, being touted as a potential rival to Sarkozy in the French presidential elections—saw its involvement in the euro zone crisis as an opportunity to re-enter the international spotlight (James, 2024: 108) after a period of marginalisation. However, the head of the IMF, given that the Fund could not institutionally and politically take over the role of the ECB in the bailout plan, set as a condition for its participation that the European side should lead the support and the Fund should be limited to a secondary role with technical assistance and limited resources (Blustein, 2015: 6).

According to Ashoka Mody (2017b), the IMF's involvement was for Angela Merkel the signal that would convince the citizens of Germany that urgent financial assistance was necessary for Greece, provided that strict discipline was imposed on its use, through the Fund. The German Chancellor's policy objectives were aligned with the strategy of the Fund's Managing Director and somehow, he added, the Fund became a "tool" of the EU, and Berlin in particular, in Greece.

Apart from the political agreement between the Europeans and the IMF, the Fund would have to go beyond the framework of its rules to be able to get involved in the Eurozone crisis. According to Blustein, Fund officials made 'legal manoeuvres' to get the IMF involved in the Greek bailout, especially after the Argentine experience, which was recorded as one of the biggest failures of the international financial institution (2015: 2). Nordström and Laiho (2023: 286) list the reasons why the IMF's participation in Greece's Stand-By Arrangement (SBA) loan programme was problematic: First, the Fund changed its own rules to formulate an exemption regime for the Greek rescue. Second, the Greek case, which was the first episode of the euro zone crisis, influenced the further management and response to the crisis by the Fund and its European partners, but also shaped the IMF's global role. Third, the painful consequences of the structural adjustment programme for the Greek economy led to a focus on the austerity policies that influenced the design of the Memorandum of Understanding (MoU).

The Fund, unlike its practice in other countries, in the case of Greece, did not have the options of devaluing the currency (to help exports and tourism) and making an autonomous monetary policy (Wroughton et al., 2015) as it is a member of a monetary union under the supervision of the ECB. Moreover, it also lost the debt restructuring option, which, as we will see, created the most complications in its involvement. Mody (2017a) also criticised the attitude of the US Treasury Secretary, Timothy Geithner, and the US government to support the European position of not restructuring Greek debt in May 2010 (so as not to harm private investors), despite warnings from Fund managers. In its assessment of the Greek programme, the IMF's Independent Evaluation Office (IEO IMF) highlighted that "the Executive Board approved the provision of financing without seeking a precautionary restructuring of the debt, which was not considered sustainable with high certainty," adding that there was no open and timely discussion of the advantages and disadvantages of all the options available to the Fund (IEO 2016: 37). The authors of the report also noted that the IMF, due to its cooperation with the Europeans in the Troika format, lost its competences as a predominant crisis manager, adding that since the Eurogroup was represented in the negotiations by the Commission, the decisions of the IMF technical teams were put early on under political pressure (IEO 2016: 38). Strauss-Kahn was expressing the IMF's restrictions within the Troika, with a view to ensuring an image of unity among the lenders, and thus preventing any public disagreement and confrontation (Blustein, 2015: 8). Former economist and former IMF historian James Boughton argued that Europe did not seem to be concerned about what would happen to the Greek economy, focusing only on the protection of the financial system of the monetary union· that was, according to him, a 'tactical error' that trapped the Fund in the Troika scheme, essentially undermining its autonomy (Wroughton et al., 2015).

The failure of Greece's first structural adjustment programme, with the non-restructuring of the country's debt as a key factor, was a foregone conclusion within the IMF. A memo from the Fund's former chief economist, Olivier Blanchard, on 4

May 2010 warned the then head of the mission to Greece, Poul Thomsen, that the Memorandum would not have a successful outcome, even if its terms were implemented with absolute consistency (Centre for International Governance Innovation, 2017).

The last Fund disbursement to Greece was in 2014, as part of the second adjustment programme. In the third programme no IMF money was disbursed, because of the Fund's disagreement with the Commission and the ECB on the sustainability of Greek debt (Thomsen, 2019). Thomsen stated that "while the bailout in 2010 was justified by systemic concerns, this, in retrospect, entailed a conversion from private to public debt that largely politicised the debt issue" and admitted that "we did not foresee the extent to which the escalating crisis between Greece and its European partners would politicise the debt issue."

In conclusion, despite the systemic risk posed by a worsening of the Greek crisis in 2010, the IMF's choice to participate in the provision of financial support to the country, contributing to the pressured design of an a priori failed and painful structural adjustment programme and to an ineffective cooperation with the EU, proved that the political criteria by which the Fund became involved in the euro zone led to very negative results (IMF 2013), hence the subsequent "correction" of the second programme.

1.3 Argentina—IMF: A Perpetual Vicious Economic Cycle

Argentina's interconnection with the International Monetary Fund is particularly long, with critics pointing to an intense and ongoing process of politicisation of the Fund's lending procedures. The Latin American country has signed 22 lending agreements since joining the members list of the international organisation in 1956.

The Fund has been criticised in the past, inter alia, because, contrary to its rules, which provide for the granting of temporary financial support, it has established a long-term relationship with some countries (Marchesi & Sabani, 2007). The practice of the Fund approving successive loans is referred to by Bird et al., (2004: 232) as "recidivism," entrenching a "routine of dependency" (Kedar, 2013: 187–184). Reinsberg et al. spoke of borrowing countries being trapped in a cycle of dependency (2022
: 1024) on IMF loans, as failure leads to a return to the Fund with new requests for financial support. According to their study, of the 763 lending programmes from 1980 to 2015, 512 faced implementation problems to the point of suspension, and 291 of these were never resumed. Kaplan and Shim (2024: 852) found that when the contagion risk of a global crisis is at a high level, the Fund tends to overlook a borrower country's non-compliance by continuing to provide financing. Conversely, when this risk does not exist it uses non-compliance with the terms of the programme to exit from it.

The culmination of Argentina's crisis was the country's bankruptcy in December 2001, which was the outcome of the implementation of the neoliberal agenda of the

Washington Consensus in the country since 1991 (Stasinopoulos, 2023: 161–163). Beyond policies, the dollarisation of the economy, with a fixed exchange rate of the Argentine peso to the US dollar (1:1), contributed to this direction. An important point was also the change in the George W. Bush administration's attitude, according to which, from that point onwards private investors would have to pay part of the economic loss as a result of their "bad" investment, rather than being repaid through public money and IMF funds on favourable terms (O'Brien & Williams, 2023: 223). According to Helleiner (2005: 965), this option, promoted by the United States, represented a catalyst for the private sector's perspective towards a broader international economic reform, as Washington and the IMF were sending a signal that they would not be willing to accept large sovereign defaults and therefore would not intervene in private debt renegotiations in the wake of defaults.

The Independent Evaluation Office of the IMF acknowledged the Fund's failures in the period 1991–2001, pointing out that the Latin American country did not only pay for its own mistakes but also for those of the IMF. At the same time, the report linked the structural reforms implemented in the country in the 1990s (such as public sector privatisation) to the aforementioned Washington Consensus, while admitting that there was no convincing evidence that the structural reforms would have a growth effect (Mateos y Lago et al., 2004: 119–116).

Rodrik, referring to the country's bankruptcy in 2001, points out that this collapse is a "humbling lesson" about "the limits of economic globalisation in an era of national sovereignty" (2003: 15). At the same time, however, a strategic error of the Fund was that it overestimated the country's growth prospects, while underestimating its weaknesses—mainly the potential for increasing public debt—despite the fact that they had already made their appearance in the 1990s when Argentina was considered as a success story (Daseking et al., 2005: 39, 42, 44).

The IMF after the Latin American country's bankruptcy was allegedly willing to follow the peculiar 'No more Argentina cases' rule, as Blustein points out, whereby the institution would prevent the provision of new loans to a country that seemed unlikely to repay its debts (2015: 2). However, as was shown in the case of Greece in the spring of 2010 mentioned above, this rule was not observed as the opt-out option was followed.

In 2018, the IMF loan to Argentina was the largest in the Fund's history (Ray et al., 2020). The fast-tracked approval of the $57 billion loan, after a total of 21 bailouts over six decades, attracted new criticism (Stott & Elliott, 2021). Rogoff (2019) argued that US President Donald Trump's pressure on the Fund to relax its lending programme, in order to support Argentine President Mauricio Macri, worsened the state of the Argentinian economy. According to a report by the US Congress, in 2018, given Macri's commitment to improving US-Argentina relations and reforming the country's economy, "the US government has been strongly supportive of the IMF's program for Argentina", even noting that this stance could change under the administration of President Alberto Fernandez "if an aggressive stance towards the Fund or US creditors were noted" (Nelson, 2020). The report adds that the Fund was mindful of the potential risks to the success of the program when it was approved.

Referring to the IMF's latest support package to Argentina in 2022, which was an attempt to correct the failed 2018 programme, former Director of the Strategy, Policy, and Review Department (SPR) of the IMF Martin Mühleisen (2022) stressed that with his move the international financial institution risks "putting geopolitical parameters above its economic principles," thus setting a dangerous precedent. Listing the reasons for this development, in addition to preventing the abandonment of the Fund's effort in the Latin American country—a confession of failure that would have crippled the image of the international financial institution—he cited the agreement of then President Alberto Fernandez during his visit to China, to have Argentina join the Belt and Road Initiative, an agreement—preceded by a stop in Russia during Fernandez's trip—which, given the intensification of international rivalries, particularly between the United States and China in recent years, was a message from Buenos Aires to Washington and the West.

In December 2023, the Biden administration guaranteed support to newly-elected President Milei in discussions with the IMF on the management of the current $44 billion loan (Jourdan, 2023), showing how the Fund can be utilised as a political lever. Moreover, following his election the Argentinian President, immediately rejected the BRICS+ member countries' invitation to Argentina to join in this bloc that, among others, includes China and Russia (Plummer, 2023).

Recently, however, new criticisms have been voiced within the international economic organisation about the continued preferential treatment of the Latin American country, while at the same time, emerging economies with macroeconomic problems, such as Zambia, Sri Lanka and Ghana, are facing more onerous support conditions (Do Rosario, 2023). The IMF's stronger involvement in Argentina than in other Latin American countries, however, is explained by the fact that this country is considered crucial for international economic stability (Pop-Eleches, 2008: 105). However, in addition to its chronic political-economic problems, Latin America's second largest country has for decades been paying the price of the external interventions that were inevitably linked to the IMF's structural adjustment programmes (Table 1).

2 Conclusions

In conclusion, the intrusion of political actors in the IMF's lending policy (and in the IMF's decision-making in general) takes place from outside as well as from within the organisation (Swedberg, 1986: 378), and depends on geopolitical factors, the aspirations of the Fund's most powerful shareholders, as well as the policies of the international economic organisation itself. The 'politicisation' of IMF lending can be reflected at multiple levels: (i) in the approval of the financial support programme; (ii) in the terms of the structural adjustment programme; (iii) in the monitoring of the implementation of the programme's terms; (iv) in the continuation of financial support.

Table 1 Concluding remarks

	Greece	Argentina
Reasons of political influence on IMF involvement	Systemic risk for the global economy, the US and the Eurozone (as the basic factor)	Geopolitical aspirations of the United States (as the basic factor)
IMF evolvement	Co-operation with the ECB and the European Commission—Problematic partnership with European partners	Autonomous presence
IMF responsibility	The Fund as a minor partner with minor funding	Full responsibility for the funding and implementation of the programme and reforms
Duration of evolvement	Medium term	Long term
Political objectives of the support (from the IMF's own point of view)	Return to the global spotlight as the most effective crisis manager	Preventing a negative image of it as an international organisation

In the case of Greece in 2010, the potential systemic risk arising from a possible collapse of the euro zone country, as well as the requirement of the EU's and the monetary union's most powerful country, Germany, led to the IMF's involvement in the provision of financial support to Athens. A support (first structural adjustment programme), nonetheless, that, being influenced by the above political factors (untimely restructuring of Greek debt), was doomed to failure in its own right. Argentina, a different case, secured a record financial support from the Fund in 2018, continuing a vicious cycle of financial dependency since the 1990s. The largest debtor of the IMF (Osborn, 2023) maintains a long-standing relationship with the international financial institution both because of US geopolitical aspirations (influence in Latin America) and the Fund's own reluctance to "give up" support for the country, further shattering its image. The case of the Argentine crisis, especially its culmination with the country's bankruptcy in December 2001, was an example to be avoided by the international organisation, especially with the intention of not getting involved again in bailing out countries with low chances of successful programmes. However, the Greek case, almost nine years later, has contradicted this informal rule of non-engagement.

In any case, overcoming the politicisation of the IMF and moving towards neutrality and decision-making based solely on economic principles and criteria is not a simple, and perhaps not even feasible, task given the structure of the international economic organisation.

The current context, characterised by intensifying international rivalries and geo-economic fragmentation, puts additional pressure on the Fund as an international organisation. Mark Rosen, former Executive Director at the IMF, speaking to a US Congressional Committee, stressed that the biggest challenge facing the IMF today is China. In particular, he referred to Beijing's lending to developing and low-

and middle-income countries under non-transparent conditions, while several IMF members are unable to repay their loans (2023: 8). Criticising Beijing's reluctance to provide debt relief to developing economies, he called on the Commission to maintain the stronger US share in the IMF above 15 per cent, which also ensures veto power, not allowing China to increase its own share and momentum within the Fund.

In these circumstances, the ongoing debate on the revision of the voting process in the Fund is of particular importance. On the one hand, there is a consistently expressed view of balancing voting percentages by strengthening the less powerful states at the expense of the more powerful ones, but on the other hand, there is also the opposite view, which posits that even if this development takes place, this politicisation will not abate.

Of course, greater transparency in the decision-making process and lending is a factor in ensuring the credibility of the international financial institution. At the same time, the further strengthening of the Fund's Independent Evaluation Office can also contribute to this.

Acknowledgements This work has been partly supported by the University of Piraeus Research Centre.

References

Bird, G., Hussain, M., & Joyce, J. P. (2004). Many happy returns? Recidivism and the IMF. *Journal of International Money and Finance, 23*(2), 231–251. https://doi.org/10.1016/j.jimonfin.2003.12.002

Blustein, P. (2015). *Laid low: The IMF, the euro zone and the first rescue of Greece.*

Boughton, J. (2014). *IMF and the force of history: Events and ideas that have shaped the global institution.* International Monetary Fund.

Broz, J. L., & Hawes, M. B. (2006). Congressional politics of financing the International Monetary Fund. *International Organization, 60*(2), 367–399.

Centre for International Governance Innovation. (2017). *IMF chief economist Blanchard warned in May 2010 Greece program was not going to work.* https://www.cigionline.org/articles/imf-chief-economist-blanchard-warned-may-2010-greece-program-was-not-going-work/. Accessed March 17, 2024.

Copelovitch, M. S. (2010). Master or servant? Common agency and the political economy of IMF lending. *International Studies Quarterly, 54*(1), 49–77.

Daseking, M. C., Ghosh, M. A. R., Lane, M. T. D., & Thomas, M. A. H. (2005). *Lessons from the Crisis in Argentina.* International Monetary Fund.

Do Rosario, J. (2023, March 15). IMF has a tough call on Argentina: force major reforms or pull the plug. *Reuters.* https://www.reuters.com/world/americas/imfs-argentina-predicament-seek-reforms-tango-or-kill-music-2023-09-15/. Accessed March 19, 2024.

Dreher, A., & Jensen, N. M. (2007). Independent actor or agent? An empirical analysis of the impact of U.S. interests on International Monetary Fund conditions. *The Journal of Law and Economics, 50*(1), 105–124. https://doi.org/10.1086/508311

Fischer, S. (1999). On the need for an international lender of last resort. *Journal of Economic Perspectives, 13*(4), 85–104.

Helleiner, E. (2005). The strange story of Bush and the Argentine debt crisis. *Third World Quarterly, 26*(6), 951–969. https://doi.org/10.1080/01436590500093002

International Monetary Fund. (2013). *Greece: Ex post evaluation of exceptional access under the 2010 stand-by arrangement*. https://www.imf.org/external/pubs/ft/scr/2013/cr13156.pdf. Accessed March 19, 2024.
International Monetary Fund. (2021). *Members' quotas and voting power, and IMF board of governors*. https://www.imf.org/en/About/executive-board/members-quotas. Accessed March 15, 2024.
International Monetary Fund. (2022a). *Articles of agreement of the international Monetary Fund*. https://www.imf.org/external/pubs/ft/aa/index.htm. Accessed March 16, 2024.
International Monetary Fund. (2022b). *IMF lending*. https://www.imf.org/en/About/Factsheets/IMF-Lending. Accessed March 12, 2024.
International Monetary Fund. (2023). *IMF conditionality*. https://www.imf.org/en/About/Factsheets/Sheets/2023/IMF-Conditionality. Accessed March 11, 2024.
James, H. (2024). *The IMF and the European debt crisis*. International Monetary Fund. https://doi.org/10.5089/9798400231902.071
Kaplan, S. B., & Shim, S. (2024). Global contagion risk and IMF credit cycles: Emergency exits and revolving doors. *Regulation and Governance, 18*, 851–873. https://doi.org/10.1111/rego.12562
Kaya, A., & Reay, M. (2019). How did the Washington consensus move within the IMF? Fragmented change from the 1980s to the aftermath of the 2008 crisis. *Review of International Political Economy, 26*(3), 384–409. https://doi.org/10.1080/09692290.2018.1511447
Kedar, C. (2013). The International Monetary Fund and Latin America: The argentine puzzle in context. *Temple University Press*. https://doi.org/10.2307/j.ctt14bs96p
Krahnke, T. (2023). Doing more with less: The catalytic function of IMF lending and the role of program size. *Journal of International Money and Finance, 135*, 102856. https://doi.org/10.1016/j.jimonfin.2022.102856
Lipscy, P. Y., & Lee, H. N.-K. (2018). The IMF As a biased global insurance mechanism: Asymmetrical moral hazard, reserve accumulation, and financial crises. *International Organization*, 1–30.
Lütz, S. (2015). From Washington consensus to flexible Keynesianism? The international monetary fund after the financial crisis. *Journal of International Organization Studies, 6*(2), 85–98.
Mandelbaum, M. (2016). *Mission failure: America and the world in the post-cold war era*. Oxford University Press.
Marangos, J. (2023). The travels of the Washington consensus: From the global financial crisis to the Greek financial crisis. *Forum for social economics* (pp. 1–20). Routledge.
Marchesi, S., & Sabani, L. (2007). IMF concern for reputation and conditional lending failure: Theory and empirics. *Journal of Development Economics, 84*(2), 640–666.
Mateos y Lago, I., Takagi, M., Martin, M., Takebe, M., & Cohen, M. (2004). *The IMF and Argentina, 1991–2001*. International Monetary Fund. https://www.imf.org/en/Publications/Independent-Evaluation-Office-Reports/Issues/2016/12/31/The-IMF-and-Argentina-1991-2001-17590. Accessed March 19, 2024.
Mody, A. (2017, February 5). *Obama Joins the Greek Chorus*. Project Syndicate. https://www.project-syndicate.org/commentary/obama-easing-greek-austerity-by-ashoka-mody-2015-02. Accessed February 25, 2024.
Mody, A. (2017, February 3). *The IMF should get out of Greece*. Bloomberg.com. https://www.bloomberg.com/view/articles/2017-02-03/the-imf-should-get-out-of-greece. Accessed March 18, 2024.
Mühleisen, M. (2022). *In Argentina, the IMF risks placing geopolitics over economics*. Atlanticcouncil.org. https://www.atlanticcouncil.org/blogs/new-atlanticist/in-argentina-the-imf-risks-placing-geopolitics-over-economics/. Accessed March 16, 2024.
Mundell, R. A. (1968). *Man, and economics*. McGraw-Hill.
Naskou-Perraki, P., Antonopoulos, K., & Sarigiannidis, M. (2019). *International organisations*. Sakkoulas Publications [in Greek].

Nelson, R. M. (2020). *Argentina's economic crisis and default*. Congressional Research Service (CRS) Reports and Issue Briefs.

Nordström, L., & Laiho, N. (2023). Explaining IMF design of 2010 Greece loan: Bricoleurs relying on fiscal space and nonlinear multiple equilibria processes. *Comparative European Politics, 21*(3), 285–307.

Oatley, T., & Yackee, J. (2004). American interests and IMF lending. *International Politics, 41*, 415–429. https://doi.org/10.1057/palgrave.ip.8800085

O' Brien, R. & Williams, M. (2023). *Global political economy: Evolution and dynamics*. Scientific Editing: Spyros A. Roukanas, Pantelis Sklias, Grigoris Zarotiadis. Athens: Papazisis Publishers [in Greek].

Osborn, C. (2023, April 14). *Why Is the IMF being flexible on argentina's loan program?* Foreign Policy. https://foreignpolicy.com/2023/04/14/argentina-world-bank-imf-spring-meetings-economy-election-massa/. Accessed March 17, 2024.

Pisani-Ferry, J., Sapir, A., & Wolff, G. B. (2013). *EU-IMF assistance to euro area countries: An early assessment* (Vol. 16). Bruegel.

Pop-Eleches, G. (2008). *From economic crisis to reform: IMF programs in Latin America and Eastern Europe*. Princeton University Press.

Plummer, B. R. (2023, March 1). Argentina pulls out of plans to join BRICS bloc. *BBC*. https://www.bbc.com/news/world-latin-america-67842992. Accessed March 1, 2024.

Ray, R., Gallagher, K. P., & Kring, W. (2020). *IMF austerity since the global financial crisis: New data, same trend, and similar determinants*. Boston University Global Development Center.

Ray, R., Gallagher, K., & Kring, W. (2022). "Keep the receipts:" The political economy of IMF austerity during and after the crisis years of 2009 and 2020. *Journal of Globalization and Development, 13*(1), 31–59. https://doi.org/10.1515/jgd-2021-0014

Reinsberg, B., Stubbs, T., Kentikelenis, A., & King, L. (2022). Compliance, defiance, and the dependency trap: International Monetary Fund program interruptions and their impact on capital markets. *Regulation & Governance, 16*(4), 1022–1041. https://doi.org/10.1111/rego.12319

Reynaud, J., & Vauday, J. (2009). Geopolitics and international organizations: An empirical study on IMF facilities. *Journal of Development Economics, 89*(1), 139–162. https://doi.org/10.1016/j.jdeveco.2008.06.001

Rodrik, D. (2003). *Argentina: A case of globalisation gone too far or not far enough?* Forum on Debt and Development (FONDAD).

Rogoff, K. (2019). Does the IMF need to refocus its role after the Argentina crisis? *The Guardian*. https://www.theguardian.com/business/2019/oct/03/does-the-imf-need-to-refocus-its-role-after-the-argentina-crisis. Accessed March 3, 2024.

Stasinopoulos, G. (2023). *The disengagement of international institutions: the systemic failure of the management of the global economy*. Gutenberg [in Greek].

Stone, R. W. (2004). The political economy of IMF lending in Africa. *American Political Science Review, 98*(4), 577–591. https://doi.org/10.1017/S0003055404041381

Stott, M., & Elliott, L. (2021). *Argentina and the IMF: the looming clash over its $57bn bailout*. Ft.com. https://www.ft.com/content/ce0d1647-0bd7-4bb4-b787-d1301a8a3bc0. Accessed March 15, 2024.

Sturm, J. E., & Lee Andresen, L. (2022). Do geopolitical interests affect how financial markets react to IMF programs? In *VfS Annual Conference 2022: Big Data in Economics*.

Swedberg, R. (1986). The doctrine of economic neutrality of the IMF and the World Bank. *Journal of Peace Research, 23*(4), 377–390. https://doi.org/10.1177/002234338602300404

Thacker, S. C. (1999). The high politics of IMF lending. *World Politics, 52*(1), 38–75. https://doi.org/10.1017/S0043887100020025

Thomsen, P. (2019). *The IMF and the Greek crisis: Myths and realities*. Speech at the London School of Economics.

Tooze, A. (2018). *Crashed: How a decade of financial crises changed the world*. Penguin.

Vreeland, J. R. (2006). *The International Monetary Fund (IMF): Politics of conditional lending*. Routledge.

Wroughton, L., Schneider, H., & Kyriakidou, D. (2015). How the IMF's Misadventure in Greece is Changing the Fund. *Reuters Investigates*. https://www.reuters.com/investigates/special-report/imf-greece/. Accessed March 5, 2024.

Jourdan, S. (2023, December 10). U.S. offers Argentina's Milei support on IMF, lithium, White House adviser says. *Reuters*. https://www.reuters.com/world/americas/us-offers-argentinas-milei-support-imf-lithium-white-house-adviser-2023-12-10/. Accesed March 18, 2024.

Rosen, M. (2023, May 25). *Statement for the record: U.S. Department of the Treasury's 2023 International Affairs Budget Request*. U.S. House of Representatives, Committee on Appropriations. https://docs.house.gov/meetings/BA/BA10/20230525/116016/HHRG-118-BA10-Wstate-RosenM-20230525.pdf. Accessed March 19, 2024.

The Impact of Socio-Demographic Characteristics on Urban Mobility Patterns in the Aftermath of a Major Earthquake: A Case Study of the February 6, 2023 Earthquakes in Turkiye

Cigdem Varol, N. Aydan Sat, Emrah Soylemez, Elif Varol, and Nazlı Tunar Özcan

Abstract Human mobility in daily life is closely related to spatial features, as well as the social contexts of individuals. Related studies emphasize that individuals tend to spend most of their time in their daily lives visiting only a few places. However, urban mobility in daily life routine differs depending on individuals' mobility behaviors during emergencies such as earthquakes. There are several studies aimed at defining the physical and social factors that affect human mobility in relation to disasters. In these studies, personal characteristics, spatial arrangements, and social networks emerge as features that affect behavioral patterns. Socio-demographic characteristics such as age, gender, marital status, and education level are reported to be associated with disaster preparedness. On the other hand, certain characteristics that provide clues about the economic structure, such as income level and homeownership, have been found to contribute positively to preparedness efforts as their values increase. In addition to social and economic features, the "disaster experience" as a significant psychological factor can significantly influence behaviors and intervention actions

C. Varol (✉) · N. A. Sat
Department of City and Regional Planning, Gazi University, Ankara, Turkey
e-mail: cvarol@gazi.edu.tr

N. A. Sat
e-mail: bnecibe@gazi.edu.tr

E. Soylemez
Republic of Türkiye Ministry of Environment, Urbanization and Climate Change, Ankara, Turkey
e-mail: emrahsoylemez@gmail.com

E. Varol · N. T. Özcan
Department of Geological Engineering, Hacettepe University, Ankara, Turkey
e-mail: elvarol@hacettepe.edu.tr

N. T. Özcan
e-mail: ntunar@hacettepe.edu.tr

I. Bartuseviciene et al. (eds.), *Building Resilience Through Digital Transformation and Sustainable Innovation*, Springer Proceedings in Business and Economics,
https://doi.org/10.1007/978-3-031-90054-9_4

during and after a disaster. When the behaviors adopted in the minutes following an earthquake are examined, the main behavioral patterns can be listed as evacuation, returning home, reuniting with family members, or resuming previous activities. These differences that emerge in studies can be explained through the seismic characteristics of the earthquake (such as an increase in protective behaviors in more strongly felt earthquakes) and socio-demographic characteristics (such as males being more inclined to evacuate buildings during earthquakes). The cultural context, which includes the willingness of the community to accept earthquake preparedness measures, trust in the government, and willingness to volunteer, also creates differences in behaviors during and immediately after an earthquake. Despite the increasing academic literature on behavioral psychology and human mobility during disasters, the temporal characteristics of individual behaviors and the relationship between emotions and mobility over time have not been thoroughly investigated. This study aims to understand the urban mobility patterns of the population living in the region during the great earthquakes that occurred on February 6, 2023, in Türkiye, and to reveal the impact of socio-demographic and economic characteristics of the population on human mobility. In this context, household surveys were conducted using a random sampling technique in two cities in the region (Malatya and Adana). In the survey studies, factors influencing the sudden and short-term urban population mobility that occurred after the earthquake were identified, and the differences between this mobility pattern and the pre-earthquake routine mobility pattern were described, highlighting the social, demographic, and economic reasons for these differences.

Keywords Human mobility · Natural disasters · Earthquake · February 6 Earthquakes

JEL Classification Code R1 · R2

1 Introduction

Human mobility encompasses all aspects of the movement of an individual or a community, regardless of context and location (Barbosa et al., 2018; Barthelemy et al., 2018). It can be realized through the use of various modes of transportation such as private vehicle use, public transportation, walking, and cycling. On the other hand, urban mobility can be characterized by the amount of travel (distances travelled and time spent travelling), regularity (frequency and number of trips), mode of transportation (walking, cycling, car, train, plane, etc.), and the reasons for travel (shopping, health, work, accompanying someone, holidays, etc.) undertaken by individuals or groups (Kaufmann, 2014). Understanding human mobility in the city provides insight into how people move within the urban area, commuting distances, the connection between people and places, and the common modes of transportation used. Therefore, characterizing mobility is not just a requirement, but a necessity for solving many urban problems (Zhou et al., 2018).

To better conceptually understand human movement, it is important to examine the concepts of "mobility" and "motility". Mobility refers to the ability to move, while motility can be explained as the set of factors/driving forces that enable mobility. The capacity to move within the city refers to "mobility" i.e. the ability to move. However, all the internal and external stimuli that set this movement in motion, direct it, or deter it are within the concept of "motility". For example, the preference for a quieter and more direct route despite heavy pedestrian traffic is a result of this stimuli. The social force model, which examines this issue in the context of "microscopic pedestrian movements" emphasizes that "sensory stimuli" leads to a behavioral response in which the individual selects alternatives that shape their benefit maximization and goals (Helbing & Molnár, 1998).

On the other hand, the patterns of mobility in emergencies, such as disasters, differ from daily mobility patterns. Several studies aim to identify the physical and social factors affecting mobility to understand human mobility in relation to natural disasters (Basile et al., 2024). Some of these studies emphasize that the actions and behaviors aimed at reducing risks during and after a disaster vary greatly according to personal characteristics and conditions (Witvorapong et al., 2015). For instance, Ayeb-Karlsson (2020) investigated how human mobility changed in Bangladesh after a natural disaster, focusing on gender and personality characteristics. This study, based on the Q-method, found that men, expected to be strong and brave during the disaster, exhibited higher mobility, while women showed more sedentary behavior by staying at home. Socio-demographic characteristics such as age, gender, marital status, number of children, and education level are associated with disaster preparedness (Dooley et al., 1992; Turner et al., 1986). Additionally, economic indicators such as income level and housing ownership seem to affect preparations for disaster risk reduction (Edwards, 1993; Mulilis et al., 2000; Russell et al., 1995).

Despite the growing academic literature on human mobility and behavioral psychology during disasters, the temporal characteristics of individual behaviors and the relationship between emotion and mobility over time have not been studied in detail (Wang & Taylor, 2018). There is a limited number of studies on behavioral patterns towards the mobility of individuals in emergencies. In these studies, personal characteristics, spatial arrangements, and social networks (Pan et al., 2007; Phithakkitnukoon et al., 2012; Wang & Taylor, 2018) stand out as features that affect behavior patterns.

According to the studies examining the seismic events in Italy, USA, Japan, Mexico and New Zealand, the dominant behavior patterns of individuals during the earthquake include evacuation, taking cover, freezing in place and protecting others (Goltz & Bourque, 2017; Jon et al., 2016; Lindell et al., 2016; Prati et al., 2012, 2013; Santos-Reyes & Gouzeva, 2020). Undoubtedly, apart from these behavioral patterns, access to information, recovery of personal belongings etc. are also emphasized. When the behaviors adopted in the minutes following the earthquake are examined; major behavioral patterns can be listed as evacuation, returning home, reuniting with family members, or resuming previous activities. These differences can be explained by the seismic characteristics of the earthquake (increased protective behaviors in earthquakes that are felt more intensely) (Jon et al., 2016; Lindell et al., 2016) and socio-demographic characteristics (male groups are more prone to evacuate buildings during earthquakes) (Goltz & Bourque, 2017; Prati et al., 2012, 2013). The cultural context, which includes society's willingness to accept earthquake preparedness measures, trust in government, and the possibility of volunteering, also creates differences in behavior during and immediately after an earthquake (Palm, 1998).

This disaster experience can change the understanding and perception of risk during disasters and encourage the taking of precautionary measures. The impact of disaster experience on self-protection behavior of individuals can vary according to different components (O'Brien & Mileti, 1992) such as the number of disasters (Russel vd., 1995), how recent the experience is (researches draw attention to post-traumatic stress disorder, which lasts 6 months to 3 years after the disaster) (Khachadourian, et al., 2015; Mileti & Fitzpatrick, 1992; Tsai et al., 2007), and disaster-related losses (Jackson, 1981). The increasing sense of loyalty and belonging of individuals/communities to each other who have experienced the same disaster develops the social capital of that region and can be a factor in determining the behavior patterns and movement preferences of individuals during disasters that may occur again (Dynes, 2002; Varda et al., 2009; Witvorapong, et al., 2015; Yamamura, 2013).

In this study, it is aimed to understand the urban mobility patterns of the population living in the region during the great earthquakes that occurred on February 6, 2023, in Türkiye, and to reveal the impact of socio-demographic characteristics of the population on human mobility. In this context, household surveys were conducted using a random sampling technique in two cities in the region (Malatya and Adana). In the survey, factors influencing the sudden and short-term urban population mobility that occurred after the earthquake were identified, and the differences between post-earthquake mobility pattern and the pre-earthquake routine mobility pattern were described, highlighting the social, demographic, and economic reasons for these differences.

2 The Case of the February 6, 2023 Earthquakes in Turkiye

On February 6, 2023, a series of two powerful earthquakes hit Southeastern Türkiye. The first earthquake, with a magnitude of 7.7 and its epicenter in Pazarcık, occurred at 04.17 am, with a focal depth was measured at 8.6 km. The second earthquake, with a magnitude of 7.6 and its epicenter in Elbistan, struck at 01:24 p.m. with a focal depth calculated at 7.0 km (AFAD, 2023). The February 6th earthquakes in Pazarcık and Elbistan triggered extensive surface ruptures along major fault zones. Following the Pazarcık earthquake, a 404 km long surface rupture was observed along various segments of the East Anatolian Fault Zone (EAFZ) and the Dead Sea Fault Zone (DSFZ) (MTA, 2023). After the Elbistan earthquake, a 167 km surface rupture was measured along the fault segments of the NAFZ (MTA, 2023). Due to the complex

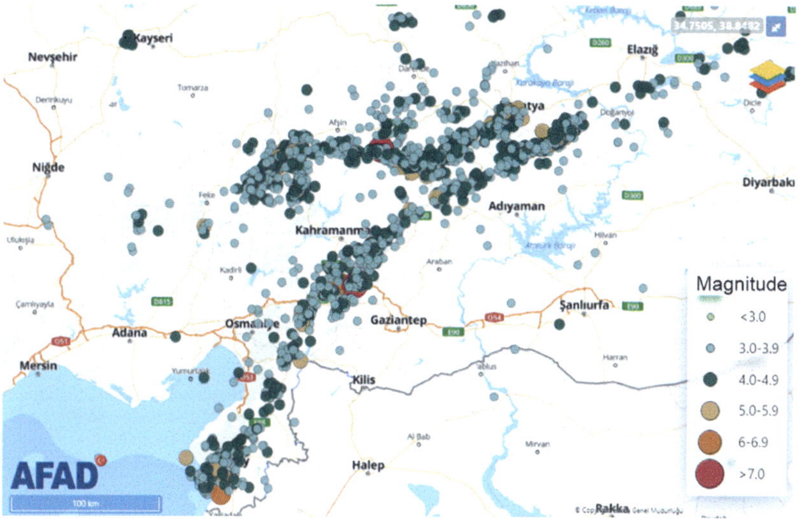

Fig. 1 Distributions of aftershocks recorded around between the 06 February 2023 and 29 May 2024. *Source* Arranged from AFAD earthquake catalogue (AFAD, 2023)

tectonic and geological features of the region, many devastating earthquakes has been experienced during the historical and instrumental periods (Ambraseys, 1989). After the main earthquakes, 62,147 aftershocks were recorded until May 29, 2024, with 668 of them having a magnitude greater than 4.0 and being felt in the nearby areas (Fig. 1).

The Disaster and Emergency Management Presidency of Türkiye (AFAD) reported that 11 provinces, including Hatay, Kahramanmaraş, Adıyaman, Malatya, Gaziantep, Osmaniye, Şanlıurfa, Adana, Diyarbakır, Kilis and Elazığ, were affected. More than 50,000 citizens lost their lives and 37,984 buildings were destroyed by the Kahramanmaraş Earthquake Series. The two cities, Adana and Malatya, affected by the Kahramanmaraş Earthquakes, were selected as the study area (Fig. 2). In Adana, 13 buildings collapsed and 418 people lost their lives, while in Malatya, 1,154 buildings collapsed and 1,346 people lost their lives. The greatest damage was observed in areas with predominantly alluvial soils. The reason behind this is that the building designs were not compatible with the soil structure in the affected areas.

3 Methodology

Human mobility behavior after major earthquakes cannot be easily predicted due to the inadequacy of the collected data or the inability of the factors defined for human mobility models to form a strong behavior model. According to the related studies, quantitative data collection and analysis methods are mainly used in the processing

Fig. 2 The affected 11 provinces in the region and the two selected cities as the study areas. *Source* Prepared by the authors, 2024

of big data and mobility analysis, but it is seen that qualitative research techniques are also very useful in this process.

In this research, both quantitative and qualitative analyses were used by conducting a household questionnaire and in-depth interviews with local actors who experienced the earthquake. The fieldwork was carried out in Adana and Malatya 4–5 months after the earthquake, in June-July 2023. Household surveys were conducted using random sampling techniques to determine the factors affecting individual and social behavior patterns. The questionnaire includes two groups of questions. The first group focuses on the personal information of the surveyed individuals and household members, including age, gender, marital status, family size and number of children, education level, job-working status, income level, disaster experience, sense of belonging, etc. These questions assist in understanding the connection between demographic and social characteristics of the population in selected provinces and their actions and behaviors. This understanding will help to mitigate risks during and after a disaster (Witvorapong et al., 2015). The second group of questions aims to reveal the mobility patterns of individuals during and immediately after the earthquake.

The destroyed buildings in the earthquake were mostly located in a specific district in Adana, while they were spread throughout the entire city in Malatya. In selection of the samples, the aim was to reach households in neighborhoods that were particularly affected by the earthquake. During the field survey, it was difficult to determine how much of the population had moved away after the earthquake for various reasons, such as destroyed homes and feelings of unsafety. Thus, in the affected areas, questionnaire was conducted for those who continue to live in the area. Heat maps, which show the most affected areas from the earthquake, were created using the ArcGIS program for

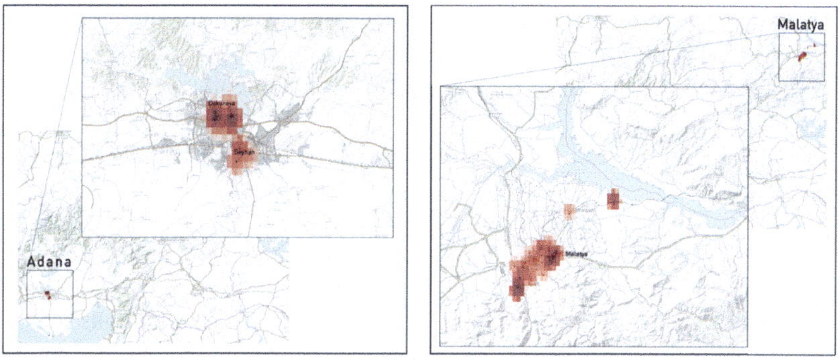

Fig. 3 Spatial distribution of the surveyed neighborhoods throughout the province of Adana and Malatya. *Source* Prepared by the authors, 2023

Adana and Malatya (Fig. 3). A total of 385 questionnaires were conducted in each city, with a 95% confidence interval and a 0.05 margin of error.

4 Results of the Study

This section presents the findings related to the demographic and social structure, economic structure, and the mobility patterns of the population surveyed in the Adana and Malatya provinces.

4.1 Demographic and Social Structure of the Population

In this section, the findings regarding the social and demographic structure of the population surveyed in Adana and Malatya are detailed.

Household Size

According to TUIK (2022), the average household size in Türkiye is 3.2 people. For Adana, this average is 3.5, and for Malatya, it is 3.4. However, among the survey participants, the household size is 2.6 for Adana and 3.4 for Malatya. This suggests that the sampled households in Adana are smaller than the regional average, while those in Malatya align closely with the overall average.

Gender

According to TUIK data from 2022, the gender distribution in Türkiye is 49.9% female and 50.1% male. In Adana, the gender distribution is exactly balanced at 50% each. Among the survey participants in Adana, however, 57.1% were women and 42.9% were men.

In Malatya, the population is 50.2% female and 49.8% male. Among the survey participants, 51.8% were women and 48.2% were men. This indicates a slightly higher female representation in the surveyed population compared to the general population.

Age Groups

The age group distributions of the survey participants were compared with the 2022 TUIK data for Türkiye and Adana province (Fig. 4). In the study area, 23% of the population is under the age of 15, which is slightly lower compared to Türkiye (22.4%) and Adana (24%). For the age group 15–65, the distributions are 68% for Türkiye, 67% for Adana, and 76% for the study area. This indicates a higher proportion of working-age individuals in the study area compared to the national and provincial averages. A notable observation is that the proportion of the population over the age of 40 is relatively low in the study area compared to Türkiye and Adana. This suggests that the surveyed groups have included relatively younger population under the age of 40.

It is seen that 31.2% of the population in the study area in Malatya is between the ages of 15–30. This rate is quite high compared to Türkiye (23%) and Malatya (22.7%). On the other hand, the ratio of the population over the age of 65 in the study area is low compared to Türkiye and Malatya. Overall, the representation of the 15–60 age group is higher in the sampling group compared to Türkiye and Malatya (Fig. 5).

Place of Birth

The survey asked about the place of registration of household heads, which provides insights into the population's origins and migration patterns. In Adana, 78.1% of respondents reported that they were born in Adana, indicating a strong local presence.

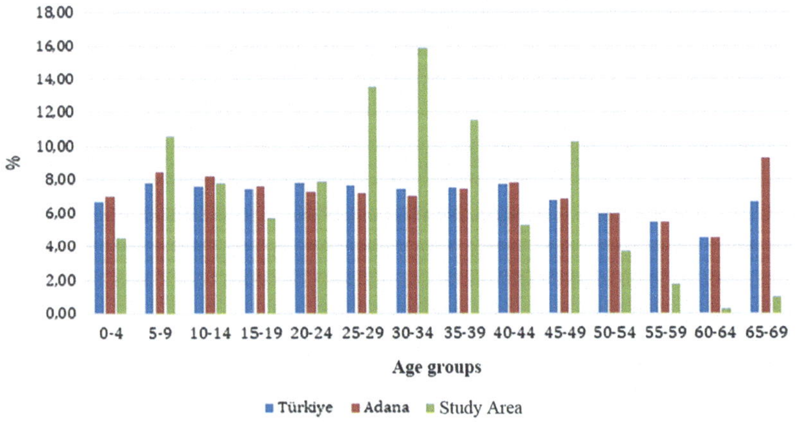

Fig. 4 Age group distributions in Türkiye, Adana and the study area (%). *Source* TUIK, 2022 and Field Survey, 2023

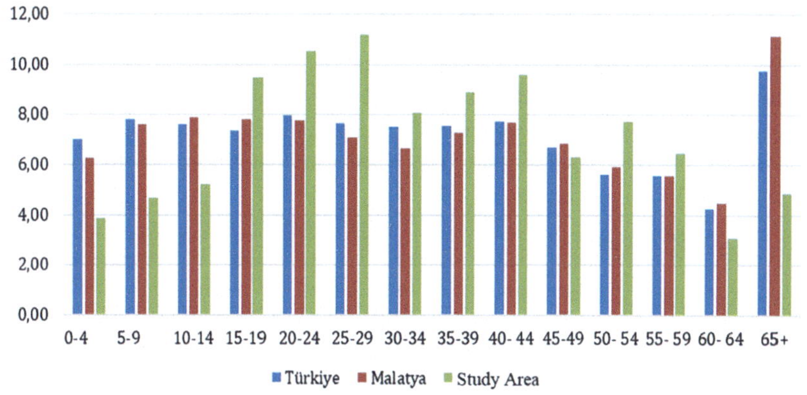

Fig. 5 Age group distributions in Türkiye, Malatya and the study area (%). *Source* TUIK, 2022 and Field Survey, 2023

Additionally, 14.1% of respondents were born in nearby provinces such as Gaziantep, Hatay, and Adıyaman. This suggests that there is some degree of regional migration. Only 7.7% of the respondents were born outside Adana and its neighboring provinces. This relatively low percentage of external births underscores the predominantly local nature of the population, suggesting that Adana has a stable, indigenous community with limited long-distance migration.

In Malatya, an even higher percentage of survey participants, 88.1%, were born in Malatya. This indicates a very strong local affiliation and a deep-rooted population. Almost all other participants were born in nearby provinces, similar to the pattern observed in Adana. This high percentage reflects minimal migration from distant regions, reinforcing the idea of a stable and local population base. The data suggest that Malatya's population has strong ties to the region, with family and social networks likely concentrated locally, contributing to community cohesion and stability.

Educational Status

Regarding educational status, more than half of the household heads in Adana are university graduates (54.0%), a rate significantly higher than the averages for Türkiye and Adana province. There is no illiteracy among the respondents in the study area, with only 1.0% not having graduated from any school.

In Malatya, the educational status of survey participants shows that primary school graduates make up 35.3%, high school graduates 31.2%, and university graduates 23.9%. The university graduation rate in Malatya is higher than the national (15%) and provincial averages (15.3%).

Marital Status

In Adana, 58.1% of the respondents are married, and 35% are single. In Malatya, these rates are 84.2% married and 7.8% single.

4.2 Economic Structure of Population

To understand the economic structure in the region, questions were asked about household income levels, home ownership, vehicle ownership and working status. The findings provide insights into the economic conditions of the surveyed populations in Adana and Malatya.

Total Household Income

The survey revealed that in Adana, more than half of the participants (56.8%) have a monthly household income between 15,501 TL and 25,000 TL (around 600$). The second highest group (25.7%) has an income between 5,501 TL and 15,000 TL (around 300$). This suggests that the survey participants in Adana generally have middle and lower-middle income levels.

On the other hand, in Malatya, nearly half of the participants (49.4%) have a monthly income between 5,501 TL and 15,000 TL. The second highest group (36.6%) has an income between 15,001 TL and 25,000 TL. No households reported an income above 40,001 TL, indicating that survey participants in Malatya generally have middle-low and low-income levels.

Home Ownership

In Adana, 50.9% of surveyed households rent their homes, and 39.1% live in their own properties. In Malatya, 20.3% live in their own properties, while 16.4% rent. Due to significant earthquake damage, many residents in Malatya (61.6%) are living in containers and tents.

Vehicle Ownership

The vehicle ownership rates also reflect the economic structure in the study area. In Adana, 17% of households do not own a vehicle, indicating that the majority do. Specifically, 72.0% own one vehicle, and 11.1% own two vehicles. In Malatya, 49.4% of households do not own a vehicle, while 48.3% own one vehicle, and 2.3% own two vehicles.

Working Status

Examining the working status, 93.8% of household heads in Adana are employed, reflecting the younger population's high employment rate. In Malatya, 80.8% of household heads are employed. The unemployment rate is below the Turkish average, with 42.4% of the unemployed population being over 65 years old. Table 1 summarizes and compares the general economic structure of the surveyed population in the case provinces.

Table 1 Comparison of economic structure of population in Adana and Malatya

Characteristics	Adana	Malatya
Total household income	Middle, and middle-lower income levels	Middle-lower, and lower-income levels
Home ownership	39.1% live in their own properties	20.3% live in their own properties
Vehicle ownership	72% of households have vehicle	48.3% of the households have vehicle
Working status	93.8% of the workable population employed	80.8% of the workable population employed

Source Field Survey, 2023

4.3 Mobility Patterns During and After the Earthquake

This section explores the mobility patterns of individuals during the time of the earthquake. Due to the earthquake occurring at 4:17 a.m., most people were at home, which contributed to the less mobility and high loss of life in the region.

At the time of the earthquake, 65.3% of people in Adana reported being with their spouse, while 25.2% were alone. In Malatya, a significant 89.8% of people were with their families. As stated before, the primary focus of the study was to understand the mobility patterns during the earthquake. Thus, survey respondents were asked about their actions at the time of the earthquake. The majority of respondents in Malatya (76.1%) reported that they experienced panic and were unable to move, mainly due to being trapped in buildings. In Adana, 65.3% of respondents reported taking action to save their family members and relatives within the building (Table 2).

Some studies emphasize that the actions and behaviors aimed at reducing risks during and after a disaster vary greatly according to personal characteristics and conditions (Witvorapong et al., 2015). Socio-demographic characteristics such as age, gender, marital status, number of children, and education level are associated with disaster preparedness (Dooley et al., 1992; Turner et al., 1986). For this reason,

Table 2 The actions at the time of the earthquake

	Adana		Malatya	
	#	%	#	%
I did not have the opportunity to move (panic, stuck in the building, etc.)	107	27.5	293	76.1
I went to rescue family members/relatives in the building	254	65.3	68	17.71
The building I was in was safe for earthquakes	6	1.5	3	0.8
I was in the open field	2	0.5	13	3.4
Other	20	5.1	8	2.1
Total	389	100.0	385	100.0

Source Field Survey, 2023

the relationship between socio-demographic characteristics and economic structures is examined more deeply.

Socio-Demographic Characteristics and Mobility Patterns

The study evaluated whether earthquake mobility patterns change according to education levels. It was found that there is no significant difference between the mobility patterns of earthquake victims with different education levels in Adana or Malatya.

When analyzing gender-related differences in mobility patterns during the earthquake, both female and male victims in Adana and Malatya reported that they could not move due to panic and being stuck in the building. Those who could move often went to rescue their family members or relatives. No significant differences were found in mobility patterns based on gender in either city. However, a higher proportion of people in Malatya were unable to move compared to Adana, likely due to the greater damage to buildings (Table 3).

Age was another factor affecting mobility patterns. The majority of earthquake victims, regardless of age, reported being unable to move during the earthquake in Malatya (76.1%). In Adana, a larger proportion of respondents (65.3%) went to rescue their family members (Table 4).

Marital status also influenced mobility patterns. In Adana, 65.4% of those who went to save their relatives were married, compared to 86.8% in Malatya. This indicates that married individuals were more likely to focus on rescuing their relatives during the earthquake (Table 5).

Different studies have yielded varied findings on how socio-demographic characteristics affect movement patterns during disasters (Dooley et al., 1992; Turner

Table 3 The actions at the time of the earthquake due to gender (%)

	Adana		Malatya	
	Woman	Man	Woman	Man
I did not have the opportunity to move (panic, stuck in the building, etc.)	27.4	27.65	80.2	70.6
I went to rescue family members/relatives in the building	66.3	64.1	13.5	23.3
The building I was in was safe for earthquakes	1.4	1.7	1.4	0.0
I was in the open field	1.0	0.0	2.3	14.9
Other	3.8	6.6	2.7	1.2
Total	100	100	100	100

Source Field Survey, 2023

Table 4 The actions at the time of the earthquake due to age (%)

Age group		I did not have the opportunity to move (panic, stuck in the building, etc.)	I went to rescue family members/ relatives in the building	The building I was in was safe for earthquakes	I was in the open field	Other	Total
Adana	15–24	25	75				100
	25–34	44.1	50.8	1.7	1.1	2.3	100
	35–44	13.1	76.8	2		8.1	100
	45–54	10.1	79.7	1.3		8.9	100
	55–64	21.4	71.4			7.1	100
	Total	27.5	65.3	1.5	0.5	5.1	100
Malatya	15–24	100					100
	25–34	75.3	17.8	1.4	2.7	2.7	100
	35–44	75.7	17.8	1.9	1.9	2.8	100
	45–54	75.5	18.6		4.9	1	100
	55–64	75.4	18.5		4.6	1.5	100
	65–74	69.6	21.7		4.3	4.3	100
	75+	100					100
	Total	76.1	17.7	0.8	3.4	2.1	100

Source Field Survey, 2023

Table 5 The actions at the time of the earthquake due to marital status (%)

		I did not have the opportunity to move (panic, stuck in the building, etc.)	I went to rescue family members/ relatives in the building	The building I was in was safe for earthquakes	I was in the open field	Other	Total
Adana	Single	57	26.8	50	100	10	35
	Married	37.4	65.4	50		85	58.1
	Wife/ Husband Died	0.9	3.1			5	2.6
	Divorced	4.7	4.7				4.4
	Total	100	100	100	100	100	100
Malatya	Single	7.2	11.8		7.7		7.8
	Married	84	86.8	66.7	69.2	100	84.2
	Wife/ Husband Died	7.8	1.5		23.1		7
	Divorced	1		33.3			1
	Total	100	100	100	100	100	100

Source Field Survey, 2023

et al., 1986). The results of the survey conducted on the February 6th Kahramanmaraş earthquakes indicate that "marital status" has a direct effect on individuals' mobility patterns. Conversely, there are no clear findings on the direct effects of "age", "gender", and "education level" on mobility patterns during the earthquake.

Economic Structure and Mobility Patterns

Studies on the effects of households' economic structures on their mobility in disaster situations are limited, and the results vary. However, there is a general acceptance that economically strong families tend to act differently in disasters because they live in more durable housing (Edwards, 1993; Mulilis et al., 2000; Russell et al., 1995). However, the survey results for the Kahramanmaraş earthquakes indicate that household income did not significantly influence earthquake mobility patterns. Households with different income levels acted similarly. Relatively higher-income households do not have confidence in the earthquake resistance of their homes. This lack of confidence is particularly noteworthy because it might be expected that wealthier families, who can afford better construction and more stringent safety measures, would feel more secure. However, the survey results reveal a different trend: middle and low-income groups in both Adana and Malatya exhibit more confidence about the structural integrity of their homes during earthquakes (Table 6).

Table 6 The actions at the time of the earthquake due to income level (%)

		I did not have the opportunity to move (panic, stuck in the building, etc.)	I went to rescue family members/relatives in the building	The building I was in was safe for earthquakes	I was in the open field	Other	Total
Adana	0–5500	66.7	33.3				100
	5501–15,000	25.9	65.9	4.7		3.5	100
	15,001–25,000	19.7	72.9	0.4		7	100
	25,001–40,000	46.9	46.9	1.6	3.1	1.6	100
	40,001+	100					100
	Total	27.5	65.3	1.5	0.5	5.1	100
Malatya	0–5500	78.3	13	4.3	4.3		100
	5501–15,000	72.6	20.5	0.5	3.7	2.6	100
	15,001–25,000	80.1	14.9		2.8	2.1	100
	25,001–40,000	77.4	16.1	3.2	3.2		100
	Total	76.1	17.7	0.8	3.4	2.1	100

Source: Field Survey, 2023

The mobility patterns of earthquake victims in their own homes compared to those in other types of housing were also similar (Table 7). Additionally, the mobility patterns after 5 min from the earthquake were analyzed according to home ownership, showing similar results across different types of home ownership in both Adana and Malatya (Table 8).

The study found no specific evidence that the economic structures of disaster survivors directly affected their earthquake mobility patterns. While the academic literature suggests that high-income households might exhibit different mobility

Table 7 The actions at the time of the earthquake due to property ownership (%)

		I did not have the opportunity to move (panic, stuck in the building, etc.)	I went to rescue family members/ relatives in the building	The building I was in was safe for earthquakes	I was in the open field	Other	Total
Adana	Own property	25.2	66.9	0.7	1.3	6	100
	Rent	32.8	60.7	1.5		5	100
	Family members'	5.6	86.1	5.6		2.8	100
	Other	100					100
	Total	27.5	65.3	1.5	0.5	5.1	100
Malatya	Own property	76.4	15.5	1.1	4.4	2.6	100
	Rent	74	24		1	1	100
	Family members'	50	50				100
	lodging	100					100
	Total	76.1	17.7	0.8	3.4	2.1	100

Source Field Survey, 2023

Table 8 Did you leave the place where you were within the first 5 min after the earthquake?

	Adana			Malatya		
	Yes	No	Total	Yes	No	Total
Own property	100.0	–	100.0	88.9	11.1	100.0
Rent	98.0	2.0	100.0	85.6	14.4	100.0
Family members'	100.0	–	100.0	87.5	12.5	100.0
Lodging	–	–	–	50.0	50.0	100.0
Other	100.0	–	100.0	–	–	–
Total	99.0	1.0	100.0	87.8	12.2	100.0

Source Field Survey, 2023

patterns during disasters, the survey results from Adana and Malatya show that economic status did not significantly impact mobility during the earthquake.

5 Conclusion

Analyzing mobility patterns following a disaster provides crucial insights that can significantly aid in mitigating the damages caused by such events. These patterns help inform crisis management strategies, including evacuation and rescue operations, and play a vital role in the rapid restoration of essential services and the resumption of social, institutional, and economic activities. The study of human behavior and movement in the aftermath of a disaster is indispensable for developing more effective disaster response plans and enhancing community resilience.

The influence of demographic and social variables on human behavior and mobility patterns during and after disasters is a key area of research. Understanding these dynamics is essential for tailoring interventions that accommodate diverse population needs. The results of our survey conducted in Adana and Malatya following the February 6, 2023 earthquakes provide valuable insights into these patterns.

One of the most significant findings from our study is the direct effect of marital status on mobility patterns during the earthquake. Individuals who were married were more likely to take action to rescue family members and relatives during the disaster. This behavior underscores the importance of familial bonds and responsibilities in influencing decision-making during emergencies. Further investigation into this finding could reveal underlying social and cultural factors that drive such behavior, offering deeper insights into how family dynamics impact disaster response.

Conversely, our study did not find clear evidence of the direct effects of age, gender, and education level on mobility patterns during the earthquake. This suggests that these demographic factors may not be primary determinants of how people respond and move in the face of disasters. While these variables are often considered in disaster preparedness and response planning, our findings indicate that other factors, such as the immediate context of the disaster and personal experiences, might play a more critical role.

Although Russell et al. (1995), Edwards (1993), and Mulilis et al. (2000) noted in their studies that economic factors significantly impact mobility patterns during an earthquake, our survey found that economic status did not significantly influence movement during the disaster. Despite expectations that higher-income households might exhibit different behaviors due to better housing conditions and resources, this was not reflected in our findings. However, economic factors do play a role in the displacement of victims in the post-disaster period. Higher-income households may have more options for relocation and recovery, while lower-income households may face prolonged displacement and greater challenges in rebuilding their lives.

These findings highlight the complexities of disaster-related movement patterns. It is essential to note that the results are based on the population surveyed following the February 6, 2023 earthquakes. The variables affecting mobility patterns can change significantly depending on the type of disaster, the cultural setting of the population, and specific characteristics of those impacted. For example, urban and rural populations might exhibit different behaviors, and cultural norms can heavily influence how communities respond to emergencies.

Furthermore, our study's limitations must be acknowledged. The survey was conducted in a specific context and time frame, which may not capture all the nuances of disaster response behaviors. The unique characteristics of the February 6 earthquakes and the surveyed populations mean that the findings might not be generalizable to all disaster situations. More extensive and diverse research is required to strengthen and validate these interpretations. Future studies should aim to include a broader range of disasters and cultural settings to build a more comprehensive understanding of mobility patterns.

In conclusion, while the conducted study provides valuable insights into the impact of socio-demographic and economic characteristics of the population on mobility patterns during disasters, it also reveals the need for a more nuanced exploration of other demographic and economic factors. By continuing to investigate these variables across different contexts, we can develop more targeted and effective disaster response strategies that address the needs of all community members. This research underscores the importance of considering a wide array of influences on human behavior to improve preparedness and resilience in the face of future disasters.

Acknowledgements The study was developed within the scope of the TÜBİTAK-SOBAG project numbered 121K919 and titled "Forecasting and Modeling of Urban Human Mobility Following Large-scale Earthquakes".

References

AFAD. (2023). *Preliminary assessment report on the 06 February 2023 Pazarcık (Kahramanmaraş) Mw 7.7 Elbistan (Kahramanmaraş) Mw 7.6 earthquakes*. Disaster and Emergency Management Presidency Earthquake and Risk Reduction General Directorate Earthquake Department Report.

Ambraseys, N. N. (1989). Temporary seismic quiescence: SE Turkey. *Geophysical Journal International, 96*(2), 311–331.

Ayeb-Karlsson, S. (2020). 'I do not like her going to the shelter': Stories on gendered disaster (im) mobility and wellbeing loss in coastal Bangladesh. *International Journal of Disaster Risk Reduction, 50*, 101904.

Barthelemy, M., Ghoshal, G., James, C. R., Lenormand, M., Louail, T., Tomasini, M., et al. (2018). Human mobility: Models and applications. *Physics Reports, 734*, 1–74. https://doi.org/10.1016/j.physrep.2018.01.001

Barbosa, H., Barthelemy, M., Ghoshal, G., James, C. R., Lenormand, M., Louail, T., Menezes, R., Ramasco, J. J., Simini, F., & Tomasini, M. (2018). Human mobility: Models and applications. *Physics Reports, 734*, 1–74.

Basile, R., Centofanti, F., Giallonardo, L., & Licari, F. (2024). Migration responses to earthquakes: Evidence from Italy. *Italian Economic Journal, 10*(1), 269–291.

Dooley, D., Catalano, R., Mishra, S., & Serxner, S. (1992). Earthquake preparedness: Predictors in a community survey. *Journal of Applied Social Psychology, 22*, 451–470.

Dynes, R. R. (2002). *The importance of social capital in disaster response*. University of Delaware.
Edwards, M. L. (1993). Social location and self-protective behavior: Implications for earthquake preparedness. *International Journal of Mass Emergencies and Disasters, 11*, 293–304.
Goltz, J., & Bourque, L. B. (2017). Earthquakes and human behaviour: A sociological perspective. *International Journal of Disaster Risk Reduction, 21*, 251–265.
Helbing, D., & Molnár, P. (1998). Social force model for pedestrian dynamics. *Physical Review E, 51*(5), 4282–4286.
Jackson, E. L. (1981). Response to earthquake hazard: The west coast of North America. *Environment and Behavior, 13*(4), 387–416.
Jon, I., et al. (2016). Behavioral response in the immediate aftermath of shaking: Earthquakes in Christchurch and Wellington, New Zealand, and Hitachi, Japan. *International Journal of Environmental Research and Public Health, 13*(11), 1137.
Kaufmann, V. (2014). Mobility as a tool for sociology. *Sociologica, 8*(1). https://doi.org/10.2383/77046
Khachadourian, V., et al. (2015). Loss and psychosocial factors as determinants of quality of life in a cohort of earthquake survivors. *Health and Quality of Life Outcomes, 13*, 1–8.
Lindell, M. K., et al. (2016). Immediate behavioural responses to earthquakes in Christchurch, New Zealand and Hitachi, Japan. *Disasters, 40*(1), 85–111.
Mileti, D. S., & Fitzpatrick, C. (1992). The causal sequence of risk communication in the Parkfield earthquake prediction experiment. *Risk Analysis, 12*(3), 393–400.
MTA. (2023). *6 February 2023 Kahramanmaraş earthquakes extended information note*. MTA Geological Surveys Department, Ankara, Türkiye.
Mulilis, J. P., et al. (2000). Tornado preparedness of students, nonstudent renters, and nonstudent owners: Issues of PrE-Theory 1. *Journal of Applied Social Psychology, 30*(6), 1310–1329. https://doi.org/10.1111/j.1559-1816.2000.tb02522.x
O'Brien, P. J., & Mileti, D. S. (1992). Natural disaster: A framework for understanding the effects of social and economic factors. *International Journal of Mass Emergencies and Disasters, 10*(2), 181–206.
Paul, O., & Mileti, D. S. (1992). Citizen Participation in Emergency Response Following the Loma Prieta Earthquake. *International Journal of Mass Emergencies and Disasters, 10*, 71–89.
Palm, R. (1998). Urban earthquake hazards: The impacts of culture on perceived risk and response in the USA and Japan. *Applied Geography, 18*(1), 35–46.
Pan, X. P., et al. (2007). A multi-agent-based framework for the simulation of human and social behaviors during emergency evacuations. *Ai & Society, 22*(2), 113–132.
Phithakkitnukoon, S., et al. (2012). Socio-geography of human mobility: A study using longitudinal mobile phone data. *PLoS ONE, 7*(6), e39253.
Prati, G., et al. (2012). Emotional and behavioural reactions to tremors of the Umbria-Marche earthquake. *Disasters, 36*(3), 439–451.
Prati, G., Saccinto, E., Pietrantoni, L., & Pérez-Testor, C. (2013). The 2012 Northern Italy Earthquakes: Modelling human behaviour. *Natural Hazards, 69*, 99–113. https://doi.org/10.1007/s11069-013-0688-9
Russell, L. A., et al. (1995). Preparedness and hazard mitigation actions before and after two earthquakes. *Environment and Behavior, 27*(6), 744–770.
Santos-Reyes, J., & Gouzeva, T. (2020). Mexico city's residents emotional and behavioural reactions to the 19 September 2017 earthquake. *Environmental Research, 186*, 109482.
Tsai, K. Y., et al. (2007). Three-year follow-up study of the relationship between posttraumatic stress symptoms and quality of life among earthquake survivors in Yu-Chi, Taiwan. *Journal of Psychiatric Research, 41*(1–2), 90–96.
TUIK. (2022). *İstatistik Veri Portalı*. https://data.tuik.gov.tr/Kategori/GetKategori?p=nufus-ve-demografi-109&dil=1
Turner, R. H., et al. (1986). *Waiting for disaster: Earthquake watch in California*. University of California Press.

Varda, D. M., et al. (2009). Social network methodology in the study of disasters: Issues and insights prompted by post-Katrina research. *Population Research and Policy Review, 28*, 11–29.

Wang, Y., & Taylor, J. E. (2018). Coupling sentiment and human mobility in natural disasters: A Twitter-based study of the 2014 South Napa Earthquake. *Natural Hazards, 92*, 907–925.

Witvorapong, N., et al. (2015). Social participation and disaster risk reduction behaviors in Tsunami Prone Areas. *PLoS ONE, 10*(7), e0130862.

Yamamura, E. (2013). Natural disaster and participation in volunteer activities: A case study of great Hanshin-Awaji earthquake. *Annals of Public and Cooperative Economics, 84*(1), 103–117.

Zhou, Y., et al. (2018). Understanding urban human mobility through crowdsensed data. *IEEE Communications Magazine, 56*(11), 52–59.

Croatian Exchange Rate Stability and Long-Term Interest Rates in Light of the Adoption of the Euro

Dijana Čičin-Šain, Martina Maté, and Anita Peša

Abstract This paper provides an overview of Croatia's preparations for joining the Eurozone through the ERM II mechanism and meeting the ECB criteria. The paper studies the fluctuations of the Croatian kuna exchange rate to the euro and the long-term interest rates from Croatia's accession to the European Union, through the ERM II mechanism towards the final entry of Croatia into the Eurozone in the beginning of 2023. Based on the conducted desk research, it can be concluded that Croatia has gone through a long and difficult process of adjusting the exchange rate and long-term interest rates to the convergence criteria.

Keywords Monetary union · Convergence criteria · Exchange rate stability · Long-term interest rate

JEL E42 · E43 · E52 · E58

1 Introduction

All EU member states have the opportunity to join the Eurozone by meeting the prescribed criteria. Some EU member states have not made such a decision and all monetary transactions there continue to take place in domestic currencies. Other countries would like to join the Eurozone but have not yet met the criteria. Bulgaria and Croatia were admitted to the Exchange Rate Mechanism (ERM II), which was

D. Čičin-Šain · M. Maté (✉) · A. Peša
Department of Economics, University of Zadar, Zadar, Croatia
e-mail: mmate@unizd.hr

D. Čičin-Šain
e-mail: dcsain@unizd.hr

A. Peša
e-mail: apesa@unizd.hr

I. Bartuseviciene et al. (eds.), *Building Resilience Through Digital Transformation and Sustainable Innovation*, Springer Proceedings in Business and Economics,
https://doi.org/10.1007/978-3-031-90054-9_5

the first step in joining the euro, while Romania never reached that step, although it is the most interested member country that wants to join the Eurozone.

Nevertheless, Bulgaria abandoned plans to introduce the euro in response to the growing economic crisis and uncertainty over the future.

The Republic of Croatia is an EU member country that has met the prescribed criteria and entered the Eurozone on January 1, 2023. The subject of this paper is the review of preparation of the entry of the Republic of Croatia into the Eurozone with regard to the exchange rate mechanism and the long-term interest rate. The goal is to investigate the convergence criteria prescribed by the EU for the entry of member states into the Eurozone on the example of the Republic of Croatia with a special focus on the exchange rate and long-term interest rate.

The topic is very actual, considering that the Republic of Croatia has just entered the Eurozone, and at a time of strong inflation present in the entire EU. The second chapter covers the literature reviews and third chapter Treaty on the Functioning of the European Union. This is followed by an overview of the convergence conditions for the entry of a country into the Eurozone, and an overview of the EBC convergence reports as well as an overview of The Exchange Rate Mechanism (ERM II). Followed by the chapter Croatian exchange rates and long-term interest rates in ERM II, inflation in the EU, discussion and conclusion.

2 Literature Review

The EMU, in addition to being an economic creation, is also a political one, because the European Commission, by expanding the common currency area, further strengthens the common space, achieving its political goal of stability, while on the other hand, many economists warn that Europe is not an optimal currency area, which can have negative consequences for the economy of the union (Mongelli, 2002). An optimal currency area refers to a unique geographical area of one or more currencies whose exchange rates are irrevocably fixed. According to Özdeşer (2020), there are several basic criteria for an optimal currency area, such as mobility of production factors, diversification of production and consumption, similar preferences of unique monetary policy, fiscal transfers and political integration. Many authors analyzed in their papers that Croatia will not adopt the euro for at least another five years, for example Čuček et al. (2020) but Croatia just entered the Eurozone on 1st of January 2023. "It is rather bad in fulfilling the real convergence because there is more focuses on nominal. Since nominal convergence, the government is currently focused on meeting public debt criteria that are still too high and other criteria not too high problem because the trends are in line with the criteria and no deterioration is expected over the years. With given its relatively high public debt, it cannot access ERM II, but it exists the possibility of easing conditions if it shows a multi-year trend of reducing public debt" (Čuček et al., 2020). In their work, Ćorić and Mesić (2012) analyzed Estonia's long-term stay in the ERM II mechanism and concluded the following: "Estonia's experience and stay in the exchange rate mechanism were marked primarily by the country's fiscal stability. In contrast, relatively high rates of economic development, such as rising commodity prices have caused a long-standing trend of high inflation. It was this fact that extended the stay Estonia in the ERM 2. Observed economic indicators, how Estonia and other accession countries do not provide a single conclusion about economic effects of staying in the exchange rate mechanism ERM 2. Despite intensifying GDP growth, Estonia, like other accession countries, has seen a strong increase external debt. Thus, the outcome of the future stay of the Republic of Croatia in the exchange rate ERM 2 is extremely uncertain because of global economic developments unfavorable" (Ćorić & Mesić, 2012).

Deskar-Škrbić and Ćorić (2020) argue that the choice of fluctuation limits is important because it largely determines the conditions under which the exchange rate stability criterion is met. Deskar-Škrbić and Ćorić (2011), stated that, although the criterion exchange rate stability de jure satisfied within fluctuations of ±15%, it de facto requires that the exchange rate stays within narrower limits of fluctuation and that there is an asymmetric treatment of the upper and lower fluctuation limits. They also refer to cde3 who pointed out that the exchange rate criterion would be satisfied within the limits of fluctuation of 2.5% in the direction of depreciation and 15% in the direction appreciation, while a depreciation greater than 2.5% would probably be considered significant pressure.

Croatia is the first country that joined ERM II since the 2008/2009 global crisis. Since the crisis, the EU has been working for more than a decade on global risk reduction, strengthening the protection of institutions against the spillover of crises and disruptions, and creating a Banking Union with two important pillars such as the Single Supervisory Mechanism (SSM) and the Single Resolution Mechanism (SRM). Joining ERM II today also means preparing for banking union (Dorrucci et al., 2020; Peša et al., 2022).

3 A Brief Overview of the Croatian Accession Process to the EU

To date, Croatia has undergone a long process of adjustment of all areas and processes necessary for EU accession including a process of economic convergence and harmonization of national legislation with the Treaty on the Functioning of the European Union for the purpose of participating in the in Stage Three of Economic and Monetary Union, i.e. the adoption of the euro. In October 2001, the Stabilisation and Association Agreement was signed between the European Community (EC) and Croatia, marking the beginning of the EU Stabilisation and Association Process. This process aimed to promote economic growth same as political stability in the whole region and was the first time that the EC and Croatia established general contractual relations. In 2003, Croatia applied for EU membership and began negotiations in 2005. On 12 June 2006, the first chapter of accession negotiations, focusing on science and research, was officially opened. After six years of negotiations, the last of the

35 negotiating chapters was closed on 30 June 2011. On 9 December 2011, EU and Croatian leaders signed the accession treaty, paving the way for Croatia to become the 28th EU member country on 1 July 2013. Croatia had active observer status in the different European Institutions, allowing it to gain insight into the workings of the EU. This helped prepare Croatia for all steps toward membership in the EU.

4 The Convergence Criteria

By signing the Treaty on the Functioning of the European Union, Croatia has committed to Protocol (No 13) on the convergence criteria as a set of guidelines that outline the conditions that Member States of the European Union must meet in order to participate in the euro currency system. These criteria are laid out in Articles 1–4 of the Protocol and pertain to price stability, government budget positions, participation in the Exchange Rate Mechanism of the European Monetary System, and the convergence of interest rates. Article 1 specifies that a Member State must have a sustainable rate of inflation that does not exceed 1 ½ percentage points of the inflation rate of the three best-performing Member States in terms of price stability. "Inflation is measured using the consumer price index on a comparable basis. Article 2 states that a Member State cannot be the subject of a Council decision under Article 126(6) of the Treaty on the Functioning of the European Union that an excessive deficit exists. Article 3 requires that a Member State must have respected the normal fluctuation margins provided by the exchange-rate mechanism of the European Monetary System without severe tensions for at least two years before the examination. Additionally, the Member State cannot have devalued its currency's bilateral central rate against the euro during this period. Article 4 stipulates that a Member State must have an average nominal long-term interest rate that does not exceed two percentage points of the interest rates of the three best-performing Member States in terms of price stability. Interest rates are measured based on long-term government bonds or comparable securities" (ECB, 2001).

5 The Exchange Rate Mechanism (ERM II)

ERM II was created in 1999 as a logical continuation of ERM with the aim of controlling fluctuations of the euro currency in relation to other currencies of EU member states and helping countries that are preparing to join the Eurozone on a voluntary basis. In principle, each such country needs to discipline its currency for at least two years before joining the Eurozone, and a fluctuation of up to 15% above or below the middle exchange rate is allowed. In order to maintain the exchange rate within the prescribed range, monetary interventions by the member National Bank in coordination with the ECB are permitted. The last countries to join the ERM II system were Bulgaria (2018) and Croatia (2019), and the same countries were accepted to join the Eurozone in 2020. Croatia joined the Eurozone on January 1, 2023, unlike Bulgaria, which refused to join the Eurozone citing concerns about the oil crisis due to the Russian-Ukrainian war.

6 The Last Report on Convergence Criteria for Croatia in 2020

For several years, the Croatian kuna has been a slightly fluctuating but stable currency, typical of tourist countries that experience an increased demand for kuna during the summer due to the tourist season, so the CNB conducted seasonal mounted operations to ensure a sufficient amount of kuna. As the season comes to an end, the pressure on the kuna was also getting weaker. If we look at the decade before the entry of the Republic of Croatia into ERM II as a waiting room for the euro, it is evident that the Croatian kuna depreciated by only 5%. In mid-2019, Croatian Institutions showed their interest in joining the ERM II mechanism, which includes a detailed plan of reforms that each country needs to implement if it wants to join the Eurozone through the ERM II preparatory system. The Croatian interest was supported by the finance ministers of the Eurozone member states, led by the Danish Minister of Finance and the Danish National Bank. The years before entering the ERM II system were followed by very low kuna volatility thanks to the interventions of the Croatian National Bank, which were usually linked to seasonal fluctuations due to the tourist season but also due to unusual situations such ase coronavirus (COVID-19). Over the reference period from April 2019 to March 2020, long-term interest rates in Croatia were 0.9% on average, significantly lower than the 2.9% reference value for the interest rate convergence criterion.

In response to the high volatility in the market for government securities caused by the COVID-19 pandemic, Croatian National Bank initiated a government bond purchase program in March 2020. This program was aimed at dampening the effects of the volatility on the market."Prior to the start of the pandemic, credit default swap spreads (a measure of investor perceptions of Croatia's sovereign risk) had declined significantly and stood at around 80 basis points in March 2020. In the first half of 2019, two of the three main international rating agencies had also upgraded the country's rating to investment grade for the first time in several years." (European Commission, 2020).

7 Croatian Exchange Rates and Long-Term Interest Rates in ERM II

We analyzed the exchange rate from July 1, 2020 to January 31, 2022, which covers the period the Croatian kuna participated in ERM II. As elaborated earlier, the Croatian kuna was very stable and traded closely to its central exchange rate against the euro of 7.53450 kuna per euro. In February 2021, an increase of 0.64% was recorded compared to the middle exchange rate, while in July 2020, a decrease of 0.7% was recorded, which coincides with the entry of the Republic of Croatia into the ERM II mechanism. Over the reference period Croatian National Bank conducted only two foreign exchange interventions (in December 2020 and June 2021) by selling domestic currency for euro and intervened once (April 2021) in foreign exchange markets by selling euro in support of the kuna (Graph 1 and Table 1).

As shown in the Graph 2, since the Croatian accession to the EU, the Croatian kuna has not deviated significantly from the ERM II central rate and has remained within the desirable limits of fluctuation of 2.5%. Certainly, in the reference period the Croatian kuna remained in a very narrow range of fluctuations to the established central rate of 7.53450 kuna per 1 euro and this criterion should be expected to remain stable until the next convergency report in June 2022.

Over the reference period observed for the purposes of this paper from July 2020 to January 2022, **long-term interest rates** in Croatia stood at 0.69% on average and thus remained well below the reference value for the interest rate convergence criterion. A Member State, in this case Croatia, must have an average nominal long-term interest rate that does not exceed by more than two percentage points that of,

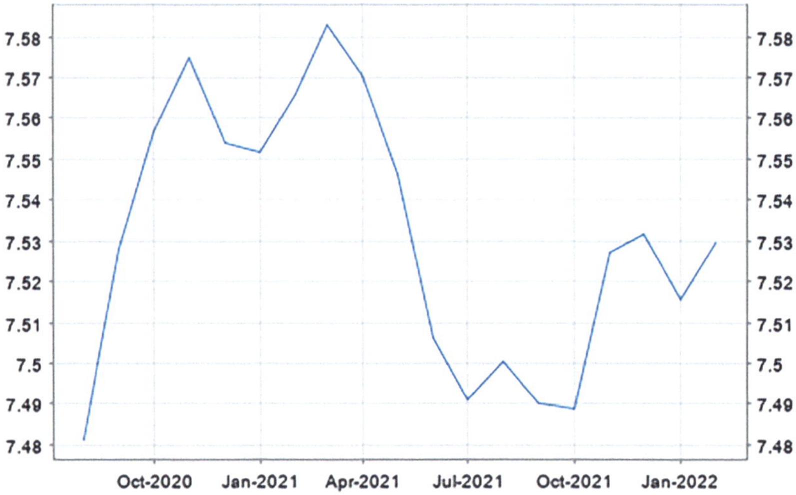

Graph 1 Exchange rates: Croatian kuna/Euro July 2020–January 2022 (European Central Bank, https://sdw.ecb.europa.eu)

Table 1 Exchange Rates: Croatian kuna/Euro July 2020–January 2022 (Authors)

Period (month)	Exchange rate	Deviation from central exchange rate in %
2020–2007	7.4815	−0.70
2020–2008	7.5280	−0.08
2020–2009	7.5565	0.29
2020–2010	7.5748	0.53
2020–2011	7.5538	0.26
2020–2012	7.5519	0.23
2021–2001	7.5658	0.42
2021–2002	7.5830	0.64
2021–2003	7.5705	0.48
2021–2004	7.5465	0.16
2021–2005	7.5062	−0.37
2021–2006	7.4913	−0.57
2021–2007	7.5003	−0.45
2021–2008	7.4900	−0.59
2021–2009	7.4889	−0.60
2021–2010	7.5270	−0.10
2021–2011	7.5315	−0.04
2021–2012	7.5156	−0.25
2022–2001	7.5293	−0.07

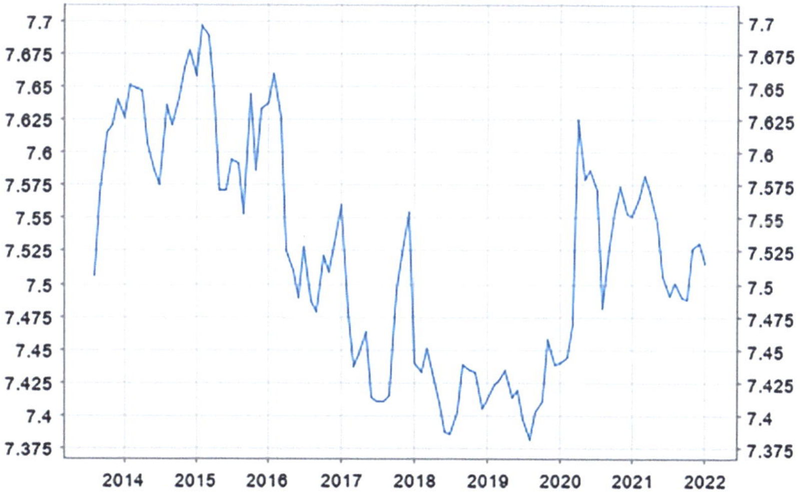

Graph 2 Exchange rates: Croatian kuna/Euro July 2013–January 2022 (European Central Bank, https://sdw.ecb.europa.eu)

Table 2 HICP and Long-term interest rate in selected countries for period March 2021–February 2022 (authors)

Country	HICP (12-months average rate of change)	Long-term interest rate (EMU convergence criterion series—monthly data)
Malta	1.3	0.80
Portugal	1.5	0.58
Greece	1.9	1.62
Average	1.57	1
Reference Value	***3.07***	***3***
Croatia	**3.6**	**0.69**

at most, the three best performing Member States in terms of price stability. As can be seen from Table 2, the three best performing Member States in terms of price stability in the period to be considered as the reference period in the next Convergence Report, but considering that January 2022 is the last available data for this analysis, are Malta, Portugal and Greece. The average long-term interest rate in these three countries stood at the end of reference period at 1%. Long-term interest rates in Croatia stood at 0.69% which means that Croatia has certainly met the long-term interest rate criteria for the next convergence report.

As shown in the Table 3 and Graph 3, since the last convergence report, long-term interest rates declined continuously from 0.9, reaching a minimum in November 2021. It should be noted that from that moment until the time of writing this paper published data show an upward trend however, Croatia still remains within the set criterion.

Since the EU accession, long-term interest rates in Croatia have declined significantly from around 5% at the beginning of that period to around 0.5% at the end of the observed period, as shown in the Graph 4. This criterion was met by Croatia in all previous convergence reports so there was no reason to expect the situation with this criterion to change drastically.

8 Discussion and Conclusion

According to the currently available data on HICP trends shown in the Table 2, Croatia didn't not fully meet the criterion of price stability and on the government debt criteria because that debt amounts is around 75 percent of GDP, significantly more than the 60 percent stipulated in Maastricht Treaty. Based on the movement of the fiscal balance of the general government budget, the share of public debt in GDP in 2021 decrease compared to the year before to 79,79% of GDP and the share of public debt in GDP is estimated to 73% in 2022. This is far more than the reference limit of 60%. Croatia did not meet this criterion in previous convergence reports either, but there was a

Table 3 Long-term interest rates: July 2020–January 2022 (European Central Bank, https://sdw.ecb.europa.eu)

Period (month)	Exchange rate
2020–2007	0.97
2020–2008	0.85
2020–2009	0.79
2020–2010	0.78
2020–2011	0.73
2020–2012	0.63
2021–2001	0.59
2021–2002	0.52
2021–2003	0.51
2021–2004	0.50
2021–2005	0.50
2021–2006	0.49
2021–2007	0.45
2021–2008	0.43
2021–2009	0.37
2021–2010	0.32
2021–2011	0.32
2021–2012	0.38
2022–2001	0.69

Graph 3 Long-term interest rates: July 2020–January 2022 (European Central Bank, https://sdw.ecb.europa.eu)

Graph 4 Long-term interest rates: July 2013–January 2022 (European Central Bank, https://sdw.ecb.europa.eu)

visible trend of decreasing the share of public debt in GDP, and it was considered that such an indicator was still satisfactory. It seems that The European Commission adopt rather arbitrarily regarding convergence criteria of economic data to political decisions in the Croatian case. However, countries differ in terms of their economic structure, they have different levels of development, institutional and informal norms of behaviour differ, so it is logical to expect that a single monetary policy will not suit everyone equally (Baimbridge et al., 2000; Krstić et al., 2020). The EU is very heterogeneous and as each EU member has 'its own story' which cannot be easily observed from only one angle, the growth and development of an EU country is influenced by many factors, not only whether it is in the Eurozone or not. It is also important for our research to mention the world crisis of 2008/2009. which to some degree was reflected in every country of the EU and/or Eurozone. Countries that implement their structural reforms faster and more efficiently record greater benefits (Dauderstädt, 2021). For this reason, peripheral countries benefit less from European integration, and the most benefits were achieved by the so-called core countries, i.e. the most developed EU countries. (Campos et al., 2019; Grabner and Hafele, 2020; Garoupa and Spruk, 2020; Mion & Ponattu, 2019). Croatia entry to Eurozone on 1.st of January 2023. This ignoring of strict prescribed convergence criteria in the case of Croatia - has its role models: Italy and Belgium were admitted to the monetary union in 1998 as founding countries despite their great indebtedness, because they somehow belonged to that circle. The time of low interest rates in the EU is behind us, which could be reflected in increased unemployment rates in the future. From the research on the determinants of unemployment in European countries, it is evident that the increase in interest rates has a strong influence on the increase in unemployment rates (Bosna, 2022).

Ironically, Covid-19 may have helped Croatia's entry into the Eurozone, because an emergency situation prevailed worldwide, and economic activities were quiet for two long years. After that, it was difficult for the European Commission to strictly adhere to the prescribed convergence criteria because it was not possible to separate the negative criteria due to the slowdown of economic activities due to Covid-19 from the possible negative internal economic indicators of the Republic of Croatia. The pandemic was quickly replaced by the energy crisis, which was further intensified by the Russian aggression against Ukraine in 2022. All those negative trends finally show their dangerous impacts in huge inflation globally.

The annual rate of consumer price inflation in Croatia continued to accelerate during June and, after reaching double-digit values in May, reached a historically high 12.1 percent in June. The average growth in consumer prices in Croatia thus amounted to 8.6 percent in the first half of 2022. Euro and inflation now go hand in hand in Republic of Croatia on the beginning of the 2023 year. Recommendations for further research include the study of double inflation that the Republic of Croatia is experiencing at the beginning of 2023; part of the inflation comes as a result of joining the Eurozone, and part of the inflation is due to global inflationary pressures due to the Russian-Ukrainian war and the energy crisis.

Funding This paper was funded by University in Zadar institutional project IP.01.2021.14.

References

Baimbridge, M., Burkitt, B., & Whyman, P. (2000). *The impact of the Euro, debating Britain's future*. Palgrave Macmillan.

Bosna, J. (2022). The determinants of unemployment: CSEE countries panel data analysis. *Scientific Papers of the University of Pardubice, Series D: Faculty of Economics and Administration (1804–8048) 30*(2022), 1; 1–9.

Brlečić Valčić, S., Peša, A., & Čičin-Šain, D. (2022). Analysis of the Eurozone's Resilience to crises and disturbances in the context of EU development strategies—Contemporary approach using Anfis. *Sustainability, 14*, 15594.

Brlečić Valčić, S. (2021). Utilisation of ANFIS in analysing impact of cost structure on Croatian maritime companies development. *Pomorstvo: Scientific Journal of Maritime Research, 35*(1), 179–185.

Campos, N. F., Coricelli, F., & Moretti, L. (2019). Institutional integration and economic growth in Europe. *Journal of Monetary Economics, 103*(2), 88–104.

Čuček, B, Grdinić, M., & Drezgić, S. (2020). Fiskalna politika i uvođenje eura. In *Održivost javnih financija na putu u monetarnu uniju, Zbornik radova znanstvenog skupa, Hrvatska akademija znanosti i umjetnosti, Odsjek za ekonomska istraživanja*, 220–235.

Ćorić, T., & Mesić, M. (2012). Tečajni mehanizam ERM 2: iskustvo Estonije. *Ekonomska Misao i Praksa, 21*(2), 621–638.

Dauderstädt, M. (2021). Cohesive growth in Europe: A tale of two peripheries. *Intereconomics, 56*(2), 120–126.

Deskar-Škrbić, M., & Ćorić, T. (2020). Pristupanje Europskom tečajnom mehanizmu ERM II: iskustva novih članica Europske Unije i slučaj Hrvatske. In *Održivost javnih financija na putu u monetarnu uniju, Zbornik radova znanstvenog skupa, Hrvatska akademija znanosti i umjetnosti, Odsjek za ekonomska istraživanja*, 252–265.

Dorrucci, E., Fidora, M., Gartner, C., & Zumer, T. (2020). The European exchange rate mechanism (ERM II) as a preparatory phase on the path towards euro adoption—The cases of Bulgaria and Croatia. *ECB Economic Bulletin, 8*(2020), 84–105.
European Commission. (2014). *Convergence report 2014*. European Central Bank.
European Commission. (2016). *Convergence report 2016*. European Central Bank.
European Commission. (2018). *Convergence report 2018*. European Central Bank.
European Commission (2020). Convergence report 2020. European Central Bank.
European Central Bank (2020). Communiqué on Croatia. European Central Bank. PRESS RELEASE 10 July 2020.
European Union. (2016). Consolidated version of the Treaty on the Functioning of the European Union. *Official Journal of the European Union, 59*(C 202), 1–361.
Garoupa, N., & Spruk, R. (2020). Does European union really matter for long-run growth and development? In search of the missing counterfactual. *SSRN Electronic Journal*.
Gräbner, C., & Hafele, J. (2020). *The emergence of core-periphery structures in the European Union: A complexity perspective* (ZOE Discussion Papers No. 6). ZOE. Institute for Future-Fit Economies.
Krstić, M. S., Filipe, J. A., & Chavaglia, J. (2020). Higher education as a determinant of the competitiveness and sustainable development of an economy. *Sustainability, 12*(16), 6607.
Mion, G., & Ponattu, D. (2019). Estimating economic benefits of the Single Market for European countries and regions. *Separate pdf Technical Appendix for Policy Paper Estimating economic benefits of the Single Market for European countries and regions*. Bertelsmann Stiftung.
Mongelli, F. P. (2002). *New views on the optimum currency area theory: What is EMU telling us?* (Working Paper no. 138). ECB Working Paper Series.
Özdeşer, H. (2020). Analysis of the Economic Impacts of the Euro, the Efficiency of the Euro in the Optimum Currency Area, and the Place of the Euro in Global Economics. *European Review, 28*(2), 258–275.
Peša, A., Maté, M., & Čičin-Šain, D. (2022). Convergence of EU banking systems: The position of euro and non-euro area countries with reference to Croatia. *Zbornik Veleučilišta u Rijeci, 10*(1), 165–183.

The Bet of Entrepreneurship, Training and Employment in the Age of Artificial Intelligence: The Case of the Manufacturing Sector in Greece

Miltiadis Staboulis, Antonios Kostas, Ioannis Tsoukalidis, and Anastasios Karasavvoglou

Abstract In the Greek labour market, a perennial problem is the gap between the provided professional education and training in relation to the needs of businesses, especially in the age of artificial intelligence. This gap results in the difficulty of finding a suitable workforce and the challenge for employees to adapt to new techno-working environments. The lack of appropriate skillsets per specialty in Greek manufacturing, delays some of the modern production processes, causing significant portions of industries to struggle with international challenges. This article, based on a study of a Greek manufacturing training institution, aims to provide a comprehensive analysis of this issue and propose a strategic framework for action. The proposed framework will focus on upgrading curricula in vocational education, formulating training protocols aligned with contemporary technocratic data, and fostering stronger networking mechanisms between educational institutions and businesses. Additionally, it will explore the implementation of a needs investigation mechanism, with the aim of a holistic approach to reduce the skills gap across critical specialties in Greek manufacturing.

Keywords Employment · Entrepreneurship · Artificial intelligence · Industries · Skillsets · Training

---

M. Staboulis (✉)
University of Macedonia, Thessaloniki, Greece
e-mail: staboulis@uom.edu.gr

A. Kostas · I. Tsoukalidis · A. Karasavvoglou
Democritus University of Thrace, Aghios Loukas, Kavala, Greece
e-mail: akostas@af.duth.gr

I. Tsoukalidis
e-mail: iotsouka@af.duth.gr

A. Karasavvoglou
e-mail: akarasa@af.duth.gr

I. Bartuseviciene et al. (eds.), *Building Resilience Through Digital Transformation and Sustainable Innovation*, Springer Proceedings in Business and Economics,
https://doi.org/10.1007/978-3-031-90054-9_6

JEL Classification Codes J21: Labor Force and Employment, Size, and Structure · M53: Training

1 Introduction

The current state of the labour market in Greek industries is characterised by the persistent mismatch between the provided technical, technological and vocational education and training, and the actual needs of Greek industries and manufacturing enterprises. This issue is exacerbated by rapid technological advancements and the emergence of artificial intelligence in production. These failures lead to a shortage of qualified candidates for open job positions, increasing the workload for current employees, raising operating expenses, and impeding the creation of novel products, services, or innovative production methods, making it difficult for many Greek industries to compete globally.

The problem arises and is exacerbated by the very nature of the digital economy. Digital transformation results in changes in the allocation of tasks between humans and machines, leading to job automation and creating new specialties and jobs. This makes digital and soft skills necessary and complementary to vertical (hard) skills. This is confirmed extensively in research. For instance, research from the Hellenic Federation of Enterprises (SEV) shows that approximately 84% of businesses prefer retraining their staff as a key tool in dealing with the changes brought about by automation, while only 3.4% considers layoffs as a preferred solution. Investing in a company's current human capital is now regarded as a top priority. Amidst the negative repercussions of the recent pandemic on employment and the resulting expansion of remote work and digital commercial transactions, enhancing the digital skills of the workforce is becoming a necessary condition for the economy's smooth advancement and the development of businesses under these new conditions (SEV, 2020a). Furthermore, the overall European labour market has undergone significant changes under the pressure of necessary technological applications in the production process. Online labour market trends and new ways of organising work, education and training indicate that digital learning and digital work are expected to become more important in the future. Cedefop's survey on online job adverts highlights that due to the recovery shown by the manufacturing sector, most online job adverts in 2020 concerned positions in manufacturing and construction sectors, with an emphasis on mid-skilled occupations and on basic to specialised digital skills (Cedefop, 2021).

A study by the Hellenic Labour Inspectorate (SEPE) entitled "White Paper-Greece of 2040", predicts dramatic changes in the nature, distribution, and organisation of work in Greece by 2040, resulting in modifications to organisational and operational structures that will depend more on coordination and decision-making services. These changes will affect the nature of these proficiencies, and future occupations will increasingly fall into the category of "superjobs", combining the use of technology with a wide spectrum of competencies and skills, necessitating accelerated the learning process for both employees and employers. The supremacy of super-jobs is connected to the expected increase in the number of Greek smart factories by 2040. In these factories, manufacturing processes will be automated to a greater extent than today, achieved, among others, through the extensive use of industrial robots, numerous data collection points (sensors of various types, interconnected devices, internet of things), and interconnected technology systems processing and exchanging information in real time. A factory's physical infrastructure will be supported by a parallel digital twin. Data will be collected from the physical world, analysed in real time in the digital world, leading to automated decision-making using artificial intelligence, which in turn will ultimately translate into specific actions in the physical world (physical-to-digital-to-physical loop). Gradually, Greek manufacturing enterprises will be digitally interconnected with different parts of their supply chain. For example, a smart factory can send automated orders to replenish intermediate goods or other materials when inventories fall below a certain level. Augmented and virtual reality tools and collaborative robotic systems (co-bots) will support logistics personnel in inventory management, while 3D printing will enable manufacturing companies will print spare parts and components on demand, reducing the related inventory carrying costs (IVEPE-SEV, 2022).

The support of the aforementioned changes is inextricably linked to the necessity of renewing and upgrading skills (reskilling, upskilling) with an emphasis on technical digital skills. Lintzeris (2020) highlights the importance of technological change, digitization, work, and skills. The use of sensors, remote monitoring mechanisms, and management of devices and facilities is widely applied in many sectors including construction professions such as technologies for remote management of electrical installations of buildings (smart buildings) assisting professions like Installers and Electricians. Policy guidelines and measures for energy conservation significantly promote the utilisation of such technologies towards the reduction of energy consumption. Mobile devices with internet access (smartphones, tablets) and device management applications, combined with communication networks and capabilities for digital interconnectivity, have led to increased demand for similar facilities and services. In the near future, more household devices and small appliances will connect to the internet, expanding the already growing market for related products and services, and changing the required skills of professionals involved in related fields and specialties. In construction and building maintenance fields (i.e., Electricians, Plumbers, Elevator Repairman, Aluminum System Installers, Refrigeration Engineers, etc.) general digital skills, specialised skills for handling devices (either on site or remotely), software programming competencies, and knowledge of management software for digital facilities, will be considered prerequisites.

The critical technical professions that play a pivotal role in achieving development objectives in manufacturing enterprises are reflected in the results of the Mechanism for Diagnosing Business Needs in Professions and Skills operated by SEV. SEV recognises that investing in the upskilling of human capital is a crucial component of any effort for the country's production restructuring efforts. Therefore, SEV developed the Mechanism for Diagnosing Business Needs in Professions and Skills identifying needs in eight important business sectors: Food, Information and Communication Technologies, Energy, Building Materials, Supply Chain, Environment, Metal industries, and Healthcare (IVEPE-SEV, 2022).

Particularly interesting are the results of the survey "Quantitative research in industrial enterprises on human resource development issues" carried out in 2018 by SEV, involving 831 Greek manufacturing enterprises operating in six sectoral ecosystems: agri-food, construction materials, energy, logistics, digital economy, and healthcare and pharmaceuticals. Approximately 36% of the total companies surveyed and about 46% of those with exports > 50% of turnover, pointed out difficulties in filling job vacancies. The most significant skill shortage is observed in medium-skilled occupations (42.6%) compared to high-skilled occupations (35.2%) and low-skilled occupations (22.2%). The most important difficulties mentioned are the shortage of appropriate skills (27.7%) and the absence of relevant work experience (21.3%). In the categories of "Technicians", "Skilled craftsmen", and "Industrial plant operators", the most important shortages are related to modern technical/professional skills. Enterprises attribute the lack of appropriate skills to the inadequacies of the technical-vocational education framework and the inadequate connection of education with the real needs of the labour market. This is confirmed by the fact that about 60% of human resources in businesses surveyed do not have a degree (graduates of higher education). Emerging professional specialisations with higher demand are not promptly recognised and incorporated. For instance, training provided does not match contemporary enterprise demands for many professions demonstrating significant dynamics in the Greek industry. Such professions, according to the international classification of occupations ISCO08, include: (a) operators of machines for the production of rubber and plastic products; (b) installers and maintainers of electrical equipment; (c) operators of machines for the production of foodstuffs and related products, and (d) metal casters, welders, sheet metal workers, metal construction workers, blacksmiths and practitioners of related professions (SEV, 2020b).

More recently, SEV's research findings in the context of its participation in the Regional Association Council with Production and the Labor Market (SSPAE) identified and highlighted dynamic professions by region and/or sector that stem from the Vocational Education and Training (VET) system. Findings include: (a) dynamic technical professions traditionally derived from Vocational Education and Training (VET) streams, showing increased job openings and offering solid career opportunities and decent salary prospects; (b) the pivotal role of Vocational Education and Training (VET) in equipping participants with the required knowledge and skills in order to facilitate labour market integration in line with productive needs of enterprises, and (c) adaptation of Vocational Education and Training (VET) to current technological and economic conditions will allow the Greek production ecosystem to counterbalance the needs in competencies and skills, enhancing employment with skilled human capital in dynamic expanding production activities and well-paid jobs (SEV, 2021).

The effectiveness of developing skills in the population through Vocational Education and Training (VET) policies, in a way that ensures the adequacy of the supply of skills, in quantity and quality, presupposes: (a) actions focused on gathering information on changes in skill demand and using that data to produce updated curricula and programmes focusing on the right blend of general and profession-specific skills, as well as improving the overall design of the education and training system. The importance of these actions is dictated by the finding that the adjustment of the supply of skills, which is shaped by the initial and continuing education and training systems, presupposes, among other things, the operation of a framework for diagnosing and forecasting the needs of the labour market at a sectoral level, and (b) actions aimed at encouraging the involvement of social partner organisations in designing and implementing skills development training programmes or adopting a clearly defined quality framework in vocational education and training, without leading to an excessive administrative burden (Lalioti, 2019).

2 Methodological Approach

This article is based on the IVEPE-SEV research study, published in 2022, titled "Report of Strategic Development of IVEPE-SEV for the Upgrading of Technical Specialties in Greek Industry", which proposes and implements a strategic framework of action (IVEPE-SEV, 2022).

IVEPE (Institute of Industrial and Business Education & Training) is a non-profit organisation created in 1980 by a consortium of major Greek enterprises to offer professional training and education. SEV took over its management in 2012, and it has since operated under the name IVEPE-SEV. Today, it serves as SEV's educational branch in the fields of Lifelong Learning and Professional Training, adding new dimensions to the organisation's function as an institutional social partner. With facilities in Athens, Thessaloniki, Volos, and Patras, and through strong educational alliances, IVEPE-SEV plays an important role in providing lifelong education programmes, some of which are not offered by other institutions in Greece. The purpose is to equip the human capital of Greek enterprises with adequate knowledge capacity and skills appropriate for the modern times.

In the context of the primary qualitative research, the main purpose was to prioritise the technical specialties of the Greek industry. The research was conducted through personal interviews via a teleconferencing platforms (Zoom, Skype, Microsoft Teams) based on an analytical guide of questions, with twenty (20) executives participating, including six (6) executives from the SEV and IVEPE-SEV and 14 executives from selected Greek industries (IVEPE-SEV, 2022).

3 IVEPE-SEV Research Results

3.1 *Results from SEV and IVEPE-SEV Executives (IVEPE-SEV Research)*

Upon inquiry on the industries most affected by the pressure to align workers' technical specialisations with job content requirements, it was found that all industry sectors have technical and technological talent shortages. The construction, metallurgy, primary food processing, pharmaceutical, and chemical and plastic manufacturing industries, all face significant challenges in recruiting qualified workers for technical positions. These shortages and the requirements for specific specialisations consist of both a deficiency in the quantity of human resources and a deficiency in quality of human capital, i.e., a lack of specific skills necessary to perform the tasks and responsibilities of each technical occupation in reference.

This shortage phenomenon is widely acknowledged to be due to the transformation of the Greek Technological Institutes (TEI), being elevated to University status, which essentially served as a talent pool that supplied manufacturing industries with workers possessing the skills necessary for jobs with technical specialisation, while semester internships provided students with the opportunity for performance evaluation. That transformation of the Technological Institutes was accompanied by the elimination of practical training and a shift towards a more theoretical curriculum, but also due to two other important dimensions: one related to the numerical disadvantage of graduates from these departments, and the other related to the expectations of those who graduate, which do not include employment in manufacturing production lines. As such, the deficit of elementary technical, technological education is gradually increasing in a population that is initially funnelled into former Technological Institutes, when the plan was to fill this gap with special two-year study programmes in universities, a measure which was not established.

At the same time, enterprises disregard Apprenticeship Vocational Schools (EPAS) and post-high school yearly apprenticeships, while Institutes of Vocational Training (IEK) are primarily a pool for specialisations engaged in the service industry (tertiary sector), which frequently includes services that support manufacturing. The relevant training manuals for the majority of IEK's technical specialisations, and the study programmes in Vocational High Schools (EPAL) do not meet the level demanded by the modern labour market or the circumstances of productive transformation in manufacturing businesses. Many young individuals, for various reasons, do not pursue technical education or training. Thus, it is not surprising that, according to research findings in the framework of the Skills4Jobs project, there are only two IEKs in the region of Attica (Greece) that offer the training specialisation in the occupation of Automation Electrician, as opposed to a plethora of those that offer specialisation in the occupation of Cook, resulting in an outflow of only 50–60 people, which is expected to fulfil the needs in all sectors of electrical engineering. Similarly, the metallurgy industry reports serious shortages of Metal Technicians.

Emerging technical talents in demand include plant maintenance workers, electrician-automators, machine operators, information technology application technicians, welders, and foremen.

It is noteworthy to mention the respondents' perceptions on technical specialties that are regarded as challenging to cover through human resources, both quantitatively and qualitatively. Specialties such as electrician, plant maintainer, automation, IT application technicians, machine drivers, supervisors, and foremen, are either in short supply or lack the necessary skills and knowledge. In fact, the profession of automation technician was mentioned as a key specialty, because the equipment installed as a result of the industries' new investments, is primarily based on the function of automation, making the lack of this specialty a significant reason for the industries' inability to respond to the orderly organisation of production lines. Furthermore, in the context of climate change and adaptation to new production standards, issues of proper energy management, environmental protection, and reducing the industry's environmental footprint are becoming more prominent, and as a result, new specialties are emerging that were barely mentioned in previous years. Examples of such specialties include the renewable energy technician, electrician-automation technician, installer-maintainer of air conditioning systems, energy management technician, technician of electrical and electronic systems and installations, and technical maintainer of industrial installations. The site foreman is another expertise for which there is a shortage of available labour. In the shipbuilding industry, shortages exist in important specialisations that do not have a strong technological profile, such as machinists, welders, lathe operators, electricians, and plumbers. In the food industry, major specialties were safety and quality management staff, who were covered from graduates of the former Technological Institutes food technology departments, food processing and production technologists, and slaughterers-meat processors.

Concerning the subject of the soft skills that present an increased or imperative demand in the industry sector includes Collaboration, Problem Solving, Adaptability, and Communication. The listed skills are regarded as necessary on a horizontal level, that is, both at the level of different professions and at the level of different sectors. In particular, the ability to work in a team and collaborate was mentioned as a primary skill by almost all participants, as the production line in the new work environments now requires teamwork, but it has been found that many employees face difficulties onboarding a new team, which is also linked to the adequacy of project management skills. Communication skills are also important, which refer to how a person learns to communicate with a client, a colleague, a supervisor, a supplier, and so on, whether it is written or oral communication. It is critical that communication abilities extend beyond the technical aspects and make the individual an active listener who is conversant with digital communication contexts and behaviours. Another key horizontal talent is the ability to address difficulties that arise during the performance of tasks, which requires that the employee has developed the ability to differentiate between correct and incorrect information, evaluate its source, think critically, analyse and synthesise data (problem solving). Additionally, the majority of participants believe that adaptability is an important horizontal talent. Because production lines and workplaces are continually changing, it is required that workers must be able to adapt to the conditions associated with the establishment of automation, digital communication techniques, high security systems, quality assurance, and environmental protection. Also, cited as a crucial horizontal skill was job empathy, or the ability for an employee to understand his/her role in the workplace and carry out his/her duties. An additional horizontal skill is the ability to self-regulate, which means that everyone understands their own strengths and weaknesses, where they fall behind, and where they excel. Finally, the lack of knowledge of a foreign language was mentioned as less common, with the major worry being mastery of the profession's technical terminology. It was noted that workers in technical specialisations must be able to read a manual for a new machine or system in a foreign language (typically English or German).

Regarding vertical skills, it is evident that these vary significantly by profession or industry. For instance, gas installation technicians must be certified in renewable energy management procedures. Similarly, plumbing, refrigeration and electrical specialties, require skills related to the green economy. For electricians, electronic installers-automatists, proficiency in the Java programming language is emerging as an important skill. Considering that today's industrial production is heavily reliant on coding procedures, the shortage of human resources in the industry, proficient in writing, editing and comprehending code and being able to configure it, configuring a robotic arm, etc., is an inhibiting growth barrier. As a result, industries, particularly those with limited in-house expertise, are spending considerable sums to outsource tasks that could be completed in a cost and time effective manner. Additionally, many technical specialties, particularly those involving operators, are in short supply, and regulatory measures ned to be developed for construction machinery operators and those skilled in new technologies such as robotic arms, robotic welding machines, etc. These emerging skills underscore the necessity for upskilling various professions as the nature and content of work continue to evolve.

In the question regarding the digital skills, modern workers in technical specialties must possess the ability to enter data on tablets and other devices that feed into massive databases. The majority of those finishing initial vocational training are uninformed on automation systems employed by the Greek industry, while there is a lack of skills connected to even basic computer knowledge, such as using Microsoft Excel or managing email communication. Among the digital skills that large corporations particularly require, is the necessary knowledge capacity in Cybersecurity matters. This gap in digital proficiency highlights the need for comprehensive training programmes to equip the workforce with the necessary skills to thrive in an increasingly digital and automated industrial environment.

3.2 *Results from Greek Industry Executives (IVEPE-SEV Research)*

When it comes to the question of identifying technological expertise that are in high demand in Greek enterprises, the following stand out as the most important: mechanical and electrical engineers, maintenance workers, lift machine operators, and welders. The specialty of mechanical–electrical engineers was highlighted by several respondents and it was stated that it is critical that they possess knowledge of automation. The specialty of mechanical engineers with hands-on experience has been proven to be essential in production lines and is associated with the maintenance of mechanical and electronic equipment. It was emphasised that the available number of human resources with a purely technical education is dropping as the transformation of Technological Institutes (being elevated to University status), resulted in the elimination of internships, which were an important route for acquiring knowledge related to real work environments and the content of mechanical engineers' jobs in Greek industries. The industry's supply of engineers in any specialisation is characterised by a lack of hands-on experience, as they do not have much familiarity with the industrial working environment. It is critical for industries to be able to recruit industrial engineers (electronics, mechanical, and electrical) with the necessary relevant experience. Maintenance workers are another crucial specialty for the Greek industry, as it is required from them to have basic knowledge of electrology, plumbing, refrigeration systems, and other technical maintenance skills granting them a multifunctional role in the field of technical maintenance, while it is also important for them to possess basic programming knowledge to use control panel applications through a monitor. The participants emphasised that, while polytechnic schools produce excellent engineers with theoretical knowledge, technical schools (EPAL) and apprenticeship vocational schools (EPAS) primarily produce technical professions (i.e., electricians, plumbers, refrigeration engineers, and so on) who can manage tasks and procedures in household rather than industrial facilities. Lifting Equipment & forklift operators, that exhibit uniqueness in their certification process, were cited as a crucial speciality. Due to the large supply of available potential candidates of this speciality in the past, certification exams have ceased to be held in recent years, resulting in shortage, while there exists now a time-consuming process in which the person must train for a year alongside a certified operator. In terms of logistics, the speciality of pickers, i.e., unskilled warehouse workers who should have basic English language skills as well as operational understanding of RF Scanners and/or Warehouse Management Systems, is regarded as critical. Industrial welders are a specialty that is difficult to supply with skilled human capital, hence needs (job vacancies) are frequently filled by persons from abroad due to a severe shortage of local labour. Another specialty that is part of the product manufacturing process is the Production Line Technician (or production line operator), being the person who operates the machines, performs technical and/or manual activities, or must comply with quality requirements.

It is worth noting that certain specialties are in high demand in specific industries. In the food industry, the most in-demand specialties are packaging machine operators, meat slicers, food technologists, and pickers in the logistics department, while in the beverage industry, brewers and maltsters are key specialties in high demand. The food and beverage sector has unique characteristics and specialisations that stem from the type and technology of the raw materials. While there are specialised institutions in Europe for the management of raw materials in food and drinks, such as Bakers schools, where flour technology is thoroughly taught, there is a significant shortage of raw material specialists in Greece. The desired specialisation is acquired through the experiential learning that comes from working in the food industry. As a result, specialised occupations such as millers and industrial bakers are lacking. In the food industry, packaging machine operator was identified as a key ability because packaging machines today rely on automation and robotic systems that cannot be managed by an inexperienced person. This shortage was covered by the outflows of the Mechanical Engineering departments. However, Polytechnic engineering graduates are no longer eager to fill such occupations, resulting in skill gaps, as unqualified or inexperienced people in the industry are hired. Particularly for this specific specialisation, there is a need for power users who are familiar with the packaging machine, can train the new employees, and handle first-level support without having to hire a specialised technician for a task as simple as this.

In terms of soft/horizontal skills that are in increased or essential demand in the industry sector, the following six soft skills emerged: (1) Teamwork; (2) Problem Solving; (3) Time Management; (4) Communication; (5) Adaptability, and (6) Code of Conduct. Teamwork is a vital horizontal talent because in industrial production lines, everyone works interrelatedly and must cooperate with each other and adapt to the conditions of each business. Teamwork must be such that they can deal with situations where there is no supervision for an extended period of time, requiring a fair division of tasks to be achieved. Time management was identified as a critical ability that involves organising one's thoughts to prioritise assigned tasks for the most effective completion within a certain time frame. Akin with this skill is the ability to solve problems, which entails analysing data and selecting the best answers. Communication skills are a horizontal talent identified by almost all respondents, as very often professionals in technical specialisations are required to communicate with colleagues (peers, subordinates or supervisors), with suppliers, etc., and may be required to present part of their work. Communication is at the heart of efficient teamwork, which is an essential component of modern production lines. It was also stated that it is important for workers in technical professions to possess skills related to Workplace Code of Conduct, meaning to be distinguished in business intelligence residing in matters of ethics, respect for the rights of others, and approaching the workplace through empathy. Finally, adaptability is a key horizontal skill since, as in recent years, changes in production lines have necessitated workers' ongoing adaptation to new job requirements. In fact, adaptability emerged as an important skill throughout the economic and health crises, and the rapid technological developments that are occurring, make human resource adaptability a crucial parameter of Greek industry competitiveness. Finally, numerous individuals mentioned proficiency in

English as a critical skill, citing the fact that manuals and machines are in English. Less frequently, business acumen was described as a vital talent that all employees should have, i.e., the reasoning surrounding entrepreneurship that allows the individual to maintain a global image of what entrepreneurship, the production process and financial results imply, and so on. Finally, horizontal skills such as consistency and responsibility, concentration on detail, devotion to the outcome, and the capacity to operate under pressure were addressed.

Regarding vertical skills, it is evident that these vary by profession or industry. For engineers, skills and expertise in automation and mechanical design are critical. Electrical engineers lack important vertical skills due to inadequate technical training in electrical engineering concepts and design, while they lack basic expertise in equipment maintenance and problem-solving in industrial machinery. Engineers working on the production lines need to understand automation and robotic systems, and possess the ability to read, understand and customise code. For welders, recognising tool terminology and applying special types of welds are essential vertical skills. For lifting machine operators, knowledge of the fundamental principles of machine operation and maintenance, the capacity to solve machine problems, the safe use of machines and responding to maintenance and inspection procedures were highlighted as critical abilities. Packaging machine operators in the food industry must have skills related to programming, monitoring, maintenance and solving technical problems and breakdowns of the packaging machine, as well as knowledge of materials technology. Meat cutters must be proficient in handling various types of meat properly. The specialty of brewer-maltster require knowledge of beer production processes and raw ingredients, as well as current quality control and packaging methods. Other technical specialties in brewing require basic electrical, mechanical, electronic, and robotics knowledge, whereas workers in technical specialties should understand the basic components of the equipment to address basic technical difficulties.

In terms of digital skills, the respondents emphasised that part of the vertical skills is related to the digitisation of production lines, and for this reason, in all branches of industry, the knowledge of automation, robotics, the use of project management platforms emerged as key skills that are used for the construction of projects. Familiarity with information systems such as SAP, ERP, widely used by Greek industries, as well as WinCC Professional (SCADA) systems, Siemens, Allen-Bradley systems, etc., is essential. However, beyond vertical digital skills, there is a shortage of horizontal digital abilities that allow workers to participate in digital technology, as the requirement for basic computer skills and efficient social media use. Finally, skills relating to the conditions of hygiene and safety in the workplace were highlighted less frequently.

Aside from the major specialties and required skills, another item investigated was the recommendation of the most appropriate method of implementing educational programmes aimed at the aforementioned specialties. The majority of respondents agree that since these are technical professions with diminishing hands-on experience, training programmes should be designed on an on-site approach to allow for the use of mechanical equipment and direct interaction with it in order to obtain practical skills. In this regard, it is fair for the training programme to include practical training in the workplace. Remote education (synchronous and asynchronous), which was proposed to primarily address the development of horizontal skills, is not excluded, but it shouldn't replace hands-on training. Almost all respondents agree that employee training programmes should not be extended in a long duration, with an indicative suggested number of total 35 training hours. All participating enterprises in the study, have developed annual staff training programmes and used various methods to examine employees' training needs, while also engaging in and supporting relevant research conducted by sectoral and other bodies. This fact is significant because it is linked to a willingness to collaborate with IVEPE to develop educational programmes that meet the needs of businesses and their employees, ensuring mutual benefit and practical application.

4 Suggestions and Value of IVEPE-SEV Research

4.1 Proposed Strategic Framework of Interventions

Based on the research results (IVEPE-SEV, 2022), the proposed interventions are categorised into two axes. The first axis covers the actions intended to be implemented by IVEPE using its own means (in-house), as follows: (1) Prioritising and developing training programmes for necessary specialties in the processing and manufacturing industries that concern new entrants. This includes automation engineers, production line engineers, electricians automation engineers, equipment maintenance engineers, hoist operators, foremen with big data management digital skills, platform and code configuration IT, etc.; (2) Developing certification programmes for individuals regarding some of the aforementioned specialisations targeting new joiners into manufacturing; (3) Establishing sectoral training agreements for the complete spectrum of duties including needs assessment, knowledge requirements, and differentiation for new entrants and existing employees for each specialty per sector; (4) Developing a forecasting mechanism to identify educational needs in technical specialisations within Greek manufacturing industries; (5) Creating a framework for researching complementing horizontal and digital skills in technical specialisations in manufacturing—leading to the formation of relevant educational programmes; (6) Developing an annual training programme implemented by IVEPE using its own resources (self-monitoring), based on the outcomes of the forecasting and needs assessment mechanism; (7) Developing an interactive electronic learning platform for employees and new joiners, to cultivate digital and horizontal skills; (8) Upgrading technical equipment in IVEPE laboratories, including simulators and educational digital platforms for programming and automation of mechanical sets, etc., based on prioritisation; (9) Developing a consultation system with vocational and technical education providers and signing programme cooperation agreements with organisations such as Hellenic Manpower Employment Organization (DYPA),

Ministry of Education, and sectoral bodies, and (10) Providing technical assistance to medium-sized manufacturing companies to help to establish training academies.

The second axis covers the following initiatives that IVEPE proposes to implement in conjunction with third parties (outsourcing), as follows (IVEPE-SEV, 2022): (1) Developing systematic educational visits to enterprises categorised by branch similarity for end-year students or university graduates, highlighting the industrial scope of operation of the speciality, and consultation on concretisation of internships in industries; (2) Enriching the information database on the development of Vocational Education and Training (VET), Initial Vocational Training (AEK) and Continuing Vocational Training (SEK) systems. This includes skills related to new technologies, quantitative ranking of specialisations in manufacturing, and the relationship between knowledge, skills, and abilities for personnel evaluation, etc., in collaboration with Hellenic Federation of Enterprises (SEV) and other similar agencies; (3) Establishing independent initiatives to assist and specialise the internship or Apprenticeship of Vocational High School (EPAL) graduates, EPAL with apprenticeship classes, Institutes of Vocational Training (IEK), and University departments (former Greek Technological Institutes) in manufacturing enterprises; (4) Creating counselling work integration in industrial businesses for newly entering trainees who participated in IVEPE training programmes; (5) Developing an integrated action plan to empower the jobless by acquiring knowledge in technical specialisations of productive firms with job placement (co-financed), and (6) Collaborating with educational institutions, with a focus on the VET and VET sectors, to further develop the ecosystem by providing specialties and skills that meet the needs of Greek manufacturing through the appropriate information dissemination and multiplier actions-forming relevant networks.

4.2 Expected Results

The expected results through the proposed interventions of the first axis include the formation of modern educational material for each speciality, intended for the introductory training of newcomers and newly hired employees. This involves the cooperation with companies for the organisation of practical training in relevant jobs, the development of a critical mass of trainers per speciality, and the feedback from the evaluation of the pilot implementation of the educational programmes, focusing on the certification of persons with cutting-edge knowledge for the modern specialties of Greek manufacturing. These efforts will result in a critical mass of certified candidate workers in chosen specialities. The establishment of a new IVEPE service or structure for predicting educational demands, and interfacing with businesses, agencies, services, and other stakeholders, can contribute to the design of training programmes through systematic monitoring of changes in the production process. These actions can gradually lead to an integrated approach to exploring educational needs in horizontal and digital skills necessary for technical specialties of manufacturing. This will contribute to standardising training services in key specialties and their interrelated required skills, aiming for the individual professional development of employees and the transformation of technological innovations into group or individual training, upgrading the value chain of the products produced through the upgrading of human capital prospects.

The expected outcomes of the actions of the second axis include the enhancement of knowledge about the operation of specialisations in a variety of industrial activities, increased internship opportunities in industrial jobs, and increased interest among graduates in employment in the Greek manufacturing industry. The creation of an integrated approach to the provision of advisory support services in conjunction with IVEPE training programmes, the strengthening of the work profile of newly joined trainees who are placed in jobs after their participation in training programmes, the better integration of new joiners in the work environment and in the industrial scope of their speciality, can enhance the attractiveness of the Greek industries as positive employers. This includes providing consulting, training, certification and offering opportunities for unemployed individuals in technical specialties of the industry. In this manner, multiplicative factors are activated for developing an ecosystem to create an employment pool of technical specialties through the use of economies of scale. This contributes to the optimal dissemination of information for the operation of an ecosystem aimed at elevating skills in technical specialties that are critical for the Greek manufacturing industry.

5 Conclusions

This article focuses on the construction of a wider strategic framework of IVEPE-SEV, aimed at upgrading training courses for specific technical specialties, through actions such as the enrichment of education protocols, the development of a network for strategic cooperation between IVEPE-SEV and tertiary education institutions and/or enterprises, the development of a permanent mechanism for researching education/training requirements, the enlarged offering of educational/training services through own IVEPE-SEV means, etc.

IVEPE-SEV is faced with the task of redefining their role in providing education in technical specialties, as there exist challenges related to the institutional framework of AEK and SEK and the necessity for developing an ecosystem of technical professional education and training that caters to evolving production systems through the adoption of new technologies. The recent application of Law 4763/2020 related to the National System of Professional Education, Training & Life-long Learning highlights this challenge.

In this vein, a series of strategic actions for IVEPE is recommended for the following 3-year period, in two basic priorities: Priority 1 includes actions recommended for IVEPE-SEV to be developed by its own means (in-house) and Priority 2 includes actions that are recommended for IVEPE-SEV to be developed in cooperation with others (outsourcing). Every priority includes side interventions that can be developed autonomously and/or in conjunction with each other. Additionally, it is feasible for more than one intervention to be joined and produce a complete project, especially if it is going to be adjusted and submitted for co-financing through National Strategic Reference Framework (ESPA) 2021-2027. In any case, the organisation can set out their priorities, in the context of a 3-year development plan, leveraging exploitable ideas to the redesign of IVEPE-SEV's role in cooperation with SEV.

In conclusion, due to the urgent need for new technologies in the Greek Processing Industry and the traditional delay of harmonisation of educational systems with the needs of the economy and job market needs, front-loaded acceleration in professional training (both intra-company and cross-enterprise) is expected.

References

Cedefop (2021). *Trends, transitions and transformation.* Briefing Note, April 2021, ISSN 1831–2462. Retrieved from https://www.cedefop.europa.eu/files/9157_el.pdf

IVEPE-SEV (2022). *Strategic growth report of IVEPE-SEV for the advancement of technical specialties in the Greek Industry.* Athens, pp. 43–53. Retrieved from https://ivepe.gr/el/

Lalioti, B. (2019). *Skill strategies: Researching their basic principles and their structural components*-EIEAD. Retrieved from https://mdaae.gr/wp-content/uploads/2023/01/Lalioti_Study_ALMPs.pdf

Lintzeris, P. (2020). *Technological advancement, digitisation, labour & competencies.* Research Texts of IME-GSEVEE. Retrieved from https://imegsevee.gr/wp-content/uploads/2020/06.pdf

SEV (2021). *Dynamic professions: Education and training towards the transformation of production.* Special Report, 11 October 2021. Retrieved from https://www.sev.org.gr/wp-content/uploads/2021/10/SR_dynamika_epaggelmata_FINAL.pdf

SEV (2020a). *Retraining and upskilling of human capital: The challenges of enhancing the workers and the development of enterprises.* Special Report, 12 October 2020. Retrieved from https://www.sev.org.gr/wp-content/uploads/2021/01/2020-10-12_SR_Reskilling_FINAL.pdf

SEV (2020b). *Vocational education and training reform: Key to a new production model with better and more job opportunities for young people.* Special Report, 9 July 2020. Retrieved from https://www.sev.org.gr/wp-content/uploads/2021/01/SR_EEK_Draft_final_new.pdf

Assessing Financial Well-Being and Migration INTentions: A Perspective from Greek Students

Goran Karanovic, Ana Stambuk, and Persefoni Polychronidou

Abstract This study explores the self-perception of financial well-being and migration intentions of Greek students. Data from 346 students were gathered thought a structured online survey distributed to economics students in Greece. The research investigates student's capacity to manage their financial routines, their adequacy of income, their perception of unforeseen financial challenges and propensity for savings. Alongside financial evaluations, this study also examines students' intentions to migrate. The results reveal significant variance in financial perception within the student population. Over 50% of the student sample are not able to cover costs of unforeseen financial expenses or save money, and 25% of the sample lack financial adequacy manage financial routines. A considerable share of surveyed students articulates a willingness to migrate to regardless of the job availability in Greece, emphasising the strong preference towards improving the living conditions through migration. Furthermore, factors such the ability of secure a job in their field of study, language barriers as well personal relationships significantly influence students' migration intention. The findings imply a complex connexion between self-perception of financial well-being and migration decisions, supported by economics status and personal aspirations for better quality of life. The study contributes to the large body of studies on youth migrations and implications of financial security, emphasising the need for inclusive policies that supports reductions of brain drain in Greece. This research sheds a new light on socio-economic factors and implications of youth migrations in Greece.

Keywords Self-perception · Financial well-being · Migrations · Students · Greece

---

G. Karanovic
Faculty of Tourism and Hospitality Management, University of Rijeka, Rijeka, Croatia
e-mail: gorank@fthm.hr

A. Stambuk
Faculty of Economics and Business, University of Rijeka, Rijeka, Croatia
e-mail: ana.stambuk@efri.uniri.hr

P. Polychronidou (✉)
Department of Economic Sciences, International Hellenic University, Serres, Greece
e-mail: polychr@ihu.gr

I. Bartuseviciene et al. (eds.), *Building Resilience Through Digital Transformation and Sustainable Innovation*, Springer Proceedings in Business and Economics,
https://doi.org/10.1007/978-3-031-90054-9_7

JEL Classification D14 · D31 · O15

1 Introduction

The Global financial crisis in late 2009 had a devastated impact to the world economy causing the collapses of banking systems and financial markets worldwide. The European Union was not exempted from these effects, which had a spillover effect on the overall economy. However, the developed northern countries managed to overcome this crisis more efficiently than the southern EU member countries. The countries that coped with the consequences for a much longer period were grouped under acronym "PIGS" Portugal, Italy, Greece and Spain. The main characterises of these countries was long run of negative GDP growth and significant rise of debt to GDP ratio.

The country that experienced of long-standing negative consequences and was most affected is Greece. Greece experienced the unsustainable debts level and in 2013 supressed 160% what was far beyond Maastricht criterion of 60% of GDP (Ozturk & Sozdemir, 2015, p. 569). The crisis exposed fiscal mismanagement and inefficiencies within the Greek economy that generated the overall economic and social turmoil. Collapse of Greek economy started with deteriorating macroeconomic fundamentals combined unsustainable fiscal finances. This was manifest trough relatively low competitiveness, account deficits, adoption of the euro and initial benefits in form of lower interest rates and expanded credit access (Arghyrou & Tsoukalas, 2011; Featherstone, 2011). All mentioned constrained the country's ability to implement swift policies to when the crisis emerged. As the result of all these circumstances to was Greece imposed austerity measures by international creditors -the so-called Troika, consisting of the European Commission, European Central Bank (ECB), and the International Monetary Fund (IMF)—only exacerbated the crisis, leading to rising unemployment, declining incomes, and severe public sector cuts (Matsaganis, 2013).

The new fiscal measures some imposed and some voluntary led to the period of seven-year deficit (2008–2016) with the exception 2014 (growth of 0.8%) and highest deficit in 2011 (–9.88) (Fig. 1).

The economic contraction and new socio-economic paradigms imposed by the Troika let to the high rates of unemployment (27.5% in 2013), cuts in earnings in all sectors no matter public or private one. Additionally, all other reforms in pensions, healthcare and labour led to cuts in pensions, decreased employment protection, reducing minimum wages, and restriction on collective agreements with unions. All imposed and voluntarily actions in that period of time were aimed at reducing welfare. This led to rise of poverty as well to increase of inequality (Matsaganis & Leventi, 2014).

Under all stated socio-economics constraints many Greeks faced limited domestic prospects, they sought emigration as mean to access better economic opportunities. Western European Union countries, as well as USA and Canada—traditional

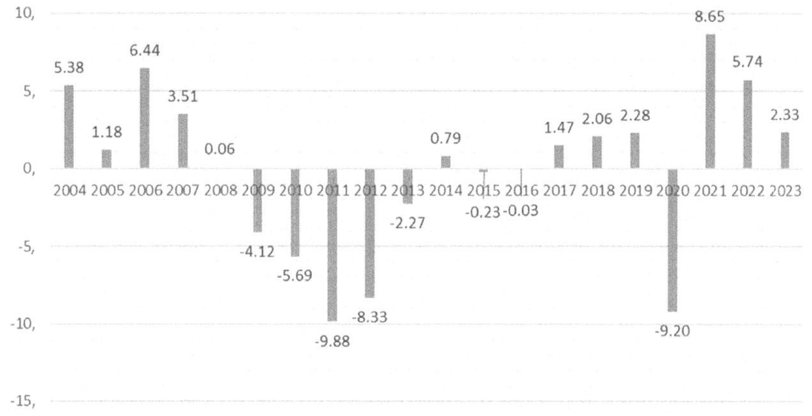

Fig. 1 Greek GDP and main components (output, expenditure and income). *Source* Eurostat

Greek emigration destination—become the final destination for numerous Greek individuals and whole families.

According to the study carried by Labrianidis and Pratsinakis (2016) those who immigrate to Britain are almost exclusively people with high education credentials, while Germany attracts a considerable number of people with low or middle educational backgrounds. The Greeks as a nation due to the diverse historical reasons experienced several weaves of (e)migration–mid-1920, mid-1950 and mid-1970–and as nation and have preferences to emigration. Unlike previous waves of emigration, which were primarily motivated by the search for better economic conditions, this "new wave" included a broader cross-section of society, incorporating highly educated individuals and entire families.

The "brain drain" phenomenon has historically affected Greece, however it surged significantly under the pressure of the Global financial crisis, particularly among the highly educated and younger population. Numerous studies have examined the economic, social, and political drivers and confirmed this trend, underlining the increased emigration intention of the skilled professionals and young population in search of better opportunities abroad (Anastasiadou, 2016; Giousmpasoglou et al., 2016; Labrianidis & Sykas, 2017; Marinakou et al., 2016; Pratsinakis, 2022; Theodoropoulos et al., 2014).

This paper aims to explore Greek students' population intentions to emigrate additionally, study examines the economic (financial) situation and its impact migration intentions of Greek students. With this study authors seek to contribute to the broader understanding of the current economic situation among the student population. As well to gain insight and better understand migration intentions "brain drain" phenomenon in Greece. Specifically, it will address the following two research questions: (1) What is current economic-financial situation among Greek student population and (2) Is there any connection among Greek students' financial situation and intentions to migrate.

Migration and migration politics have been central political and social issue within the European Union last two decades lasting from Global financial crisis to the Arab spring, war in Syria and Ukraine and migrations crisis. This topic is in the spotlight of the European Union due to current global economic and political instability and conflicts, demographic shifts and labor market disparities among member states.

The study findings will provide essential information for policymakers and scholars to further expand the understandings of the dynamics of student Greek migrations and their intentions to migrate. Furthermore, the conclusion may help to reflect the broader implications of trends for Greece's demographic structure as well as changes in policy paradigms to mitigate negative large-scale emigration.

This paper consists of four sections. Section 1, the Introduction, provides overview and literature review on the topic on students' migrations, Sect. 2 describes the Research Methodology followed by the Results and Discussion in Sect. 3, Sect. 4 Concludes the paper.

2 Research Methodology

This paper attempts to examine Greek students' financial situation and attitude toward emigration intentions. In order to explore the relations between migrations variables and financial situation variables authors have employed Spearman's rank-order correlation coefficient. This non-parametric statistical test is commonly used for analysing the degree of monotonic association between two variables, particularly when data do not meet assumptions of normality or linearity required for parametric tests. Spearman's rank correlation is robust to outliers and can capture non-linear but monotonic relationship and it is useful to non-parametric data in this study.

To carry this non-parametric analysis data was gather by survey that was distributed among undergraduate and postgraduate economics students of International Hellenic University, Department of Economics Sciences located in Serres. Questionnaire was created in lime survey software and distributed among students e-mails in period of one month–May–in academic year 2023/2024.

A convenience sample of 346 respondents was selected for this study, representing approximately 6% of the total population. This sampling method was employed due to the accessibility and willingness of the participants to engage in this research. The sample size is considered sufficient to provide initial insights into the research questions. Out of 346 respondents, 250 were from undergraduate study program and 96 from graduate study program. From the total sample 271 (63%) are females and 217 (37%) were males. Although, the sample seams unbalanced the share of female population in the whole student population is 60%.

The questionnaire consists of multiple items and for the purpose of this study we have used only items connected to the financial situation and variables related to the migration intentions. The items were taken from the paper (Štambuk et al., 2024) who investigated level of Croatian economics students competences and attitudes towards migration.

3 Results and Discussion

Data used for this study included items that have assessed Greek students' financial situation and their migration intentions. The financial items (Q018-Q020, see Table 1) examined students' ability to cover monthly expenses, their capacity to handle unexpected financial expenses like expenses for new laptop due malefaction of existing one, and possibility to save money on monthly basis. From these three items authors created latent financial variable (QL00) and employed it for Spearmans' rho analysis.

The migration intentions authors investigated with questions linked to students' personal characteristics. The thirteen items were investigated in this section. These personal characteristics included items that analyzed intentions quitting studies and moving abroad, perception of finding jobs and related intention to migrate, knowledge on foreign language and intention to migrate, desire to go abroad, perception on own

Table 1 Data on financial situation among Greek students

Q018-FIN_I have sufficient financial resources to cover my monthly expenses					
		Frequency	Percent	Valid percent	Cumulative percent
	1 strongly disagree	30	8.7	8.7	8.7
	2	66	19.1	19.1	19.1
	3	107	30.9	30.9	30.9
	4	69	19.9	19.9	19.9
	5 strongly agree	74	21.4	21.4	21.4
	Total	346	100	100	100
Q019-FIN_I am able to cover an unexpected financial expense (e.g. theft of a laptop/computer)					
		Frequency	Percent	Valid percent	Cumulative percent
	1 strongly disagree	87	25.1	25.1	25.1
	2	77	22.3	22.3	22.3
	3	73	21.1	21.1	21.1
	4	50	14.5	14.5	14.5
	5 strongly agree	59	17.1	17.1	17.1
	Total	346	100	100	100
Q020-FIN_I manage to save some money every month					
		Frequency	Percent	Valid percent	Cumulative percent
	1 strongly disagree	77	22.3	22.3	22.3
	2	82	23.7	23.7	46
	3	86	24.9	24.9	70.8
	4	50	14.5	14.5	85.3
	5 strongly agree	51	14.7	14.7	100
	Total	346	100	100	

Source Authors

assimilation on life abroad, perception on future in Greece, migration intentions due partner and perception of stay due a family/partner/friends. For each item authors employed 5-point Liker scale that ranged from 1-Strongly disagree to 5-Strongly agree.

From Table 1 we may conclude that 28% of the examined population disagreed with having sufficient financial resources to cover their monthly expenses, while 40% agreed. This suggests that nearly 30% of the examined student population face challenges in meeting their monthly expenses, indicating considerable financial vulnerability. When examining the capacity to cover unexpected expenses 47% of respondents expressed difficulty covering unexpected expenses. On the other hand, 31% of students felt confident, with 17,1 strongly agreeing they could handle such financial difficulty. These results suggest a significant divide in the financial status of the students. In terms of monthly saving 46% of respondents express an inability to save regularly on monthly basis, while almost 30% of students expressed their ability to save.

Overall, the results uncover mixed financial status among Greek students. Minority students have a perception of financial stability, while almost half of the population struggles with unexpected costs and regular saving.

In order to examine relation on financial situation but also personal characteristic and emigration intention authors have performed the Spearman's rank-order correlation. Also, in the survey authors have examined students' intention to migrate abroad in the next 5 years. Data and results are provided in Table 2. From the results it may be concluded that all financial items, except ability to regularly save money are significant to emigration intentions. There is negative correlation on all financial items suggesting that students with more financial stability are less likely to plan migration.

Items from Q50-Q52 indicates positive corelation to migrations. Those who have tendency to migrate for better quality life are more likely to emigrate (Q50), students thinking about leaving studies are more prone to migrate (Q51) and last item suggests that job unavailability is significant driver of migration intentions (Q52).

Furthermore, items negative correlations are Q53-Q57. Students with higher desire to live in hometown are less likely to migrate, also job prospects i.e., ability to find a job in Greece after studies negatively impacts intentions for migrations. The students that are prone accepting any job, not int the field, are less likely to migrate. Financial stability in terms of possibility acquiring real estate have negative impact to the migration intentions. Not knowing the languages revealed as migration barrier.

Items from Q58-Q61 had positive correlation on intention to emigrate. Strong desire to go abroad had very positive correlation coefficient reflecting that those student with high desire to migrate are very likely to migrate. Students that are confident in adapting to life abroad are prone to migrate, as well as students whose see no future in Greece. Also, migration intentions may be motivated by relationships due a partner.

Negative correlation has items Q62 family or social relations, and those students with strong family or social ties are less prone to emigrate from Greece.

Table 2 Spearman's rank-order correlation coefficient between financial and migration variables

Variables	*Q063-PER_In the next 5 years, I plan to migrate abroad*		
	Corr. Coeff	Sig.(2-tailed)	N
QL00-LAT00_FIN_Latent_finance	–0.125*	0.020	346
Q018-FIN_I have sufficient financial resources to cover my monthly expenses	–0.140**	0.009	346
Q019-FIN_I am able to cover an unexpected financial expense (e.g., tsheft of a laptop/computer)	–0.140**	0.009	346
Q020-FIN_I manage to save some money every month	–0.028	0.602	346
Q050-PER_Regardless of the possibility of finding a job in Greece, I would migrate for a better quality of life in another country	0.589**	0.000	346
Q051-PER_I am thinking about quitting my studies to go abroad	0.262**	0.000	346
Q052-PER_The impossibility of finding a job in Greece would encourage me to migrate	0.638**	0.000	346
Q053-PER_After finishing school, I want to live in the city where I grew up	–0.373**	0.000	346
Q054-PER_I have the possibility to find a job in my field in Greece after completing my studies	–0.220**	0.000	346
Q055-PER_If I could not find a job in my field in Greece, I would rather do some other job than migrate	–0.343**	0.000	346
Q056-PER_I would not migrate because I do not know the foreign language of another country	–0.171**	0.001	346
Q057-PER_I have the possibility to buy real estate after finding a job in Greece	–0.142**	0.008	346
Q058-PER_I have a strong desire to go abroad	0.623**	0.000	346
Q059-PER_I could easily live abroad	0.493**	0.000	346
Q060-PER_I do not have a good future if I stay in Greece	0.509**	0.000	346

(continued)

Table 2 (continued)

Variables	*Q063-PER_In the next 5 years, I plan to migrate abroad*		
	Corr. Coeff	Sig.(2-tailed)	N
Q061-PER_I would migrate to a foreign country because of my partner	0.256**	0.000	346
Q062-PER_I would stay in Greece because of my family/partner/friends	–0.199**	0.000	346

* Correlation is significant at the 0.05 level (2-tailed)
** Correlation is significant at the 0.01 level (2-tailed)

The analysis reveals significant insight into pulling and pushing factors influencing Greek students' migration intentions. The financial insecurity, especially inability to cover unexpected expenses and ability to not to save monthly, have positive corelation of migration. Also, dissatisfaction with job opportunities in Greece significantly influents students' migration intentions while personal ties and stability reduce migration tendencies.

All this suggests that dissatisfaction with economic opportunities and desire for a better life are key drives of migration intention within the Greek students.

4 Conclusion

This study offers important insights into the financial and personal factors propelling migration intentions among Greek students. We may conclude that there are three pivotal factors in anchoring the individual to their home country. First one is financial stability, the analysis carried out clearly suggests that migration intentions are strongly linked to the financial insecurity. Students who struggle with meet basic monthly expenses or ability to cover unexpected financial expenses. The data reveals the half of examined student population have fragile financial-economic situation.

Second one is economic perspectives and future opportunities. Also, there is positive strong correlation between migration intentions and dissatisfaction of job opportunities in Greece. A significant portion (46%) of the students indicated they would migrate even if employment were available in Greece. Their intentions of migration are driven by perception that better quality life lies abroad.

Third one is private connections and interconnected to a family, friends and personal relationships as strong anchor, reducing the migration intentions. Analysis, revealed that students who have strong family and friends' ties are less prone to emigrate, even contrary to economic difficulties (financial stability and economics perspective). We may conclude that importance of social connections in context of migration intentions plays important role. Strengthening social and community ties may play significant role in reducing migration intention into individuals. Likewise, social ties can influence negatively if partner of individual aspire to emigrate or is already abroad.

In conclusion, the results of the study indicate that migrations intentions among Greek student are affected by complex personal, financial, economic and social elements which often intertwine in positive and negative directions. Economics factors remain main driver, personal relationships and perception of future opportunities also have significant impact to the decision to migrate. These findings could help policymakers to finely calibrate target policies to address both economic and social implication of these policies. To mitigate the “brain drain” phenomenon, based on this study, policymakers should focus on improving job perspective and enhancing financial stability among young population. All these policies should reduce migration intention of young individuals, ensuring that young people see their future in their home country.

Acknowledgements This paper was funded under the project line ZIP UNIRI of the University of Rijeka, for the project ZIP-UNIRI-2023-17

References

Anastasiadou, S. (2016). Economic crisis in Greece and the consequential “Brain Drain”. In A. Karasavvoglou, Z. Arandelovic, S. Markinovic, & P. Polychronidou (Eds.), *Contributions to Economics*. Springer Science and Business Media Deutschland GmbH, pp. 113–120.

Arghyrou, M. G., & Tsoukalas, J. D. (2011). The Greek debt crisis: Likely causes, mechanics and outcomes. *The World Economy, 34*(2), 173–191.

Featherstone, K. (2011). The JCMS annual lecture: The Greek sovereign debt crisis and EMU: A failing state in a Skewed Regime. *Journal of Common Market Studies, 49*(2), 193–217.

Giousmpasoglou, C., Marinakou, E., & Paliktzoglou, V. (2016). Economic crisis and higher education in Greece. In P. Ordóñez de Pablos & R. D. Tennyson (Eds.), *Impact of Economic Crisis on Education and the Next-Generation Workforce*. IGI Global, pp. 120–148.

Labrianidis, L., & Sykas, T. (2017). Why high school students aspire to emigrate: Evidence from Greece. *Journal of International Migration and Integration, 18*(1), 107–130.

Marinakou, E., Giousmpasoglou, C., & Paliktzoglou, V. (2016). The brain drain phenomenon in higher education in Greece: Attitudes and opinions on the decision to immigrate. In *3rd Annual International Conference on Humanities & Arts in a Global World*. Athens.

Matsaganis, M., & Leventi, C. (2014). Poverty and inequality during the great recession in Greece. *Political Studies Review, 12*(2), 209–223.

Ozturk, S., & Sozdemir, A. (2015). Effects of global financial crisis on Greece economy. *Procedia Economics and Finance, 23*, 568–575.

Pratsinakis, M. (2022). *Challenging mobilities in and to the EU during times of crises*. IMISCOE. IMISCOE Research Series. Cham: Springer International Publishing.

Štambuk, A., Arbula Blecich, A., & Karanović, G. (2024). Perceived level of competence and attitudees of university students towards migration. In: S. Drezgić, A. Host, M. Tomljanović, & S. Žiković (Eds.). University of Rijeka, Faculty of Economics and Business.

Theodoropoulos, D., Kyridis, A., Zagkos, C., & Konstantinidou, Z. (2014). ‘Brain Drain’ Phenomenon in Greece: Young Greek scientists on their Way to Immigration, in an era of “crisis”. Attitudes, Opinions and Beliefs towards the Prospect of Migration. *Journal of Education and Human Development, 3* (4).

Regulation of Short-Term Rentals: Policy Responses from Europe

Tania Pantazi and Vasileios Vlachos

Abstract This study reviews short-term rentals regulation in five countries of the European Union- France, Greece, Italy, Portugal and Spain- and investigates the role of European law, in order to examine regulatory choices, similarities and differences and the suitability of regulation to mitigate negative effects of short-term rentals. Although the literature has provided comparative studies on short-term rental regulation at the regional or city level, very few studies focus at the country level or discuss the role of European law. The present paper aims to address this gap with a narrative review of theoretical and empirical literature on country level STR regulation from various disciplines, placing emphasis on legal and economic research and including official EU documents. The study concludes that countries follow a diversified and fragmented approach, divided between the national and the local level and do not address a number of important issues, such as distinction between professional and non-professional providers and health and safety conditions. The effect of European law is limited to the regulation of digital services and consumer protection.

Keywords Airbnb · Sharing economy · Economic impact · Regulation · Policy · European Union · Short-term rentals

JEL Classification K20 · Z38

T. Pantazi (✉)
Hellenic Open University, Patra, Greece
e-mail: pantazi.soultana@ac.eap.gr

V. Vlachos
Department of Economic Sciences, International Hellenic University, Serres, Greece
e-mail: vlachosuk@ihu.gr

I. Bartuseviciene et al. (eds.), *Building Resilience Through Digital Transformation and Sustainable Innovation*, Springer Proceedings in Business and Economics,
https://doi.org/10.1007/978-3-031-90054-9_8

1 Introduction

Short-term rentals via online platforms have seen an unprecedented increase in the last decade. Airbnb has been the pioneer of this revolution, with a promise of offering an authentic and cheaper alternative to travel accommodation options. Along with the explosive development of short-term rentals, scientific research in the field has equally increased and originates from multiple disciplines, such as tourism studies, urban planning and development, economics and management, public policy and legal studies. Short-term rentals (STRs) have been an additional source of income for residents, especially for crisis-hit capitals (Balampanidis et al., 2021). They have been generally seen as major contributor to tourism growth and tourism related-employment (Dogru et al., 2020). The findings of these studies suggest that the rise of STRs has been a source of investment in post-crisis Europe, especially in countries that lag behind in investment expenditure, such as Greece (Vlachos & Bitzenis, 2019, 2021). Nonetheless, the development of short-term rentals has had major consequences for cities; displacement of residents and gentrification as a result of overtourism (Celata & Romano, 2022), as well as rises on housing prices and rents (Barron et al., 2020).

The upsurge of STRs was accompanied by unique challenges for regulators, as the main question that arose was whether restrictions are desirable. Digital platforms have succeeded in questioning traditional legal norms and establishing the opinion that they are by default legal (McKee, 2017). Although the rights to property and provision of services are legally recognized, short-term rentals have also brought tensions among co-owners and questions of equal treatment with professional accommodation providers, mainly hotels. The approach taken by regulators across the globe has been substantially diverse (Guttentag, 2019) with European cities found to be more lenient than their American counterparts (Colomb & Moreira de Souza, 2023). Enforcement has proven problematic as platforms do not take action on listings that are according to local laws illegal and often refuse to share their data with authorities, making the measurement of the activity almost impossible.

Previous studies have focused on regulation with a comparison of policy choices at the city level (for example, Aguilera et al., 2021; Colomb & Moreira de Souza, 2021; Nieuwland & van Melik, 2020; von Briel & Dolnicar, 2020). The literature has not focused on country level regulation and important questions on policy choices for STRs, such as distinction between peers and professionals, have not been specifically addressed. In addition, the role of the European Union as a supranational regulator has not been explored, despite discussions on EU action, such as the urgent call for EU regulation by municipal authorities of major European cities (Eurocities, 2022).

This chapter seeks to investigate whether EU countries have similarities in the way they regulate STRs at the country level, whether regulatory choices are suitable for the problems that have been identified in literature and whether uniform EU mandated regulation is feasible. In order to answer the above questions, the research focuses on five EU member states of the Mediterranean –France, Greece, Italy, Portugal and Spain. The selection of countries is based on their popularity as tourist destinations as well as the fact that they are among the largest EU markets for short-term rentals in terms of nights spent.[1] The research is based on secondary sources, including official EU documents and reports, and follows an interdisciplinary approach relying on studies from various fields, with an emphasis on legal and economic literature.

The rest of the chapter is structured as follows: Sect. 2 provides a brief literature review of empirical studies on the impact of short-term rentals on destinations. Section 3 presents the unique challenges that STRs pose for regulators. Section 4 provides an overview of regulation in five EU member states. Section 5 examines the question of whether regulation is possible at the EU level. The final section summarizes the findings and provides recommendations for policy makers.

2 The Impact of Short-Term Rentals (STRS) on Tourism Destinations: Evidence from Empirical Research

Reviews of the literature on peer-to-peer accommodation (Belarmino & Koh, 2020; Dolnicar, 2019; Prayag & Ozanne, 2018; Sainaghi, 2020), on Airbnb (Dann et al., 2019; Guttentag, 2019; Hati, 2021; Yang et al., 2021), as well as more recent empirical studies (for example, Shabrina et al., 2022), indicate that the impact of STRs on tourism destinations can be broadly categorized according to its effect on:

i. hotel industry revenue / occupancy / daily rates: STRs are a substitution threat to hotels and their negative effect on the revenue of (almost) all different hotel types prevails in most empirical investigations.
ii. tourism industry employment: STRs have a positive effect on tourism and tourism-related employment in almost all empirical investigations.
iii. real estate prices: Increasing supply of properties for STRs leads to higher rental rates and house prices in all empirical investigations.

The consensus arising from empirical findings in regions with developed tourism infrastructure is that STRs have a negative effect on the performance of small traditional accommodation providers and a positive effect on the income of destinations' residents at the cost of collective displacement. However, research has also shown that, in less popular tourist destinations, the impact of STRs on the hotel industry performance is manifestly positive (Leick et al., 2021; Strømmen-Bakhtiar & Vinogradov, 2019) and supports the claim that STRs can have a positive effect when they fill the gap of underdeveloped tourism infrastructure (Adamiak, 2018; Cvelbar & Dolnicar, 2017).

The effect of STRs on long-term housing stock is also connected with gentrification, where lower income population is replaced by one of a higher status, and touristification, where the increase in tourist activity leads to the loss of residents

[1] According to the data of Eurostat, available at: https://ec.europa.eu/eurostat/statistics-explained/index.php?title=Short-stay_accommodation_offered_via_online_collaborative_economy_platforms&oldid=584207 (accessed on 27.05.2024).

(Jover & Díaz-Parra, 2020). Several qualitative studies (for example, Balampanidis et al., 2021; Jordan & Moore, 2018) and studies performing socio-spatial analysis (for example, Celata & Romano, 2022; Morales-Pérez et al., 2020) indicate the occurrence of these negative effects on residents through the process of collective displacement (substitution of residential life with tourism).

3 The Peculiarities of Short-Term Rental Market for Regulators

Short-term rentals via online platforms present some unique challenges for regulators and legal scholars. At first, the issue was examined within the context of 'sharing economy' or 'collaborative economy', as an opportunity for home owners to gain an additional income through peer-to-peer transactions (for example, Hatzopoulos & Roma, 2017; Cauffman & Smits, 2016). Nonetheless, short-term rentals now cover a wide range of activities, from renting an individual room within one's own home to the exploitation of entire blocks of apartments, which would otherwise qualify as tourist accommodation services. An increasing number of empirical studies indicate that short-term rentals are becoming professional, alienated from the concept of 'sharing economy' (for example, Cocola-Gant, Jover et al., 2021; Dogru et al., 2020; Gyódi, 2019) and imposing an additional layer of complexity to the efforts for their regulation. As Iacovone (2023) clearly demonstrates, professionalization of STRs is particularly evident in Mediterranean cities and this aspect is not taken into consideration by policy makers.

Another major challenge that short-term rentals pose is their three-dimensional character. In contrast to traditional contracts for the provision of services or tenancy contracts for residential property, in which there are two distinct parties-the consumer and the trader in the first case, the lessor and the lessee in the second case- in short-term rentals the intermediary online platform plays a vital role. The platform often imposes its own terms and conditions and the lines between different markets and types of contracts are blurred (Ulfbeck et al., 2018). Digital platforms themselves enjoy freedoms and are subject to regulations as digital services providers, especially within the EU legal framework (Chapuis-Doppler & Delhomme, 2022; Kramer & Schaub, 2022). In addition, the actual short-term rental contract between the host and the guest, which belongs to the 'downstream' market as it is often called (in contrast to the digital 'upstream' market), may not always fit to previously distinct categories in national legal orders, since national law will most probably draw a distinction between B2C contracts between consumers and service providers and peer-to-peer contracts for rental of residential property.

Restrictions to short-term rentals may be seen as a restraint on the right to property use. It is argued that short-term letting is a right to share the burden of ownership and restrictions to this right may be deemed unconstitutional (Jefferson-Jones, 2015). The use of property may also be voluntarily restricted by adhering to community of owners' agreements or regulations in multi-apartment buildings: co-owners often seek to restrict short-term rentals and the legitimacy and interpretation of respective agreements, which were sometimes drafted well before the upsurge of STRs, troubles courts in many countries (for example, Kochan, 2018; Martinez-Nadal, 2019).

Tourist accommodation services on the other hand are usually subject to public law provisions. Health and safety (e.g. fire safety) as well as quality standards apply for hotels, as states seek to ensure the high level of their tourism services. Most countries require mandatory registration of guests for immigration control and national security purposes. Hotel guests are protected as consumers under EU consumer law, which only applies to contracts between consumers and professionals. Hotel associations often raise issues of equal treatment and unfair competition with STR providers, since similar services are treated differently, for example in terms of taxation, or STRs are listed indistinguishably with traditional accommodation service providers (Aguilera et al., 2021; Guttentag, 2017; HOTREC, 2022).

In view of the above, regulators find it hard to regulate STRs and authorities find it even harder to enforce existing regulations (Guttentag, 2017). Traditional concepts of market composition and dynamics seem inadequate to regulate STRs (Tedds et al., 2021). Even with compulsory registration schemes in place, authorities often do not have access to full data owned by platforms and rely on a variety of self-improvising strategies in order to assess the impact of STRs in their territory and design their regulatory response (Colomb & Moreira de Souza, 2023). Little evidence is available on the effect of regulations, but stringent regulation appears to be effective in reducing listings of entire apartments (Bei & Celata, 2023).

The following section reviews STR regulations in five EU member states of the Mediterranean and makes references to adverse impacts of STRs in these countries, as they have been reported in academic literature. Taking into consideration the preceding analysis, the focus is placed on five key aspects of regulation: the existence of registration schemes for STRs, health and safety or other quality standards, distinction between peers and professional providers, specialized tax legislation for STRs and regulations limiting or prohibiting the activity, whether by local authorities or other interested parties, such as co-owners or neighbors. The review also investigates whether STRs are regulated at the national or local level, in order to better understand policy choices, as regulation of tourist accommodation in Europe often lies within the competence of local authorities.

4 Regulation of STRs in Five EU Member States

4.1 France

Regulation on STRs exists in France since the 1960s (Aguilera et al., 2021). Various pieces of legislation regulate different aspects of STRs, such as registration of properties, changes of use and obligations of platforms (Colomb & Moreira de Souza, 2021).

French legislation distinguishes between primary residence, secondary residence and tourist flats or 'tourist accommodation' (Kaźmierczyk, 2019).

STR of primary residence is only allowed for less than 120 days a year. Rentals should be declared to the municipality and dwellings are subject to minimum standards on 'decent housing'. Hosts should also collect data on foreign guests (Colomb & Moreira de Souza, 2021). More stringent rules apply for accommodation rented out to tourists for more than 120 days a year, in which case the property qualifies as 'tourist accommodation': apart from mandatory registration, in municipalities with more than 200,000 inhabitants, change of use of residential premises is subject to prior authorization from the municipality (from residential to commercial). Municipal authorities are entitled to limit the change of use by making it subject to 'offset requirement', i.e. the concurrent conversion of non-residential premises into housing; such a restriction is in place in various cities, including Paris (European Court of Justice, 2020). If the property is part of a condominium, the consent of co-owners is also required for the change of use (European Commission, 2018c). With regard to taxation, when the annual income from STRs exceeds 23,000 EUR or is higher than income from other sources, it is taxed as income from professional activities (European Commission, 2018d).

French law requires that all properties available for rent should comply with minimum health, safety and comfort standards, such as minimum size of rooms (which is also dependent on the number of guests), natural ventilation and the existence of a smoke detector. These rules also apply to all types of short-term rentals (European Commission, 2018c).

Empirical research on French cities shows that professional STR activity significantly affects rents and justifies the introduction of stricter regulation (Ayouba et al., 2020). Paris, as the most popular Airbnb destination worldwide, has been the object of numerous studies, showing, for example, that STRs are not in direct competition with hotels (Heo et al., 2019) and that the majority of listings on Airbnb platform cannot be classified as sharing economy activity (Gyódi, 2019).

4.2 Greece

Tourist accommodation services in Greece are regulated at the national level. Dwellings certified as tourist accommodation (hotels, flats and tourist villas) should fulfill certain technical, safety and environmental conditions. Rules on the contract between the provider of tourist accommodation services and the customer are also in place (Kardoulia, 2020).

In contrast, properties rented in the STR market do not qualify as tourist accommodation. Specialized regulation for STRs was introduced in 2016. The Greek law includes definitions for 'sharing economy', 'digital platforms' and 'short-term rentals', making it the only piece of legislation in the European Union to provide such definitions (European Commission, 2018d). According to the definitions, STR is 'the rental of immovable property via digital platforms for a specific limited time, less than a year'. Immovable properties which can be an object of short-term rentals are apartments, detached houses, single rooms and every other type of autonomous dwelling. No restrictions apply with regard to the size of the property or its characteristics.

Owners or managers are obliged to register their property in a database operated by the fiscal authorities and demonstrate its registration number on the platform. In addition, a list of concluded contracts should be submitted to a dedicated database in the beginning of the subsequent month. Administrative fines are in place for lessors who do not fulfill their obligations. Individuals who engage in STR were not considered professionals or traders, and their activity is treated as a special category of residential lease (Amore et al., 2020). Nonetheless, a new law passed in 2023 provides that, if an owner leases more than three properties, the income is considered to be income from professional activity and taxed accordingly. The law also submits STRs to tourist taxes similar to hotels, introducing thus a limited distinction between peers and professionals for tax purposes.

The Greek law also stipulates that STRs *may* be restricted in certain geographical areas with a Joint Ministerial Decision. However, no such decision has been issued so far. A limited number of cases have reached the Greek courts and they are all concerned with questions arising from the disturbance of co-residents in blocks of flats. The position of Greek courts has been controversial, with the majority of them ruling that STR is a property use that should be allowed.

Hotel owners in Greece complain about differentiated treatment, as STR appears to negatively affect their revenues (Apergis et al., 2021). Evidence from Greece also shows an increased professionalization of the activity, far from the concept of 'sharing economy' (Katsinas, 2021).

4.3 *Italy*

In Italy, national legislation passed in 2017 establishes a nationwide system of registration of properties for tax purposes, as well as the mandatory display of the registration code in listings. The law has been challenged before the European Court of Justice, which ruled that the obligations imposed on platforms to share data with tax authorities and withhold taxes are legitimate, although a tax representative in Italy should not be required (European Court of Justice, 2022b). Moreover, national legislation obliges service providers to contact the identity of their guests to a national police database for border control purposes (European Commission, 2018c; Colomb & Moreira de Souza, 2021). With regard to taxation, an optional flat rate tax applies to STR providers (Colomb & Moreira de Souza, 2021).

Apart from the aforementioned issues, regulation of short-term rentals in Italy, as a tourism activity, lies within the competence of regional authorities. Regional legislation is in place in the areas of Lazio, Tuscany and Milan. In Lazio, providers are obliged to submit a registration request with technical details of the building to the municipality and verify that the property is in compliance with applicable laws concerning health and safety (Colomb & Moreira de Souza, 2021). Local regulations in Tuscany further provide a distinction between peer and professional providers, stating that peer providers cannot rent more than two apartments or pursue a total of more than 80 rentals per year. However, local rules not specifically address health and safety issues (European Commission, 2018c). In Milan, the subject of short-term rentals has been an issue of great controversy between stakeholders, which has led to minimum regional legislation obliging owners to register in a local database, facilitating also the collection of tourist taxes (Aguilera et al., 2021; Amore et al., 2020).

STR as a driving factor of overtourism has brought about tensions and concerns in a number of Italian cities, which call for stricter regulation; authorities in Florence and Bologna have announced their intention to limit the conversion of residential dwellings into tourist accommodation (Celata & Romano, 2022). Regarding the effects of STR on hotel performance, the evidence from Milan and Rome indicates the absence of direct competition and the emergence of a substitution threat only during weekends and holiday periods when the attracted market segment is leisure clients (Sainaghi & Baggio, 2021). Another study on 13 Italian cities also indicated that STRs are not in direct competition with large hotels (Roma et al., 2019).

4.4 Portugal

Short-term rentals in Portugal are regulated by national specialized legislation on ‘local accommodation’ since 2014 (Carvalho & Policarpo, 2018). The law distinguishes between individual houses, apartments, sets of rooms (and hostels) and rooms. Registration of the property in a national registry is compulsory. The Mayor has the right to object to registration in case legal requirements are not met. Health and safety conditions as well as minimum quality standards are in place at the national level, such as the presence of fire extinguishers, window and complaints book (European Commission, 2018c). There is also mandatory reporting of foreign guests in a national database for border control purposes. With regard to taxation, the income is subject to VAT if exceeding 10.000 EUR annually.

The question of whether the association of residents can forbid the use of an apartment for STRs has troubled Portuguese courts (Carvalho & Policarpo, 2018). A Supreme Court decision in 2017 found that this in principle is not allowed, as the use of the property for tourist accommodation does not affect its ‘residential’ character (European Commission, 2018c).

With legislation passed in 2018, local authorities can restrict STRs in particular areas in order to preserve social conditions and housing offer. Under the new regime, the city of Lisbon has suspended new licenses in certain areas (Colomb & Moreira de Souza, 2021). Moreover, a local tourist tax applies in Lisbon and Porto. There is no explicit distinction between peer and professional providers in Portuguese law. However, it is argued that the increased registration requirements point to the conclusion that the provider will almost always be a trader (Carvalho & Policarpo, 2018).

Liberalization of STRs in Portugal was fostered by economic adjustment programs in the 2010s, as tourism was seen as a major contributor to economy. The steep increase of STRs has been the matter of significant academic research, as it has caused tensions among residents, local authorities and service providers in various cities and particularly Lisbon (Amore et al., 2020; Pereira, 2022). The above-mentioned national legislation of 2014 is believed to have facilitated to a great extend the operation of STRs and to have contributed to the fourfold increase of registered STR properties between 2014 and 2017, further resulting in a considerable rise in property prices and rents (Franco & Santos, 2021), as well as insecurity and displacement concerns for tenants (Cocola-Gant & Gago, 2021). Recent evidence also suggests increased professionalization of STR activity in Portugal (Cocola-Gant et al., 2021).

4.5 Spain

The tourism sector in Spain is subject to the regulation of the autonomous communities, since, by legislation passed in 2019, tourist accommodation is explicitly excluded from national law (Vallejo, 2019). However, national legislation allows the assembly of owners in a particular property to limit the exercise of business activity with regard to tourist accommodation with a majority of 3/5 of owners who in turn represent 3/5 of participation quotas (Martinez-Nadal, 2019). In general, regulations on STRs in Spain do not explicitly distinguish between peer and professional providers, although some local regulations set thresholds of days per year, above which the host is considered to be a professional (Vallejo, 2019). If the host offers services besides accommodation (e.g. meals, cleaning), the income is considered to be income from professional activity and it is subject to VAT. A national tax law obliging platforms to share data was contested in court but it is expected to be redrafted (Colomb & Moreira de Souza, 2021). In any case, in the end of 2018 Airbnb agreed to cooperate with Spanish tax authorities (Martinez-Nadal, 2019).

Within this context, specialized legislation on STR is in place in various Spanish communities and cities including Barcelona, Madrid and the Balearic Islands. Barcelona has repeatedly attracted the attention of scholars and the media for its restrictions on STRs and severe fines on digital platforms for advertising unregistered properties (Aguilera et al., 2021; Garcia-López et al., 2020). A number of general rules apply in the whole region of Catalonia: commencement of activity needs to be submitted to the local authorities, the dwelling must comply with technical and quality conditions, information on guests should be contacted to the police within 24 h, and the provider should offer a telephone contact for inquiries and complaint sheets (European Commission, 2018c). In the city of Barcelona, a zoning system is in place, which further requires mandatory authorization for STRs. Different conditions apply depending on the territorial position of the dwelling. The restrictions reach upon the total ban of the activity in certain areas of the city (Martinez-Nadal, 2019). Legislation passed in 2020 established a separate category of 'shared home', for which local authorities are authorized to introduce additional regulation (Colomb & Moreira de Souza, 2021).

Similar restrictions are in place in the Balearic Islands, with a practical ban on short-term rentals in Palma (Martinez-Nadal, 2019). In Madrid, there are specific technical requirements for the dwellings, such as separate access and the existence of particular rooms. The activity is subject to prior notification of 'commencement of activity'. The regulations apply if the provider exercises the activity for more than 90 days per year (European Commission, 2018c). A legislation requirement for a minimum stay of 5 days has been declared invalid by Spanish courts (Martinez-Nadal, 2019).

Empirical evidence indicates that STRs contribute to increases on average rents and housing prices in Barcelona (Garcia-López et al., 2020). Social impacts related to economic and social sustainability have also been found in Madrid, Barcelona, and Palma de Mallorca (García-Ayllón, 2018).

5 Summary of Regulatory Choices in Five Countries

The following table (Table 1) provides a summary of the previous analysis of STR regulation in five member states:

The assessment reveals that the five countries have a different legal regime for STRs in relation to traditional accommodation providers. Registration schemes exist in all member states, but some of them are regional, which does not allow for a uniform policy drafted at the country level. Safety and quality standards are regulated at the local level in Spain and Italy, but are totally absent in Greece. No clear distinction between peers and professional exists, except for different categorization of the activity in France. The distinction between peers and professionals is critical, as professional providers are subject to different taxation and consumer protection rules. Member states follow different approaches with regard to STR taxation: for example, Greece and Spain impose VAT and consider the income to be one of a professional activity only in case the provider offers additional services, while Portugal and France set an income threshold. In general, STRs are treated in a fragmented and inconsistent way by national legislators, which does not allow for the activity to be measured and controlled. Finally, even well-designed regulation at the national level, namely in Portugal, cannot eradicate negative STR effects on affordable housing.

5.1 Overview of the STR Market in Relation to the Hotel Industry in the Five Countries Under Study

An overview of data on STRs in each of the above studied countries would contribute to a better understanding of the development of the STR market and its position in

Table 1 Regulatory aspects of STRs in EU member states

		France	Greece	Italy	Portugal	Spain
Registration scheme	National	Yes	Yes	Yes (challenged)	Yes	No
	Local	Yes	No	Yes	No	Yes
Safety and quality standards	National	Yes	No	No	Yes	No
	Local	No	No	Yes	No	Yes
Taxation	Specific STR rules	No	Yes	Yes	No (VAT)	No
	Local tourist tax	Yes	Yes	Yes	Yes	Yes
Distinction between peers and professionals	National	Yes	Only for tax purposes	No	No	No
	Local	No	No	No (except Tuscany)	No	No
Legislation allowing authorities to restrict STR under certain circumstances	National	Yes	Yes- Not implemented	No	Yes	Yes
	Local	Yes	No	No	Yes	Yes
Legislation allowing co-owners to restrict property use for STR	National	Yes	No	No	Complaint to the mayor	Yes
	Local	No	No	No	No	No

relation to the hotel industry. Figure 1 presents bar charts showing tourism data from 2014 to 2023 for France, Greece, Italy, Portugal, and Spain. The dark and light gray bars represent nights spent at tourist accommodations and short-term rentals respectively (left-hand axis in millions), and the dashed line indicates hotel occupancy rates (right-hand axis in percentages). A legend explains the symbols used and notes define accommodation types. Figure 1 indicates that nights spend at all tourist accomodation establishments showed a rising trend after the pandemic in all five countries. In relation to their pre-pandemic peak in 2019, they increased between 2.4% and 9.4% in 2023 (no data for Greece in 2023). Nights spend at short-term rentals also showed a rising trend after the pandemic. In relation to their pre-pandemic peak in 2019, however, they had a significant increase, which ranged between 27.2% and 60% in 2023 (no data for Greece in 2023). These indicators reveal that short-term rentals have grown much faster after the pandemic in all five countries. Taking into consideration that the change of hotels' occupancy rates between 2019 and 2023 was marginal (for example, -0.1% in Spain, 0% in France, 0.9% in Portugal), it can be assumed that the increase of short-term rentals may have been at the expense of traditional accommodation. Furthermore, although country-level data such as those presented in Fig. 1 may indicate possible effects of short-term rentals on the hotel

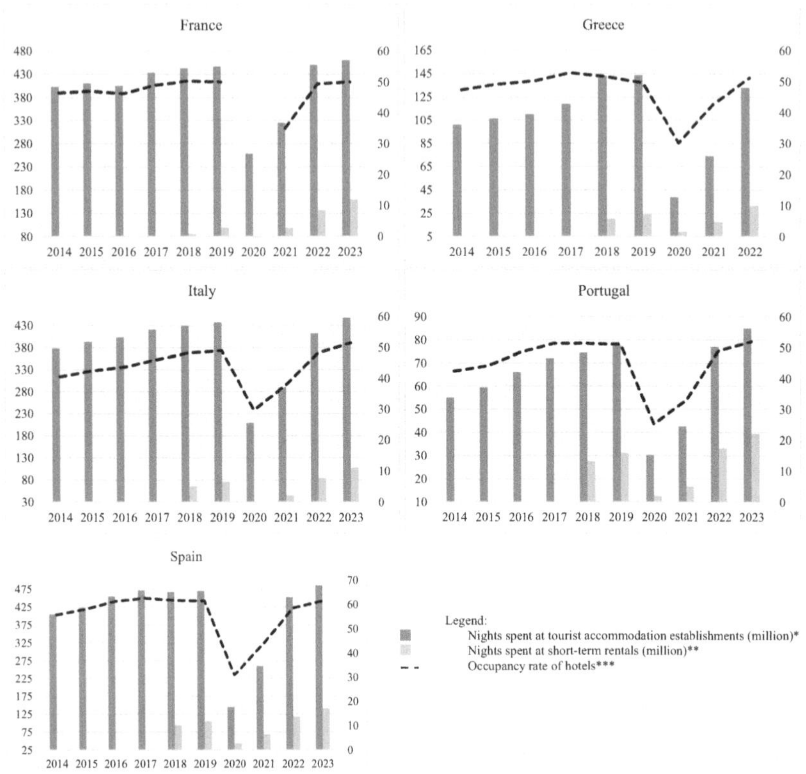

Fig. 1 Hotels vs. Short-term rentals in France, Greece, Italy, Portugal and Spain. *Notes** Hotels; holiday and other short-stay accommodation; camping grounds, recreational vehicle parks and trailer parks. ** Offered via collaborative economy platforms. *** and similar accommodation. *Source* Authors' elaboration with data from Eurostat (https://ec.europa.eu/eurostat/data/database), accessed Sep. 2024

industry, it is not easy to present effects on housing prices and rents, because in this case regional data would be required. Such regional data are not available in Eurostat and thus not presented here.

6 The Effect and the Limits of EU Legislation

The issue of whether the EU has a mandate to regulate STRs is a critical one, as it would allow for a uniform and possibly more efficient approach. The first official EU document on aspects of STR regulation was the European Commission's 'Agenda for the collaborative economy' (European Commission, 2016), which in general concluded that market access requirements for collaborative economy providers should be justified on grounds of public interest and suggested that private individuals should not automatically be treated as professionals. The Agenda captured considerable attention in legal literature (Cauffman, 2016; Hatzopoulos & Roma, 2017).

In 2018, the European Commission mandated a study on the regulatory aspects affecting the collaborative economy in the tourist accommodation sector (European Commission, 2018a). The study found that 22 out of 28 Member States had introduced licensing or registration schemes for STR providers. It also interestingly pointed out that 'purely economic reasons, such as the protection of competitors' cannot justify restrictions on the STR market and concluded that STRs had no negative impact on traditional accommodation providers-a fact that, as already mentioned, is not verified by empirical studies. Another study for the European Commission (2018b) examined the business and regulatory environment of member states and concluded that the majority of them had a favorable business environment. In 2020, four peer-to-peer platforms agreed to share statistical data on short-term rentals with Eurostat (European Commission, 2020a).

Four judgments of the European Court of Justice from 2019 to 2022 have a significant effect on the issue of STR regulation: In *Airbnb Ireland*, the Court ruled that Airbnb should be treated as an 'Information Society Service provider' according to the E-commerce Directive, and thus it could not be subject to French laws on real estate agents, as it had been argued by French hoteliers (European Court of Justice, 2019; Chapuis-Doppler & Delhomme, 2022). In *Cali Apartments*, the Court was asked to assess whether local regulations in Paris restricting STRs could be justified under the Services Directive. The Court concluded that member states are allowed to impose restrictions for reasons of public interest, such as combating housing shortage, as long as they are justified and proportionate (European Court of Justice, 2020; Hatzopoulos, 2021; Pantazi, 2021). In case C-674/20, a Belgian law obliging Airbnb to provide data to tax authorities was validated by the Court (European Court of Justice, 2022a). In the most recent case, C-83/21, (European Court of Justice, 2022b- mentioned also above in Sect. 4.3), the Court ruled that the Italian law obliging platforms to share data and withhold taxes is compatible with the Services Directive.

The Digital Services Act (Regulation 2022/2065) introduced two important obligations for platforms: online intermediaries are now required to obtain information on the identity and contact details of traders and also cooperate with national authorities on the removal of illegal content (Busch & Mak, 2021). Furthermore, amendments to consumer protection Directives have imposed the obligation of platforms to act on the prevention of false reviews, as well as make a distinction between peer and professional providers, although the platform is only required to display the information that the host has declared to it (Cauffman, 2019; Pantazi, 2021).

Finally, in April 2024, Regulation 2024/1028 on data collection and sharing relating to short-term accommodation rental services was published. The legal basis of the new rules are the provisions on the functioning of the internal market. The Regulation obliges national authorities to provide user friendly online registration schemes for STRs and platforms to automatically share data with authorities via a 'singe digital entry point' and also delete unregistered listings. The new rules will solve some of the problems that authorities currently encounter in their relationship with digital platforms, but it appears that its main aim is to improve transparency rather than introduce substantive obligations.

What follows from the preceding analysis is that the European legislation only marginally affects STRs. In contrast to other tourism sectors, such as passenger rights and package travel, regulation of tourism accommodation services lies within the exclusive competence of member states and there is no uniform European legislation on the field. According to Article 195 of the Treaty for the Functioning of the European Union, EU action in tourism is complementary and only aims to the creation of a favorable business environment and the promotion of cooperation among member states. Taxation is also an issue regulated at the national level. The EU is only competent to introduce legislation on consumer protection and digital services. Consequently, the prospect of harmonized EU legislation on STRs is dim. It should be noticed, though, that the initial liberal approach taken by the European institutions towards STRs a few years ago is obviously becoming more stringent; the European Court of Justice has adopted a restrictive approach and the EU is not hesitant to examine intervention in the field within the limits of its legislative powers.

7 Conclusions

STRs are a complex issue that preoccupies multiple disciplines. As the impact of STRs is both positive and negative and does not affect all destinations in the same manner, a one-size fits all regulatory approach should not be deemed appropriate.

STRs were originally examined in the context of sharing economy. Nonetheless, the activity is increasingly becoming professional and often serves as a substitute to traditional accommodation services. The principle of equal treatment and reasons of public interest, such as health and safety and consumer protection, require legislators to draw a distinction between persons that generate an additional income through the sharing of their property and professional accommodation providers. Regulation on issues of health and safety, consumer protection, distinction between peers and professional should be therefore drafted in a non-discriminatory manner. On the other hand, affordable housing or environmental concerns as a result of overtourism may also serve as reasons of public interest in order to justify restrictions on STRs; in this case regulation should be carefully elaborated at the local level.

The comparative study of regulations in five member states reveals that countries take a completely different approach on STRs. In some cases, registration is required only at the local level, a fact that does not allow the measurement of the activity and the accurate evaluation of its effect on places. In most cases, restrictions also only apply at the local level and they do not always take public interest considerations into account.

The European Union does not have a general mandate to legislate in matters of tourist accommodation services, but it is becoming increasingly interested in regulating aspects of digital services and consumer protection. An important requirement imposed by EU law on STR regulation is that restrictions should be carefully justified and proportionate. In any case, uniform EU legislation on STRs is not feasible.

STR regulation is a rapidly evolving field and research inevitably mirrors the situation at one point in time (von Briel & Dolnicar, 2020). Nonetheless, comparative approaches are needed to develop explanations about the differences in policy responses to STRs (Aguilera et al., 2021). In contrast to extant literature which focuses at the regional level, the present study examined STR regulation in five mediterranean countries focusing at the country level and revealed the differences and the failures in policy responses. The study is based on secondary sources; future research may rely on primary legal sources or focus on specific issues, such as the distinction between peer and professional providers in national legislation, the different regimes of STR taxation and their consequences, the variances in STR regulation among regions with a different level of tourism development and, most importantly, the effect of existing regulations on the negative externalities of STRs.

References

Adamiak, C. (2018). Mapping Airbnb supply in European cities. *Annals of Tourism Research, 71*, 67–71. https://doi.org/10.1016/j.annals.2018.02.008

Aguilera, T., Artioli, F., & Colomb, C. (2021). Explaining the diversity of policy responses to platform-mediated short-term rentals in European cities: A comparison of Barcelona, Paris and Milan. *Environment and Planning a: Economy and Space, 53*(7), 1689–1712. https://doi.org/10.1177/0308518X19862286

Amore, A., de Bernardi, C., & Arvanitis, P. (2020). The impacts of Airbnb in Athens, Lisbon and Milan: A rent gap theory perspective. *Current Issues in Tourism, 25*(20), 3329–3342. https://doi.org/10.1080/13683500.2020.1742674

Apergis, N., Hayat, T. & Saeed, T. (2021) Airbnb and hotel revenues in popular Greek destinations. *Journal of Economic Studies, 48*(4), 804–816. https://doi.org/10.1108/JES-11-2019-0512

Balampanidis, D., Maloutas, T., Papatzani, E., & Pettas, D. (2021). Informal urban regeneration as a way out of the crisis? Airbnb in Athens and its effects on space and society. *Urban Research & Practice, 14*(3), 223–242. https://doi.org/10.1080/17535069.2019.1600009

Barron, K., Kung, E., & Proserpio, D. (2020). The effect of home-sharing on house prices and rents: Evidence from Airbnb. *Marketing Science, 40*(1), 23–47. https://doi.org/10.1287/mksc.2020.1227

Bei, G., & Celata, F. (2023). Challenges and effects of short-term rentals regulation: A counterfactual assessment of European cities. *Annals of Tourism Research, 101*, Article 103605. https://doi.org/10.1016/j.annals.2023.103605

Belarmino, A., & Koh, Y. (2020). A critical review of research regarding peer-to-peer accommodations. *International Journal of Hospitality Management, 84*(102315). https://doi.org/10.1016/j.ijhm.2019.05.011

Busch, C., & Mak, V. (2021). Putting the digital services act in context. *Journal of European Consumer and Market Law, 10*(3), 109–114. Retrieved from https://kluwerlawonline.com/journalarticle/Journal+of+European+Consumer+and+Market+Law/, https://doi.org/10.3/EuCML2021025

Carvalho, J. M., & Policarpo, P. (2018). Regulating Airbnb in Portugal. *Journal of European Consumer and Market Law*, *7*(6), 256–258. Retrieved from https://kluwerlawonline.com/journalarticle/Journal+of+European+Consumer+and+Market+Law/7.6/EuCML2018051

Cauffman, C. (2016). The commission's European Agenda for the collaborative economy –(Too) platform and service provider friendly? *Journal of European Consumer and Market Law*, *5*(6), 235–243. https://kluwerlawonline.com/journalarticle/Journal+of+European+Consumer+and+Market+Law/5.6/EuCML2016054

Cauffman, C., & Smits, J. (2016). The sharing economy and the law: Food for European lawyers. *Maastricht Journal of European and Comparative Law, 23*(6), 903–907. https://doi.org/10.1177/1023263X1602300601

Cauffman, C. (2019). New EU rules on business-to-consumer and platform-to-business relationships. *Maastricht Journal of European and Comparative Law, 26*(4), 469–479, (476). https://doi.org/10.1177/1023263X19865835

Celata, F., & Romano, A. (2022). Overtourism and online shortterm rental platforms in Italian cities. *Journal of Sustainable Tourism, 30*(5), 1020–1039. https://doi.org/10.1080/09669582.2020.1788568

Chapuis-Doppler, A., & Delhomme, V. (2022). Regulating composite platform economy services: Examining the applicable legal framework in light of recent judicial developments. *Legal Issues of Economic Integration, 49*(1), 43–70. https://doi.org/10.54648/leie2022003

Cocola-Gant, A., Hof, A., Smigiel, C., & Yrigoy, I. (2021). Short-term rentals as a new urban frontier—Evidence from European cities. *Environment and Planning a: Economy and Space, 53*(7), 1601–1608. https://doi.org/10.1177/0308518X211042634

Cocola-Gant, A., Jover, J., Carvalho, L., & Chamusca, P. (2021). Corporate hosts: The rise of professional management in the short-term rental industry. *Tourism Management Perspectives, 40*, Article 100879. https://doi.org/10.1016/j.tmp.2021.100879

Colomb, C., & Moreira de Souza, T. (2021) Regulating short-term rentals. Platform-based property rentals in European cities: The policy debates. Property Research Trust. https://doi.org/10.52915/KKKD3578

Colomb, C., & Moreira de Souza, T. (2023). Illegal short-term rentals, regulatory enforcement and informal practices in the age of digital platforms. *European Urban and Regional Studies*. https://doi.org/10.1177/09697764231155386

Cvelbar, L. K.., & Dolnicar, S. (2017). Filling infrastructure gap. In: Dolnicar, S. (Ed.), P*eer-to-Peer Accommodation Networks: Pushing the boundaries,* pp. 98–108. Goodfellow Publishers. https://doi.org/10.23912/9781911396512-3607

Dann, D., Teubner, T., & Weinhardt, C. (2019). Poster child and guinea pig—Insights from a structured literature review on Airbnb. *International Journal of Contemporary Hospitality Management, 31*(1), 427–473. https://doi.org/10.1108/IJCHM-03-2018-0186

Dogru, T., Mody, M., Suess, C., McGinley, S., & Line, N. D. (2020). The Airbnb paradox: Positive employment effects in the hospitality industry. *Tourism Management, 77*(104001). https://doi.org/10.1016/j.tourman.2019.104001

Dolnicar, S. (2019). A review of research into paid online peer-to-peer accommodation: Launching the annals of tourism research curated collection on peer-to-peer accommodation. *Annals of Tourism Research, 75*, 248–264. https://doi.org/10.1016/j.annals.2019.02.003

Eurocities. (2022). Short-term rentals: cities ask Europe's help. Retrieved from https://eurocities.eu/latest/short-term-rentals-cities-ask-europes-help/

European Commission. (2016). Communication of the commission—A European agenda for the collaborative economy, COM/2016/0356 final. Retrieved from https://eur-lex.europa.eu/legal-content/EN/TXT/?uri=COM%3A2016%3A356%3AFIN

European Commission. (2018a). Study on the assessment of the regulatory aspects affecting the collaborative economy in the tourism accommodation sector in the 28 Member States (580/PP/GRO/IMA/15/15111J): Final report. https://data.europa.eu/doi/https://doi.org/10.2873/649335

European Commission. (2018b). Study to monitor the business and regulatory environment affecting the collaborative economy in the EU: final report. https://data.europa.eu/doi/https://doi.org/10.2873/972344
European Commission. (2018c). Study on the assessment of the regulatory aspects affecting the collaborative economy in the tourism accommodation sector in the 28 member states (580/PP/GRO/IMA/15/15111J): Task 2 report. https://data.europa.eu/doi/https://doi.org/10.2873/428928
European Commission. (2018d). Study on the assessment of the regulatory aspects affecting the collaborative economy in the tourism accommodation sector in the 28 Member States (580/PP/GRO/IMA/15/15111J): Task 1 report. https://data.europa.eu/doi/https://doi.org/10.2873/78753
European Commission. (2020). Commission reaches agreement with collaborative economy platforms to publish key data on tourism accommodation. Retrieved from https://ec.europa.eu/commission/presscorner/detail/en/ip_20_194
European Commission. (2022). Proposal for a regulation of the European parliament and of the council on data collection and sharing relating to short-term accommodation rental services and amending Regulation (EU) 2018/1724, COM/2022/571 final, Retrieved from https://eur-lex.europa.eu/legal-content/EN/TXT/?uri=CELEX%3A52022PC0571
European Court of Justice. (2019). Case C-390/18 Airbnb Ireland, ECLI:EU:C:2019:1112
European Court of Justice. (2020). Joined cases C-724/18 and C-727/18, Cali Apartments, ECLI:EU:C:2020:743
European Court of Justice. (2022a). Case C-674/20, Airbnb Ireland UC v Région de Bruxelles-Capitale, ECLI:EU:C:2022:303
European Court of Justice. (2022b). Case C-83/21, Airbnb Ireland UC, Airbnb Payments UK Ltd v Agenzia delle Entrate, ECLI:EU:C:2022:1018
Franco, S. F., & Santos, C. D. (2021). The impact of Airbnb on residential property values and rents: Evidence from Portugal. *Regional Science and Urban Economics, 88*(103667). https://doi.org/10.1016/j.regsciurbeco.2021.103667
García-Ayllón, S. (2018). Urban transformations as an indicator of unsustainability in the P2P mass tourism phenomenon: The Airbnb case in Spain through three case studies. *Sustainability, 10*(8), 2933. https://doi.org/10.3390/su10082933
Garcia-López, M. -À., Jofre-Monseny, J., Martínez-Mazza, R., & Segú, M. (2020). Do short-term rental platforms affect housing markets? Evidence from Airbnb in Barcelona. *Journal of Urban Economics, 119*(103278). https://doi.org/10.1016/j.jue.2020.103278
Guttentag, D. (2017). Regulating innovation in the collaborative economy: an examination of Airbnb's early legal issues. In: Dredge, D., Gyimóthy, S. (Eds.), *Collaborative Economy and Tourism. Tourism on the Verge*. Springer, Cham. https://doi.org/10.1007/978-3-319-51799-5_7
Guttentag, D. (2019). Progress on Airbnb: A literature review. *Journal of Hospitality and Tourism Technology, 10*(4), 814–844. https://doi.org/10.1108/JHTT-08-2018-0075
Gyódi, K. (2019). Airbnb in European cities: Business as usual or true sharing economy? *Journal of Cleaner Production, 221*, 536–551. https://doi.org/10.1016/j.jclepro.2019.02.221
Hati, S. R. H., Balqiah, T. E, Hananto, A., & Yuliati, E. (2021). A decade of systematic literature review on Airbnb: The sharing economy from a multiple stakeholder perspective. *Heliyon, 7*(10), Article e08222. https://doi.org/10.1016/j.heliyon.2021.e08222
Hatzopoulos, V., & Roma, S. (2017). Caring for sharing? The collaborative economy under EU law. *Common Market Law Review, 54*(1), 81–127. https://doi.org/10.54648/cola2017004
Hatzopoulos, V. (2021). Disarming Airbnb—Dismantling the Services Directive? Cali Apartments. *Common Market Law Review, 58*(3), 905–928. https://doi.org/10.54648/cola2021054
Heo, C. Y., Blal, I. & Choi, M. (2019) What is happening in Paris? Airbnb hotels and the Parisian market: A case study. *Tourism Management, 70*, 78–88. https://doi.org/10.1016/j.tourman.2018.04.003
HOTREC. (2022). *Position paper on EU-wide regulation of short-term rentals (Full Report).* Retrieved from https://www.hotrec.eu/wp-content/customer-area/storage/8086fb0898d771b

564773a81471d8d4e/HOTREC-position-paper-on-EU-wide-regulation-of-Short-Term-Rentals-FULL.pdf

Iacovone, C. (2023). Debate on regulation and professionalisation in the short-term rental housing market. *Geoforum, 146*, Article 103870. https://doi.org/10.1016/j.geoforum.2023.103870

Jefferson-Jones, J. (2015). Airbnb and the housing segment of the modern sharing economy: Are short-term rental restrictions an unconstitutional taking. *Hastings Constitutional Law Quarterly, 42*, 557–576.

Jordan, E. J., & Moore, J. (2018). An in-depth exploration of residents' perceived impacts of transient vacation rentals. *Journal of Travel and Tourism Marketing, 35*(1), 90–101. https://doi.org/10.1080/10548408.2017.1315844

Jover, J., & Díaz-Parra, I. (2020). Gentrification, transnational gentrification and touristification in Seville, Spain. *Urban Studies, 57*(15), 3044–3059. https://doi.org/10.1177%2F0042098019857585

Kardoulia, E. (2020). Public and private tourism law in Greece. *Tourism Law in Europe,* ESHTE / INATEl / USAL. Retrieved frm https://intranet.eshte.pt/tourismLawInEurope/tlie6/

Katsinas, P. (2021). Professionalisation of short-term rentals and emergent tourism gentrification in post-crisis Thessaloniki. *Environment and Planning A: Economy and Space, 53*(7), 1652–1670. https://doi.org/10.1177%2F0308518X21988940

Kaźmierczyk, A. (2019). Issues of short-term rental in light of EU and member states' regulations. *PWWPM-Review of International European and Comparative Law, 17,* 180–198. https://doi.org/10.26106/5gev-2c68

Kochan, D. J. (2018). The sharing stick in the property rights bundle: The case of short-term rentals and HOAs. *University of Cincinatti Law Review,* pp. 893–922.

Kramer, D., & Schaub, M. (2022). EU law and the public regulation of the platform economy: The case of the short-term rental market. *Common Market Law Review, 59*(6), 1633—1668. https://doi.org/10.54648/cola2022114

Leick, B., Kivedal, B. K., Eklund, M. A., & Vinogradov, E. (2021). Exploring the relationship between Airbnb and traditional accommodation for regional variations of tourism markets. *Tourism Economics, 28*(5), 1258–1279. https://doi.org/10.1177%2F1354816621990173

Martinez-Nadal, A. (2019). Regulating Airbnb in Spain. *Journal of European Consumer and Market Law, 8*(1), 42–45.

McKee, D. (2017). The platform economy: Natural, neutral, consensual and efficient? *Transnational Legal Theory, 8*(4), 455–495.

https://doi.org/10.1080/20414005.2017.1416516

Morales-Pérez, S., Garay, L., & Wilson, J. (2020). Airbnb's contribution to socio-spatial inequalities and geographies of resistance in Barcelona. *Tourism Geographies, 24*(6–7), 978–1001. https://doi.org/10.1080/14616688.2020.1795712

Nieuwland, S., & van Melik, R. (2020). Regulating Airbnb: How cities deal with perceived negative externalities of short-term rentals. *Current Issues in Tourism, 23*(7), 811–825. https://doi.org/10.1080/13683500.2018.1504899

Pantazi, T. (2021). Regulating short-term rentals: Joined cases C-724/18 and C-727/18 Cali Apartments. *Maastricht Journal of European and Comparative Law, 28*(4), 573–581. https://doi.org/10.1177/1023263X211014688

Pereira, S. M. (2022). Regulation of short-term rentals in Lisbon. *Urban Research & Practice, 15*(4), 477–504. https://doi.org/10.1080/17535069.2020.1842901

Prayag, G., & Ozanne, L. K. (2018). A systematic review of peer-to-peer (P2P) accommodation sharing research from 2010 to 2016: progress and prospects from the multi-level perspective. *Journal of Hospitality Marketing & Management, 27*(6), 649–678. https://doi.org/10.1080/19368623.2018.1429977

Regulation (EU) 2022/2065 of the European Parliament and of the Council of 19 October 2022 on a Single Market For Digital Services and amending Directive 2000/31/EC (Digital Services Act). retrieved from https://eur-lex.europa.eu/legal-content/EN/TXT/?uri=celex%3A32022R2065

Regulation (EU) 2024/1028 of the European Parliament and of the Council of 11 April 2024 on data collection and sharing relating to short-term accommodation rental services and amending Regulation (EU) 2018/1724. Retrieved from https://eur-lex.europa.eu/legal-content/EN/TXT/?uri=OJ%3AL_202401028

Roma, P., Panniello, U., & Lo Nigro, G. (2019). Sharing economy and incumbents' pricing strategy: The impact of Airbnb on the hospitality industry. *International Journal of Production Economics, 214*, 17–29. https://doi.org/10.1016/j.ijpe.2019.03.023

Sainaghi, R. (2020). The current state of academic research into peer-to-peer accommodation platforms. *International Journal of Hospitality Management, 89*(102555). https://doi.org/10.1016/j.ijhm.2020.102555

Sainaghi, R., & Baggio, R. (2021). Are mom-and-pop and professional hosts actually competing against hotels? *International Journal of Contemporary Hospitality Management, 33*(3), 808–827. https://doi.org/10.1108/IJCHM-08-2020-0882

Shabrina, Z., Arcaute, E., & Batty, M. (2022). Airbnb and its potential impact on the London housing market. *Urban Studies, 59*(1), 197–221. https://doi.org/10.1177%2F0042098020970865

Strømmen-Bakhtiar, A., & Vinogradov, E. (2019). The effects of Airbnb on hotels in Norway. *Society and Economy in Central and Eastern Europe, 41*(1), 87–105. https://doi.org/10.1556/204.2018.001

Tedds, L., Cameron, A., Khanal, M.,& Crisan, D. (2021). Why existing regulatory frameworks fail in the short-term rental market: Exploring the role of regulatory fractures. *University of Calgary-The School of Public Policy Publications, 14*(1). https://doi.org/10.11575/sppp.v14i1.72317

Ulfbeck, V. G., Petersen, C. S., & Hansen, O. (2018). Platforms as private governance systems—The example of Airbnb. *Nordic Journal of Commercial Law, 1*, 38–60. https://doi.org/10.5278/ojs.njcl.v0i1.2484

Vallejo, A. O. (2019). Contractual relationships in collaborative economy platforms. *European Review of Private Law, 27*(5), 995–1022. https://doi.org/10.54648/erpl2019055

Vlachos, V., & Bitzenis, A. (2019). Post-crisis growth prospects in the European Union. In V. Vlachos & A. Bitzenis (Eds.), *European Union*, pp. 1–16. Palgrave Macmillan, Cham. https://doi.org/10.1007/978-3-030-18103-1_1

Vlachos, V., & Bitzenis, A. (2021). Competitive position and dynamics of the Greek economy. In V. Vlachos, A. Bitzenis, & B. S. Sergi (Eds.), *Modeling economic growth in contemporary Greece*, pp. 13–27. Emerald Publishing Limited, Leeds. https://doi.org/10.1108/978-1-80071-122-820211003

von Briel, D., & Dolnicar, S. (2020). The evolution of Airbnb regulation—An international longitudinal investigation 2008–2020. *Annals of Tourism Research, 87*, Article 102983. https://doi.org/10.1016/j.annals.2020.102983

Yang, Y., García, M. N., Viglia, G., & Nicolau, J. L. (2021). Competitors or complements: a meta-analysis of the effect of Airbnb on hotel performance. *Journal of Travel Research, 61*(7). https://doi.org/10.1177%2F00472875211042670

Sustainability, Circular Economy, and Innovation

Digitalisation: Catalysing the Transition to a Circular Economy in Ukraine

Tetiana Gorokhova

Abstract Digitalization can contribute to the shift towards a sustainable circular economy (CE). Digitalization not only refines business processes but also emphasizes waste curtailment, prolonging product life, and slashing transaction costs. Therefore, digitalization supports the growth of circular economy business models by aiding in closing the loop, decelerating the material cycle, and narrowing the cycle by improving the efficiency of resource utilization. However, fully leveraging this integration presents challenges, with clear gaps hindering the fluid adoption of digital-backed circular business models. Despite its significance, there's a dearth of comprehensive literature on digitalization's potential and challenges. This research aims to explore the main benefits and obstacles of applying digitalization in CE business models in Ukraine, focusing on identifying opportunities and challenges and finding ways to overcome these hurdles. The study involved online interviews with business representatives, researchers, NGOs, and students (a total of 36 participants) during the thematic training course according to the Erasmus + program in an online format in Ukraine (December 8–10, 2023). One of the activities during the training course was finding answers to four questions relevant to the research aim in small groups for 40 min for 7–8 participants. The data was recorded and subsequently examined using MAXQDA software for qualitative data analysis. I identified challenges related to the integration of circular principles into existing business models, data ownership, data sharing, data integration, collaboration, and competence requirements. The post-war rebuilding and modernizing of industries towards sustainability, visualization, and innovation in product design, enhancement in resource efficiency, and optimization of logistics process collaboration with stakeholders and implementation of digital technologies were noted as main opportunities in adopting business models based on CE in the Ukrainian perspective. This research uncovered less recognized or previously unexplored prospects linked to digitalization in the context of transitioning to

T. Gorokhova (✉)
Centre for Advanced Internet Studies (CAIS), Bochum, Germany
e-mail: tetiana.gorokhova@cais-research.de

Pryazovskyi State Technical University, Dnipro, Ukraine

I. Bartuseviciene et al. (eds.), *Building Resilience Through Digital Transformation and Sustainable Innovation*, Springer Proceedings in Business and Economics,
https://doi.org/10.1007/978-3-031-90054-9_9

a CE. One of the new opportunities is virtualization in business models can influence on reduce costs, conserve resources, and provide reliable data. The research underscores the significant role of digitalization in enabling the transition towards a circular economy in Ukraine's business sector. While there are considerable opportunities for innovation and modernization, the challenges of integration, collaboration, data management, and skill gaps cannot be overlooked. Addressing these challenges through targeted educational programs, strategic partnerships, and supportive policies will be pivotal in harnessing the full potential of digitalization in advancing circular economy models.

Keywords Digitalization · Circular economy · Sustainability · Ukraine

JEL Classification A12 · Q5 · O3

1 Introduction

Digitalization is recognized as a key driver in the advancement of the CE, enhancing product and asset management through increased visibility and intelligence. This includes tracking the location, status, and availability of assets. Central to CE-oriented business models is the concept of not selling but rather leasing, renting, or sharing durable products wherever feasible (Ellen MacArthur Foundation, 2013). This shift towards Product Service Systems (PSS) is crucial for propelling the CE forward, with digitalization playing a significant role in this shift (Guzzo et al., 2019).

Integrating cyber-physical systems, Big Data, data analytics, the Internet of Things (IoT), and innovative business models presents significant opportunities for sustainable industrial value creation and capture within the CE framework (Raynor et al., 2015; Stankovic et al., 2017). The adoption of digital technologies like artificial intelligence and blockchain enhances the traceability and transparency across the lifecycle of products. Such technologies enable manufacturers to remotely monitor, manage, analyse, and optimize product performance while gathering data on product use.

Recent studies have emphasized the intertwined nature of Industry 4.0 and CE as a significant area of research. Rosa et al. (2020) explored how Industry 4.0 intersects with CE studies and devised an innovative framework that introduces concepts like Circular I4.0 and Digital CE to underline their connection. Pham et al. (2019) demonstrated through electric scooter-sharing platforms how Industry 4.0 could facilitate the sharing economy, thus enhancing sustainability within the manufacturing realms in a CE framework. Dev et al. (2020) developed a decision-making model for sustainable reverse logistics, integrating Industry 4.0 with CE in real-time operations. Furthermore, Yadav et.al. (2020) proposed a model aimed at addressing the challenges in sustainable supply chain management by leveraging solutions derived from Industry 4.0 and CE.

In support of CE, various innovative business models have been suggested (Pieroni et al., 2019). Digital Twins (DTs) contribute to achieving circular objectives through integrated monitoring, control, optimization, and automation. Ingemarsdotter et al. (2019) highlighted the role of the Internet of Things (IoT) in enabling companies to monitor products across their life cycles, thereby facilitating strategies such as reuse, remanufacturing, recycling, and sharing. Alcayaga et al. (2019) took a comprehensive approach to CE, IoT, and smart PSS, creating a framework that explores the dynamic interactions between smart circularity systems, circular PSS, and smart PSS. Finally, Kristoffersen et al. (2020) crafted a strategic framework based on DTs to aid manufacturing companies in achieving the United Nations' Sustainable Development Goal 12, as part of the 2030 Agenda for Sustainable Development.

Real-time data on product location boosts accessibility and supports effective end-of-life management strategies such as collection, refurbishment, remanufacturing, and recycling. Understanding a product's condition allows for predictive and condition-based maintenance, which utilizes advanced diagnostics and prognostics to increase product reliability and lifespan, thereby supporting remanufacturing efforts with historical product data. Moreover, knowing a product's availability facilitates its shared use via digital platforms and marketplaces, enhancing recycling processes.

However, to fully realize the benefits outlined above, numerous challenges and obstacles remain that impede the implementation of circular business models supported by digital technology. Presently, there is a scant amount of research addressing the opportunities and challenges posed by digitalization in transforming the CE. Consequently, our qualitative and exploratory study aims to shed light on these issues and provide clearer insights.

In the context of Ukraine, the implementation of circular economy principles faces numerous structural and practical challenges. One of the key obstacles is the complexity involved in designing and implementing green processes and systems. Many Ukrainian businesses are still heavily reliant on traditional, linear economic models that prioritize short-term profits over long-term sustainability (Shpak et al., 2020). Transitioning to CE requires substantial redesign of production processes, which demands both technical expertise and significant financial resources.

Moreover, the lack of regulatory support further hinders progress. While some policies exist that touch on environmental protection, there is no comprehensive, strategic framework specifically aimed at promoting CE practices. This creates uncertainty for businesses that might otherwise be interested in adopting circular models, as there is little guidance or incentive from government authorities (World Bank, 2022). Without supportive regulations, businesses face difficulties in navigating the transition, especially when it comes to compliance with global sustainability standards.

Consumer support is also insufficient, as public awareness about the benefits of CE remains low in Ukraine. Many consumers are still unfamiliar with concepts such as product leasing, sharing, or remanufacturing, and there is a general reluctance to move away from the conventional ownership model (Kirchherr et al., 2017; Udovyk, 2021). This lack of demand for circular products and services stifles innovation and discourages businesses from adopting circular practices, which are often perceived as risky in the absence of strong market demand.

High investment costs and low immediate economic returns further complicate the shift to CE. Many Ukrainian companies, especially small and medium enterprises (SMEs), operate with limited financial capacity and are reluctant to invest in new technologies or processes that may not yield quick returns. Implementing CE practices requires significant upfront investments in green technologies, infrastructure, and training, which, without financial incentives or rewards systems, appears unattractive to many firms (Saarinen et al., 2023). Additionally, suppliers often lack motivation, as there are few, if any, reward mechanisms to encourage the use of sustainable materials or processes.

The uncertainty of green outcomes also plays a role. Due to the relatively nascent state of CE in Ukraine, many businesses are unsure about the long-term benefits and viability of adopting circular practices (Ruda et al., 2021) There is a lack of clear data and case studies within the Ukrainian context to demonstrate the tangible benefits of CE, which breeds scepticism among companies hesitant to move away from familiar, profit-driven models.

Furthermore, Ukraine faces shortages of green materials, processes, and technologies essential for CE implementation. The country is still developing its infrastructure for waste management, recycling, and the production of renewable energy, which are critical components of a functioning circular economy (Tanveer et. al., 2022; Meidl, 2021). This lack of infrastructure is compounded by insufficient access to advanced technologies such as smart sensors, automation, and digital platforms, which are necessary for the efficient monitoring, optimization, and integration of circular processes.

Finally, businesses often lack the flexibility to switch to green systems. Many industries, particularly in manufacturing and heavy industry, have long-standing operational practices that are difficult to alter (Madu, 2022). Existing machinery, supply chains, and production methods are often incompatible with circular models, and the transition requires costly and time-consuming overhauls (Jensen, 2024; Khan et al., 2023). Without clear pathways or external support, businesses face significant obstacles in making these changes.

These factors, collectively, represent substantial barriers to the widespread adoption of circular economy principles in Ukraine. Overcoming them requires concerted efforts from both the public and private sectors, including regulatory reform, financial incentives, technological advancement, and a shift in consumer attitudes toward sustainability (Hadi et al., 2021).

Additionally, there is a lack of know-how and needed technology for implementing urban mining, which is an important aspect of the circular economy (Kazançoğlu et al., 2020; Shpak et al., 2020). Furthermore, there is a substantial uncertainty and scepticism surrounding the rise in energy prices and capital costs, as well as concerns about environmental capacity and ecological safety risks. Lastly, there is a lack of comprehensive policy and regulatory frameworks that support and promote circular economy practices (Ruda et al., 2021).

Considering these facts, the aim of this research is to develop insight into the principal benefits and obstacles associated with applying digitalization to the transition towards a circular economy models in business sphere in Ukraine.

Accordingly, I formulated two research questions:

1. What principal opportunities and challenges does digitalization create when applying it to business models based on the circular economy?
2. In what ways can the obstacles linked to digitalization be overcome to effectively implement business models based on the circular economy?

Structure of the paper. The Introduction section provides an overview of the important role that digitalization plays in driving the transition towards a CE, particularly in the context of Ukraine's post-war rebuilding. It emphasizes the importance of Industry 4.0 technologies like IoT and AI in enhancing resource efficiency and transparency, which are crucial for achieving sustainability goals. In the Sect. 2 "The Literature Review" explores the intersection of digitalization and CE, reviewing key studies that link digital tools to sustainable business models. It highlights gaps in the existing literature, particularly regarding Ukraine's adoption of CE principles, and sets the foundation for the research. In the section "Methodology" the study outlines a qualitative approach, involving interviews with stakeholders across business, academia, and NGOs. The data is analysed using MAXQDA software, providing insights into the opportunities and challenges of integrating digitalization into CE in Ukraine. The section "Results" uncovers both the barriers, such as issues with data management and collaboration, and the opportunities, including the virtualization of business models and improved resource efficiency. These insights are important for understanding the practical implications of digitalization on CE. The section "Discussion" contextualizes the findings within Ukraine's socio-economic and regulatory landscape, highlighting the need for supportive policies, strategic partnerships, and educational programs to fully realize the potential of digital technologies in CE. Finally, the section "Conclusion" summarizes the contributions of the study, emphasizing digitalization's role in transforming business models towards sustainability. It contextualizes the findings within Ukraine's socio-economic and regulatory landscape, highlighting the need for supportive policies, strategic partnerships, and educational programs to fully realize the potential of digital technologies in CE.

2 Literature Review

2.1 *Digitalization Enhances the Shift Toward the Circular Economy Business Model. Opportunities and Challenges*

Adopting circular business models not only promotes sustainability but also provides a competitive edge for companies (Androniceanu et al., 2017). A business model can be described as follows:

> It is a unit of analysis separate from the product, the company, or the network, centred around a focal company yet extending beyond its boundaries.
> It emphasizes a systemic view in explaining business operations.
> It details both the creation of value and its capture (Zott et al., 2011).

Beyond the well-established body of literature on business models, there is an emerging focus on sustainable business models and innovations in this area, which suggest that the creation of economic value should also consider the environmental and social value for stakeholders, thereby contributing to sustainable development both for the business and wider society (Boons et al., 2013).

Additionally, a circular business model is conceptualized as "the logic through which an organization creates, delivers, and captures value in closed-loop material cycles" (Mentink, 2014). Such models inherently rely on networking and necessitate collaboration among various stakeholders to achieve shared goals. It is important to recognize the shifts in value creation that these models bring, often leading to significant transformations in business practices. Circular business models are categorized into three types: slowing, closing, and narrowing the loop. "Slowing the loop" focuses on extending the product's life through thoughtful design and maintenance. "Closing the loop" revolves around effective recycling processes, which can be facilitated through practices like industrial symbiosis. "Narrowing the loop" involves reducing resource use per product, which can be enhanced by smart technologies (Beattie et al., 2013; Bocken et al., 2016. These strategies often overlap, with circular business models typically incorporating elements of all three to reinforce each other (Fig. 1.)

Shifting business perspectives from a linear to CE presents numerous challenges that demand effective management of sustainable production and consumption,

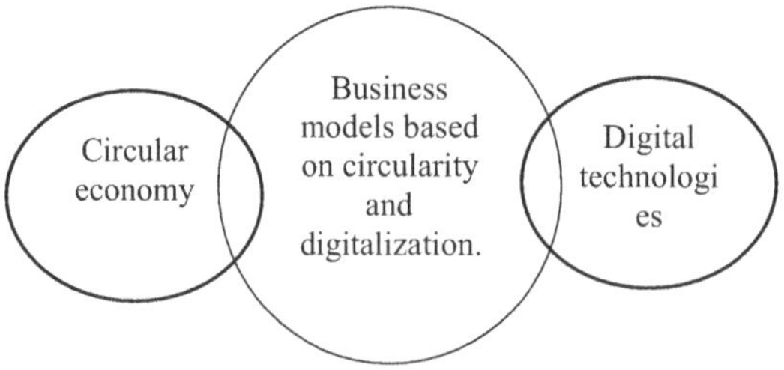

Fig. 1 Integration of circular economy and digital technologies in business models

closed-loop supply chains, and PSS. Grafström et al. (2021) investigated the obstacles to adopting CE through four dimensions: technology, market, system, and cultural barriers. In their research, Rajput et al. (2019) applied principal component analysis to explore the elements connecting Industry 4.0 with the adoption of CE, pinpointing artificial intelligence and service and policy frameworks as key facilitators. Furthermore, Abdul-Hamid et al. (2020) assessed the difficulties that Industry 4.0 faces in implementing CE and proposed solutions to these challenges.

PSS are configurations that blend both tangible products and intangible services, strategically designed to satisfy the ultimate needs of customers. These systems emphasize the development of products that are durable, efficiently utilized, and both cost- and material-efficient. While PSS itself does not constitute a circular business model, it promotes similar objectives, encouraging firms to adopt practices that are pivotal for achieving circularity in business operations (Deineko et al., 2018; Ferasso et al., 2020). Digitalization within PSS frameworks play a crucial role by facilitating the collection and analysis of data, which enhances product innovation and customer satisfaction. Furthermore, the efficient use of data opens up new business models, such as monetizing data by selling it to third parties. Despite these advancements, significant challenges remain in fully understanding and capitalizing on the business opportunities that arise from the integration of PSS, digitalization, and the circular economy.

The significance of digitalization in facilitating the CE is well recognized. The deployment of digital technologies and interconnected devices could lead to a reduction in resource consumption and support the development of circular systems. Nevertheless, research exploring how digitalization could foster the shift toward a CE remains relatively scarce (Bressanelli et al., 2018; Pagoropoulos et al., 2017; Tseng et al., 2018).

Pagoropoulos et al. (2017) conducted a literature review that yielded 12 articles discussing the intersection of digital technologies and the circular economy. Gorokhova et al. (2024) categorised 1855 relevant scientific articles in Web of Science from 2015 to the first quarter of 2023 including key words, author, year, research methods, content. To examine the trends in published articles focused on the circular economy and digitalization over different years, a bar chart analysis was conducted, and chose 135 articles.

The digitalization of industries enhances resource efficiency, enabling the use of fewer resources more effectively. Intelligent technologies facilitate the reduction of energy use and improve the efficiency of logistics and capacity utilization (Kagermann et al., 2015). Digitalization provides transparent access to data on product resource usage, allowing for optimization of product lifecycles and advancing the transition to the CE. Technologies like RFID are crucial for gathering usage data on products, which is essential for PSS business models. Such data is invaluable for assessing the condition of returned products and streamlining their reintroduction into product lifecycle management.

Researchers like Bressanelli et al. (2018) have examined how the Internet of Things (IoT), Big Data, and analytics support the CE transition, identifying eight key functionalities enabled by these technologies. These include enhancing product design, attracting specific customers, monitoring product usage, providing technical support and maintenance, optimizing product use, upgrading products, and improving renovation and end-of-life processes.

CE systems feature interconnected cycles of large data sets. Digitalization opens new pathways to this data, which is critical for making decisions about product lifecycle stages, material reuse, logistical needs, and identifying stakeholders in the value network (Ferasso et al., 2020).

Furthermore, digitalization fosters the virtualization of distribution channels, allowing companies to deliver value via digital platforms like online stores and digital products, thereby reducing environmental impact and promoting circular business models.

In the CE, managing the flow of materials and information is vital. Digital technologies are instrumental in maintaining comprehensive data on the quantity and quality of products and their material compositions, thereby supporting the use of waste as a resource.

The integration of digital intelligence into CE practices offers numerous benefits, including the dissemination of knowledge, structuring, and customization at various levels, which enhances sustainable customer and user relationships. Moreover, digital solutions facilitate circular business models by automating the monitoring, control, and optimization of resource and material flows (Moreno et al., 2016).

Previous research on the obstacles to adopting the circular economy (CE) has highlighted several challenges that diminish the potential benefits of digitalization. These challenges can be categorized into financial obstacles (assessing financial gains and profitability), structural obstacles (lack of information sharing, unclear distribution of responsibilities), operational obstacles (infrastructure, supply chain management), and attitudinal obstacles (perceptions of sustainability, risk aversion). Additionally, technological barriers also persist, particularly in product design and the integration of digital technologies within production processes.

Despite the advances in digitalization, which have enhanced the volume, accuracy, and costs of information, significant gaps remain. Currently, informational issues are among the primary barriers to implementing the CE. These include problems like the limited availability of information, higher transaction and search costs, and a general lack of knowledge. The importance of data integration is often overlooked in studies focusing on digital solutions in the CE. This oversight is crucial, as the optimal use of data to facilitate the shift from linear to more circular business models is not always clear. Data integration is vital for business applications; it merges distinct information sources with the strategic objectives of stakeholders and their practical business applications.

3 Methods

The data for this research was collected during the training course "European Circular Economy and Social Entrepreneurship: Steps of Own Idea Development," conducted as part of the Erasmus + program from December 8–10, 2023, in an online format in Ukraine. The course involved 36 participants representing a diverse range of sectors: 14 from business, 11 from academia and research projects, 6 from NGOs, and 4 students. This diverse group contributed to a broad perspective on the challenges and opportunities in digitalizing circular economy (CE) models.

To ensure a thorough exploration of the research questions, the participants engaged in structured group activities. Divided into small groups of 7–8 participants, they were tasked with answering four key questions over a 40-min period:

1. What key business prospects are associated with the Circular Economy?
2. How does digitalization facilitate the capitalization of these opportunities?
3. What are the primary challenges encountered in circular business models and digitalization within organizations, and what strategies can be employed to address these challenges?
4. What resources are needed to solve these challenges?

Each group presented their findings, followed by a reflection session to encourage further insights and dialogue.

The collected data was transcribed and analysed using MAXQDA software, a robust tool for qualitative data analysis. The analysis followed a systematic coding process, where initial codes were assigned to segments of the transcriptions. These codes were then refined and categorized into broader themes. The categorization process was informed by existing literature, but new categories were also introduced as necessary based on the data. This approach ensured that the analysis was grounded in both established knowledge and the specific insights emerging from the participants' responses.

To enhance transparency, it is important to clarify that participants included representatives from SMEs, large business, which presented different economic sectors of Ukraine and NGOs actively involved in CE initiatives. This diversity strengthens the relevance and breadth of the findings but should be understood within the context of a qualitative exploratory study, where the goal is to uncover insights rather than make broad statistical generalizations.

4 Results

Digitalisation is not only a technological shift but a transformative force that facilitates the transition towards a circular economy in Ukraine. This shift is crucial for rebuilding and modernizing industries with an emphasis on sustainability. As highlighted by previous studies (Bocken et al., 2016; Pieroni et al., 2019), digital tools provide robust infrastructure for tracking resources, managing complex supply chains, and fostering effective communication between diverse stakeholders. For example, the development of sharing economy platforms and marketplaces, as demonstrated by Pham et al. (2019), enables better utilization of assets and reduces waste by facilitating the reuse and repurposing of products.

The respondents recognized that digitalization is crucial for creating new opportunities and modernizing industries toward sustainability in Ukraine and especially during the rebuilding period. By offering detailed data on the location, condition, and availability of products, digitalization supports decision-making processes with open, accurate, and expansive datasets. Furthermore, it underpins the development of novel digital platforms that facilitate the creation of new market types, largely based on the virtualization of products and processes. This transformation is particularly evident in the agricultural sector, where digital tools are leveraged to adopt circular practices that improve soil health and generate value from agricultural waste.

Digitalization enhances networking, facilitating more effective collaboration and joint efforts with diverse stakeholders, such as customers. It enhances consumer involvement in product and service innovation, aligning with findings by Kristoffersen et al. (2020), which show that social media and digital platforms play a critical role in driving engagement and sustainable practices.

Moreover, the impact of digitalization extends to marketing strategies, which are becoming increasingly interactive and intelligent, allowing for more precise consumer targeting and engagement. This shift is vital in areas such as post-war rebuilding phases, where the traceability of goods and optimization of logistics are critical. Digital tools not only support these functions but also contribute to significant enhancements in resource efficiency and cost reduction, underpinning the broader goals of transitioning to a circular economy and promoting sustainable practices across industries.

The respondents also highlighted primary challenges for linked to CE and digitalization encompass several pivotal areas in Ukraine, including business models, data dynamics, collaboration, and competence requirements. Shifting existing business models to integrate circular principles necessitates a profound change in mindset from linear to circular thinking. This transformation is essential not only for redefining business strategies but also for securing financing for innovative business ideas and transitioning from product-oriented to service-oriented models.

Data-related issues are especially significant. Challenges include accessing data and resolving concerns over data ownership. The exchange of data between competing businesses introduces further complications, such as ensuring the privacy and property rights of information and overcoming a general lack of trust among stakeholders. Moreover, the technological challenges associated with implementing digital tracking and analytics systems are exacerbated by a lack of standardization and interoperability, complicating the integration of big data from multiple sources and the management of information flows.

Collaboration also poses a considerable challenge, requiring the organization of partnerships between diverse entities. Defining shared processes and finding suitable collaborators who can merge different areas of expertise and perspectives are critical for effective communication from companies to consumers.

Additionally, there is a notable skills gap in both digitalization and sustainability. This gap highlights a widespread lack of understanding of the importance of digitalization and basic CE concepts among stakeholders. Addressing these challenges is crucial for advancing the integration of CE principles and harnessing the full potential of digitalization in sustainable business practices.

However, several challenges were identified in implementing CE through digitalization, which align with findings from Grafström et al. (2021), Rajput et al. (2019), and Abdul-Hamid et al. (2020). These studies also highlighted obstacles like shifting business models, data-related issues, and collaboration hurdles. Shifting from linear to circular models requires a profound change in business strategies, as companies need to transition from product-oriented to service-oriented approaches. Securing financing for these innovative business models adds another layer of complexity, as also noted by Pieroni et al. (2019).

The respondents also proposed solutions for the challenges. Education and awareness initiatives are vital for embedding a circular mindset among businesses and consumers. The development of partnerships between government, industry, and academia is instrumental in driving innovation within CE technologies and practices. Such collaborations can enhance the co-creation process, where sharing expertise between organizations and amalgamating competencies from diverse actors across various sectors—including both small and large entities—is deemed highly effective.

Further, implementing supportive policies and incentives is crucial to motivate businesses to embrace circular and digital solutions. These measures not only foster an environment conducive to sustainable practices but also reinforce the commitment to a circular economic model.

Networking also plays a significant role in overcoming challenges associated with CE. By expanding connections with international partners, such as businesses and NGOs, as well as enhancing networking with domestic partners, stakeholders can unlock new possibilities for addressing the challenges inherent in CE. Engaging in collaborative research projects that bring together companies from different backgrounds can further bolster opportunities for networking, facilitating a broader exchange of ideas and solutions that drive the principles of circular economy forward.

Tre results of qualitive data analyse were presented in Table 1.

5 Conclusion

In the study, I uncovered novel or lesser-known opportunities of digitalization related to the transformation towards CE. Notably, digitalisation emerged as a key enabler in adopting circular business models based on the principles of slowing, closing, and narrowing the loop. Digitalisation contributes significantly to cost reduction, resource conservation, and the provision of reliable data, which are essential for designing modular and repairable products that can be updated—a critical factor

Table 1 Digital transformation for circular economy resilience in Ukraine. The results of qualitive data analyse

Digitalization as a catalyst	Challenges	Solutions for the challenges
- CE is seen as an opportunity to rebuild and modernize industries towards sustainability in Ukraine; - potential for innovation in product design; - the agricultural sector in Ukraine could adopt circular practices to improve soil health and create value from agricultural waste; - digitalization is pivotal for transitioning to a CE as it provides the infrastructure for tracking resources, managing supply chains, and enhancing communication between stakeholders; - development of sharing economy platforms and marketplaces; - enhancement in resource efficiency and cost-cutting; - digital tools can support the traceability of goods and optimize logistics, particularly in post-war rebuilding of Ukraine	- the integration of circular principles into existing business models, requiring a shift in mindset from linear to circular thinking; - data ownership, data sharing, data integration, collaboration and competence requirements; - technological challenges in implementing digital tracking and analytics systems due to a lack of standardization and interoperability; - difficulties in accessing data and issues pertaining to who owns the data; - the obstacles of exchanging data among competing businesses, safeguarding privacy and ownership rights, and a general lack of trust; - cooperation among various stakeholders; - the gap in the skills of digitalisation and sustainability-related	- education and awareness campaigns are crucial to fostering a circular mindset among businesses and consumers; - developing partnerships between government, industry, and academia to foster innovation in CE technologies and practices; - implementing supportive policies and incentives to encourage businesses to adopt circular and digital solutions; - networking with international partners (e.g., business, NGOs) would bring additional opportunities to create solutions to the identified challenges

in the successful adoption of circular business models. My findings indicate that the circular business model is not about a single company closing the loop, but rather, it involves an ecosystem approach where networking and collaboration with stakeholders and new partners play crucial roles. Additionally, consumers are pivotal in the transition towards the CE as adopters of innovative products and services. Digitalization facilitates this by enhancing the ability to reach and communicate with consumers effectively, thereby enabling the creation of innovative circular business models through a shift from traditional one-way to dynamic two-way marketing communications.

Also, this study provides an exploration into the integration of digitalization within CE business models in Ukraine, revealing both substantial opportunities and formidable challenges. The respondents underscore the important role digitalization plays in modernizing and rebuilding industries towards sustainable practices, particularly in the post-war context. By facilitating enhanced resource management, product lifecycle optimization, and stakeholder collaboration, digital technologies offer a robust platform for implementing CE principles effectively.

The opportunities, respondents highlighted include innovation in product design, improvement in resource efficiency, and the development of sharing economy platforms, which collectively contribute to a more resilient economic framework. However, the transition towards a circular economy is hindered by significant challenges, including issues related to data ownership, sharing, and integration, as well as the need for a shift in business and consumer mindsets from linear to circular thinking.

Addressing these challenges will require a multifaceted approach involving targeted educational programs, strategic partnerships across government, industry, and academia, and the implementation of supportive policies and incentives. These efforts will not only help overcome the barriers but also harness the potential of digitalization to advance circular economy models in Ukraine, contributing to sustainable development goals.

Ultimately, the successful integration of digital technologies within CE practices hinges on a collective commitment to innovation, collaboration, and education, aimed at fostering a sustainable future through the efficient and ethical use of resources.

This study represents an initial step on the research path towards understanding the role of digitalization in implementing CE-based business models. To build on these findings, further studies incorporating real company cases with both qualitative and quantitative data are necessary to deepen our comprehension and refine the strategies needed to leverage digitalization effectively in the circular economy.

Acknowledgements This research was supported by Centre for Advanced Internet Studies (CAIS), Bochum, Germany.

References

Abdul-Hamid, A. -Q., Ali, M. H., Tseng, M. -L., Lan, S., & Kumar, M. (2020). Impeding challenges on industry 4.0 in circular economy: Palm oil industry in Malaysia. *Computers & Operations Research, 123*, 105052.

Alcayaga, A., Wiener, M., & Hansen, E. G. (2019). Towards a framework of smart-circular systems: An integrative literature review. *Journal of Cleaner Production, 221*, 622–634.

Androniceanu, A., & Popescu, C. R. (2017). An inclusive model for an effective development of the renewable energies public sector. *Administration and Management Public, 28*, 81–96.

Beattie, V., & Smith, S. J. (2013). Value creation and business models: Refocusing the intellectual capital debate. *British Accounting Review, 45*, 243–254. https://doi.org/10.1016/j.bar.2013.06.001

Bocken, N. M. P., de Pauw, I., Bakker, C., & van der Grinten, B. (2016). Product design and business model strategies for a circular economy. *Journal of Industrial and Production Engineering, 33*, 308–320. https://doi.org/10.1080/21681015.2016.1172124

Boons, F., & Lüdeke-Freund, F. (2013). Business models for sustainable innovation: State-of-the-art and steps towards a research agenda. *Journal of Cleaner Production, 45*, 9–19. https://doi.org/10.1016/j.jclepro.2012.07.007

Bressanelli, G., Adrodegari, F., Perona, M., & Saccani, N. (2018). Exploring how usage-focused business models enable circular economy through digital technologies. *Sustainability, 10*(639). Retrieved from https://doi.org/10.3390/su10030639

Deineko, L. V., & Tsyplinska, O. O. (2018). Tsyrkuliarna ekonomika yak napriam promyslovoi modernizatsii: yevropeiskyi dosvid [Circular economy as a direction of industrial modernization: European experience]. *Ekonomika: realii chasu [Economy: the realities of time], 5*(39), 30–40.

Dev, N. K., Shankar, R., Qaiser, F. H. (2020). Industry 4.0 and circular economy: Operational excellence for sustainable reverse supply chain performance. *Resources, Conservation and Recycling, 153,* 104583.

Ellen MacArthur Foundation. (2013). *Towards the Circular Economy: Economic and business rationale for an accelerated transition*, vol. 1. https://doi.org/10.1162/108819806775545321

Ferasso, M., Beliaeva, T., Kraus, S., Clauss, T., & Ribeiro-Soriano, D. (2020). Circular economy business models: The state of research and avenues ahead. *Business Strategy and the Environment, 29*(8), 3006–3024.

Gorokhova, T., Kravchenko, M., Muterko, H., Korostova, I., & Lukash, M. (2024). Exploring the integration of circular economy and digitalization: current research progress and trends. *Amazonia Investiga, 13*(73), 297–306. Retrieved from https://doi.org/10.34069/AI/2024.73.01.25

Grafström, J., & Aasma, S. (2021). Breaking circular economy barriers. *Journal of Cleaner Production, 292*, Article 126002.

Guzzo, D., Trevisan, A. H., Echeveste, M., & Costa, J. M. H. (2019). Circular innovation framework: Verifying conceptual to practical decisions in sustainability-oriented product-service system cases. *Sustainability, 11*, 3248.

Hadi, S. P., Prabawani, B., & Qomariah, A. (2021). Circular initiatives for industrial sustainability. *E3S Web of Conferences, 317,* 01078. https://doi.org/10.1051/e3sconf/202131701078

Ingemarsdotter, E., Jamsin, E., Kortuem, G., & Balkenende, R. (2019). Circular strategies enabled by the internet of things—A framework and analysis of current practice. *Sustainability, 11*, 5689.

Jensen, H. H. (2024). *How manufacturers could lead the way in building the circular economy.* World Economic Forum. https://www.weforum.org/agenda/2024/02/how-manufacturers-could-lead-the-way-in-building-the-circular-economy/

Kazançoglu, Y., Ada, E., Ozturkoglu, Y., & Ozbiltekin, M. (2020). Analysis of the barriers to urban mining for resource melioration in emerging economies. *Resources Policy, 68*, Article 101768.

Khan, S., Zaman, S. I., & Mubarik, S. (2023). Obstacles in disruption and adoption of green supply chain management (GSCM) practices by manufacturing industries. In Qudrat-Ullah, H., & Ali, S. I. (Eds.), *Advanced technologies and the management of disruptive supply chains* (pp. 165–183). Springer, Cham. https://doi.org/10.1007/978-3-031-45229-1_7

Kirchherr, J., Hekkert, M., Bour, R., Huijbrechtse-Truijens, A., Kostense-Smit, E., & Muller, J. (2017). *Breaking the barriers to the circular economy* (White Paper). European Circular Economy Stakeholder Platform. Retrieved from https://circulareconomy.europa.eu/platform/sites/default/files/171106_white_paper_breaking_the_barriers_to_the_circular_economy_w hite_paper_vweb-14021.pdf

Kristoffersen, E., Blomsma, F., Mikalef, P., & Li, J. (2020). The smart circular economy: A digital-enabled circular strategies framework for manufacturing companies. *Journal of Business Research, 120*, 241–261.

Madu, C. N. (2022). Sustainable manufacturing: Strategic issues in green manufacturing. In C. N. Madu (Ed.), *Handbook of environmentally conscious manufacturing*. Springer, Cham. https://doi.org/10.1007/978-3-030-75834-9_1

Meidl, R. A. (2021). *Waste management and the energy transition: The path to sustainability and a circular economy.* Baker Institute for Public Policy. Retrieved from https://www.bakerinstitute.org/research/waste-management-and-energy-transition-path-sustainability-and-circular-economy-1

Mentink, B., 2014. *Circular Business Model Innovation: A process framework and a tool for business model innovation in a circular economy.* Delft University of Technology & Leiden University.

Pham, T. T., Kuo, T. -C., Tseng, M. -L., Tan, R. R., Tan, K., Ika, D. S., & Lin, C. J. (2019). Industry 4.0 to accelerate the circular economy: A case study of electric scooter sharing. *Sustainability, 11,* 6661.

Pieroni, M. P., McAloone, T. C., & Pigosso, D. C. (2019). Business model innovation for circular economy and sustainability: A review of approaches. *Journal of Cleaner Production, 215*, 198–216.

Rajput, S., & Singh, S. P. (2019). Connecting circular economy and industry 4.0. *International Journal of Information Management, 49*, 98–113.

Raynor, M. E., & Cotteleer, M. J. (2015). The more things change: Value creation, value capture, and the Internet of Things. *Deloitte Review*, pp.50–65. https://doi.org/10.1089/pho.2011.9920

Rosa, P., Sassanelli, C., Urbinati, A., Chiaroni, D., & Terzi, S. (2020). Assessing relations between circular economy and industry 4.0: A systematic literature review. *International Journal of Production Research, 58*, 1662–1687.

Ruda, M. V., Yaremchuk, T. S., & Bortnikova, M. (2021). Circular economy in Ukraine: Adaptation to European Integration. *Lviv Polytechnic National University Science Journal*. Retrieved from https://science.lpnu.ua/smeu/all-volumes-and-issues/volume-3-number-1-2021/circular-economy-ukraine-adaptation-european

Saarinen, A., & Aarikka-Stenroos, L. (2023). Financing-related drivers and barriers for circular economy business: Developing a conceptual model from a field study. *Circular Economy and Sustainability, 3*(3), 1187–1211. https://doi.org/10.1007/s43615-022-00222-5

Shpak, N., Kuzmin, O., Melnyk, O., Ruda, M., & Sroka, W. (2020). Implementation of a circular economy in Ukraine: The context of European integration. *Resources, 9*, 96. Retrieved from https://doi.org/10.3390/resources9080096.

Stankovic, M., Gupta, R., & Figueroa, J. (2017). Industry 4.0 - *Opportunities behind the challenge*. UNIDO Background Paper.

Tanveer, M., Khan, S. A. R., Umar, M., & et al. (2022). Waste management and green technology: Future trends in circular economy leading towards environmental sustainability. *Environmental Science and Pollution Research, 29*(58), 80161–80178. https://doi.org/10.1007/s11356-022-23238-8

Tseng, M.-L., Tan, R. R., Chiu, A. S. F., Chien, C.-F., & Kuo, T. C. (2018). Circular economy meets industry 4.0: Can big data drive industrial symbiosis? *Resources, Conservation and Recycling, 131*, 146–147.

Udovyk, O. (2021). *Testing circular economy approaches in Ukraine*. United Nations Development Programme. https://www.undp.org/ukraine/blog/testing-circular-economy-approaches-ukraine

World Bank. (2022, December 6). *World Bank releases its first report on the circular economy, says decoupling growth from resource use in Europe achievable within a decade*. https://www.worldbank.org/en/news/press-release/2022/12/06/world-bank-releases-its-first-report-on-the-circular-economy-says-decoupling-growth-from-resource-use-in-europe-achievab

Yadav, G., Luthra, S., Jakhar, S. K., Mangla, S. K., & Rai, D. P. (2020). A framework to overcome sustainable supply chain challenges through solution measures of industry 4.0 and circular economy: An automotive case. *Journal of Cleaner Production, 254*, 120112.

Zott, C., Amit, R., & Massa, L. (2011). The business model: Recent developments and future research. *Journal of Management, 37*, 1019–1042. https://doi.org/10.1177/0149206311406265

Building a Circular Economy Strategy in the Healthcare Organisations: The Role of the Group Purchasing Organisations

Michela Bobini, Caterina Cavicchi, Mario Del Vecchio, Anna Romiti, and Emidia Vagnoni

Abstract The UN strategy 2030 calls all actors to contribute to the achievement of the Sustainable Development Goals; among them the sustainability of healthcare systems represents a relevant target as they are considered responsible for 4%–5% of the emissions of greenhouse gases worldwide (Rodríguez-Jiménez et al., Journal of Advanced Nursing 79:2830–2844, 2023).

In England, over 1.4% of supply chain emissions are due to single-use devices, some of which could be refurbished and reused, saving both carbon and money. The healthcare systems could reduce emissions from their supply chain in three ways: more efficient use of supplies; low-carbon substitutions and product innovation; and by ensuring our suppliers are decarbonising their own processes (Delivering a "Net Zero" National Health Services, Policy paper. https://www.england.nhs.uk/greenernhs.).

To this regard, the extension of the lifetime of medical equipment and devices through practices like sharing, maintenance, repair, and refurbishment have been

M. Bobini · M. Del Vecchio
SDA Bocconi School of Management, 10 Via Sarfatti, 20136 Milan, Italy
e-mail: michela.bobini@unibocconi.it

M. Del Vecchio
e-mail: mario.delvecchio@unifi.it; mario.delvecchio@unibocconi.it

C. Cavicchi · E. Vagnoni
Department of Economics and Management, University of Ferrara, 11 Via Voltapaletto, 44121 Ferrara, Italy
e-mail: cvccrn@unife.it

E. Vagnoni
e-mail: emidia.vagnoni@unife.it

M. Del Vecchio · A. Romiti (✉)
Department of Experimental and Clinical Medicine, University of Florence, 48 viale Morgagni, 50134 Florence, Italy
e-mail: anna.romiti@unifi.it

I. Bartuseviciene et al. (eds.), *Building Resilience Through Digital Transformation and Sustainable Innovation*, Springer Proceedings in Business and Economics,
https://doi.org/10.1007/978-3-031-90054-9_10

acknowledged (Wuyts, W. et al., 2020. Circular economy as a COVID-19 cure? Resources, Conservation and Recycling, Vol. 162, 105,016.).

The healthcare industry is characterised by a complex supply chain; this is key to contribute to the overall performance of the industry and to support the successful implementation of circular economy (CE) strategies (Hazen et al., The International Journal of Logistics Management 32:510–537, 2021). In this context, the relationship between the supply chain members is a key determinant of the healthcare system. The original equipment manufacturers and healthcare organisations often see a third actor in the group purchasing organisations, an intermediate entity responsible for specific functions.

In the healthcare setting, a variety of authors have attempted to address how the CE practice may contribute to improve the environmental sustainability (Quintana-Gallardo et al., Polymers 15:1130, 2023). Nevertheless, the implementation of CE practices faces several challenges: for instance, recycling hazardous waste requires a huge revision of the collection infrastructure and logistics, accompanied by a risk-cost–benefit and environmental impact analysis (Wuyts, W. et al., 2020. Circular economy as a COVID-19 cure? Resources, Conservation and Recycling, Vol. 162, 105,016.). Other barriers to the CE in healthcare include liability, costs, and complexity of developing and an in-house reprocessing infrastructure for single-use devices, obsolescence, and practices to discourage the disassembly by original equipment manufacturers, lack of clear standards for reusable devices reprocessing, lack of clarity on devices' infection risks (MacNeill et al., Health Affairs 39:2088–2097, 2020).

Consequently, fostering the transition of healthcare systems towards a circular economy requires collaboration among various stakeholders (MacNeill et al., Health Affairs 39:2088–2097, 2020).

Based on the above premise the aim of the paper is to investigate the extent to which specific green and CE practices could be extensively routed in the government funded healthcare system and the challenges experienced in the public sector.

To this regard, a qualitative study has been designed and conducted in the Italian healthcare setting, where the healthcare system is government funded, diversified on a regional base, and highly regulated. Data have been collected through online semi-structured interviews to leading actors of purchasing intermediate entities in the sector.

The interviews have been recorded and transcribed and analysed through deductive thematic analysis approach (Fereday and Muir-Cochrane, International Journal of Qualitative Methods 5:80–92, 2006) to provide an overview of the extent to which it is feasible for public healthcare system to adopt CE and greening actions to contribute, through their procurement process, more effectively to mitigate the climate change.

The study contributes to the stream of literature about sustainability management providing a discussion of the type of CE practices relevant to enhance the contribution of the public healthcare system to the sustainable goals, from a managerial perspective.

Keywords Circular economy · Group purchasing organisations · Refurbishment · Supply chain · Healthcare systems · Environmental sustainability

jel Classification Q01 Sustainable development · Q53 Air pollution · Water pollution · Noise · Hazardous waste · Solid waste · Recycling · I1 health

1 Introduction

The World Health Organisation (WHO, 2021) forecasts that between 2030 and 2050, the impacts of environmental factors are projected to result in roughly 250,000 additional deaths annually. The WHO's Global Strategy on Health, Environment, and Climate Change underscores the critical intersection of health and environmental conditions. This strategy asserts that enhancing environmental health could markedly reduce global mortality and disease burden. Key elements for this enhancement include maintaining a stable climate, ensuring clean air and water availability, safe chemical usage, effective sanitation and waste management, and biodiversity preservation.

The healthcare system is vital in safeguarding the health and welfare of a nation's population. Encompassing a broad network of organisations, these systems deliver crucial healthcare services across diverse geographic regions. Despite their essential role in national development, healthcare systems also contribute significantly to environmental degradation, primarily through substantial carbon emissions and waste production. The healthcare sector, as the largest emitter of CO_2 among service sectors and a significant waste producer—particularly of plastics and hazardous materials—faces the dual challenge of mitigating potential environmental contamination and harnessing its capabilities to reduce these impacts through strategic operational changes. According to Rodríguez-Jiménez et al. (2023), healthcare systems worldwide are responsible for approximately 4–5% of global greenhouse gas emissions, largely due to their extensive infrastructure, waste generation, and consumption of medical supplies.

The commitment to mitigate healthcare's environmental impact is gaining global momentum. The United Nations' 2030 Agenda highlights the Sustainable Development Goals (SDGs), with a particular focus on the sustainability of healthcare systems. The recent global disruptions, including the COVID-19 pandemic, have accentuated the vulnerabilities of healthcare systems and underscored the need for resilient, climate-adaptive strategies to mitigate environmental and public health damage, increase healthcare costs, and expose supply-chain vulnerabilities as discussed by Fournier et al. (2022) and MacNeill et al. (2020). In addition, following the United Nations Climate Change Conference (COP26), over 50 countries have pledged to develop health systems that are climate-resilient and low-carbon. A notable example is the United Kingdom's National Health Service (NHS), which has committed to achieving net zero carbon emissions by 2040 for direct emissions and by 2045 for indirect emissions from its supply chain. This commitment is part of a broader strategy aimed at achieving decarbonization across the economy by 2050. The NHS estimates that over 1.4% of supply chain emissions are due to single-use devices, some of which could be refurbished and reused, saving both carbon and money. Healthcare systems can reduce emissions from their supply chain in three ways: by using suppliers more efficiently, making low-carbon substitutions and product innovation, and ensuring that suppliers are decarbonising their own processes (NHS, 2020). In Europe, including the European Union (EU), several member states such as Italy, Sweden, and Germany, as well as the UK and Norway, have implemented initiatives or issued guidelines to foster a circular economy, as exemplified by COM (2015). Green public procurement is regarded as a significant strategy to achieve these objectives, involving the procurement of goods, services, and works that have a minimized environmental footprint. Notably, some of these procurement efforts are specifically directed at suppliers within the healthcare sector, which is significant considering that healthcare expenditure constitutes approximately 9% of governmental spending across OECD countries.

Among the different approaches to achieve sustainability targets, Circular Economy is highly emphasized by both scholars and practitioners. CE has been defined as "an economic system that uses the reuse of products and materials as a starting point, as well as the conservation of natural resources, where economic, social, and environmental values are relevant in all aspects of the system" (Reike et al., 2018; van Boerdonk et al., 2021). CE practices have been identified as beneficial for business as it aims to minimize environmental degradation and energy consumption without hampering economic growth or social and technical progress (Marconi, Germani et al., 2019). It is expected that CE practices may promote business opportunities, increase job opportunities, and minimize waste and material consumption.

To this regard, the extension of the lifetime of medical equipment and devices through practices like sharing, maintenance, repair, and refurbishment (Guzzo et al., 2020; Wuyts et al., 2020) have been acknowledged by the literature. Furthermore, there are evidence of healthcare firms adopting circular strategies (Van Boerdonk et al., 2021; Kirchherr et al., 2017; Lieder & d Rashid, 2016) to design and provide medical devises based on reprocessing and to adopt refurbishment solutions (Wilson & Kishk, 2013). For instance, Short et al. (2010) addressed new build initiatives and refurbishment to reduce carbon emissions showing more sustainable energy consumption figures for the refurbishment cases.

The healthcare industry is characterised by a complex supply chain; this is key to contribute to the overall performance of the industry and to support the successful implementation of circular economy strategies (Hazen et al., 2021). In this context, the relationship between the supply chain members is a key determinant of the healthcare system; the original equipment manufacturers and healthcare organisations often see a third actor in the group purchasing organisations (GPOs).

The Circular Economy (CE) approach can be effectively applied across multiple stages of the healthcare supply chain (Mahjoob et al., 2023). The authors have outlined three pivotal actions for optimizing waste management from a CE perspective.

Firstly, there's the management of reuse, which can be seamlessly integrated between the disposal and healthcare provider stages. Secondly, remanufacturing emerges as a crucial step, occurring between the healthcare provider stage and the manufacturing stage. Lastly, recycling plays a vital role wherein raw materials are returned to the supplier for recycling purposes, positioned between the healthcare provider and supply stages.

Therefore, the role of Group Purchasing Organisations (GPOs) in healthcare in Italy, which act as intermediary between healthcare organisations and various stages of the supply chain (supplier and manufacturers), has become increasingly critical in implementing CE practices such as reuse, remanufacturing and recycling. As key actors in the healthcare supply chain, GPOs have the unique capability to influence and enact sustainable practices across the sector. Thus, the role of GPOs can be particularly relevant in terms of Sustainable Public Procurement' choices. Based on this approach (Walkers & Phillips, 2008), GPOs have the opportunity to balance and consider environmental, social, and economic objectives in their procurement decisions. By leveraging their considerable purchasing power, GPOs can promote environmentally friendly products and services, thus driving the adoption of CE principles within the healthcare organisations. CE practices not only aim to reduce waste and material consumption but also strive to minimize environmental degradation and energy usage without compromising economic growth or technological and social progress.

Research focusing on the role of public sector green procurement in the development of the circular economy is still in its early stages (Wijayasundara et al., 2022). To address this gap, a qualitative study has been designed and conducted in the Italian healthcare setting, where the healthcare systems is government funded, diversified on a regional base, and highly regulated. The GPOs have been defined as intermediate entities responsible for specific functions (such as purchasing, logistics, etc.) depending on the regional regulation. Data have been collected through online semi structured interviews to leading actors of purchasing organisations in the sector. The overall population of the GPOs is made of 25 entities (Baldino et al., 2023), each of them characterised by a specific governance structure.

Based on the above premise, the aim of the paper is to investigate the extent to which specific green and CE practices could be extensively routed in the government funded healthcare system and the challenges that the public sector experiences.

The study contributes to the stream of literature about sustainability management providing a discussion of the type of CE practices relevant to enhance the contribution of the public healthcare system to the sustainable goals, from a managerial perspective, and of the challenges associated with the adoption of such practices. The paper is structured as follows: Sect. 2 delves into the academic debate on *Circular Economy and Public Green Procurement in Healthcare*; Sect. 3 provides an overview of the Italian healthcare system and the dynamics related to procurement processes; Sect. 4 outlines the methodology employed in the study; Sect. 5 presents the findings and discussion; and finally, Sect. 6 offers concluding reflections.

2 Circular Economy and Public Green Procurement in Healthcare

In the healthcare setting, authors have addressed how circular economy practices can contribute to improving environmental sustainability. Quintana-Gallardo et al. (2023) considered the environmental impact of disposable nonwoven fabrics to identify sustainable solutions. Dolatab et al. (2022) presented an approach to enhance the circular supply chain in intensive care units, while Harding et al. (2021) investigated how to reduce operating room waste through circular economy practices.

Nevertheless, the implementation of CE practices faces several challenges. For instance, recycling hazardous waste, such as face masks, requires a significant revision of collection infrastructure and logistics, accompanied by a risk-cost–benefit and environmental impact analysis (Wuyts et al., 2020). Other barriers to CE in healthcare include liability issues, costs, and the complexity of developing in-house reprocessing infrastructure for single-use devices, obsolescence, practices that discourage disassembly by original equipment manufacturers, lack of clear standards for reprocessing reusable devices, and ambiguity regarding the infection risks of these devices (MacNeill et al., 2020).

In the public sector, adopting a circular economy approach can significantly impact the environmental sustainability, particularly when integrated into the organisational procurement processes. Public procurement, the process by which the public sector purchases goods, services, or tasks from the private sector, represents an average of 13% to 20% of GDP (World Bank, 2020). In Italy, the healthcare sector had the highest number of tenders in the past year (2022) for medical equipment, pharmaceuticals, and personal care products, totaling 1,257 tenders. In terms of value, this sector ranks second, with tenders worth 2.4 billion euros, only behind the construction sector (https://opentender.eu/it/dashboards/market-analysis). The importance of the healthcare sector for the implementation of Green Public Procurement (GPP) has been emphasized by various authors (Ahsan & Rahman, 2017; Chiarini et al., 2017).

Unfortunately, the introduction of CE practices in the procurement processes of public healthcare organisations faces several limitations. Ahsan and Rahman (2017) developed a framework for addressing challenges in implementing GPP based on previous research on public and sustainable procurement. This framework identifies five categories of challenges for the public health sector: (i) familiarity with green issues, (ii) organisational green issues, (iii) perceived cost/benefits by the organisation, (iv) government, NGO, and public-related issues, and (v) supplier issues. In their research on the Australian public health sector, they found that the most critical issues are strategic, including the lack of legislation on green procurement, insufficient support from senior management, lack of government incentives for green purchases, and inadequate financial support.

In public health procurement, another barrier can stem from the primary objectives of the purchasing group, upon which organisations rely for a significant portion of their procurement processes. Research indicates that supplier and product choices are often driven by a priority on cost savings, which takes precedence over environmental considerations (Bentahar et al., 2023). The authors observed three distinct approaches to Green Supply Chain (GSC) adoption in healthcare settings, varying in the degree of GSC practices diffusion.

A reactive approach exhibits a low level of GSC adoption, primarily influenced by legislation. A receptive approach entails a moderate level of GSC diffusion, involving only a few aspects of purchasing. Conversely, a proactive approach reflects a high level of GSC adoption across various supply chain domains. Therefore, the purchasing group, responsible for a significant portion of health organisations' procurement, can play a pivotal role by opting for a proactive approach to implementing green supply chain practices (Bentahar et al., 2023).

A proactive approach necessitates innovation within procurement processes, such as incorporating green criteria into the supplier selection criteria for tender submissions. However, these innovations are currently experiencing limited adoption and, notably, carry little weight in the final supplier selection decision (Igarashi et al., 2015). This is largely attributed to the lack of environmental knowledge and awareness among public procurers, coupled with their risk-averse behavior, which discourages the inclusion of environmental criteria in supplier selection (Cheng et al., 2018).

Furthermore, budgetary constraints pose a significant challenge, as green products are often perceived as more expensive from a short-term perspective.

To overcome these barriers, cooperation among various stakeholders—including hospitals, healthcare providers, regulators, industry representatives, purchasing organisations, and professional bodies—is imperative to facilitate the transition of healthcare systems towards green procurement and Circular Economy practices (MacNeill et al., 2020). This collaboration is essential for fostering innovation investment in green products, leveraging the purchasing power of public authorities to drive sustainable procurement practices (Li & Geiser, 2005).

3 Institutional Background

The Italian National Health Service (SSN) was conceived by Legislative Decree No. 502/92 as a regionalised healthcare system. Since the 1990s, a process of progressive devolution of responsibilities to the Regions in the management and financing of healthcare has been initiated. This process culminated in 2001 with the amendment of Title V of the Constitution, which entrusted the Regions with the "protection of health," while the State was tasked with determining and monitoring the essential levels of care to be uniformly guaranteed throughout the national territory. With the reform of Title V, the responsibility for economic and financial balance was de jure attributed to the Regions. Concomitant with these institutional changes, a proliferation of intermediary entities has emerged within the Regional Health Services (SSR). These intermediary entities were established to pursue two main objectives. Firstly, the new institutional bodies were created to support the regional Health Departments in the exercise of governance functions, understood as the overall coordination of the system of healthcare providers, and to provide support through the centralisation of typically back-office technical-operational services, as purchasing function.

The objective of rationalising expenditure has profoundly impacted the methods of acquiring production factors, considering that expenditure on goods and services is the largest item of expenditure for the Italian national healthcare system (SSN), even exceeding personnel costs. Centralisation can be accounted among the main directions of change in procurement policy; this would take shape through the establishment and strengthening of national and regional procurement centers and/or the promotion of consortia. Centralisation over time has led to the establishment of specialised entities at the national, regional and territorial levels.

The intermediary entities performing procurement functions in the healthcare sector in the Italian regions are depicted in the Table 1. In addition to the entities listed in the table, the following procurement centers operating within the public sector operate in the country: SUA Abruzzo, SUA Calabria, CUC Molise, Direzione Acquisti Regione Lazio, SUA Marche, CUC Sicilia, APAC Trento, and SUA Basilicata.

Traditionally, the purchasing bodies have been responsible for managing tenders, leaving individual entities responsible for analysing needs and managing and executing contracts. Through standardization, efforts have been made to reduce the variance in procurement behaviors (tenders, specifications, contractual clauses), the

Table 1 Italian intermediary entities

Name	Region	Sector	Date of institution
ARIC	Abruzzo	Public	2000
Azienda 0	Calabria	Healthcare	2021
Soresa	Campania	Public	2004
Lepida ScpA	Emilia Romagna	Public	2019
Intercenter	Emilia Romagna	Public	2004
ARCS	FVG	Healthcare	2019
Lazio.0	Lazio	Healthcare	2021
A.li.sa	Liguria	Healthcare	2007
ARIA	Lombardia	Public	2019
ACP	PA Bolzano	Public	2011
SCR	Piemonte	Public	2007
Azienda Zero	Piemonte	Healthcare	2022
InnovaPuglia SpA	Puglia	Public	2008
ARES	Sardegna	Healthcare	2020
ESTAR	Toscana	Healthcare	2014
Umbria salute e servizi	Umbria	Healthcare	2014
Azienda Zero	Veneto	Healthcare	2016

diversity of which is not always based on genuine differentiation needs. The underlying assumption of this reasoning is that standardising tenders and specifications allows for the comparison of procurement results among administrations, reducing informational asymmetry and creating reference benchmarks, mainly aimed at cost containment.

4 Methodology and Methods

Given the research aim to investigate the extent to which specific green and CE practices could be routed in the government funded healthcare system and the challenges of the public sector setting, a qualitative study has been designed and conducted in the Italian healthcare system.

The Italian healthcare system has been considered a relevant setting for the study as it is government funded, thus the role played by the public sector to adopt sustainability practices might be key compared to other context; furthermore, it is a highly regulated and diversified system on a regional base, signifying that the effect of the regulatory context might be explored and eventually different approached to CE captured. The study focuses on key actors playing a critical role regarding the procurement process in healthcare: the intermediary entities as purchasing organisations.

The selected intermediary entities are from three highly populated regions in Italy—Veneto, Toscana, and Emilia Romagna —which are recognized as advanced examples of regional procurement practices within the country (Marraccini, 2014). Moreover, these regions demonstrate high levels of centralized purchasing within their healthcare systems, which is a critical factor in understanding how sustainability practices are integrated. Specifically, the percentage of centralized purchases as a proportion of total regional procurement is very high in all three regions in 2022: 93% in Toscana, 70% in Veneto and 65% in Emilia Romagna (Vecchi, 2023). These figures underscore the strategic importance of centralized procurement and make these regions ideal for studying the adoption of CE strategies in a highly regulated public sector environment. It is also important to note that the intermediary entities selected for the study operate exclusively within the healthcare sector. This deliberate choice allows the study to isolate awareness and challenges specifically related to CE practices in healthcare, as opposed to other intermediary entities that serve multiple areas of public administration. By focusing on organizations solely dedicated to healthcare procurement, the study ensures a more targeted and relevant understanding of sustainability practices within this critical sector. Data have been collected through online semi-structured interviews to leading actors of three purchasing organisations, each of them running the procurement in a single region. Furthermore, archival data from the purchasing organisations' website have been collected to provide a more holistic understanding of their approach, objectives, purchase contracts (Dunwoodie et al., 2023). An interview guide, outlined in Table 2, was designed to facilitate data collection by focusing on key areas such as the general understanding the role

Table 2 Interview guide

Area of inquiry	Interview questions
Role of the intermediate entity and interviewee's experience	• What is your current role within the company, and what positions have you held in the past? • What are the main activities carried out by the organization you work for?
Environmental sustainability and organizational approach	• What is your organization's approach to environmental sustainability? • Do you personally support these practices?
Adoption of circular economy strategies	• Does your organization consider purchasing refurbished products, i.e., previously used and renewed items, for specific product categories? To what extent is this practice implemented?
Barriers and enablers of CE strategies and more in general green procurement	• What are the primary obstacles to the adoption of green procurement practices, particularly those related to Circular Economy (CE) strategies, within your organization? • What factors do you consider crucial in promoting the integration of environmental sustainability into procurement practices?

of intermediary entities, their approaches to supplier selection, the degree to which Circular Economy (CE) strategies are being adopted, and the challenges associated with implementing CE practices in this context. The interviews have been conducted with the manager responsible for planning purchases at Intercent-ER; the director of Department of Pharmaceutical and Logistics and the director of the Department of Health Technologies at Estar; the director of the Procurement unit at Azienda Zero.

The all interviews lasted for 4.5 h. The interviews have been recorded and transcribed and analysed through deductive thematic analysis approach (Fereday & Muir-Cochrane, 2006) to provide an overview of the extent to which it is feasible for public healthcare system to adopt CE actions to contribute more effectively to mitigate the climate change.

5 The Findings and Discussion

Legislation has strongly influenced the green orientation of procurement organisations both by providing incentives and by setting limits. From the point of view of enhancing the green procurement, an important incentive came from the adoption of the recovery plan; based on this plan, the European Union granted funds based on the adherence to specific green criteria.

In the opposite direction is the transposition by the Italian law of the EU regulation 2017/745 and 746; based on this, according to D. Lgs 5/8/22 n.137, in Italy reconditioning of disposable devices and further use is prohibited. This regulation significantly restricts the development of CE practices.

Beyond the restrictions provided by the public procurement regulatory framework, the intermediary entities explored prove the attempts to enhance both green public procurement practices and circular economy ones. The inclusion of green criteria to choose the services and products' providers is considered in the three experiences, the Estar in Tuscany, the Intercent-ER in Emilia Romagna and Azienda Zero in Veneto. This is done wedging into the gap left by the national regulation in terms of 'essential' green criteria which are twofold: the basic specifications (to comply with the standard nationally defined) and the further specifications (that might be used to better score environmentally friendly providers).

The subsections 5.1, 5.2 and 5.3 provides a snapshot of the experience of each intermediary entities investigated.

5.1 Tuscany Region Intermediary Entity: ESTAR

ESTAR, the Technical Administrative Support Entity for Tuscan Healthcare, is an intermediary entity established in 2014 (Regional Law No. 26 of 2014) and became operational in 2015. Currently, ESTAR undertakes a wide range of activities, including procurement of goods and services, warehouse and distribution logistics, information and communication technologies, healthcare technologies, competitive and selective procedures for recruiting healthcare personnel, payroll processes for healthcare staff, and management of tender procedures for maintenance, disposal, concession, and leasing of healthcare property assets. The process leading to the establishment of ESTAR began in the early 2000s when the Tuscany Region created a centralised system for purchasing goods and services and distributing consumer goods for healthcare facilities. Specifically, in 2002, three Consortia of Vast Areas (CAVs) were established: Centro, Nord-Ovest, and Sud-Est. In 2005, these Consortia were transformed into Entities for Technical-Administrative Services of Vast Areas (ESTAVs). Subsequently, the three ESTAVs were unified into a single intermediary entity named ESTAR, to which an increasing number of specialised technical functions were assigned.

The main actions undertaken by ESTAR in terms of Green Public Procurement (GPP) can be attributed to three areas that will be shown separately below: structural and technology park investment; investments in robotics; purchase of goods and services.

In terms of structural and technology park investment, in recent years Estar's focus on green procurement has been significantly influenced by regulations tied to funding from European frameworks, particularly the Next Generation EU initiative aimed at supporting countries affected by the pandemic. To be eligible for these funds, certain priorities must be met, such as dedicating at least 30% of the NextGenerationEU Recovery Plan to supporting climate change and green projects (EU commission).

In Italy, the "National Recovery and Resilience Plan" outlines the objectives, reforms, and investments to be achieved using European funds. The plan aims to make Italy a more equitable, green, and inclusive country, with a stronger, more competitive, dynamic and innovative economy. Notably, at least 37% of the EU funding must support the green transition.

To access EU funding, the Tuscany region devised a plan (Piano Operativo Regionale) identifying the required funds and their intended purposes. This Plan includes investments in healthcare sector aimed at supporting green projects such as energy-efficient buildings and the digital modernization of hospital technology parks. The procurement criteria for these projects prioritize environmental sustainability, guided by principles such as "Do no significant harm" based on the EU Taxonomy for sustainable finance.

About investments in robotics Estar's attention to the environment matter is proven by the evaluation criteria for technical offer in recent tenders, such as the procurement of robotic surgical systems (Resolution of the general director n. 227 of 26/05/2023). These criteria include assessing the environmental impact of the equipment, particularly focusing on energy consumption levels and adherence to CE practices. Additionally, there's an emphasis on multi-purpose instruments to reduce waste generated from equipment. In summary, when organising the tender there is the possibility to assign a weight to the environmental impact of the equipment, with 9 points out of the 75 total. This weight concerns the evaluation of three aspects, each of which can be assigned up to a maximum of 3 points. Two of the criteria concern energy consumption levels, and one refers to CE practices. Specifically, the first criterion concerns the power consumed by the equipment in operation. The second criterion concerns the power consumed by the equipment in standby mode. The third criterion concerns multi-purpose instruments, with a focus on reducing waste from equipment. For this criterion, the lower weight of waste generated annually in relation to the total of surgical procedures in Urology and Gynecology will be positively evaluated based on a quantitative score deduced from a mathematical formula.

Considering the purchase of goods and services, Estar's commitment to green procurement is also reflected in tender design, such as the inclusion of green and socially responsible criteria in the evaluation of suppliers for the purchase of medical gloves, a product that is highly polluting. These criteria go beyond legal requirements, demonstrating Estar's proactive stance towards sustainability. Aligned with this, out of the 70 points assigned to the various criteria, in same case (which differ according to the type of gloves) up to 11% of points concern the compliance with green criteria: the low environmental impact and the reduction and disposal of waste; the limitation of polluting emissions; the presence of environmental sustainability plans; the recognition of third-party environmental sustainability bodies; the use of eco-sustainable packaging; third-party certifications for the adoption of ethical behaviors throughout the supply chain; membership in international collaborations and advanced audit programs (Fiumalbi et al., 2023; Determination of the director of the Department acquisition of goods and services of Estar, 2022).

Arpat, the regional environmental protection agency, provided guidance on defining the above-mentioned criteria, facilitating sustainability knowledge transfer in green practices.

Collaboration with other regions such as Umbria, aims to spread this environmentally conscious approach.

An interviewee also affirms that, although the path towards Green Public Procurement (GPP) and Socially Responsible Public Procurement (SRPP) has begun, it is not without significant obstacles. On the one hand, there is a lack of in-depth expertise within the institution, which needs to decide whether to "make or buy" green competencies. This means that Estar should decide whether to develop the skills internally or to acquire them externally in the future, as in this tender. On the other hand, the tender raised several issues in awarding the contract. The tender faced several appeals and access requests to the proceedings after the winner was identified, primarily due to the innovations expected from the tender for which the market was not yet ready as affirmed by an interviewee.

5.2 Emilia Romagna Region Intermediary Entity: Intercent-ER

In 2004 the Emilia Romagna region gave the birth to the Intercent-ER (Regional Law 24.5.2004 n.11), a regional agency created with the aim to improve the efficiency of the procurement function for the entire public sector in the region, especially in the healthcare one, the latter accounting for 80% of the value of the overall purchases. Although nowadays, the agency is well committed to the sustainability principles, its original drivers were related to efficiency, standardization of goods and services provided, and enhancement of the use of digital platforms to root the e-procurement practices in the public sector organisations.

The Agency accomplishes its functions given the national and European regulatory frameworks. To this regard the European Union has greatly promoted the introduction of environmental sustainability criteria in purchasing procedure since 2010. That has enhanced the national green public procurement plan and the definition of the essential green criteria (CAM) at the national level. Intercent-ER is a well-established organisation that is fully aware of its role as an intermediary agency at the centre of a network of players: the healthcare organisations as the main served sector on a side, and the enterprises, both large and small sized ones, being the producers of goods and services. The agency can affect the players' strategic criteria when introducing environmental sustainability criteria in their purchasing procedure (as from 2010) or even social sustainability criteria (for instance the employees protection and workplace safety compliance) as in the last few years. Considering the overall categories of goods and services that are part of the agency's business and that could fulfil the 'green' option, 92% of the purchase by Intercent-ER is the object of procedure that have at least one sustainable criterion. As a consequence of the above-mentioned commitment to the sustainability, the agency discloses both the procurement contracts and the sustainability related results in terms of impact on the emissions through the official website (amount of renewed electricity provided, transports, reused waste bins, reconditioned toner for printers, etc.).

When considering medical devises and equipment, for instance, it is needed to point out that the focus of the agency is mainly on services and goods functional to any public sector organisation. Nevertheless, the CE practices represent a challenge for such an organisation highly committed to the 2030 Agenda for different reasons. Firstly, the national regulation requires not to restrict the tenders to narrow the competition among enterprises; as a consequence, for some categories of products (such as reconditioned medical technologies) the availability of a few players only could compromise the purchasing procedure.

Secondly, the agency involves clinicians from the regional healthcare areas (three in the region, each of them comprising a few healthcare organisations) in a formal team to identify the 'specifications' for each product and service to be purchased. The clinicians' professional culture results to be a key determinant of the criteria adopted to identify the product or service's specifications. The clinicians might opt for products that would be 'better received' and accepted by the colleagues throughout the region. The process adopted to identify the products' specifications is consistent with one of the pillars of the agency mission, the standardization of the product and services used across the organisations, as this would leverage the efficiency criterion based on the economy of scale principles.

Thirdly, the project managers' approach might result in an impediment to adopt CE strategies. Tenders' project managers are mainly trained on the national regulation; therefore, they may lack to challenge the innovation of the process or to find out regulatory space to introduce new criteria to identify the products.

Beyond the above challenges associated to the operational procurement process of Intercent-ER as intermediary entity, some improvements might be identified to facilitate the adoption of CE strategies. It emerged that the definition of national criteria for reconditioned, reusable, recycled products would be an effective measure in a context that is highly related to the national regulatory framework. Alternatively, enhancing the CE culture among clinicians would be a desirable determinant of a change of practices to identify the products' specifications. Furthermore, supplementing the tenders' project manager with sustainability matters related to the procurement process might be another action to improve the CE strategy. For instance, those involved in managing tenders should be skilled in terms of life cycle assessment and methods of consultation of players functional to introduce products sustaining the circularity. Finally, it has emerged the option to pursue a gradual approach to the adoption of CE actions; for instance, a quota of purchases might be reserved to CE-related products, or a higher weight might be given to the enterprises offering CE-related products to facilitate their access to the market.

Overall, beyond the commitment to the sustainability principle, the adoption of circular economy actions seems to be opposed by the regulatory spaces, the culture of practices, and the original aim of the agency. However, some ways forward have been identified as consistent with the agency approach.

5.3 Veneto Region Intermediary Entity: Azienda Zero

In the Veneto Region, the governance of the Regional Health Service (SSR) follows a model that emerged from the centralisation of the decision-making process and the expenditure rationalization over recent years. Specifically, Regional Law no. 19 of October 25, 2016, introduced a new organisational structure, which included reducing the number of Local Health Units (Aziende ULSS) from twenty-one to nine, and establishing a new intermediate entity named Azienda Zero.

The governance functions of the health entities have been distributed between the Healthcare Department and Azienda Zero. The latter plays a role in centralized health management alongside numerous administrative functions which have been progressively absorbed from other entities. However, from the regulatory framework, it emerges that the Health and Social Care Sector of the Department continues to hold a directive role, by issuing regional guidelines and setting socio-health programming objectives that must be met by the Health Agencies, such as those concerning Essential Levels of care (LEA). Therefore, the responsibility for the governance of the regional health system remains with the Department, albeit technically supported by Azienda Zero. Specifically, the technocratic structure of Azienda Zero manages numerous technical-specialist activities, including centralized purchasing, personnel selection procedures, clinical risk management, the development of information systems and data flows, the management of accreditation procedures, warehouse and logistics, and Health Technology Assessment (HTA) domain. The CRAV is the unit within Azienda Zero that, as a regional procurement hub and central contracting authority, aims to optimize public spending of the Regional Health Service (SSR) through the centralized and standardized management of delegated purchasing functions. This includes reference to the annual planning of contractual activities and the subsequent rationalization of purchases, as well as managing the tender procedures for the company's own requirements.

In response to environmental sustainability, Azienda Zero strictly adheres to European legislation, implementing the essential green criteria (CAM) across all operations, thus integrating predetermined sustainability requirements. Within the context of the Central Regional Purchasing Agency (CRAV), there is provision for the procurement of refurbished products for specific types, particularly commodities such as recycled paper or recycled material packaging, which are indeed viable requests. However, the practice is not common in the field of medical devices, where attempts have been made, including costly procedures like harvesting from cadavers for prosthetic devices. Yet, regulatory challenges persist, as current laws do not comfortably permit the reuse of these items, causing concerns from both a regulatory and health safety perspective, despite multiple proposals.

It emerges from the interview how the transition to green procurement faces different impediments: regulatory frameworks; competency development; and the need to keep the market open while balancing environmental sustainability with other criteria in the procurement tenders. The staff at CRAV predominantly includes administrative profiles, thus two administrative directors and a lead pharmacist overseeing the pharmaceutical area, along with various employees skilled in administrative tasks. These team members are essential in drafting tender documents and managing technical groups tasked with developing specialized specifications. Technical support from clinicians and pharmacists is selected regionally from healthcare companies to bolster the development of tender documents. Mastery in environmental sustainability is critical and non-trivial. A cautious approach is necessary to avoid excessively constraining the market, as over-stringent criteria may limit the number of participating operators (enterprises), adding complexity from both technical and market analysis perspectives. The key challenge lies in the lack of expertise necessary to set and evaluate "green" criteria effectively. To address this, efforts are being made to involve environmental regulatory agencies (ARPAV) to enhance awareness and understanding of relevant issues.

6 Summary of Findings and Discussion

The explorative qualitative study on the adoption of circular economy actions to fulfill the sustainability strategy of the healthcare organisations from the perspective of the intermediary entities engaged with services and good procurement leaves a narrow space to CE to innovating the public procurement in healthcare. Nevertheless, the intermediary entities have shown commitment to the sustainability criteria; to this regard the driving force behind the integration of environmental sustainability seems to be predominantly the EU legislation. The interviewees clearly converged on the relevant role of the European Union policies and regulatory framework to introduce green criteria in the procurement practice. This is consistent with the results shown by Chiarini et al. (2017) whose study focused on the green public procurement from a different angle, the local healthcare organisations.

Additionally, the analysed purchasing groups attempt ad adopting proactive approaches towards the development of green policies (Bentahar et al., 2023) as some actions are taken with the regulatory space.

Given the peculiarities related to the public healthcare system, a government funded that needs to fulfill common principles although regionally organised, the regulation represents an impediment to adopt circular economy strategies with regard at the medical products.

Our study confirms that in the absence of predetermined standards, the implementation of a formal qualification process for suppliers enables the exploitation of the potential of public procurement opportunities for the implementation of circular economy actions (Alhola et al., 2019).

This is clearly based on safety and efficacy standards that needs to be fulfilled, and on risk management issues. Nevertheless, the evidence gathered prove the attempts of the intermediary entities to introduce CE with regard at different types of products, not medical ones. As from Guzzo et al. (2020) the healthcare sector is composed of devices with rather specific lifecycles and impacts: imaging equipment that eventually become electronic waste, sophisticated invasive devices that require sterilisation before reprocessing, and potentially infected single-use devices that hinder recycling possibilities. Furthermore, the EU and national regulation limit the adoption of such strategies.

Moreover, the development of green practices in the healthcare sector in Italy results from the expertise, knowledge, and awareness of decision-makers acting within the purchasing groups. This has been clearly stated by all interviewees; someone has also highlighted the cross-fertilization process that might arise from collaborating with environmental agencies to upgrade the procurement employees' skills and challenge the sustainability innovation of the process. Consistent with previous research, our findings confirm the benefits of fostering a workplace culture of innovation in influencing environmentally friendly choices (Gormly, 2014). As a matter of facts, scholars have begun to discuss the potential of knowledge, training and intellectual capital for the achievement of sustainability in public sector organisations only recently (Allee, 2000). In Italy, Botturi et al. (2015) argued that sustainable healthcare systems can be achieved if urgent action is taken, among the others, to develop professionals' competences devoted to innovation for sustainability.

Overall, a cultural change is needed to tackle the CE strategy and the sustainability principles from different perspectives, the clinicians and health professionals on a side and the procurement managers and enterprises on the other side. The intermediary entities represent the center of a network where the above players converge; thus, a common efforts and awareness is needed to innovate the procurement strategies.

7 Conclusion

This study explores the critical role of Group Purchasing Organizations (GPOs) in implementing Circular Economy (CE) strategies within government-funded healthcare systems, focusing on the Italian context. Despite increasing public pressure for sustainability, the full implementation of green procurement practices in the healthcare sector faces several obstacles.

These challenges include difficulties in translating environmental principles into regulatory frameworks relevant to the practice, which expose public administrators to risks and uncertainties. In absence of a clear and specific mandate, green procurement processes rely on the discretion, personal commitment, risk appetite and knowledge of the individuals responsible for purchasing process (Wijayasundara et al., 2023). There is a clear need for enhanced expertise and awareness among procurement managers, clinicians, and other healthcare professionals. The integration of CE strategies is impeded by a lack of specific training and a cultural shift towards sustainability (BeWell, 2023).

Moreover, sector-specific complexities, the absence of measurement systems, and competency gaps within purchasing groups pose significant hurdles. In the public healthcare sector, the lack of knowledge acts as a barrier to advancing greener procurement practices (Faracik, 2018) along with the absence of a structured evaluation process (Lindfors & Ammenberg, 2021), as demonstrated in previous studies across other sectors.

Furthermore, competing priorities, such as economic savings (which may not always align with green objectives) and equipment effectiveness (which can carry professional status implications) further complicate the transition to green procurement. Our study also confirmed that green procurement for a circular economy is perceived as time-consuming and requires additional efforts to justify any potential extra costs, as it competes with other non-environmental organisational priorities (Wijayasundara et al., 2023).

Addressing these challenges requires coordinated efforts to enhance regulatory clarity, develop measurement standards, build competency and balance competing priorities effectively.

The study contributes to unfold the complexity of the greening and CE actions in the healthcare organisations' supply chain, and more clearly on key players such as the intermediary entities. More studies on these entities would improve the identification of sustainability actions in the healthcare sector and raise awareness on the gaps to be filled.

This contribution presents the limitations associated to the research design that has been chosen. In particular, the research group conducted a few interviews with intermediary entities' managers, limiting the data gathering process. However, the empirical research on the topic, from the perspective of the intermediary entities, is a lack although their role to adopt practices to mitigate the climate change is an important one. A more in-depth study will be carried out in the future through a multiple case study approach to broaden the knowledge on the topic and deepen the understanding of the plus and mines of the circular economy actions considering different perspectives within the diversified governance structure of the entities.

Acknowledgements The authors thank the mangers from the group purchasing organisations interviewed, for their willingness to participate to the study.

References

Alhola, K., et al. (2019). Exploiting the potential of public procurement: Opportunities for circular economy. *Journal of Industrial Ecology, 23*(1), 96–109.

Allee, V. (2000). The value evolution: Addressing larger implications of an intellectual capital and intangibles perspective. *Journal of Intellectual Capital, 1*(1), 17–32.

Ahsan, K., & Rahman, S. (2017). Green public procurement implementation challenges in Australian public healthcare sector. *Journal of Cleaner Production, 152*, 181–197.

Baldino, L. et al. (2023). La diffusione e l'eterogeneità degli enti intermedi. In "Enti Intermediari SSR: elementi di studio ed analisi", *I quaderni di Monitor*, supplemento, pp. 23–28.

BeWell - Blueprint Alliance for a future health workforce strategy on digital and green skills. (2022, June). Skills Strategy for the digital & green upskilling and reskilling of the health and care workforce. https://bewell-project.eu/skills-strategy.

Bentahar, O., et al. (2023). A green supply chain taxonomy in healthcare: Critical factors for a proactive approach. *The International Journal of Logistics Management, 34*(1), 60–83.

van Boerdonk, P. J. M., et al. (2021). New business models in circular economy: A multiple case study into touch points creating customer values in health care. *Journal of Cleaner Production, 282*, Article 125375.

Botturi, D., et al. (2015). Investing in social capital in Emilia-Romagna region of Italy as a strategy for making public health work. *Social Capital: Global Perspectives* (pp. 197–219). Nova Science Publishers, Hauppauge, NY.

Cheng, W., et al. (2018). Green public procurement, missing concepts and future trends—A critical review. *Journal of Cleaner Production, 176*, 770–784.

Chiarini, A., et al. (2017). Public healthcare practices and criteria for a sustainable procurement: A comparative study between UK and Italy. *Journal of Cleaner Production, 162*, 391–399.

COM. (2015). 614 final. Comunicazione della commissione al parlamento europeo, al consiglio, al comitato economico e sociale europeo e al comitato delle regioni. *L'anello mancante - Piano d'azione dell'Unione europea per l'economia circolare*. https://eur-lex.europa.eu/legal-content/

Dolatabad, A. H., et al. (2022). Analyzing the key performance indicators of circular supply chains by hybrid fuzzy cognitive mapping and Fuzzy DEMATEL: Evidence from healthcare sector. *Environment, Development and Sustainability*. https://doi.org/10.1007/s10668-022-02535-9

Dunwoodie, K., et al. (2023). Qualitative interviewing in the field of work and organisational psychology: Benefits, challenges and guidelines for researchers and reviewers. *Applied Psychology, 72*(2), 863–889.

Faracik, B. (2018). Non-legal barriers to sustainable public procurement in Poland. *Eur. Procurement & Pub. Private Partnership L. Rev, 13*, 184.

Fereday, J., & Muir-Cochrane, E. (2006). Demonstrating rigor using thematic analysis: A hybrid approach of inductive and deductive coding and theme development. *International Journal of Qualitative Methods, 5*(1), 80–92.

Fiumalbi, E. et al. (2023). Green public procurement e socially responsible public procurement: le due dimensioni della sostenibilità, *Bollettino SIFO, Società italiana di farmacia ospedaliera e dei servizi farmaceutici delle aziende sanitarie, 69*(2), 79–80.

Fournier, A., et al. (2022). Impact of the COVID-19 pandemic on the mental health of professionals in 77 hospitals in France. *PLoS ONE, 17*(2), Article e0263666.

Gormly, J. (2014). What are the challenges to sustainable procurement in commercial semi-state bodies in Ireland? *Journal of Public Procurement, 14*(3), 395–445.

Guzzo, D., et al. (2020). Circular business models in the medical device industry: Paths towards sustainable healthcare. *Resources, Conservation and Recycling, 160*(104904), 1–15.

Harding, C., et al. (2021). Design opportunities to reduce waste in operating rooms. *Sustainability, 13*(4), 2207.

Hazen, B. T., et al. (2021). Supply chain management for circular economy: Conceptual framework and research agenda. *The International Journal of Logistics Management, 32*(2), 510–537.

Igarashi, M. et al. (2015). Investigating the anatomy of supplier selection in green public procurement. *Journal of Cleaner Production, 108*(Part A), 442–450.

Kirchherr, J., et al. (2017). Conceptualizing the circular economy: An analysis of 114 definitions. *Resources, Conservation and Recycling, 127*, 221–232.

Lieder, M., & Rashid, A. (2016). Towards circular economy implementation: A comprehensive review in context of manufacturing industry. *Journal of Cleaner Production, 115*, 36–51.

Li, L., & Geiser, K. (2005). Environmentally responsible public procurement (ERPP) and its implications for integrated product policy (IPP). *Journal of Cleaner Production, 13*(7), 705–715.

Lindfors, A., & Ammenberg, J. (2021). Using national environmental objectives in green public procurement: Method development and application on transport procurement in Sweden. *Journal of Cleaner Production, 280*, Article 124821.

MacNeill, A. J., et al. (2020). Transforming the medical device industry: Road map to a circular economy: Study examines a medical device industry transformation. *Health Affairs, 39*(12), 2088–2097.

Mahjoob, A. et al. (2023). Healthcare waste and sustainability: implications for a circular economy. *Sustainability, 15*(10, 7788), 1–20.

Marconi, M., et al. (2019). Applying data mining technique to disassembly sequence planning: A method to assess effective disassembly time of industrial products. *International Journal of Production Research, 57*(2), 599–623.

Marraccini, L. (2014). Le forniture sanitarie tramite le centrali di committenza. *Rivista di Diritto Amministrativo, 7*(8), 3–13.

NHS. (2020). *Delivering a "Net Zero" National Health Services,* Policy paper. https://www.england.nhs.uk/greenernhs.

Quintana-Gallardo, A., et al. (2023). The environmental impacts of disposable nonwoven fabrics during the COVID-19 pandemic: Case study on the Francesc de Borja Hospital. *Polymers, 15*(5), 1130.

Reike, D., et al. (2018). The circular economy: New or Refurbished as CE 3.0? Exploring controversies in the conceptualization of the circular economy through a focus on history and resource value retention options. *Resources, Conservation and Recycling, 135*, 246–264.

Rodríguez-Jiménez, L., et al. (2023). The carbon footprint of healthcare settings: A systematic review. *Journal of Advanced Nursing, 79*(8), 2830–2844.

Short, C. A., et al. (2010). Low energy refurbishment strategies for health buildings. *Journal of Building Performance Simulation, 3*(3), 197–216.

Vecchi, V., Cusumano, N., Callea, G., Amatucci, F., Brusoni, M., Zurlo, F., ... & Longo, F. (2023). Acquisti sanitari: Stato dell'arte e percorsi evolutivi verso logiche di valore. In Rapporto OASI 2023 (pp. 615–650). Egea.

Walker, H., & Phillips, W. (2008). Sustainable procurement: Emerging issues. *International Journal of Procurement Management, 2*(1), 41–61.

Wijayasundara, M. et al. (2022). Green procurement for a circular economy: What influences purchasing of products with recycled material and recovered content by public sector organisations? *Journal of Cleaner Production*, 377.

Wilson, G., & Kishk, M. (2011). Meeting sustainability requirements in the refurbishment of hospitals. In C. EGBU and E.C.W. LOU, eds. Proceedings of the 27th Annual ARCOM conference. 5–7 September 2011. ARCOM, pp. 1095–1104.

WHO. Published online 2021. https://www.who.int/news/item/09-11-2021-countries-commit-to-develop-climate-smart-health-care-at-cop26-un-climate-conference.

World Bank, Publised online 2020. Global Public Procurement Database (GPPD). https://www.globalpublicprocurementdata.org

Wuyts, W. et al. (2020). Circular economy as a COVID-19 cure? *Resources, Conservation and Recycling, 162,* 105016.

ESG and Business' Organisation: Evidence from Italy

Claudio D'Alonzo

Abstract The aim of this paper is to examine the impacts of Environmental, Social and Governance (ESG) factors on a business' organisation in Italy. The carrying out of a business and the subsequent increase in production creates, first of all, positive effects. However, it is crucial to verify if a business should be sustainable. The findings show that over the last few years attention towards social and environmental sustainability has increased both in the economic field and in all aspects of daily life; this is both a reply to environmental disasters that occurred and keep happening and a consequence of Covid-19 which made clear that there is a need for a future based on a different social and economic system. A sustainable business affects the organisation of a company; sustainability and ESG factors should be both parts of a business' organisation and its target. In addition, the findings of the research highlight that running a sustainable business requires a change in the planning of a company's structure, which has been created since the setting up of the company itself, and the adoption of necessary measures to achieve the objective of the company.

Keywords ESG · Sustainability · Business-organisation

JEL Classification Code K22

1 Introduction. The Issue of Sustainability

The carrying out of entrepreneurial activities and the consequent increase in production entails, first and foremost, positive effects. In fact, a flourishing business leads to an increase in the assets of single enterprises, which is related to an increase in the value of the investments made by the shareholders. However, the advantages outlined above are counterbalanced by negative elements that, in the long run, may far outweigh the positive ones; in other words, an immediate benefit may be followed

C. D'Alonzo (✉)
Catholic University Our Lady of Good Counsel, Tirana, Albania
e-mail: c.dalonzo@unizkm.al

I. Bartuseviciene et al. (eds.), *Building Resilience Through Digital Transformation and Sustainable Innovation*, Springer Proceedings in Business and Economics,
https://doi.org/10.1007/978-3-031-90054-9_11

by a long-term disadvantage (Denozza, 2021). Therefore, it is necessary to investigate whether a business activity should be sustainable. The concept of sustainability in itself appears neutral and its meaning may vary depending on the specific context to which it refers (Maugeri, 2021; Sepe, 2021; Zammitti, 2021). With reference to a business, sustainability recalls, first and foremost, the idea of the continuity of the business itself and thus its stability over time (Cerrato, 2022; Stella Richter jr., 2021). However, the issue can also be approached from a different angle that differs from that of the duration to which every enterprise generally tends and which is left to the statutory autonomy. The reference is to the consequences for the environment resulting from a massive production activity carried out solely with a view to obtaining the highest possible profit. In this sense, the concept of sustainability seems to imply the need to bring a business closer to the protection of more general interests, such as the environment and human life (Pacchi, 2023). Of course, the two different meanings of the term sustainability belong to separate levels whose aims do not necessarily coincide.

Regarding environmental sustainability, it seems appropriate to bear in mind that every company conducts its business with the objective of generating profits rather than losses; moreover, it is nothing new that the profit motive serves as a criterion for company management choices, albeit with the exceptions of mutual and consortium companies (Cian, 2021; Maugeri, 2019; Tombari, 2019). However, it seems no longer possible to remain insensitive to the issues of environmental protection and sustainability. It seems essential to react to the problems that may arise, ensuring both a business-friendly environment and an attractive climate for investors (Amatucci, 2022). Hence the need felt by many to adopt all necessary instruments and precautions to reduce, if not eliminate, harmful consequences for the environment. Of course, this kind of task is entrusted to governments and the attribution of it to private actors with market power is in contradiction with the principles of democracy (Barcellona, 2022; Brescia Morra, 2022); the role of a government is fundamental both for the protection of general interests, such as the environment, and for monitoring the possible transition to a different type of economic system (Genovese, 2022). Nevertheless, a business can make its voice heard in order to contribute to the management of general problems, making discretionary choices that may be decisive in the production of a given result and possibly sacrificing part of its own profit. For example, measures can be taken to control and prevent pollution, as well as to recycle, manage and reduce waste; likewise, the management of natural resources in a sustainable manner, the optimal use of assets such as land and water, and the adoption of clean production methods through the promotion of efficient use of energy and environmentally friendly technologies, appear fundamental.

The current historical moment seems favourable to a synergy between business, environment and society, which is able to place social and environmental issues at the centre of business activity and not at the margins of it (Maurutto, 2023). The idea is that environmental and social issues are vital for successful business management. In fact, sustainability has taken on such a decisive role that it is no longer confined solely to specific sectors closely connected to the environment, but has become a point of reference for business activity as well (Calderazzi, 2022).

The purpose of this paper is to examine the impacts of Environmental, Social and Governance factors on a business' organisation in Italy. Being the topic of sustainability relevant not only in the economic field, the research is carried out from a legal point of view. As a consequence, the methodological approach adopted takes into consideration both existing legislation and literature; however, it seems not possible to refer to case law or examples. The findings show that over the last few years attention towards social and environmental sustainability has increased both in the economic field and in all aspects of daily life. Additionally, it emerges that running a sustainable business requires a change in the planning of a company's structure.

The paper is organised as follows. Section 2 presents a brief description of the European intervention on sustainability. Sections 3 and 4 deal with ESG factors and their impact on the organisation of a business. Section 5 is about the relationship between sustainability and CSR. Section s6 and 7 discuss the purpose of a business. The last part presents the conclusions.

2 The European Intervention on Sustainability

In recent years, the focus on social and environmental sustainability has increased not only in the economic sphere, but in all aspects of daily life (Stella Richter jr, 2021); this is both a reply to environmental disasters that occurred and keep happening and a consequence of Covid-19 which made clear that there is a need for a future based on a different social and economic system (Natoli, 2021; Stanzione, 2022). Both national lawmakers and individuals have felt the need to set a new pace in their daily lifestyles and, consequently, in the legal and economic spheres, seeking a balance in the relationship between the rules dictated by business and the impact on the environment. With this in mind, the European Union has directly addressed the issue of environmental sustainability, attempting to steer businesses towards adopting virtuous behaviour and changing production models (Semeraro, 2021). To this end, a new growth strategy has been identified, through the introduction of rules aimed at reducing emissions from human activities and pursuing climate neutrality in Europe by 2050, creating a fair and prosperous society where economic growth does not go hand in hand with resource use. This project, called the European Green Deal, is not merely a set of technical rules, but sees an economic and social transition as its goal. The aims pursued, although already contained in various provisions of the European Treaties and in the EU Charter of Fundamental Rights, are based on the awareness that finance, the economy and the ecosystem are not isolated phenomena, but are closely connected to each other, and must therefore be changed together (Cavaliere, 2022). For this reason, non-financial aspects must be more integrated into business life, so that the financial system and investors are increasingly oriented towards sustainable investments and informed about the sustainability of those already made, bringing about a transformation of the current social and economic system (Maurutto, 2023). The goals of climate neutrality and the creation of a better environment have seen further steps forward through the enactment of European climate legislation, as well as multiple proposals driven by the realisation that immediate action is needed to prevent the unfortunate consequences of current inaction from falling on future generations (Ammannati, 2021).

The management of environmental and social sustainability transcends size barriers and directly or indirectly involves all businesses in the production context in which they operate. Pursuing sustainability goals today appears fundamental to review business models and create new ones, guaranteeing businesses a solid and competitive position in the market.

Sustainability and environmental protection have also affected the field of State aid, the purpose of which is now mainly to promote intelligent and sustainable economic growth, protecting free competition and the environment. To this end, the European Commission has approved the Regional Aid Map for Italy for the period 2022–2027, by which Italy is allowed both to help less favoured regions catch up and to reduce disparities in terms of economic welfare, income and unemployment (Strianese, 2022).

3 ESG Factors

The topic of sustainability is closely linked to the phrase environmental social governance (ESG), which defines its contents. The term ESG is rather recent and dates back to 2004 when the UN asked a number of financial institutions to produce a report containing recommendations aimed at integrating environmental and social concerns into asset management and investment activities (Brescia Morra, 2022). Although one might think that the term ESG recalls vague concepts (Cerrato, 2022; Stella Richter jr., 2021), it actually refers to three different factors, namely environmental, social and governance.

In this regard, the reference to the environment (E) implies the need to look at everything related to it and, therefore, gas emissions, water, reduction of waste production, circular economy, biodiversity and species extinction.

Conversely, the social factor (S) refers to certain rights such as equality and non-discrimination, recognised as fundamental by the Italian Constitution and all evolved legal systems, as well as inclusion, human rights, mental health in all environments (especially work) and education in terms of quality and gender equality. However, it should be noted that the social issue is not unambiguous, but varies according to the historical moment and place in which it is addressed; as a consequence, it is inevitably influenced by cultural, religious and political traditions (Brescia Morra, 2022).

Finally, the third factor comes into consideration, namely governance (G), which, unlike those previously mentioned, does not affect the life of a business from the outside, but from within. Governance (G) concerns, first and foremost, matters relating to the management of a company and, consequently, the increase in the value of the shareholdings of the shareholders, who have invested in a company; this circumstance seems to imply that there is an inevitable contrast between the factor under consideration and the other two, since they are all aimed at protecting conflicting interests (Cerrato, 2022). The relationship between external and internal profiles affecting the organisational structure of an enterprise raises the question of what the purpose of a business is.

However, it is possible to approach the question from a different point of view and state that the governance factor stands alongside the environmental and social factors and is a precondition for them, since only if a business is managed efficiently can the results listed above be achieved; any business can only effectively tackle environmental and social challenges if its governance is sound. From this, one seems to be able to draw the conclusion that corporate governance bodies must also pay attention to environmental and social profiles and be able to deal with any crises that may occur. If the above considerations are true, it follows that the meaning of the term ESG is to be prepared for crises that may occur in the future and to manage them appropriately. Inevitably, among the risks that may arise in the course of doing business are those related to climate change, which must be considered with a view to profit and return in the medium and long term (Brescia Morra, 2022). This specific task must be carried out not only to allow a business to profitably carry out its activity, but also to allow investors to assess the performance of the operation carried out, through clear and timely information on the social and environmental consequences of the choices made by the management bodies.

4 The Impact of ESG Factors on the Organisation of a Business

From what has been said so far, it emerges that the term ESG identifies scenarios in which sustainable actions and investments are carried out; this is done by paying attention not only to the environment, but also to human activities and business management (Cerini, 2022). The circumstance that operating within a short time horizon is considered the cause of negative effects (Goergen et al., 2019), such as environmental degradation and reduced investment in research and development, implies the adoption of appropriate reaction instruments (Denozza, 2021). It seems imperative that businesses plan their activities over the long term and carry them out according to a sustainability objective that allows them to effectively face any possible difficulties and overcome them. However, it is worth noting that, on the one hand, the concept of the long term appears to be undefined and seems to vary inevitably according to the activity actually carried out; on the other hand, there is nothing to prevent a business from planning a time horizon for carrying out its activity that is not necessarily long and that gives an immediate return on the investments made. This implies that even the pursuit of a short-term economic advantage is not necessarily detrimental (Stella Richter jr., 2021).

In any case, the foregoing considerations lead one to believe that conducting a business in a sustainable manner affects the organisational dimension of the business itself (Pellegrini & Davola, 2021) and, consequently, raises various questions in terms of the applicable rules. In Italy there is a growing conviction that any business should be carried out with ESG criteria in mind and that these factors are the end of it (Calderazzi, 2022; Maugeri, 2019); in other words, sustainability and ESG factors should be an integral part of the organisation of a business and serve as an additional goal of it. However, at the moment it seems not possible to provide examples. To the aim of achieving the highest possible profit would be added that of pursuing secondary results, which converge towards the realisation of a better economic and social environment (Celati, 2021). To opine to the contrary does not seem possible, considering that the adoption of ESG factors takes quite a long time and that the comparison between the sacrifices to be made currently and the benefits to be obtained in the future leads one to believe that the latter are certainly greater than the former. Of course, this would not be reduced solely to compliance with the rules contained in the sector legislation, as it is clear that the violation of specific rules is a source of liability in civil and possibly even criminal law; otherwise, the application of ESG factors would require taking into account higher interests deemed relevant to the community. From this perspective, the European Green Deal can be the instrument through which sustainable economic growth can be pursued in light of existing environmental challenges, overcoming traditional economic and social models (Cavaliere, 2022); this, even though it is not a transversal regulation, but a regulation that only intervenes in a single sector (Passalacqua, 2021).

Conducting a business in a sustainable manner necessarily implies a change in the planning and coordination of the entrepreneurial structure, which has been in place since the inception of the business itself, as well as the adoption of all the means necessary to achieve the desired end. The method to be adopted would not be univocal, but would vary according to the nature and size of the enterprise. By way of example, it would seem possible to include specific clauses in the articles of association delimiting the sustainability objectives pursued, indicating both the operations that may be performed and those that are precluded, and consequently providing for remuneration instruments that are proportionate to the results achieved. The former would include those that identify the expected results and burden the management body with precise tasks, as well as those that set out the ethical and social principles to which a company adheres and with which the directors must comply (Cian, 2021).

In any case, the adoption of ESG factors requires that directors operate with foresight, carrying out an adequate evaluation between costs and benefits and, if necessary, modifying management policies; it appears necessary not only to correctly identify risks and prevent them, but also to consider the consequences that may affect the entire organisation. From this point of view, a solution to the problem can be provided, first of all, by the creation of organisational, administrative and accounting structures, as referred to in Article 2086 of the Italian Civil Code, and their periodic review in the light of any changes in the nature and size of an enterprise. In fact, the concept of a business encompasses two different characteristics: the organisation needed to carry out a business and the characteristics of a business itself, which inevitably entail risks, among which are also those linked to ESG factors (Pacchi, 2023).

Sustainable management also implies a change in accounting processes and policies to reflect the implications of environmental issues (Loizzo et al., 2022). Furthermore, it is conceivable to diversify management bodies (Calvosa, 2022) through the creation of specific committees, which, based on the nature and size of a business, would be entrusted with the pursuit of sustainability objectives and the management of related risks. In this way, the choices made by the management body should be subject to the opinion of the individual committee, although it should be understood that the decisions taken cannot be questioned on their merits and are not open to censure if taken in a diligent and informed manner; this means that directors' actions are unquestionable provided they have acted in accordance with the so-called duty of loyalty and duty of care. Likewise, it seems necessary to rely on external consultants for the drafting of sustainability documents. Choices of this kind inevitably entail an increase in costs, but in the long run they can help to increase the value of a business and, consequently, of the investments made in it.

5 Sustainability and CSR

The legislative intention seems to be that it is no longer acceptable for a business to generate profits without taking into account the consequences of its actions (Makandar, 2018). In other words, without prejudice to the profit motive to which businesses tend, attention to the environment and the social context is becoming increasingly important.

Legislative interventions have also influenced another aspect of business activity, namely corporate social responsibility (CSR), understood as the adoption of a behaviour that harmonises economic objectives with the social and environmental objectives of the territory where a business activity is. In fact, the pursuit of such ambitious objectives leads to the conclusion that it is desirable to integrate aspects such as safety and CSR into the creation and management of every business, so that businesses distinguish themselves by their social responsibility objectives.

CSR is relevant for all types of enterprises, whether large or small and without distinction with regard to the activity carried out, since they contribute significantly to the development of the economy. Of course, CSR is not uniform, but varies according to political traditions, social reality and the way in which certain social and environmental issues are regulated by law; hence, CSR must be adapted to the peculiarities of each nation.

The application of CSR standards is grounded in a European, if not global, context in which, as mentioned, awareness of the environment and its protection is increasing so much that the solution of problems related to it is considered to play a fundamental role (Daccò, 2022). To this end, a prominent role is assumed by the theme of sustainability, which presupposes the adoption of certain voluntary behaviours necessary to achieve the objectives pursued. Sustainability is reflected in the goals of the UN 2030

Agenda for Sustainable Development, with the consequence that business conduct and responsible development become the basis for a new corporate social responsibility aimed at increasing cooperation between individuals (Capriglione, 2022). Identifying the negative effects that a business can have on third parties and the environment and combating them sets the boundaries of CSR, which is not necessarily linked to long-term or short-term policies (Amatucci, 2022).

CSR is made up of several elements that combine the typical aims of each business with additional goals, the fulfilment of which affects a business' strategy; these goals are represented by the observance, mostly on a voluntary basis, of ethical and social rules, environmental balances and human rights (Capriglione, 2022; Rossi, 2021). The aim of obtaining an asset advantage in the long term and not only in the short term can be achieved by paying as much attention to the interests of third parties in general as to those of protecting the value of the assets of a business (Porter et al., 2011). In this way, a business is no longer only relevant as an economic factor, but also as a social institution (Capriglione, 2022). Investments directed towards the creation of a society in which there is development of human capital, protection of the environment and an increase in the capacity to relate to third parties are the objectives of businesses that intend to be socially responsible (Capriglione, 2022). This should apply not only to big enterprises, but also to smaller ones, which are more widespread and make up the Italian entrepreneurial fabric. The demands of users would make it essential to set precise environmental protection standards, as well as attention to corporate social responsibility.

As previously mentioned, the carrying out of business activities in an environmentally and socially sensitive manner has taken place on a voluntary basis, being left to the discretion and impulse of companies that have sought to be active in environmental and social policies. However, it is necessary to point out that some European legislative interventions have been contributing for some time now to ensure that CSR goes beyond the voluntary and non-binding features that characterise it to become an essential element of business management (Angelici, 2018; Vessia, 2019). To this end, non-financial information is considered the main tool for implementing sustainability policies (Pacchi, 2023). The primary role assumed by non-financial information has led to the recent enactment of the Corporate Sustainability Reporting Directive (CSRD), inspired by principles of completeness, comparability and reliability (Passador, 2023). The Directive, in order to put sustainability and financial information on an equal footing, has imposed sustainability reporting obligations on all large companies and on all companies with securities admitted to trading on regulated markets, with the exception of micro companies only. Companies are required to consider both the consequences of their activities on third parties and the environment, as well as the way in which sustainability issues affect the companies themselves, disclosing relevant information from both perspectives, as well as pertinent information from only one of them (Maurutto, 2023); the sustainability data that each company is required to provide must be relevant, comparable and reliable (Pacchi, 2023), and must be compiled according to specific rules. Furthermore, in order to protect European investors and to avoid situations of competitive disadvantage for European companies, the Directive also envisages its application to companies not based in the European Union that have shares listed on European regulated markets (Genovese, 2023). It follows the presence of a transparent and truthful reporting duty of a company's activity in favour of third parties, which is based on the three ESG factors.

6 The Purpose of a Business

The relevance of the topic of environmental sustainability and related issues leads one to address, albeit briefly, that of the purpose of a business. The decision to look not only at profit, but also at other issues is not new and dates back at least to the last century when the interests of a company were opposed to those of its shareholders. The issue that arose was whether or not, especially for large companies, it was necessary to pursue not only the interests of the shareholders, but also those of other parties (stakeholders), such as employees, suppliers and all third parties in general towards whom corporate management could have positive or negative consequences. Initially, it was argued that a company conducts its business in the interests of the shareholders, with the consequence that its main purpose is to share the profits made (Hansmann et al., 2000; Mayer, 2021), provided that shareholders do not decide to pursue different interests (Cerrato, 2022). This orientation, also known as 'shareholderism', identifies the valorisation of the capital invested by the shareholders, considered to be the owners of a company, as the main objective to which a company must tend. According to this idea, it is possible to consider interests other than those of the shareholders only where a company can benefit from them in the medium to long term (Cian, 2021); in this way, the possibility of a sacrifice in terms of profit is excluded.

This theory has been countered by the theory of the so-called 'stakeholderism', according to which a business does not necessarily have to be oriented towards the maximisation of profit and the remuneration of capital (Denozza, 2022); according to this order of ideas, directors should take into account the impact on interests other than those of the shareholders, i.e. those of the stakeholders, who are involved in various ways by a business (Amatucci, 2022; Merrick Dodd, 1932; Stout, 2008). From this it would follow the possibility of renouncing a share of profit, if this is necessary to protect higher interests.

This is not the place to return to the complex debate that has developed and the arguments in support of one or the other thesis, although it seems possible to state that the purpose of a business is the composition between the interest that the various categories of shareholders wish to pursue and that of stakeholders (Montalenti, 2022). However, starting from the consideration that in a company, especially a large one, there is always a contraposition between different and even conflicting interests (Tombari, 2019), it is necessary to observe that the notion of business' purpose is not static, but changes according to the historical, economic and social context and has become increasingly diversified. In recent years, the question of business' purpose and corporate social responsibility has come to the fore again (Hansmann et al., 2000;

Montalenti, 2022; Portale, 2018), not least because of a European economic policy aimed at competition and globalisation (Fortunato, 2019). In addition, ecological and environmental disasters as well as the Covid-19 pandemic have played a decisive role in the debate on business' purpose, which have inevitably changed the lives and interests of individuals. Thus, the opposition between the proponents of the supremacy of the interests of shareholders and those of the interests of stakeholder has become more heated (Brescia Morra, 2022). The idea that a company, especially a large one, must take into account the interests of its main stakeholders and look after those of the community has made its presence felt again (Bebchuck et al., 2020; Spiesshofer, 2018), and perhaps the reason lies in the fact that the issue of sustainability and that of the purpose of entrepreneurial activity appear intimately connected. In Italy, the debate has mainly focused on the concept of CSR and in particular on the duty of administrative bodies to safeguard interests other than those of shareholders (Angelici, 2018; Calderazzi, 2022; Stella Richter jr., 2021). The basis of this discussion seems to find its justification in the consideration that the violation of stakeholders' interests inevitably translates into a decrease in the value of a company, whose capacity to entertain relations is compromised (Maugeri, 2019; Pacchi, 2023).

Stakeholders' attention is increasingly focused on socially responsible behaviour to protect the environment and human rights by companies rather than on making profits; as a consequence, directors are given the additional task of balancing the interests of shareholders with those of stakeholders. Consequently, in addition to complying with legal and contractual obligations, management bodies should strive to operate in an ethical and socially responsible manner in order to gain benefits in terms of corporate image and reputation (Branch et al., 2017). The reputation of a company is determined by the behaviour it engages in, which will enable it to maintain a relationship with its various stakeholders based both on trust and the belief that the company will continue to operate in a respectful and fair manner (Troisi, 2022). In this way, a company would be able to increase its value and consequently its profit, by attracting talented workers, improving coordination with the supply chain by reducing waste, simplifying access to finance and retaining investors and customers (Palmieri, 2023).

7 The Enlightened Shareholder Value

The importance of interests other than those of the shareholders has been confirmed by some national legislative interventions, which have adopted the vision of the so-called 'enlightened shareholder value', according to which profit is to be pursued in a way that is compatible with the long-term consequences of a company and with the interest of third parties in not being prejudiced by a company's activities (Amatucci, 2022; Bruno, 2017). In this way, foreign legislation has introduced new rules of conduct for directors, imposing a balancing act between the interests of shareholders and those of stakeholders and requiring that the latter be given due consideration (Amatucci, 2022; Cian, 2021). More specifically, the management bodies of a company are required to pay attention to the interests of the various stakeholders, with the dual aim of ensuring sustainable company growth and averting the risk of new crises.

In this regard, the English Companies Act of 2006 comes into consideration, which was the first to implement a form of empowerment of directors with respect to the governance of the multiple interests that revolve around the corporate operation; in fact, Sect. 172 establishes the obligation for directors to reconcile the interests of a company and its shareholders with those of the environment and third parties in general (Keay, 2012), without prejudice to the duty to perform their duties for the benefit of the company (Libertini, 2013). English law provides that the administrative body of a company, as part of a general duty of good faith, must act in such a way as to promote the success of the company for the benefit of the shareholders (Calandra Bonaura, 2011), taking into account, among other things, the possible consequences of any long-term decision, the impact of the company's operations on the community and the environment, and the need to foster the company's business relations with third parties (Angelici, 2011). In the same vein is French legislation, where the Loi Pacte and the Code de Commerce attach importance to the social and environmental problems associated with businesses (Cerrato, 2022) and introduce into French company law the notion of the company's raison d'être, understood as a further objective to be pursued in the long-term conduct of a business (Riolfo, 2023). Similarly, in Germany, the Gesetz über die unternehmerischen Sorgfaltspflichten in Lieferketten - Lieferkettensorgfaltspflichtengesetz was enacted, which, through the provision of rules of conduct, requires large corporations to protect human rights and the environment in product and service distribution chains.

The tendency to carry out a business in a manner other than exploiting every opportunity to benefit shareholders, taking into account the interests of those with whom a company interferes, can also be found in the so-called soft law regulations, which dictate principles and recommendations to be followed by management bodies. As an example, one may recall the UK Corporate Governance Code of 2018, which mandates directors to promote the sustainable success of a company from a long-term perspective, generating value for shareholders and contributing to a wider society. Similarly, the Deutsche Corporate Governance Kodex requires directors to systematically identify and assess risks and opportunities related to social and environmental factors, as well as the ecological and social impacts of their activities. In addition to long-term economic objectives, German law requires that corporate strategy also take ecological and social objectives into proper consideration and that planning include financial and sustainability objectives. Finally, the Italian Corporate Governance Code of 2020 establishes that directors guide the company by pursuing its sustainable success, understood as an objective that creates value for the benefit not only of shareholders, but also of other stakeholders relevant to a company; to this end, they are asked to promote dialogue with shareholders and stakeholders in the forms they deem most appropriate, without, however, giving any indication as to their identification. The choice of whether to pursue these objectives is left to the administrative body, but the provision may be contained in the articles of association, thus conditioning the actions of the directors (Daccò, 2022).

8 Conclusion. The Relationship Between Business and Stakeholders

From what has been said so far, it emerges how the different legislative interventions have turned their attention to sustainability, establishing rules of conduct for the governing bodies of each company and highlighting that the aim they must strive for is to create a balance between the interests of shareholders and the social demands of sustainability born by stakeholders; this approach has also been accepted by the Italian law, albeit at a regulatory level and with reference to listed companies. Thus, a broadening of a business' purpose seems to emerge, which would not be limited solely to the achievement of a financial advantage, but would also consist in safeguarding the interests of third parties that come into contact with it (Cossu, 2022; Daccò, 2022). Nevertheless, it seems possible to state that the rule affects the object and not the purpose, which remains profit. The contrast between the interests of shareholders and those of third parties sees as its own battleground the choices made by the management body (Cian, 2021). The identification of the stakeholders whose interests deserve protection appears to be left to the discretion of directors, which is thus broadened (Ventoruzzo, 2020); in this way, the role of directors is no longer aimed solely at pursuing the company's interest, but extends to become that of arbiters of the entrepreneurial operation and of weighing the interests of all the stakeholders potentially exposed to the company's negative externalities. It seems possible to hypothesise that the choices made by the governing body should look to a broad horizon, seeking, on the one hand, to address the various crises that have occurred in recent years, including the economic, climate and energy crises, and, on the other, to prepare for those that may arise in the future. This once again implies an intervention in the organisational component of the company through the creation of specific structures and the elaboration of plans that allow for the efficient use of resources.

However, it is not clear whether in sifting through the stakeholders' demands, directors must also mediate them with those of the shareholders (Calvosa, 2023). The doubt seems to be answered by the consideration that the balancing activity entrusted to the administrative body does not exclude that its main duty is to act in the best interests of the company and to allow the shareholders to obtain a return on their invested capital; should this not be the case, directors could be held liable for the breach of their duties. Adherence to this interpretation implies that the interests of shareholders and stakeholders can coexist without excluding each other, even if they are not on homogeneous levels. In fact, the preference given to the protection of the former does not seem to give rise to the possibility for stakeholders to bring an action to invoke directors' liability; it will be sufficient for the latter to prove that they have carried out a reasonable balancing act between the various opposing interests, it being understood that the margins of reviewability of their actions are reduced (Denozza, 2022).

Otherwise, the exclusive focus on the interests of stakeholders is at odds with the business' purpose and therefore exposes the administrative body to claims for damages for breach of its duties; in any case, the care of such interests does not seem censurable by unwise shareholders who prefer to forego greater future profits, even at the risk of some economic sacrifice, and wish to have higher dividends in the immediate future. If the foregoing is true, then it follows that the pursuit of sustainable success is instrumental to the profit motive and, therefore, functional to the satisfaction of shareholders. The demands of third parties must not necessarily be accommodated; in fact, directors are only required to take them into account in their role as arbitrators of the various conflicting positions. In other words, directors enjoy a discretionary power that may affect the realisation of the various interests at stake; the management strategies adopted must take into account the interests of stakeholders, but always with the ultimate perspective of the pursuit of profit.

As previously mentioned, the theme in consideration is important not only from an economic point of view, but also from a legal one. This means that the investigation on the impact of ESG factors on the organisation of a business may be implemented and new conclusions may be reached. In fact, an additional area of investigation may be that related to new pieces of legislation, such as the Corporate Sustainability Due Diligence Directive (CSDD).

References

Amatucci, F. (2022). Considerazioni introduttive. In F. Amatucci & C. Fontana (Eds.), *L'impatto delle zone economiche speciali sugli ordinamenti giuridici nazionali europei* (pp. 9–23).

Ammannati, L. (2021). Energia e ambiente: regolazione per la transizione. In M. Passalacqua (Ed.), *Diritti e mercati nella transizione ecologica e digitale* (pp. 169–182).

Angelici, C. (2011). Responsabilità sociale dell'impresa, codici etici e autodisciplina. *Giur. comm, 2*, 159–176.

Angelici, C. (2018). Divagazioni sulla "responsabilità sociale" d'impresa. *Riv. soc, 1*, 3–19.

Barcellona, E. (2022). La sustainable corporate governance nelle proposte di riforma del diritto europeo: a proposito dei limiti strutturali del cd. stakeholderism. *Riv. soc., 1*, 1–52.

Bebchuck, L. A., et al. (2020). The illusory promise of stakeholder governance. *Cornell Law Review, 106*, 91–177.

Branch, B., et al. (2017). *Fiduciary duty and social responsibility* (pp. 1–17). www.westga.edu/~bquest/2017/fiduciary2017.pdf

Brescia Morra, C. (2022). Chi salverà il pianeta: Lo Stato o le grandi corporation? ESG: Una formula ambigua e inutile. *Rivista Trimestrale di diritto dell'economia, Addition to No., 4*, 78–99.

Bruno, S. (2017). The 'enlightened shareholder value' in UK companies ten years later: What the European Directive N. 2014/95/EC Can Do. In F. Annunziata, A. Brobel Dorsman, B. François, & F. Pernazza (Eds.), *Le droit comparé des affaires au XXIe siècle. Mélanges à la mémoire de Claude Ducouloux-Favard, Bruylant-Larcier and Minerva Bancaria* (pp. 313–326).

Calandra Bonaura, V. (2011). Responsabilità sociale dell'impresa e doveri degli amministratori. *Giur. comm, 5*, 526–548.

Calderazzi, R. (2022). La sostenibilità nell'impresa bancaria. *Rivista Trimestrale di Diritto Dell'economia, Addition to No., 4*, 168–192.
Calvosa, L. (2022). La governance delle società quotate italiane nella transizione verso la sostenibilità e la digitalizzazione. *Riv. soc, 2–3*, 309–321.
Calvosa, L. (2023). La sfida della sostenibilità: Grandi imprese, Pmi e corporate governance. *Bancaria, 7–8*, 64–82.
Capriglione, F. (2022). *Responsabilità sociale* d'impresa e sviluppo sostenibile. *Rivista Trimestrale di Diritto Dell'economia, Addition to No., 4*, 22–45.
Cavaliere, S. (2022). Il green deal e il tempo delle crisi. *Rivista Trimestrale di Diritto Dell'economia, Addition to No., 4*, 526–542.
Celati, B. (2021). Diritto per lo sviluppo economico nella transizione climatica. In M. Passalacqua (Ed.), *Diritti e mercati nella transizione ecologica e digitale* (pp. 271–286).
Cerini, D. (2022). From "green" to "blue": l'assicurazione tra sostenibilità e regole di mercato. *Assicurazioni, 1*, 9–46.
Cerrato, S. A. (2022). Appunti per una «via italiana» all'ESG L'impresa «costituzionalmente solidale» (anche alla luce dei «nuovi» artt. 9 e 41, comma 3, Cost.). *Analisi Giuridica dell'economia, 1*, 63–114.
Cian, M. (2021). Clausole statutarie per la sostenibilità dell'impresa: spazi limiti e implicazioni. *Riv. soc., 2–3*, 475–507.
Cossu, M. (2022). Tassonomia finanziaria e normativa dei prodotti finanziari sostenibili e governo societario. *Banca Impresa Società, 3*, 433–487.
Daccò, A. (2022). Spunti di riflessione su capitalismo sostenibile e strumenti a disposizione. *Banca Borsa 3*, 372–393.
Denozza, F. (2021). Incertezza, azione collettiva, esternalità, problemi distributivi: Come si forma lo short-termism e come se ne può uscire con l'aiuto degli stakeholders. *Riv. soc, 2–3*, 297–321.
Denozza, F. (2022). Due concetti di stakeholderism. *Orizzonti dir. comm 1*, 37–67.
Fortunato, S. (2019). L'informazione non-finanziaria nell'impresa socialmente responsabile. *Giur. comm, 3*, 415–428.
Genovese, A. (2022). Bilanci di sostenibilità, tassonomia UE delle attività economiche ecosostenibili e governo societario. *Orizzonti dir. comm, 2*, 497–560.
Genovese, A. (2023). L'armonizzazione del reporting di sostenibilità delle imprese azionarie europee dopo la CSRD. *Contratto e Impresa, 1*, 88–111.
Goergen, M., et al. (2019). Introduction to special issue on sustainable corporate governance. *British Journal of Management, 1*, 3–9.
Hansmann, H., et al. (2000). The end of history for corporate law. *Discussion Paper N., 280*, 1–34.
Keay, A. (2012). *The enlightened shareholder value. Principle and corporate governance*. Routledge.
Libertini, M. (2013). Economia sociale di mercato e responsabilità sociale dell'impresa. *Orizzonti dir. comm, 3*, 18–45.
Loizzo, T., et al. (2022). ESG disclosure: Regulatory framework and challenges for Italian banks. In *Questioni di economia e finanza* (pp. 5–41) (Occasional papers, No. 744).
Makandar, N. B. M. (2018). Special economic zones and social responsibility. *International Journal of Advance Research and Development, 3*(1), 212–217.
Maugeri, M. (2019). Informazione non finanziaria e interesse sociale. *Riv. soc, 5–6*, 992–1031.
Maugeri, M. (2021). Sostenibilità ed Engagement degli azionisti istituzionali. *Riv. soc, 5–6*, 1350–1371.
Maurutto, S. (2023). Dalla società benefit alla CRSD: modelli e paradigmi in bilico tra imprenditorialità sostenibile e green washing. *Ilcaso.it*, 1–27.
Mayer, C. (2021). *The governance of corporate purpose* (pp. 1–13) (European Corporate Governance Institute—Law Working Paper No. 609/2021).
Merrick Dodd, E. (1932). For whom are the corporate managers trustees. *Harvard Law Review, 45*(7), 1145–1163.

Montalenti, P. (2022). Società, mercati finanziari e fattori ESG: Ultimi sviluppi. *Riv. Corporate Governance, 1*, 9–25.

Natoli, R. (2021). Impresa e responsabilità nel prisma del Green New Deal europeo. In M. Passalacqua (Ed.), *Diritti e mercati nella transizione ecologica e digitale* (pp. 287–300).

Pacchi, S. (2023). Sostenibilità, fattori ESG e crisi d'impresa. In *Ristrutturazioni aziendali* (pp. 1–36).

Palmieri, M. (2023). L'informazione non finanziaria e il bilancio di sostenibilità. In *Orizzonti dir. comm., 1*, 273–302.

Passador, M. L. (2023). Sull'utilità della ESG disclosure e sul ruolo dei comitati rischi e sostenibilità. *Banca Impresa Società, 1*, 135–181.

Passalacqua, M. (2021). Green New Deal e transizione digitale verso un diritto eventuale. In M. Passalacqua (Ed.), *Diritti e mercati nella transizione ecologica e digitale* (pp. 3–30).

Pellegrini, M., & Davola, A. (2021). Il ruolo dello Stato nella transizione della finanza verso la sostenibilità. In M. Passalacqua (Ed.), *Diritti e mercati nella transizione ecologica e digitale* (pp. 83–98).

Portale, G. B. (2018). Diritto societario tedesco e diritto societario italiano in dialogo. *Banca Borsa, 5*, 597–612.

Porter, M. E., et al. (2011). Creating shared value. *Harvard Business Review*, 62–67.

Riolfo, G. (2023). Sostenibilità sociale/ambientale dell'attività d'impresa: La proposta di direttiva sul "dovere di diligenza ai fini della sostenibilità" e l'esperimento delle società benefit. *Contratto e Impresa, 1*, 184–224.

Rossi, S. (2021). Il diritto della corporate social responsibility. *Orizzonti dir. comm, 1*, 99–134.

Semeraro, M. (2021). Fattori di sostenibilità ambientale e politiche creditizie: rischio climatico e accesso al credito. In M. Passalacqua (Ed.), *Diritti e mercati nella transizione ecologica e digitale* (pp. 253–270).

Sepe, M. (2021). Sviluppo, sostenibilità e sana prudente gestione in ambito finanziario. In M. Passalacqua (Ed.), *Diritti e mercati nella transizione ecologica e digitale* (pp. 63–82).

Spiesshofer, B. (2018). *Responsible enterprise*. Beck/Hart.

Stanzione, D. (2022). Scopo e oggetto dell'impresa societaria sostenibile. *Giur. comm., 6*, 1023–1051.

Stella Richter, jr. M. (2021). Long-termism. *Riv. soc., 2021*(1), 16–52.

Stout, L. A. (2008). Why should we stop teaching Dodge v. Ford. *Virginia Law and Business Law Review, 3*(1), 164–190.

Strianese, L. (2022). Zone franche verdi in Italia tra principi costituzionali, aiuti a finalità regionale e sostenibilità. In F. Amatucci & C. Fontana (Eds.), *L'impatto delle zone economiche speciali sugli ordinamenti giuridici nazionali europei* (pp. 213–237).

Tombari, U. (2019). *"Potere" e "interessi" nella grande impresa azionaria*. Giuffrè Francis Lefebvre.

Troisi, A. (2022). Enforcement e normative di contrasto al fenomeno del greenwashing. *Giur. comm, 5*, 1262–1273.

Ventoruzzo, M. (2020). Il nuovo Codice di Corporate Governance 2020: le principali novità. *Società*, 439–447.

Vessia, F. (2019). Towards consumer social responsibility. *Journal of Economics and Management, 38*, 157–181.

Zammitti, M. V. (2021). Long-termism e short-termism nella ricerca di strategie di sostenibilità. *Orizzonti dir. comm, 1*, 255–274.

What Kind of Sustainability for the Economy? Entropy and Financial System

Savvas Zachariadis and Georgios Makris

Abstract The contemporary growth pattern is related to the desired term of sustainability. The latter could be broadly defined as the simultaneous achievement of GDP growth, social cohesion, and environmental protection. In practice, nevertheless, the above sustainability constitutes an important challenge or even utopic. The targets are often contradictory, or one cannot assure the other's pursuance. Certain fundamental drawbacks have impeded the progress in economics. An eloquent example is the disinclination to acknowledge the boundaries of economic activity. Traditional theories pay little attention on stylized facts on economic growth and environment in terms of available energy. The perpetual exponential economic growth conflicts with the restraints on energy limitations. These have been established by the two physical laws of Thermodynamics. The First Law of Thermodynamic states that total energy is preserved. Economics is a social science in compliance with physical laws. This implies that excessive use of resources may lead to stagnation or even degrowth. The above view introduces no novelty since the roots could be traced with the Second Law of Thermodynamics, or the entropy law. It refers to finite natural resources, whenever organized systems are progressively moving towards the disorder state and simultaneously are transforming their free energy to bound energy. The generalized principle of entropy is applicable to natural systems but also to economic systems. Many models accentuated growth perpetuity, but stagnation, recessions, and crises comprise frequent phenomena at the international economy. This immanent direction of the economy is not easily detectable but moves imperceptibly to growing entropy. Consequences become evident at later stage when natural restoration is unfeasible and economic recovery too costly. This paper brings together the entropic challenges with sustainability. It reports the historical development of the entropy concept linking it with the contemporary sustainability challenges. By entropy is not only ascribed the natural resources scarcity but also any kind of excessive use, practice, or policy with eventual potential threats for stagnation. A representative example is witnessed in the function of financial system, where more emphasis is given. The financial sector in its broadest sense has increasingly infiltrated into the

S. Zachariadis (✉) · G. Makris
University of Macedonia, Thessaloniki, Greece
e-mail: szachariadis@yahoo.gr

I. Bartuseviciene et al. (eds.), *Building Resilience Through Digital Transformation and Sustainable Innovation*, Springer Proceedings in Business and Economics,
https://doi.org/10.1007/978-3-031-90054-9_12

functioning of real economy systems. Therefore, it is difficult to establish a separation among them, as the financial system affects the way economic systems produce and manage natural resources. Entropy law operates ineluctably as for the matter transformation, but for economic systems there are margins to resist against entropy by their own means, linking their readiness to this scope. Thus, the restructuration towards sustainability encompasses a sound update of various interacting factors, processes, behaviours, and perceptions which altogether form the economic system. The actual question is whether there could be real hope for sustainability and in what terms. The financial system could be endogenously directed to the emergence of new structural socio-economic conditions ensuring the necessary investments that would allow sustainability.

Keywords Sustainability · Entropy · Resources · Energy · Financial sector

JEL Classification Codes G01 · B26 · Q01

1 Introduction

The basic role of heat had been recognized during the first industrial revolution and the construction of the steam engine (heat engine) by James Watt (1769) through the need to extract the motivating force from nature. The emergence of the importance of heat engines was initially interpreted mechanistically by Sadi Carnot (1824), but eventually led to the need for creating a relevant theory which would explain the relation between mechanics and heat. This need had been then fulfilled with the use of the term "thermodynamics" (motive power of heat) by William Thomson (1851), laying the foundations of the relevant theory as an independent and distinct branch of the earlier "mechanics" (Rudolf Clausius, 1879). The key issue on thermodynamics debate had been the energy conservation of a system and the reversibility of the transformations that take place during the processes within it. The formulation of Clausius concerns isolated systems that exchange neither energy nor matter with the outside world, but only operate cyclical processes within the system. However, further research resulted in the introduction of the "entropy" concept, which increases continuously until thermodynamic equilibrium is reached. Thomson (1851) from his part, preferred the term "degradation of the energy". The outcome of all the empirical and theoretical path was the formulation of two basic thermodynamics laws. The first law was called the "energy conservation principle" stating that the amount of energy in the universe remains constant. The second law was called the "energy degradation principle" or "entropy", stating that energy, although constant, is increasingly transformed into non-reusable energy in the system operation process. It should not be ignored, nevertheless, the fact that these thermodynamics laws originally concerned isolated closed systems (such as machines) and not systems which are affected by their external environment. The introduction of entropy into thermodynamics made "...easy the application to open systems where energy and matter are exchanged with the outside world" (Prigogine, 1978, p. 778). Apart from thermodynamics, the entropy concept can be also found in other scientific fields such as physics, chemistry, biology, economics, sociology, climate change and information systems.

From this point on and deviating from the classicals' pessimism, the working group's conclusions under D. Meadows for the Club of Rome (Meadows et al., 1972) or even from degrowth[1] literature and its limitations, it would be useful to consider primarily the initiative of the application of entropy theory in the economy as proposed by the mathematician, economist, and philosopher Nicholas Georgescu-Roegen (1906–1994).[2] From the beginning of 1950s, Georgescu-Roegen was already concerned with the critical treatment of the dominant neoclassical theory and particularly with the fact that marginal utility theory had been influenced by Newtonian mechanical physics, and consequently the consumer theory (utility maximization) where the approach of quality change is absent. From the same perspective and in the context of the cyclical production-consumption relation, he also points out the absolute absence of natural resources role in the economic process (1977). In other words, he criticizes the neoclassical theory for adopting the logic of mechanics, a fact attributed to the similarity of the terms and ignoring the conceptual differences (Mirowski, 2001). Indeed, traditional economic theory had integrated the first law of thermodynamics dictating the law of the conservation of Matter and Energy but had discarded the second law. This perception has led to the development of theories, models, and production factors that have not treated energy as a scarce and finite factor. The prevailed approach was that economic growth remains unaffected by the scarcity of resources in the long run because of the technological progress and the continuous capital investment (Solow, 1974). At this point it should be noted the importance of the remark of Fr. Perroux[3] (1977) where the analytical framework of an emerging science should not be adopted by another science under the pretext of being successful for the latter, as was for neoclassical theory the mechanics, but it should only serve as an inspiration source. For Georgescu-Roegen, his analysis

[1] The term was proposed by André Gorz in the context of a debate on the relationship between growth and capitalism organized by the Nouvel Observateur in 1972. Gorz demonstrated that the limit of the needs of individuals to be satisfied is constantly moving away in the context of modern economies. See Gorz A., 1988. Métamorphoses du travail, Quête du sens, Critique de la raison économique, Galilée. Paris.

[2] Best known for his work The Entropy Law and the Economic Process (Cambridge, MA Harvard University Press, 1971) N. Georgescu-Roegen had quite a significant impact with the publication of his article Energy and Economic Myths in 1975, as well as with his selected works in 1979 (with a 3rd edition in 2006) in French under the title La décroissance: Entropie–Écologie–Économie, which was perhaps not entirely justified as an inspiration source for the later socio-academic degrowth or the post-growth movement. See Grinevald, Jacques (Paris, 18–19 April 2008). "Introduction to Georgescu-Roegen and Degrowth". In Flipo, Fabrice and Schneider, François (eds) (in French), Proceedings of the First International Conference on Economic De-Growth for Ecological Sustainability and Social Equity, pp 14–17. Also, Markantonatou, M. 2013. "From The Limits to Growth to Degrowth. Discourses of Critique of Growth in the Crises of the 1970s and 2008", DFG-KP Working Paper 5, ISSN 2194-136X.

[3] Perroux Fr., 1977. "La rénovation de la théorie de l'équilibre économique général", in "L'idée de régulation dans les sciences", Maloine, Paris.

brought him into conflict with the neoclassical school which had strongly criticized[4] him.

Based on this reflection and considering the climate crisis urgency, the paper seeks to explore the major issue of the sustainability under the context of the entropic historical development arising questions about contemporary challenges of the human economic activity. For this purpose, it argues that the main way to deal with the issue is by reforming the current operational manner of the international financial system, which is inextricably linked to the real economy and is approached from the perspective of the theory of complex systems.

2 Entropy and Complex Systems

Georgescu-Roegen's originality lies on the fact that he managed to generalize with scientific rigour the application of the second law of thermodynamics to the economy, i.e., rendering it anthropomorphic. As he now refers it as "entropy law", Georgescu-Roegen argues that energy and matter also undergo qualitative irreversible transformations[5] in the macroscopic world. Therefore, the entropy of a system increases during the economic process until it reaches a maximum point that characterizes the system's thermodynamic equilibrium and the irreversible dissipation of its usable energy. In this way, he introduces the "bioeconomy" concept, as he terms it since 1975, where the economic process is considered as a continuation of the biological activity. It consists of a pattern with high-value material and energy resource inputs (low entropy) and low-value waste outputs (high entropy), where it enters the economy once these flows acquire monetary value. This scheme which refers to Carnot's degradation of the used energy has the implication of leading to the concept of the total metabolism of our bio-economic activity which is inscribed in the wider system of matter and energy, i.e., the Earth. The reasonable arising question thus is whether the Earth could be considered as an open system. Earth certainly receives solar energy. However, its natural resources remain finite and absolute recycling is impossible, even if technological progress allows the increasingly improved substitution of production factors.[6]

The second law of thermodynamics for a system states that its entropy increases. Whenever the entropy of an organism-system is low, this could only mean that the entropy of its external environment is increasing. As technological progress evolves,

---

[4] Daly, H. E. 1999. "How long can neoclassical economists ignore the contributions of Georgescu-Roegen?" in Daly, Herman E (ed), Ecological Economics and Sustainable Development. Selected Essays of Herman Daly, Cheltenham: Edward Elgar, ISBN 978-1-84720-101-0.

[5] Georgescu-Roegen N.1979. "La Décroissance", 2e éd. fr., Paris, Sang de la terre, 1995.

[6] Technological progress that includes the recycling of waste to save non-renewable resources is related to the rebound effect or Jevon's paradox, where the result is an increase in the use of non-renewable resources, due to the activities which frame this progress. See. York R. and McGee J. A, 2016. Understanding the Jevon's Paradox, Environmental Sociology, vol. 2, Issue 1, pp 77–87.

human activity puts more and more pressure on the exploitation of available productive resources. Life necessities for material constructions require the absorption of matter and energy from the natural environment for their operation and maintenance, thus causing entropic degradation.

In retrospect Georgescu-Roegen realized that the entropy law, unlike energy, does not apply to matter at the macroscopic level, an error for which he was severely criticized. He endeavoured to correct it with the proposal of "fourth law of thermodynamics" (although L. Onsager[7] principle had already been numbered as such), where he asserts that absolute recycling of matter is impossible (1979, p. 1034).[8] However, the 'fourth law of thermodynamics' debate has created an ambiguity about the possibility, as R. Ayres (1999) suggested, of achieving a steady state in which the supply of matter will be limited but the energy flow will be continuous, and additionally, the required for recycling technological equipment will be integrated into the production capacity allowing the volume of waste to remain constant.[9]

Therefore, entropy corresponds to the tendency for disorganization, degradation, and disorder. To wit, it is a process where an open system tends to exhaust its dynamics as well as its ability for self-maintenance or self-renewal. Entropy increment adjusts the relationship of living beings with their environment. The development though of the concept of dissipative structures by Ilya Prigogine[10] provided with new impetus to the way of dealing with entropy. It is specifically argued that while the principle underlying classical thermodynamics concerns necro mass (dead matter), non-equilibrium thermodynamics concerns living systems. In other words,

---

[7] Onsager (Nobel prize award in chemistry 1968) proved that in certain irreversible thermodynamic systems the equality of certain relations between fluxes and forces indicates the existence of local equilibria outside thermodynamic equilibrium. See Onsager L., 1931. Reciprocal Relations in Irreversible Processes, I, Phys. Rev. 37, 405.

[8] His position was strengthened by physicist Max Planck's work (Nobel Prize in Physics 1918), who had developed the concept of "matter dissipation", regarding the existence of irreversible physical processes.

[9] Closely related to thermodynamics (and mechanics) is the concept of exergy. It was first described by J. W. Gibbs in 1873 and named as exergy by Z. Rant in 1956. According to the Gouy-Stodola theorem, in thermodynamics the destroyed exergy rate during the production process is proportional to the rate of entropy created which is based on the second law of thermodynamics and defined as the maximum usable energy-work that a system can provide in an equilibrium state with its environment. In modern literature, there has been an increasing interest in the application of the exergy concept in ecological economics and particularly in the subject of exergy and resource availability, as for example in the work of J. Szargut "Exergy Method: Technical and Ecological Applications", 2005, WIT Press, where the concept of "thermo-ecological cost" is introduced. In this regard, a useful tool could be the application of the Gouy-Stodola theorem in ecophysics and especially in the study of ecosystems. According to the Gouy-Stodola theorem, in thermodynamics the destroyed exergy rate during the production process is proportional to the rate of entropy created. In the case of open and complex systems such as ecosystems, it helps to measure with greater accuracy the creation of entropy as well as the irreversibility of the processes of individual systems, and thus their sustainability due to human economic activity. See e.g. Díaz-Méndez,S. et al., 2011. A general exergy-based environmental impact index, Journal of Mechanical Science and Technology, 25(8), pp.1979–1985.

[10] See Prigogine, I., 1972, "La thermodynamique de la vie", La Recherche, vol. 3, n°, 24, pp. 547–562.

they involve open systems striving to reduce their entropy[11] as they exchange energy and entropy with their environment away from the thermodynamic equilibrium point where entropy is maximized. This fact[12] potentially allows the creation of complex structures that are stabilized precisely by absorbing more and more energy from their environment. The interest arises from the upshot that these systems, after a maturity stage, can shew the ability for auto-organization. In this sense, economic systems also endeavour to control their entropy at the expense of their environment, but also to self-organize in an evolutionary way.[13] Introducing this schema into economic analysis signifies the acceptance of the historical time and uncertainty and thus the explanation of economic disturbances and crises (Lavoie, 1983). Contrary to the attainment of Walrasian equilibrium, notwithstanding, as Henri Guitton (1979, p. 73) states, "when we approach reality, we move away from equilibrium". In this direction, Jacques Lesourne (1991, 2002) contributed in a fundamental way to the study of the interaction of the behaviour of economic actors among themselves and their role in the operation and evolution of a more complex economic system.

The entropy law presents a worth noted characteristic. Even though it states the general processing direction[14] it does not reveal the exact level of degradation, nor does it indicate the certain level of threshold. It only assures of a slow and constant process, not facilitating the prediction of the consequences in near future. Nevertheless, Georgescu-Roegen's contribution to the integration of entropy into the theoretical edifice of economic science as well as Prigogine's boost for comprehending the function of open systems have decisively enabled us to understand the modern problem of man's relationship with the natural environment.[15]

[11] See Bailly Fr. and Longo G., 2009. Biological organization and anti-entropy, Journal of Biological Systems, 17 (1), pp. 63–96.

[12] According to Prigogine (1972), in the field of thermodynamics, the appearance of diffusion structures at the microscopic level depends on fluctuations of a random character. In an open system though with a non-equilibrium stable state, the exchange of energy and matter with its environment, these fluctuations could possibly lead to the creation of stable macroscopic structure.

[13] See on Bertalanffy L., 1968. General Systems Theory: Foundations, Developments, Applications (revised ed.), Braziller, New York. In addition, Foster J., 2005. From Simplistic to Complex Systems in Economics, Cambridge Journal of Economics, 29(6):873–892.

[14] The entropy law expressed as $\Delta S > 0$, where S is the entropy, indicates only the increase in entropy.

[15] That also concerns one of human's weaknesses concerns one of human's weaknesses, namely, the reluctance to recognize mankind's limitations in relation to space, to time, and to matter and energy. The main implication inclines on future generations who are likely to be in lower standards of living due to scarcity of resources that could provoke unsustainable levels of consumption and investment.

3 From the Dominant Growth Paradigm to Sustainability

From the undesirable stationary state by David Ricardo (1817) to the beginning of the debate about the relation between economic growth and economic development after the Second World War, to the publication of the Meadows Report on the Club of Rome[16] (Meadows et al., 1972) and to Brundtland Report (UN) on Environment and Development by the World Commission in 1987, which introduces the concept of sustainable development and describes how it can be achieved, the road had been long. The notion of the continuous economic growth and the policy framework that is implemented are now in the past.

Georgescu-Roegen's intellectual heritage no longer allows to deal with the universe, besides in terms of evolution and irreversibility. However, the undoubtedly progress made in the relation between the complexity theory and the systems theory essentially contributes to overcome the obstacles for comprehending the nature of the challenges that modern society faces. Specifically, while the systems theory deals with the structure and interdependence of the elements that form a system, complexity theory focuses on the investigation of the subsystems of an organized complex system, and consequently, on the behaviours that could change its function and the final produced result.

It is not namely about two extraneous or conflicting theories, as has occasionally been mentioned in the literature,[17] but for the consideration of complexity as a condition for understanding the function and the evolution of a system. That gives rise to the concept of a "complex system", i.e., a group or organization that consists of many interacting parts and from which the emerging behaviours are hardly or not at all related to those of the parts that compose it, and which influence the evolution of the system itself, (Richardson, 2004), such as an ecosystem.[18]

The entire course of the entropy concept was accompanied by a multitude of theoretical biocentric and anthropocentric approaches as well as ecological movements that question the sustainability of the dominant economic development model. The subject's main idea is degrowth (Gorz, 1972),[19] which has gained many followers but has also been regularly criticized.[20] The disclaimer of development and productivism

---

[16] Where the first of a series World3 system dynamics model was developed for computer simulation and consists of interacting parts such as: food system, industry, population, non-renewable resources and pollution, resulting in pessimistic predictions. See. Meadows D. L., 1974. Dynamics of growth in a finite world, Wright-Allen Press, Cambridge, Mass.

[17] Phelan S. E., 1999. A note on the correspondence between complexity and systems theory, Systemic Practice and Action Research, 12(3), pp. 237–246.

[18] See Mitchell M. and Newman M., April 17, 2001. Complex systems theory and evolution, Santa Fe Institute, Retrieved 2024-04-03.

[19] See above.

[20] The principal inspirer of the movement is rather wrongly considered to be Georgescu-Roegen, who expressed reservations about the approach of many degrowth theorists, where the solution to the problem of the unlimited and environmentally destructive growth will be either stagnation or a steady-state economy. By contrast, he argues that it should be in a declining state (Georgescu-Roegen, 1975). Furthermore, as Antoine Missemer (2017, p. 499) mentions, Georgescu-Roegen

collides with two obstacles that set limits to the implementation of the ambitions of the degrowth movement: the demographic evolution, which is linked to hard living conditions of world's population large part, and the human needs themselves, which do not conform to any "natural" order but depend on individual behaviours. It is thus reasonable that the economic, social, and ecological sustainable development is humanity's greatest challenge.

The sustainability concept appears in modern literature at the end of the twentieth century,[21,22] closely linked to the three shaping pillars in the popular diagram of the three circles: economy-society-environment (Barbier, 1987; IUCN's World Conservation Strategy, 1980). Barbier advocates for the goal maximization of the three subsystems through mutual interactions and adaptations. Contrary to the dominant neoclassical theory of economic development in the 1960s and the frequent conflation of growth with development, we were led to the report of human activity impact on the environment (UN Conference on the Human Environment, Stockholm, 1972) and to the "sustainable development", a term that is now officially used by a large part of the scientific community and international organizations, such as the Brundtland Report (UN, 1987) on Environment and Development, where it is termed as the "development which fulfils the needs of present generations without putting at risk those of future generations to meet their own needs" or the 1992 Earth Summit in Rio (UNCED)[23] and subsequent ones.

3.1 *Sustainability: Conceptual and Policy Confusions*

The notion of sustainability has been established in the contemporary time and already integrated within institutional communication. It has become an essential meaning of the legitimacy of all economic and political action. Sustainability includes the core economic pillar, where growth is the main element accompanying with increased levels of consumption, investment, productivity etc. The ecological or environmental pillar which is linked to bioeconomy or environmental economics and underlines the maintenance of a stable resource system, the use of renewable resources and the avoidance of overexploitation of non-renewable ones. That also encompasses the preservation of the landscape, the flora and fauna, and the productive land.[24] The social pillar concerns the promotion of social justice and cohesion

---

does not deal with an ahistorical degrowth but only with the degrowth of certain production factors, such as fossil fuels and the development of new technologies related to the energy. See Dincer I. and Rosen M. A., 2012. Exergy—Energy, Environment and Sustainable Development, 2nd ed., Elsevier.

[21] See above «Meadows Report, The limits of Growth, 1972».

[22] Sachs and Passet have already used the term "eco-development" since 1979, essentially describing sustainable development.

[23] The Rio Declaration, which was subsequently published, contains 27 rules that must be followed for the success of sustainable development.

[24] The latter is at great importance considering the arable land abatement during the last decades. It should not be also forgotten that land is deemed as a production factor and agriculture consists

which is chiefly achieved by the means of an equal distributional system. The goal of income distribution in a fair and equal manner requires the restructure of the entire economic, financial, and institutional system.

The elaboration of the rules and the construction of indicators that followed both the various summit meetings (UN—Commission on Sustained Development sessions, OECD) and the academic literature, which evolved in parallel, regarding the specific measures for the implementation of a sustainable development policy, provide with a rather confusing overview. Despite the often-repeated belief about the correctness of the three sustainable development pillars, neither the relation among them nor the policy to be followed for the relevant goals achievement, seem to have become clear. Is it the pursuit of separate goals that correspond to the pillars or for a systemic approach, i.e., interaction between subsystems and the behaviour over time of a complex non-linear system (Barbier, 1987; Cocklin, 1989)? Purvis et al. (2019) suggest that the concept of sustainability based solely on the social, economic, and environmental pillars is not realistic, but it was simply an historical outcome of relative studies, where there is not any actual intersection between these pillars.[25] Moreover, it is observed a gap between some academic literature view, which argues that there should be limits to economic growth for the selection of sustainable development goals (Redclift, 1987; Tulloch & Neilson, 2014), and the view, as for example of the United Nations, where the priority of the economic pillar seems to dominate for transmitting the results to the other fields of the system.

The sustainable development term is now a dominant example of the environmental thought, weakening the relation with sustainability, a concept of which it constitutes logically a part. At the same time, in the context of the necessary adjustments between the pursuits of the pillars, the importance of economic activity is reinforced, maintaining the traditional concept of economic growth.

The actual sustainability entails in a controversy of the current system operation, where it is aligned with changes on actors' behaviour, inputs, structures, and processes. These imbalances provide with thoughts for a radical questioning of the current market economy in its globalized version, which is based on both ecological and social concerns. This questioning could take multiple directions with various purposes and modalities, whether it comprises environmental issues, common financial practices, and the standardization of modes of lifestyles.

---

of the main activity of economic primary sector. Certainly, the concept of sustainable development varies among economic sectors. In agricultural, for instance, reproduction of a constant crop yield can be assured under proper cultivation. This constant reproduction does not apply in other sectors where their production depends on the use of mine or other non-renewable resources.

[25] Despite the efforts to explain sustainability, Parris and Kates (2003) argue that sustainability has not been explicitly defined and therefore the relative data and methods could vary. Barrow (1995) emphasizes the poor implementation of sustainable development and the fact that it is related to the mankind's behaviour.

3.2 Sustainability and Growth

The traditional unlimited growth models have only prevailed in a theoretical world, whereas stagnation and recession have been repeatedly appeared in world economy, among other factors, also due to the operation of entropy. The latter is not only limited in the excess use of energy type of fossils or coal but also to excessive low entropic use in specific sector of economy (e.g., financial system). The second law of thermodynamics has implications in economic production which could in turn impose constrains to growth. Growth theories are based on the traditional factors of production. That consists of physical resources as well as human labour and knowledge. Even if total output is quite satisfactory still the input flow needs to be examined.

The main factors of production have been traditionally defined as land, capital, and labour.[26] Energy possesses high productive power for all energy-converting systems, as it involves labour (people) and capital (machines). Environment provides with low entropy, i.e., energy, which plays a vital role on the production process. The energy could be considered as the sole physical and finite input, whilst capital could be regarded as the only endogenous factor of production because it can take the form either of money or tangible assets used in the production process, always in combination with exergy and labour. During the economic process, the available low-entropy, or exergy is not conserved, where in fact, it is truly consumed. Since exergy is indispensable in the economic process and is also not produced, then it consists of a tantamount factor of production like capital and labour. The human factor cannot produce or create exergy and that generates further debates about the technological progress factor and how the latter is integrated and interpreted in economic growth theories. Deficiencies in the production thus are related to its factors, where capital and labour may not be available at a certain time due to various reasons and so energy flows. Economic activity will eventually suffer from these deficiencies. Consequently, the acknowledgement of production factors is necessary for understanding the meaning and chiefly the realization of sustainability.[27]

[26] Land refers to the natural resources that are used to produce goods and services, besides parcel fields. In the eighteenth century, labour and land were regarded as factors of production, where capital has been an intermediate produced from labour (Ayres 1996). The Marxist theory supports that capital is the accumulation of labour surplus where labour is the only true factor of production. Neoclassical theory only regards capital and labour as the production factors of modern economies, where land has gradually been demoted.

[27] An alternative growth type refers to human factor as primary source of output integration the minimum possible use of physical resources. The latter could be a result of advanced technology, structural organisation, and final consumers' preferences. There are numerous examples such as recycled materials, limited printing, intensive use of electronic procedures and filing. The above concept is like the endogenous growth theories mainly developed by Romer (1990). The basic feature of knowledge is in rivalry with environment and thus not affected by entropy because knowledge yields to innovation and to further knowledge and ideas. Additional knowledge requires investment and time, nevertheless, its importance to the sustainability is not perceived by all economic systems in the same manner.

4 Financial System

The financial system analyses the way individuals, firms or governments make an economic decision in a specific context. It encompasses activities related to banking, capital markets, investments, and debt. It enables the optimization of resources and expenses, but mainly generates added value. Profits tend to increase the wealth, which will be beneficial to its expansion and sustainability.

The financial system furnishes the economy and society with the monetary means to increase the consumption and investments levels, necessary for the maintenance of the economic activity and social prosperity.[28] The financial system can be perceived as an organised economic system which exercises a significant influence on the economy. It is relevant for the sustainability because its actual size cannot be ignored.

4.1 *Globalization and Financialization*

Globalization describes the interconnection and interdependence among countries in terms of trade, technology, information, finance etc. Convergence policies have been observed during the last three decades where countries have opened their boundaries for trade and capital mobility. The concept of globalisation captures the economic, social, and environmental changes.[29] What is more interested are the consequences of globalization on available resources.

For financialization there is no concrete definition since it comprises aspects from the financial markets' globalization, the shareholders' value, and the income increment from financial investment. Epstein defines financialization as "the increasing role of financial motives, financial markets, financial actors, and financial institutions in the operation of the domestic and international economies (Epstein, 2005)". Binswanger (1999) supports that financialization has encouraged higher rates of financial investments relative to real investments. Davidson (1978) stresses the importance of the financial motive into the economy's function. If growth is mainly depending on investment which in turn depends on capital granted by financial institutions, then finance has essential role in economic activity. Orhangazi (2008) indicates two aspects of financialization with negative effects on real capital accumulation. First, the increased financial investments at the expense of real investment and, secondly, the increased financial payments that can reduce the amount of available funds. Dore (2008) suggests that financialization resembles globalization because

[28] It also provides the opportunities for financing a society's part that is usually excluded, such as middle or even low-income households as well as to small and medium size enterprises. The provision of funds is taken place through a variety of financial instruments, which broadly include the equity finance, debt, pension funds, derivatives, and stock options.

[29] It can be described by many views including the aspect of "colonization" of the lifestyles of "less developed" countries by developed countries. The meaning of life of the affected countries is distorted at its essence core and few manage to maintain their authenticity.

it is a suitable term for structural changes in the involved economies. Like globalization, these changes are interlinked and have the same implications on wealth distribution and in economic growth pattern.

Financialization refers to the financial sector growth[30] and its dominant role in the economy path.[31] As Dünhaupt (2016) argues, financialization[32] is not simply an effect but the real cause. It affects the economy through income distribution, capital stock investment, debt, net exports, and current account balances. It lessens investment in capital stock, deteriorates the income equality and stimulates indebtedness. This entropic process takes place gradually and even not apparently because increased consumption through wealth effect can temporarily sustain growth.[33] Financialization favors the emergence of profits with no investment mainly driven by debt-led consumption, a process which is susceptible to crises and disorder.

The actual information and communication technologies facilitate capital transfers from one country to another in zero time. In this way, the financial sector of

---

[30] The financial sector has already become dominant in terms of capital accumulation. The size of the financial sector augments over time and its impact on the economy is significant. Wray reports that for US economy finance became too big where at its peak in 2008, it captured 40% of all corporate profits and about a fifth of the total US GDP (Wray, 2011). Accounting only for US economy, household debt to GDP rose from 48% in 1980 to 100% in 2008, the private sector debt from 123 to 290% and overall, the financial sector debt augmented from 22% to GDP in 1981 to 117% in 2008 (Crotty, 2008). International financial transactions, including derivatives on exchange rates and interest rates, have increased 281 times from 1977 to 2007 (Panico et al., 2012). Similarly, big banks have augmented their size where "the total assets of the top 25 global banks in 1990 estimated approximately to USD 7,000 billion, which accounted for about 30% of the worldwide GDP and just before 2007, their total assets rose up to almost USD 40,000 billion, 70% of the worldwide (Dombret & Lucius, 2013)".

[31] Hein (2014) suggests that financialization could generate three different growth regimes. The 'finance-led growth' with a positive impact on growth mainly through the debt-financed consumption related to the wealth effect, where the accelerator mechanism also boosts investment. The 'profits without investment' regime with the difference that investment is not a matter of interest. This regime is possible only if demand stems from another element other than investment, such as consumption, deficits, or export surpluses. Finally, the 'contractive regime' which functions inversely because the increment in the corporates and households' payoff ration dampens profits, savings, consumption, and overall utility. The above regimes describe in a precise manner the various impacts on growth. Nevertheless, the positive regimes are more related to the short or medium term, where eventually all of them could end up to the contractive regime.

[32] For financialisation see also, Akcay, Ümit, et al. "Financialisation and Macroeconomic Regimes in Emerging Capitalist Countries Before and After the Great Recession," International Journal of Political Economy, Vol. 51, Iss. 2, 2022, pp. 77–100; Palley, Thomas "Financialization: What It Is and Why It Matters", The Levy Economics Institute and Economics for Democratic and Open Societies Washington, D.C., December 2007, Working Paper No. 525; Sawyer, Malcolm. "What Is Financialization?" International Journal of Political Economy, vol. 42, no. 4, 2013, pp. 5–18.

[33] Stockhammer (2004) tests the argument that financialization can lead to a slowdown. Based on post-Keynesian theories, the development of a market for creating shareholder value leads to a reduction in the growth rate, which also denotes the tradeoff between growth and profits. The shareholder revolution will result in the adoption of management policy closer to shareholders' preferences, i.e., profitability to growth. The implication of profitability selection is that investment will be lower. His empirical tests for the business sector for USA, France, UK, and Germany showed that financialization causes a slowdown in accumulation for the first two countries.

a nation becomes part of the international financial sector rather than a part of the domestic economy. Likewise, the financial markets could be also regarded as decentralized economies which comprise many interacting agents in a heterogeneous, autonomous and competitiveness environment. In the current highly financial globalized economy, therefore, finance and globalization are two concepts intertwined while the most serious consequences emanate from possible disorder and distortions of the financial system. The reasons are the strong linkages between finance and real economy and from the exceedingly global integration of financial markets. Households, firms, governments, banks, all of them have liabilities which require cash flows that could be derived either from income, sales of goods and services, profits from investments or financial instruments. The latter implies more finance. The result is even greater global dependence on financial fluctuations because of the amplification of the financial sector in economy.

It is quite paradoxical that whilst financial globalization cannot be considered as the entropy cause, nevertheless, it consists of a formidable accelerator of the existing imbalances inscribed in the conventional regime fueled by mass consumption. In addition, globalization expands the entropic implications mainly from the developed to developing countries. The most profitable systems of advanced countries have always been the pattern for successive imitation in order to "converge". However, this convergence also hints the extensive use of the pattern that consumes its free energy and moves towards disorder.

4.2 Financial System and Entropy

The function of the financial system affects the real economy. Many economists support that the operation of the current financial system is not stable but inherently flaw (Bagelot, 1873; Kindleberger, 1989; Lavoie, 1983; Minsky, 1986; Wray, 2011). The financial system could be currently deemed as complex system and thus it coincides with a complex system's entropy. The entropy of complex systems formalizes our understanding of many complex processes including their development as applied in the financial system.[34] The origin of instability and crises is the endogenous entropic tendency. Corporates and households finance their investment through an indebtment process in the anticipation of future profits for repayment. The entropy of the financial system is the unperceivable movement from a stable to an unstable financial environment. That depends though upon the financial system structure. During prosperous periods, profit generations cultivate positive expectations that in turn induce financial institutions to increase credit access and availability. Investment and debt leverage increase, but also future commitment obligations. This process is endogenous and could turn to an excessive practice use with capital concentration. In this case, entropy increases and accelerates the move towards drainage and disorder.

[34] See Prigogine I., 1978, Time, Structure and Fluctuations, Science, vol. 201, no 4358, pp. 777–785.

Another matter of consideration is the behavior of corporates and individuals. Entropy increases at a higher pace because of the imitation of behaviors. This kind of externality is transmitted during boom periods when everything seems to operate well. When higher profits are created and credit is available, enterprises are willing to increase their debt level instead of disburdening it, since investment continues to pay off. A similar role is played by the derogatory depreciation policy which in combination with the tax policy, could lead to a pro-cyclical multiplier effect (Lohmann-Rüchti effect). In fact, depreciations that are faster than the equipment's economic life lead to a reduction in investment in the event of a reversal of the circumstance, whilst it is not certain that the accrual funds are channelled to the capital investment, but rather to financial activities.[35] Success from financial activities encourages other agents to imitate similar behavior, but it also nurtures a disregard of the possibility of failure. Financial products are offered to the public with the implicit conviction that their prices could only rise. The development of a euphoric economy, where short-term financing of long positions is available, curbs agents from raising awareness of the potential risks. It is remarkable that the process is not quite visible during the prosperous period, but it becomes a normal way of life convincing everyone for a constant stability.[36] The above-described process could be attributed as the operation of entropy law in the financial system, where the entropy of this complex system corresponds to the endogenous instability of the financial system.

The accumulation of finance could direct the economy in stagnation. Accumulation favors merges and acquisitions and the progressive emergence of large oligopolistic and monopolistic patterns and as a result this emergence results in an increase of the overall profit share and capital accumulation. The lack of opportunities and the concentration of capital will discourage investment demand. At the same time, notwithstanding, these oligopolistic corporations will avoid overproduction to shun price reduction and maintain the profit margins. Therefore, investment in capital stock will be low even if huge profits are generated but that will finally lead to stagnation.[37] Reduction on investment in capital stock has inversely effect on growth, which was instead sustained through indebtedness from the financial sector's funds. After almost four decades most of the advanced countries have been heavily indebted stimulating further the instability and uncertainty.

Entropy and instability are both qualitative concepts, where entropy leads to the point of maximum instability. This is the point when everyone becomes fully aware that indebtedness had reached its peak and repayments cannot be easily fulfilled. As soon as a financial distortion appears then growth is ultimately blocked. Households and corporations seek to reduce their indebtedness, lowering consumption and

---

[35] See also. Abraham-Frois G., 1989, Dynamique Économique, 6ème éd., Dalloz, Paris, pp. 342–343.

[36] This overoptimistic psychological behavior is transparent both from borrowing and lending size, implicitly indicating that the system's discipline has been lessened.

[37] Foster and McChesney (2009) attributed the crisis of 1970s as the result of overaccumulation and stagnation. Thereafter, huge amounts of capital have been channelled into financial products instead of fixed capital investment (Magdoff & Sweezy, 1987).

investment.[38] It is the moment when borrowers can no longer finance their debts, expectations change, the financial system can no longer provide with credit and is forced to contraction and inertia. The peak cannot be predicted because it also depends on psychological, institutional, and social factors. However, entropy will be at maximum level when the financial system's endogenous instability causes an irreversible crisis. The traditional macroeconomic theory preconizes financial system's stability which can be only perturbed by short term external shocks, nevertheless, this perception neglects the apparition of several financial crises that had led to stagnation and disorder. The operation of entropy which is the intrinsic recurrent of boom/busts dynamics cycles is ignored. It accelerates the growth path through the boom phase with overproduction and super profit maximization but eventually leads to stagnation and disorder. The implication is a chaotic state, where consumption, lending, investment, and production are all stagnated. Thus, the term entropy can be viewed as the measure of disorder and uncertainty reflecting the features of financial instability.

4.3 Financial System and Sustainability

From the above is observed the process of a socioeconomic system reproducing itself identically towards same pattern, where its entropy depends on the evolution of structures. A silent but still a constant grow of the system's entropy has less chances for perpetuity or sustainability. Thus, sustainability cannot be achieved if investment and consumption depend upon a great extent on credit availability and profits creation for the repayments of past obligations or on rollover debts because it is quite likely that these conditions cannot always be met.

The emergency of the sustainability implicitly indicates a tradeoff with profits generation that corporates need to tackle. Entropy and sustainability consist of two non-fully intersecting concepts where sustainability is mainly hindered by ecological disturbances and limitation of natural resources. Climate change risk and the overall environmental degradation are actually the outcome of the entropy law operation.

Therefore, the available options for sustainability are either to allow entropy law, which would move the system towards a quasi-stationary state, because of energy degradation, or to discover new reaction processes. Financial system has an important impact on sustainability since its influential size could direct the economy to the sustainability path. The stability of the financial system can assure a sufficient investment and production level to maintain economy activity. The key factors are the provision of financial services on a stable and continuous process and the financing of sustainable projects. The role of the financial system is to motivate investment compatible with the sustainability. King and Levine (1993) support that the development of financial system is a prerequisite for sustainability. The financial system seems to be adequate in supporting sustainability as for the dimension of economic

[38] Whilst banks refrain from conveying the almost zero liquidity received from central banks since they are highly risk averse.

growth, less for the social cohesion and even less for the environment (Ozili, 2023). Financial institutions are currently viewed as cruel operators of money circulation and creation without any social or environmental sensibilities. For this reason, financial institutions should invest on social trust which could be achieved with the cultivation of new relations with the society within an enhanced friendly environmental approach. That implies the reorientation from profit maximization to sustainability maximization. This reorientation encompasses technological advancements, regulatory influence, economic theory, consumer preferences and investor behavior. As a process, a sustainability strategy should be first designed, following by sustainability innovation leading to the introduction of new sustainable financial instruments. Hence, the involvement and engagement of stakeholders supported by new regulatory environment finally inducing a sustainable consumer demand and investor behavior. Access on financial instruments could be available for the sustainable projects that comprise the environmental preservation. These could include credit availability or loans in quite attractive rates oriented to meet sustainability targets such as poverty alleviation, environmental protection and restoration, promotion of renewable use of resources, clean water, affordable and clean energy, reduced inequality, responsible consumption and production.

Even though the above argument may sound utopic, notwithstanding, financial institutions have started to show an increased interest on the sustainability. The insertion of the fear that climate change has put on the financial institutions has forced them to realize that the pursuance of sustainability would also assure their existence.

4.4 Willpower of the Financial System

As for all systems, the entropy of the financial system constantly increases. What matters though is the pace of the entropy increase and the degree of resistance. Entropy law moves an organized system to disorder consuming at the same time its available energy. Afterwards the system attempts, intentionally or not, to restore some degree of order to avoid complete finality. Therefore, economic systems do possess some degree of intuitive resistance to entropy that turns up in periods of distortions. Based on Daloz's (1974) graphical structure, Fig. 1 summarizes the entropy of the system.

According to the complex systems theory, socioeconomic systems could be considered as decision making systems, which also refers to the structural features of each system. In that sense, the willpower of the financial system could be reoriented towards new structural conditions subject to internal new processes and behaviors that would deter or delay the operation of entropy law. Financial institutions constitute a main component of the financial system, where entropy is associated with the traditional financial traits such as liquidity, credit, market solvency as well as with the financial institutions that are confronted with the challenge to transform their business chains.

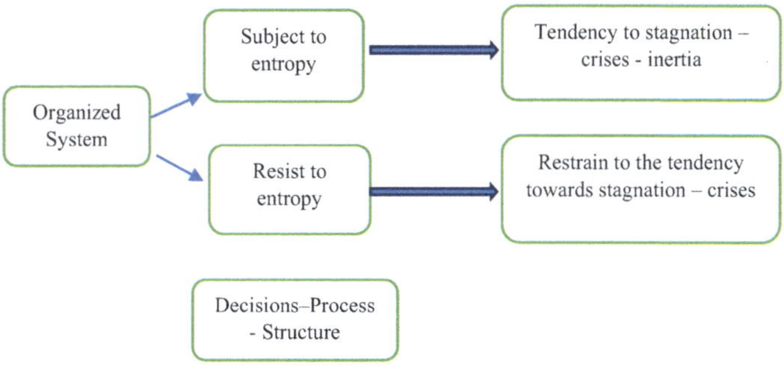

Fig. 1 Entropy operation. *Source* Daloz (1974) and authors' elaboration

The restructure of the financial system should aim to securing a stable investment level with the development of sound and sincere social relations. Being a main influential of economic activity, the investment boost from the financial system depends upon three factors. Firstly, the managerial attitudes that reflect subjective positions and optimism of the economy. Secondly, the financial status of individuals and corporates, interpreted by their level of indebtedness, expectations, and interest rates levels. Thirdly, it is the set of profit thresholds that depend on the forecast of economy growth path.

Entropy thus arises some the plausible questions on how and to what degree could the financial system be transformed[39] in order to avoid disorder and ecological collapse, and if this transformation is already launched or would the system be finally forced to change.

5 What Kind of Sustainability?

Therefore, the important question that the paper raises is the kind of sustainability. Daly (1992) states that if the economic system is perceived as a Biosphere subsystem, then economic growth is not durable. Finance and economics, notwithstanding, is a part of social sciences and is related to the behavior and interaction of the actors in the market. The profound subtle relationship of economic activity with physical laws uncovers the anthropomorphic character of entropy.

Economic activity consists of an interaction between human factor and physical resources. An advanced and high-quality human factor level in terms of knowledge and technology designates the most efficient use of physical resources in the production process. The relationship of sustainability between biological and

[39] The structures must be internally evolved to establish the greatest possible self-sufficiency of the system. It is quite important the safeguard of the system, the decision-making, and certainly the matter of capital allocation. Hence, the stability of an influential and powerful system will be externalized to other systems contributing thus to an overall stability. The above process could allow the achievement of the sustainability goal.

economic activities reveals the material foundation of human society (Couix, 2015). The primary source of the produced prosperity via current economic activity is the "low entropy" resources, which provides with a prospect of a combined development of economic process and the bioeconomy. Therefore, actual sustainability is linked to this combination. The bioeconomic aspect puts human activities, structures, institutions, and preferences in a harmony within natural and physical conditions.

Energy and matter are subject to physical laws, and entropy constantly operates in the biophysical sphere. Apart from physical input, socioeconomic systems also rely on human factor that contains technology, knowledge, and preferences. The technology develops advanced combinations of natural physical inputs and knowledge to produce goods and services.[40] However, could new technologies evolve and decelerate the entropic tendency? The ever-increasing trend for stock buybacks, apart from reinforcing income inequality, does not encourage investment in the real economy and the development of new technologies.[41] Even if technology plays an important role in growth theories, its concept is quite generic and cannot be easily quantified.[42]

Besides the production process, economic entropy is highly linked to the products' utility and the preferences. This circular chain indicates that action could be also taken from the demand side because sustainability is also related to preferences and choices. The real value of a financial product is the enjoyment of life where the main objective of an economic activity should be the self-preservation of the human beings. The self-preservation is only associated with the satisfaction of well-known basic needs, such as the self-maintenance, development, replication, protection of the environment and other species. Low entropy and economic value are interlinked with the basic but necessary needs and under this scope, the need for production of luxurious products is perhaps contestable. Sustainability cannot coincide with the fulfillment of preferences beyond reason. Jean Baudrillard (1972, pp. 83–94) states that actual productive system has been adjusted according to the needs of each socioeconomic class.[43] If there were less or even one homogenous class, then production will have been only driven by one main demand force.

Utility maximization was first developed by the utilitarian philosophers Jeremy Bentham and John Stuart Mill. It is an optimal decision problem mostly referred in consumer theory. Besides income and prices, utility also depends on consumers

---

[40] Technology has been always included as potential factor in the traditional growth models that would assure sustainable growth.

[41] See Lazonick W., 2009, Sustainable Prosperity in the New Economy? Business Organization and High-Tech Employment in the United States, Kalamazoo, MI:W.E. Upjohn Institute for Employment Research. (2010 Schumpeter Prize).

[42] The substantial term of advanced technology in an economy is not quite clear, where. it mainly refers to innovations occurred in certain domains or processes of economic activity, where each innovation partly contributes to the development of each domain but cannot simply be regarded as a global enhanced technology that stimulates growth. For the financial sector, innovation was principally linked with the introduction of new financial products that further stimulated securitization and hence the instability entropic process.

[43] There is a differentiation of needs based on each class structure. That seems to be quite relevant considering the eager of each class to improve its economic status and reach to the next higher class. This pursuit even constitutes an established goal.

preferences. The dominant economic theory is based on the fundamental principle that the purpose of the system is to satisfy as many needs as possible despite the scarcity of available resources. The adoption of the view made the concept of scarcity to disappear. The process that determines the levels of consumption, investment, employment, income, portfolios occur within an institutional structure, where is assumed that consumers are rational seeking the most benefit for themselves. Rationality though can be bounded or complex to prevent them from making the optimal choices. Gazing deeper though it puts pressure on the entropy within the system. The reasons are the growing demand for addable and redundant processes and the demand for further money creation through extra opportunities of financial products. The latter also entails huge losses which will certainly not be advertised. The actual financial system operates in that manner encouraging the entropic operation.

When sustainability or irreversibility enters in the argumentation, preferences could be analogously modified. The demand side can thus promote real sustainability. The preferences should be formed into the concept of responsibility, modesty, and periodization of the needs. Jonas (1979) adopts the principle of responsibility towards future generations, where the existence requires the continuation of its existence.[44] Rahnema underlines that populations "are subject to merciless propaganda for new and often "addictive" needs, which make them passive witnesses to their condemnation to misery" (2003, p. 265). Coméliau (2006) points out the confusion between needs and desires, where needs can bring enjoyment but there are also limited, whilst desires are potentially endless. The use of the latter therefore makes it possible to justify the claim of indefinite growth.[45] Gorz indicates that current rationality excludes the notion of "sufficient" (1988, p. 142). However, it is no longer easy to determine what is necessary and sufficient, but it seems that there no limits on utility maximization or satisfaction. Instead, the prevailed dogma encourages greediness and unstoppable mania for more and more. The right for free trade and transactions has been misinterpreted with a useless abundance that distorts sound thinking rather than promotes sustainability. The economic and financial system provides goods and services to satisfy the needs of the society. However, these needs are increasing throughout time pushing up further the production system without questioning the means to meet these needs.

The challenges of sustainability fall essentially into the broad categories of natural imbalances and social characteristics. Before the sustainability emergence, it was deemed that abundance would be available for everyone without considering that was simply an intense exploitation of non-renewable resources and a prodigious acceleration of entropy. Therefore, the abundance can only be for short-run, or concern only a tiny minority for the long term. However, habits and preferences have been

[44] He proposes the renunciation of the "wasteful" lifestyle of some part of the population of developed countries.

[45] Coméliau refers that as utilitarian obsession that forms the social behaviour and contemporary culture. The society is fascinated by wealth increase of its individuals which signifies the progress of well-being enhancement. He summarizes it in the formula the "more is equal to better". However, a society of abundance leads to the need for increased consumption, production and thereafter for the pursuit of more, even though that could be illusory or even destructive.

adopted, evolved but also become entropic and non-sustainable. Fortunately, it has been much raised awareness of the sustainability aspect,[46] but the problem is that the conventional foundations of the cause are only marginally discussed. The various strategies envisaged in the name of sustainability do not call into question these conventional foundations simply because of the reluctance to abstain from all the comfortable but non-sustainable "habits". Thus, the entropic movement cannot be constrained.

6 Conclusion

Research on entropy in sustainable economics and finance now has gained attention for its innovative approach to understanding complex socio-economic systems, their uncertainty, and information dynamics. It reveals how energy and resource flows affect economic sustainability, i.e. the efficiency of resource utilization and the long-term sustainability of economic activities. Entropy as a measure of uncertainty and disorder is used to quantify the uncertainty or disorder within economic and financial systems leading to their unstable growth. It helps in assessing the unpredictability and complexity of market dynamics.

Consequently, sustainability becomes more complex depending not only on the preservation of natural resources but also on the sound development of the human knowledge and action. The interaction of human factor with natural resources represents the process of sustainability. The goal requires the economy to be placed in a steady stationary state aligned with environmental conditions. The financial system currently fails to adequately channel funds at a steady pace towards long term productive investment in the economy. As a complex system, nevertheless, the financial system cannot be simply carried away by instability that its entropic nature dictates. The reform of the financial system reform is needed at global level, not only to improve financial stability but hence to ensure that finance is redirected towards productive activities and assists countries to address the new environmental challenges and overall, sustainability. The interplay of social, economic, biophysical, psychologic factors will finally designate the expedience of sustainability. The attempt to oppose to the dynamics of the system in the name of social justice and environmental protection i.e., sustainability, could turn us back to the ethical issue and the reassessment of the laisser-faire right.

As the main influential factor of the economy, the financial system should be a pioneer steering resources to simultaneously deal with climate change, social cohesion, and sustainable development challenges. Instead of providing credit based on

[46] There are several publications on the subject, such as e.g., Harris J. M. and Roach B., 2022, Environmental and Natural Resource Economics. A Contemporary Approach, 5th ed., Routledge. Επίσης, Tietenberg T. and Lewis L., 2018, Environmental and Natural Resource Economics, 11th ed., Routledge.

investors' fit, rely on expectations and depend on the uncertainty, the current multilateral financial system can be transformed by sweeping reforms to reduce debt burdens, and channel private finance to both climate and sustainable development. It is really hard to conceive that these global goals could be achieved without devising the most effective financial instruments.

Given the urgency and magnitude of the sustainability and climate change, the world cannot risk more time waste. It is emphasized that the sustainability must be confronted at global level. Climate risks are complex and interlinked, where the impact of the climate change in one country may spill over to neighbouring countries. To make progress towards more equitable and climate-resilient the world demands change and interventions to address cross-border systemic risk. If sustainability is to be both effective and fair, then it must happen globally and forthwith.

In this paper we referred to the newly emerging concept of entropy from the nineteenth century, which led to the awareness of the effects of human economic activity on the natural environment and the risks that arise. The approach through the theory of complex systems has allowed us to place conceptually on a new basis the approach to the enormous environmental challenge of the international community. Despite all the efforts that are being launched, we argue, as conclusion, that the reform of the international financial system based mainly on the criterion of collective responsibility towards environment i.e., ultimately a moral and political problem, constitutes the principal way of dealing with the sustainability of economic activity in the modern world.

References

Ayres, R. (1996). *Eco-thermodynamics: Economics and the Second Law*, 96/51/EPS, CMER, INSEAD Fontainebleau, Paris.

Ayres, R. (1999). The second law, the fourth law, recycling and limits to growth. *Ecological Economics, 29*(3), 473–483.

Bagelot, W. (1873). *Lombart Street: A description of the Money Market*. Henry S King.

Barbier, E. B. (1987). The concept of sustained economic development. *Environmental Conservation, 14*(2), 101–110.

Barrow, C. J. (1995). Sustainable development: Concept, value and practice. *Third World Planning Review, 17*(4), 369.

Baudrillard, J. (1972). *Pour une critique de l'économie politique du signe*. Gallimard.

Binswanger, M. (1999). *Stock markets, speculative bubbles and economic growth*. Edward Elgar.

Brundtland Report (UN). (1987). *World commission on environment and development*. Oxford University Press.

Carnot, S. (1824). *Réflexions sur la puissance motrice du feu*. Chez Bachelier.

Chen, J., & Calbraith, J. (2022). *Economics: A biophysical theory* (UTIP, Working Paper 78).

Clausius, R. (1879). *The mechanical theory of heat*. MacMillan and co.

Cocklin, C. R. (1989). Methodological problems in evaluating sustainability, *Environmental Conservation, 16*(4), 343–351. Retrieved 8 April 2024.

Comeliau, C. (2006). *La Croissance ou le progrès ? Croissance, décroissance, développement durable*. Seuil.

Couix, Q. (2015). Entropie et économie, dans le tournant théorique de Nicholas Georgescu-Roegen, Economies et finances. dumas-01404779f.

Crotty, J. (2008). *Structural causes of the global financial crisis: A critical assessment of the 'new financial architecture* (UMASS Amherst, Working Paper No. 14). Amherst, MA: Department of Economics, University of Massachusetts Amherst.

Daloz, J. P. (1974). Inflation et entropie du système économique. In Économie appliquée, tome 27 n°1,1974. Inflation, secteurs, plan. pp. 5–26.

Daly, H. E. (1987, December). The Economic Growth Debate: What some economists have learned but many have not. *Journal of Environmental Economics and Management*, reprinted in A. Markandya and J. Richardson (Eds.), *The Earthscan reader in Environmental Economics*. London 1992.

Daly, H. E. (1992, janvier–février). Il n'y a pas de croissance durable. *Transversales Science/Culture, 13*, 10–11.

Davidson, P. (1978). *Money and the real world* (2nd ed.). Macmillan.

Dombret, A., et al. (2013). *Stability of the financial system—Illusion or feasible concept*. Edward Elgar.

Dore, R. (2008). Financialization of the global economy. *Industrial and Corporate Change, 17*(6), 1097–1112.

Dünhaupt, P. (2016). Financialization and the crises of capitalism. *Hochschule für Wirtschaft und Recht Berlin* (Working Paper, No. 67/2016). Institute for International Political Economy (IPE), Berlin.

Epstein, G. (2005). Introduction. In G. Epstein (Ed.), *Financialization and the world economy*. Edward Elgar.

Farrell, K. N. (2019). Producing ecological economy. *Real-World Economics Review, 87*. Universidad del Rosario.

Fetter, F. A. (1905). *The principles of economics, with applications to practical problems chap, vi*. The Century Co.

Fisher, I. (1930). *The theory of interest, as determined by impatience to spend income and opportunity to invest it* (p. 3). Macmillan.

Foster, J. B., & McChesney, R. W. (2009). Monopoly-finance capital and the paradox of accumulation. *Monthly Review, 61*(5).

Georgescu-Roegen, N. (1971). *The entropy law and the economic process*. Harvard University Press.

Georgescu-Roegen, N. (1975). Energy and economic myths. *Southern Economic Journal, 41*(3), 347–381.

Georgescu-Roegen, N. (1977). What Thermodynamics and Biology can teach economists. *Atlantic Economic Journal, 5*(1), 13–21.

Georgescu-Roegen, N. (1979). Energy analysis and economic valuation. *Southern Economic Journal, 45*(4), 1023–1058.

Georgescu-Roegen, N. (2006). *La décroissance: Entropie–Écologie–Économie*. Ellébore—Sang de la terre, 3ème éd. revue et augmentée, Paris.

Gorz, A. (1988). *Métamorphoses du travail, Quête du sens, Critique de la raison économique*. Galilée.

Guitton, H. (1979). *De l'imperfection en économie*. Calman-Lévy.

Harribey, J. M. (2007, mars–avril). Les théories de la décroissance: enjeux et limites. *Cahiers français, Développement et environnement, 337*, 20–26.

Hein, E. (2014). *Distribution and growth after Keynes: A post-Keynesian guide*. Edward Elgar.

Herrmann, P. C. (2010). *Rethinking evolution, entropy and economics: A triadic conceptual framework for the maximum entropy principle as applied to the growth of knowledge* (Working Paper Series, No. 146). Frankfurt School of Finance & Management.

International Union for Conservation of Nature and Natural Resources. (Ed.). (1980). World Conservation Strategy (IUCN): Living Resource Conservation for Sustainable Development. IUCN–UNEP–WWF.

Jakimowicz, A. (2020). *The role of entropy in the development of economics.* Entropy 22, no. 4: 452. Department of World Economy, Institute of Economics, Polish Academy of Sciences, Palace of Culture and Science.
Jonas, H. (1979). *Le principe responsabilité, Une éthique pour la civilisation technologique*, éd. fr. Paris, Ed. du Cerf.
Kindleberger, C. (1989). *Manias, panics and crashes: A history of the financial crises.* Macmillan.
King, R. G., & Levine, R. (1993). Finance and growth: Schumpeter might be right. *The Quarterly Journal of Economics, 108*, 717–737.
Kümmel, R., et al. (2010). Thermodynamic laws, economic methods and the productive power of energy institute for theoretical physics and astrophysics. *Journal of Non-equilibrium Thermodynamics, 35*(2), 145–179.
Kümmel, R., & Lindenberger, D. (2020). Energy, entropy, constraints, and creativity in economic growth and crises. *MDPI Review, Entropy, 22*(10), 1156.
Latouche, S. (2010). *Farewell to growth.* Polity.
Lavoie, M. (1983). Loi de Minsky et loi d'entropie. *Economie Appliquée, tome XXXVI*(2–3), 287–331.
Lesourne, J. (1991). *L'économie de l'ordre et du désordre.* Economica.
Lesourne, J., Orléan, A., & Walliser, B. (2002). *Leçons de microéconomie évolutionniste* (O. Jacob, Ed.).
Marshall, A. (1927). *Principles of economics: An introductory volume.* Macmillan.
Magdoff, H., & Sweezy, P. M. (1987). *Stagnation and the financial explosion.* Monthly Review Press.
Meadows, D., et al. (1972). *The limits to Growth: A report for the Club of Rome's project on the predicament of mankind.* Universe Books.
Minsky, H. P. (1986). *Stabilizing an Unstable Economy.* Mc Graw Hill.
Mirowski Ph. (2001). *Plus de chaleur que de lumière: l'économie comme physique sociale, la physique comme économie de la nature.* Economica.
Missemer, A. (2017). Nicholas Georgescu-Roegen and degrowth. *European Journal of the History of Economic Thought, 24*(3), 493–506.
Nieto, J., et al. (2020). An ecological macroeconomics model: The energy transition in the EU. *Energy Policy, 145*(C). Elsevier.
Orhangazi, Ö. (2008). Financialisation and capital accumulation in the non-financial corporate sector: A theoretical and empirical investigation on the US economy: 1973–2003. *Cambridge Journal of Economics, 32*(6), 863–886.
Ozili, P. K. (2023). *Financial inclusion, sustainability and sustainable development* (MPRA Paper 118880). University Library of Munich.
Panico, C., et al. (2012). Income distribution and the size of the financial sector: A Sraffian analysis. *Cambridge Journal of Economics, 36*(6), 1455–1477.
Parris, T. M., & Kates, R. W. (2003). Characterizing and measuring sustainable development. *Annual Review of Environment and Resources, 28*(1), 559–586.
Prigogine, I. (1978). Time, structure and fluctuations. *Science, 201*(4358), 777–785.
Purvis, B., Mao, Y., & Robinson, D. (2019). Three pillars of sustainability: In search of conceptual origins. *Sustainability Science, Springer Link, 14*, 681–695.
Rahnema, M. (2003). *Quand la misère chasse la pauvreté.* Fayard/Actes Sud.
Redclift, M. R. (1987). *Sustained development: Exploring and contradictions.* Routledge.
Ricardo, D. (1817). *On the principles of political economy and taxation.* J. McCreery.
Richardson, K. A. (2004). Systems theory and complexity: Part 1. *E:CO Issue, 6*(3), 75–79.
Romer, P. M. (1990). Endogenous technological change. *Journal of Political Economy, 98*, s71–s102.
Solow, R. M. (1974). The economics of resources or the resources of economics. *The American Economic Review, 64*(2). Papers and Proceedings of the Eighty-sixth Annual Meeting of the American Economic Association (May 1974), pp. 1–14.

Stockhammer, E. (2004). Financialisation and the slowdown of accumulation. *Cambridge Journal of Economics, 28*(5), 719–741.

Thomson, W. (1851). On the dynamical theory of heat. *Transactions of the Royal Society of Edinburgh, 20*, 261–288.

Tulloch, L., & Neilson, D. (2014). The neoliberalisation of sustainability. *Citizenship Social and Economics Education, 13*(1), 26–38.

UN Conference on the Human Environment Report, Stockholm. (1972). United Nations.

Wray, R. (2011). Lessons we should have learned from the global financial crisis but didn't (Working Paper No 681). Levy Economics Institute of Bard College.

An Assessment of the Greek Farmers' Motives to Adopt Bio-Pesticide Products

Achilleas Kontogeorgos and George Tsiamis

Abstract European Green Deal aims to reduce the use and risk of chemical pesticides by 50% by 2030, although it is still undefined, on the one hand, whether a reduction in chemical pesticides could be feasible in different farming systems and situations and on the other, if farmers are willing to quit chemical pesticides in favour of other solution. A solution towards reducing chemical pesticides are the pesticides derived from natural materials such as animals, plants, bacteria, and fungi named in general, Biopesticides. The prospects for biopesticides are quite promising, and they are expected to play an increasingly important role in sustainable agriculture and pest control in the future since they demonstrate some potential advantages like environmental sustainability, reduced chemical residue, less adverse health problems for farmers and so on. Having this in mind the prospects for Biopesticides to acquire a significant market share in the pesticides market are quite promising. Nevertheless, biopesticides, as any new technology in agriculture, should be adopted and promoted by the farmers themselves. For this reason, it is crucial to examine farmers' perception about biopesticides, their attributes and to conclude if they are willing to move towards to reduce chemical pesticides in favour of biopesticides. This paper aims to provide a first investigation about the perceptions of farmers in Greece about biopesticides. For this reason, a questionnaire examining farmers' perceptions was prepared and distributed in farmers in northern Greece. The main goal of this research is to find out what could motivate Greek farmers to adopt more environmentally friendly practices and more specific if they are willing to adopt and use biopesticide products. A special part of the questionnaire was devoted to rank and evaluate by using the best—worst scaling approach 11 advantages, and 7 disadvantages derived by the international bibliography about biopesticides. Best—worst scaling approach provides more accurate results about ranking biopesticides properties. Another part of the questionnaire devoted to investigating Greek farmers' willingness to pay for

---

A. Kontogeorgos (✉)
Department of Agriculture, International Hellenic University, Thessaloniki, Greece
e-mail: akontoge@ihu.gr

G. Tsiamis
Department of Sustainable Agriculture, University of Patras, Patras, Greece
e-mail: gtsiamis@upatras.gr

I. Bartuseviciene et al. (eds.), *Building Resilience Through Digital Transformation and Sustainable Innovation*, Springer Proceedings in Business and Economics,
https://doi.org/10.1007/978-3-031-90054-9_13

biopesticides products by applying Stoetzel's approach of min and max price. The results of this research could help policy makers and biopesticides companies to formulate a communication strategy to approach farmers to increase the willingness to adopt biopesticides.

Keywords Green Deal · Environment protection · Greece

JEL Classification Codes Q18 · Q16 · Q56

1 Introduction

European Union (EU) has long pursued a leading role in policies to tackle climate change (Siddi, 2020). In this direction, in 2019, the European Commission presented the European Green Deal committing to climate neutrality by 2050. To achieve this goal, Green Deal sets out an action plan aimed at achieving two initial targets: boosting resource efficiency by moving to a clean, circular economy, and restoring biodiversity and reducing pollution (Refaat, 2021). The European Green Deal can be seen as an important step that will improve the environment, but, at the same time, will pervert the competition and the entrepreneurial activities within the EU due to its interventionist dimension. Therefore, the responsibility of political actors will increase, not only in the environmental area, but also in market processes and daily life (Bogoslov et al., 2022).

The Green Deal includes several strategies for achieving its objective, with the Farm to Fork strategy as at its heart aiming to make food systems fair, healthy and environmentally friendly (EC, 2020). This strategy includes specific actions: ensuring sustainable food production; stimulating sustainable food processing, wholesale, retail, hospitality, and food services' practices; promoting sustainable food consumption, facilitating the shift toward healthy, sustainable diets; and reducing food loss and waste. In this direction two main key quantitative targets of the Farm to Fork strategy to be reached by 2030 is a) reduce the use and risk of chemical pesticides by 50%, b) reduce the use of more hazardous pesticides by 50%.

Many authors have discussed the economic implications of the Farm to Fork strategy especially those actions linked to quantitative targets like the above (see for example Wesseler, 2022). Such economic assessments prove and quantify the evident conclusion that by such substantial reduction in crop production inputs, such as fertilizers—fertilizer use has a yield-increasing effect—and pesticides—pesticide use has a yield-securing effect—agricultural output and income will face significant loses. This is obvious for farmers too resulting in a series of protests across all European capitals struggling to avoid such policy measures (Hilmi & Frison, 2024). So even if, European Farm to Fork strategy and Green Deal represents a bold and necessary step towards sustainability, its implementation faces significant challenges that has to be examined in order to be successfully implemented.

In this direction, this work examines the role of biopesticides as an alternative solution to chemical pesticides acting as a mean to protect and assure agricultural production and agricultural incomes, Biopesticides are products originating from living organisms, such as microbes and nematodes, as well as plant-derived products, secondary metabolites from microorganisms, insect pheromones, and genes used to induce natural resistance in crops (Copping & Menn, 2000). Based on the nature and origin of the active ingredients, biopesticides fall into several categories such as botanicals, antagonists, compost teas, growth promoters, predators and pheromones (Lengai & Muthomi, 2018). However, biopesticides are limited in comparison to chemical pesticides because of high manufacturing costs, poor storage stability, and efficacy problems, among other issues (Ortega et al., 2023). Biopesticides still require research and development, but these products generally have a lower environmental impact than chemical pesticides, making them viable alternatives to conventional pesticides (Kumar et al., 2021). Nevertheless, biopesticides may be a viable option for meeting the Farm to Fork Strategy's 2030 objectives.

However, the acceptance of the European Green Deal among European farmers varies widely and is influenced by several factors, including the perceived benefits and challenges associated also with the biopesticides' implementation. Even critical factor is the perceived cost to adopt sustainable practices which may involve significant upfront costs for new equipment, technology, and changes in farming methods. On the other hand, many farmers recognize the long-term benefits of sustainable agricultural practices, such as reduced pesticide use and organic farming, which can improve soil health and fertility. Therefore, environmental awareness and behaviour among farmers should be examined since it can affect adoption of environmentally friendly practices and in this way determine policy measures adoption and success (Kontogeorgos et al., 2015).

Examining adoption of environmental policies is crucial to ensure they would be effective, equitable, and economically viable. It also helps identify best practices, areas for improvement, and could ensure that these policies finally meet their intended goals without unintended negative consequences. This scrutiny is vital for building a sustainable future that balances environmental health, economic growth, and social well-being. Hence, the main objective of this paper is to assess the perceptions of farmers on alternative pesticide solutions and mainly for biopesticide products in a wider scope of adopting Grean Deal goals. Moreover, use and adoption of such products will be examined, and an attempt will be made to identify factors that affect adoption of such products. These factors can be considered as indicators of a broader environmental attitude that affect not only adoption of biopesticide products but also determining a wider ecological behaviour and what is most the broader adoption of the environmental policy—Green Deal—of the common agriculture policy. To facilitate farmers perceptions about biopesticides the following issues were also examined: Advantages and disadvantages of biopesticides according to farmers along with an attempt to measure their willingness to pay for such products.

Such analysis and research is quite important, since the last period farmers are protesting against Green Deal, that become an easy target instead of the serious structural problems of the European agricultural sector. The acceptance of the European Green Deal among farmers is mixed, with many seeing both opportunities and challenges. Successful implementation requires addressing the concerns of farmers through adequate support, clear communication, financial incentives, and robust infrastructure. Ensuring that farmers have the knowledge, tools, and resources to transition to sustainable practices will be crucial for achieving the Green Deal's ambitious goals.

2 Methodology

This survey was conducted in the period September–November 2023 in the region of Central Macedonia (mainly in the prefectures of Serres). A questionnaire was filled through interviews by farmers. Farmers were approached through farmers associations and professional networks mainly providing agricultural supplies. The only prerequisite for someone to participate in the survey was to state that was occupied professionally in farming sector. Respondents had to answer a series of questions about their cultivation and environmental practices, their perceptions of farmers responsibilities and had to rank a series of attributes assigned to pesticides and finally they had to consider their willingness to pay for such products. Through the whole procedure more than 75 farmers were interviewed, however, in the statistical analysis of the survey only 60 completed questionnaires were used, while more than 15 incomplete questionnaires were omitted from the analysis.

Three research pillars were used in this survey, the first one concerns the use of biopesticides products among the participant farmers in the survey. More specific an attempt was made to formulate a model capable to predict use and consequently adoption of biopesticide products among Greek farmers. In the second research pillar, best worst scale was applied to rank a series of biopesticide advantages and disadvantages that were collected through literature review (see Soutar et al., 2015). Finally, a third pillar concerns willingness to pay for biopesticide products among Greek farmers based on Stoetzel's idea was that there is a maximum and minimum price for each product which can be elicited by directly asking the customers (see for example Breidert et al., 2006).

3 Data Analysis and Results

This part presents the data analysis and the results of this survey. The results are presented in this subsection similar to research pillars described in the methodology part.

3.1 *Participants' Perceptions About Environmental Protection*

Firstly, the demographic of the participants in this survey should be reported. Most participants are men (53.3%) married (48.3%), less than 40 years old (51.7%), who have graduated from high school (47.6%), are employed exclusively in agriculture (81.6%), have more than 12 years of previous experience in agriculture and almost half of them (41.7%) claim that their annual income is less than 10,000€. It is worth mentioning that more than half of them (51.6%) of the respondents claimed that they have used at least once, biopesticides products. Nevertheless, it must be noted here that many farmers are traditionally using sulfur and copper products that are classified as biopesticide products. The demographic profile of the respondents is presented in Table 1.

Despite the frequent use of demographic variables and employing them to model human behaviour, there is very little certainty as to how these relationships are

Table 1 Demographic data of the participants

Respondents' features	Count/mean	Percentage
Gender		
Male	32	53.3%
Married		
Yes	29	48.3%
Age		
< 40	31	51.7%
> 40	29	48.3%
Full time farmer	51	81.6%
Farming Experience	12.63 years	10 (years)
Use of Biopesticide product		
At least once	31	51.7%
Never	29	48.3%
Education		
< 9 years (Basic)	3	5.0%
9–12 Years (High School)	28	46.7%
12–14 years (College)	20	33.4%
15–16 years (Higher)	9	15.0%
Annual income (from agricultural activities):		
< 10,000 €	25	41.7%
10,001 to 20,000 €	15	25.0%
20,001 to 30,000 €	10	16.7%
> 30,001€	10	16.7%

occurring making important to examine persistently these relationships (Kontogeorgos et al., 2015). The most examined demographics determining environmental behaviour are age, education, farming experience and farm size. Most studies examining the relationship between age and education level on environmental behaviour suggest that younger farmers and more educated are more likely to undertake programs or environmental enhancements than older and less educated farmers. Burton (2014) has provides a useful and detailed review on this subject.

In the next section of the analysis, respondents were asked to point out some of their perceptions and beliefs as well as to reveal some their daily practices that could be used to protect environment. This part of the research was performed by using a five-point Likert scale ranging according to the question from (1) that is "not important" or "not aware" to (5) "very important' or "highly aware". The results of these section are presented bellow (Tables 2, 3, and 4).

It is worth mentioning, that participating farmers claim that they are aware of the climate change accepting in a high level that pesticides used in agriculture cause serious environmental contamination while at the same they agree also that Pesticides residues that remain in or on food at the time of purchase pose a serious risk to the health of consumers.

In the next section, farmers were asked to report their perceptions of the Farmers'—their—role about food safety. Briefly to comment the highest level of agreement goes to the statement that farmers' have the ability to control food safety, even though the mean value of this agreement is 3.07 over 5, the maximum possible value. All the other statements about the farmers' role on food safety lies in lower values, showing that are not considering or accepting food safety as one of their responsibilities.

Following with the presentation of the results, the next table (Table 4) presents a series of generally accepted practices that could be used to protect the environment. Three main practices categories were chosen to be examined that is buying local

Table 2 Respondents' awareness and perceptions about using chemical pesticides

Respondents' awareness (self-reported)	Mean*	Standard dev
About the climate change	4.02[a]	1.066
The consequences of pesticides on the environment	3.93[b]	0.989
The existence of bio pesticides / environmentally friendly pesticides	3.62[c]	1.290
Respondents' perceptions (self-reported)		
Pesticides residues that remain in or on food at the time of purchase, pose a serious risk to the health of consumers	4.10	0.986
Pesticides used in agriculture production cause serious environmental contamination	3.98	1.000

*min = 1, max = 5

*Wilcoxon Signed-Rank tests: a to b sig = 0.435, a to c sig = 0.005, b to c sig = 0.003, (there are differences in the distributions of these two related variables)

Table 3 Respondents' perceptions about farmers' role on food safety

Respondents' perceptions (self-reported)	Mean[a]	Mean rank[2]
Farmers and producers of agricultural products have the ability to control food safety	3.07	4.22
Farmers and producers of agricultural products care about food safety	3.03	4.05
Farmers and producers of agricultural products care about their consumers' health	2.82	3.64
Farmers and producers of agricultural products have the necessary knowledge to ensure food safety	2.55	3.12
Farmers and producers of agricultural products are honest / ethic about food safety	2.52	3.01
Farmers and producers of agricultural products inform public authorities about food safety issues	2.48	2.97

[a]min = 1, max = 5
[b] Friedman Test: Chi-Square: 40.55, df = 5, Asymp.Sig = 0.00

Table 4 Respondents' general practices to protect environment

Respondents' environmental practices (self-reported)	Mean[a]	Mean rank[b]
How often you use the following activities: Buying locally produced food products or groceries	*3.68*	6.59
How often you use the following activities: Buying locally produced products	*3.48*	6.03
How often you use the following activities: Recycling materials (like glass, metals etc.)	3.40	5.95
How often you use the following activities: Buying eco-labelled products	*2.98*	4.75
How often you use the following activities: Reducing the consumption of disposable items (eg plastic bags et packaging, etc.)	*2.98*	4.66
How often you use the following activities: Recycling materials—Making Compost	*2.80*	4.38
How often you use the following activities: Choose an environmentally friendly mode of transport (walking, cycling, public transport)	*2.78*	4.38
How often you use the following activities: Reduction of water consumption	*2.87*	4.24
How often you use the following activities: Reducing energy consumption (i.e. by using low energy consumption devices or fuel efficient machinery)	*2.78*	4.03

[a]min = 1, max = 5
[b]Friedman Test: Chi-Square: 72.585, df = 8, Asymp. Sig = 0.00

products (food and other products), reducing consumption of energy; water; and fuels and a third one about recycling different materials. All these practices have been ranked with low rates by the respondents since the highest value was assigned to the practice of buying locally produced food products or products in general.

All the above answers and farmers' statements were used to create a model capable to predict adoption and use of biopesticides. For this reason, binary logistic regression was applied. Binary logistic regression widely used when someone wants to model the event probability for a categorical response variable with two outcomes (Field, 2005). For example, one or zero, true or false, yes or no and for this case to predict adoption/use of biopesticides by using as the dependent variable in this model one of the demographic variables concerning use (at least once) of biopesticide products. The logistic regression model is a type of generalized linear model that extends the linear regression model by linking the range of real numbers to the range 0–1. Since the probability of the described event (users and non-users of biopesticides) must lie between 0 and 1, it is unrealistic to model probabilities with linear regression techniques, because the linear regression model allows the dependent variable to take values greater than 1 or less than 0. All computations were performed with the statistical software Jamovi ver.2.3.21. and R studio ver. 24.04. The results of binary logistic regression are presented in the following tables (Tables 5 and 6).

Table 5 Binary logistic regression analysis

Variables (Farmers' perceptions)	B	S.E	Statistic Wald	Wald Sig	Exp(B)
How aware are you with the climate change	1.143	0.377	9.207	0.002*	3.137
Farmers and producers of agricultural products have the necessary knowledge to ensure food safety	1.143	0.377	9.207	0.014*	0.214
Farmers and producers of agricultural products should be honest / ethic about food safety	1.154	0.619	3.474	0.06***	3.172
Constant Term	−3.555	1.923	3.417	0.065***	0.029

Estimation Method = Forward Stepwise (Likelihood Ratio)
R^2 = 0,484 (Chi^2 7.445, df = 78—Hosmer & Lemeshow), 0.270 (Cox & Snell); 0.360, (Nagelkerke).
Significance: $^{*}p < 0.01$, $^{**}p < 0.05$, $^{***}p < 0.1$

Table 6 Classification table of the binary logistic regression model (α)

Observed use of biopesticides	Predicted use of biopesticides		Percentage Correct
	Yes	No	
Yes	22	7	75.9%
No	7	24	77.4%
Total			76.7%

α: The cut value is 0.5

It should be noted that all examined questions about farmers' environmental awareness, perceptions and practices affecting environment were used as input variables in the attempt to come up with a prediction model of biopesticide use/adoption. However, during the stage of building up a predictive model forward stepwise method was applied to estimate the most important variables of the model. In this way, only three variables formulated the predictive model, that is aware of the climate change; have the necessary knowledge to ensure food safety and a third one concerning ethics in agriculture/ food production.

Different types of R^2 (pseudo R^2, for binary logistic regression) and the following classification table (Table 6) suggest that the estimated model adequately fits the data. The estimated model can correctly predict something more that 3 out of 4 cases. More specific the model can correctly classify 75.9% of the users of biopesticides products and 77.4% of the non-users. Having verified that the estimated model is statistically acceptable we can proceed to the interpretation of the results. All variables are statistically significant and affect positively the possibility to belong to the group of famers who have used at least once a biopesticide product.

The variables that affect more the use of biopesticide products are climate change awareness and ethics on agriculture production. For both variables holds that they have an increased "Exp(B)" or odds ratio. The odds ratio is the predicted change in odds for a unit increase in the predictor variable. When odds ratio is greater than 1, increasing values of the variable correspond to increasing odds of the event's occurrence that is to adopt /use biopesticide products. In simple words, if odds ratio is greater than 1 there is a positive association (i.e., higher number for the predictor means group 1 in the outcome), and an odds ratio less than 1 means a negative association (i.e., higher number for the predictor means group 0 in the outcome). So, an increase by 1 unit in one predicting variable results in (Exp(B) $- 1 \times 100$)% more changes to belong into predicting group. Thus, for this case if climate change awareness increased among farmers, then the adoption of biopesticide products will be significantly increased. The same holds true for raising ethics in agriculture production (i.e. using appropriate chemicals, or by following chemical products application rules i.e. time and quantity of application). On the other hand, odds ratio for education on food safety issues is less than one, which means educating farmers on food safety issues then the use of biopesticides will decrease. A first explanation but needs further examination, is that farmers with food safety education feel confident using chemical pesticides so they don't worry about food safety issues.

3.2 Ranking Biopesticides Advantages and Disadvantages

In this part of the analysis, respondents were asked to rank a series of advantages and disadvantages mentioned in previous studies about biopesticides (i.e. Ayilara et al., 2023; Essiedu et al., 2020; Fenibo et al., 2021; Kanatas et al., 2022) along with information derived from official European Union Sites about Green Deal and also

Environmental Protection Agency of US. In this way, 9 advantages and 7 disadvantages were selected for biopesticides. Best Worst Scaling (BWS) was applied to rank these attributes assigned to biopesticides. BWS is a survey method for assessing individuals' priorities: what they view as best and worst among a set of items (Flynn & Marley, 2014), so BWS can identify the relative importance of a series of attributes.

Farmers participated in the survey were asked to indicate in sets of 3, like the example of Fig. 1, which advantage is the most important, the less important and consequently which one is indifferent. Respondents were shown 12 such comparisons, therefore they had to evaluate each advantage, in total, 4 times and in combination with all others one time.

The whole design is an example of balanced incomplete block design that statistically assures the appearance of the attribute sets (Doehlert, 1965; lee et al., 2008) The whole design was made with "Crossdes" Package that can create balanced incomplete block design in R studio. A similar procedure was followed for the selected disadvantages however the total number of sets were 7 and farmers had to evaluate each disadvantage, in total, 3 times and in combination with all others one time, due to lower number of disadvantages to be evaluated.

BWS gathered data were analysed as frequency counts for the number of times each attribute—advantage or disadvantage—was chosen as most important and less important across the series of 12 sets and 7 sets presented to each respondent, and as a standardized "score" for each attribute named as the Best Worst Index (BWI). The BWI score was calculated as the difference between the frequency of being chosen as most important vs less important divided by the availability of each attribute (meaning the number of times it appeared across the design, that is 4×60 the number of respondents $= 240$). If a BWI score of an attribute is two times bigger than another attribute, it can be interpreted that it is twice as more important. These results are presented in Table 7 for biopesticide advantages and Table 8 for biopesticide disadvantages.

It is clear, that the most important advantage for participants in this survey is that biopesticides have no adverse effects on farmers health. This advantage is in fact

Comparison 1

	Less Important	Indifferent	Most Important
* Groundwater pollution is not a problem for BIO - pesticides	○	○	○
* Genetics of plants are not getting altered through the use of BIO pesticides	○	○	○
* Use of BIO - pesticides have no long-term effects	○	○	○

Comparison Cons 1

	Less Important	Indifferent	Most Important
* Use of BIO – pesticides could decrease food production	○	○	○
* BIO – pesticides use new (not sufficiently tested) technology	○	○	○
* BIO – pesticides could not be available in all countries	○	○	○

Fig. 1 Sample question used for the best worst scaling

Table 7 Best–Worst Index (ranking) for the selected biopesticides Advantages

Biopesticides advantages	Best	Worst	Indifferent	Best–Worst	BWI
Use of Biopesticides have no Adverse health effects on farmers	106	60	74	46	0.24
Use of Biopesticides do not affect useful insects	106	67	67	39	0.18
Use of Biopesticides do not create problems for pollination	98	81	61	17	0.16
Groundwater pollution is not a problem for Biopesticides	93	83	64	10	−0.02
Use of Biopesticides have no long-term effects	68	86	86	−18	−0.07
Use of Biopesticides can reduce soil pollution	80	99	61	−19	−0.08
Use of Biopesticides is not Problematic for the local flora and fauna	70	91	79	−21	−0.08
Genetics of plants are not getting altered through the use of Biopesticides	46	71	123	−25	−0.104
Use of Biopesticides do not create Ecological imbalance	53	82	105	−29	−0.212

33%—calculated as [(0.24 – 0.18) /0.24 = 0.333]—more preferable that the second one which state that Biopesticides do not affect useful insects. In the same way all examined advantages could be ranked and evaluated. Briefly to comment that the most important disadvantage is that biopesticides are not so effective compared to chemical pesticides. What is more this disadvantage is 165%—calculated as [(0.178 – 0.067)/ 0.067 = 1.65]—more important than the second one which state that biopesticides are rather expensive.

3.3 Willingness to Pay for Biopesticide Products

In the third and last part of the analysis respondents were asked to demonstrate their willingness to pay for biopesticide products. It has been already mentioned that a direct approach was chosen to measure farmers' willingness to pay for biopesticide

Table 8 Best–Worst Index (ranking) for the selected biopesticides disadvantages

Biopesticides disadvantages	Best	Worst	Indifferent	Best–Worst	BWI
Biopesticides are not so effective	91	59	30	32	0.178
Biopesticides are rather expensive	80	68	32	12	0.067
Use of Biopesticides could decrease food production	60	48	72	12	0.067
Use of Biopesticides could increase food prices	61	64	55	−3	−0.017
Biopesticides use new (not sufficiently tested) technology	47	52	81	−5	−0.028
Biopesticides could not be available in all countries	45	69	66	−24	−0.133
Biopesticides need special storage conditions	36	60	84	−24	−0.133

products. The whole concept is based on Stoetzel's idea that there is a maximum and minimum price for each product which can be elicited by directly asking the customers the following two questions formulated by Marbeau back in 1987 (mentioned by Breidert et al., 2006).

These questions are the following and reconstructed accordingly to fit this survey.

1. "Above which price would you definitely not buy the product, because you can't afford it or because you didn't think it worths the money?
2. Below which price you would not buy the product because you would start to suspect its quality?"

For the purposes of this survey respondents were shown two well-known chemical pesticides (one herbicide priced at the survey period at 20€ per litre and one insecticide priced at the survey period at 40€ per litre) of the Greek and European market and were asked the above two questions for each product. The results of the analysis are presented in Table 9.

In general, min price that determines biopesticides products in terms of efficiency as this was the most important disadvantage was ranging from 25 to 40% lower than the chemical products. On the other hand, when it concerns max price that farmers are willing to pay for biopesticides it is worth mentioning that there are many outliers indicating that are farmers who are willing to pay 2 and 3 times more for biopesticide products like chemical ones (assuming with the same effectiveness). In any case, our sample is quite small and cannot be used to conduct a cluster analysis or a similar

Table 9 Respondents' willingness to pay for biopesticide products (min and max mean price and their distribution)

Biopesticide insecticide product compared to a chemical one with price 40 € per littre	
Max Mean Price: 50.10€ (sd 10.40€)	**Min Mean Price: 25.90€ (sd 9.04€)**
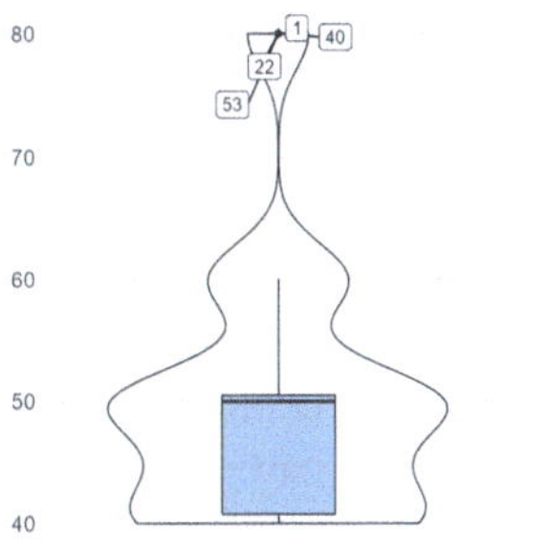	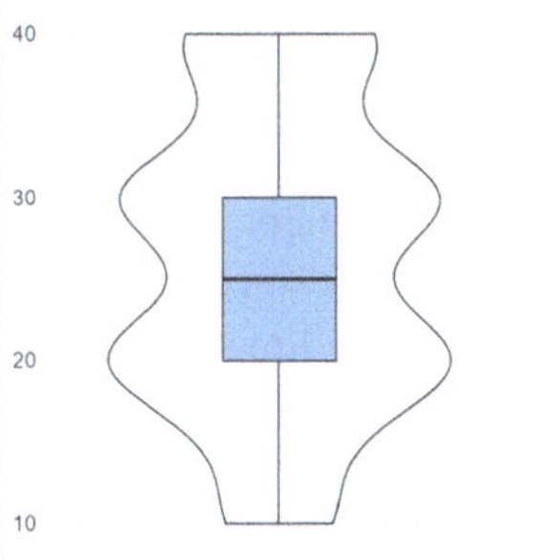
Biopesticide herbicide product compared to a chemical one with price 20 € per litre	
Max Mean Price: 33.40€ (sd 15.00€)	**Min Mean Price: 14.10€ (sd 5.34€)**
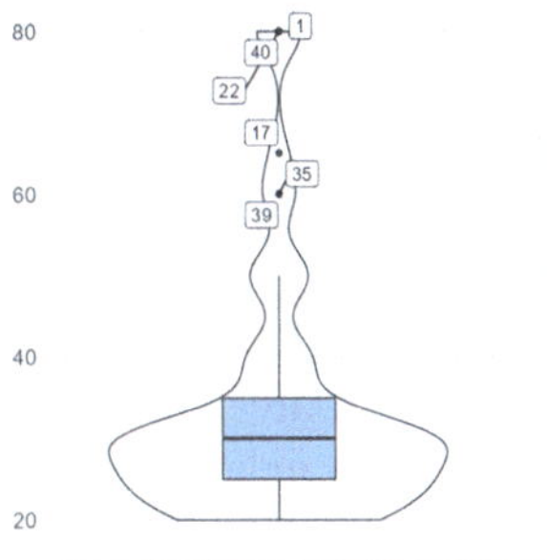	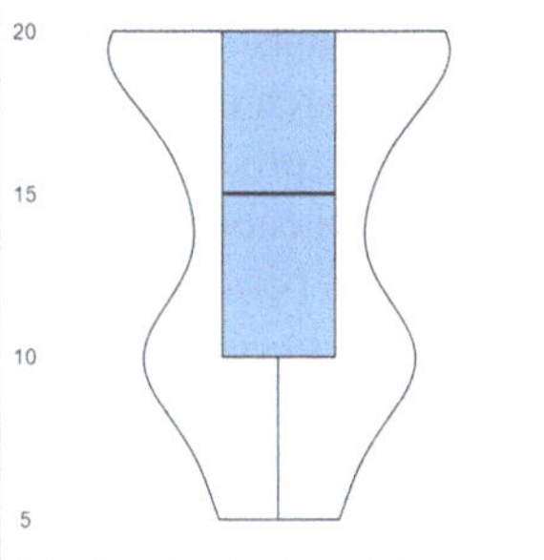

approach to investigate more on the characteristics of those who are willing to pay that much for biopesticide products. In any case, further analysis is required to investigate such a research question.

4 Conclusion

According to European Common Agricultural Policy and farm to Fork strategy, the link between healthy people, healthy societies and a healthy planet is the Green Deal that promotes sustainable agriculture production and sustainable food systems. Under the Green Deal farmers would have to halve pesticide use by 2030, reduce fertilisers, double organic farming and rewild landscapes to increase biodiversity. However, these measures named as Green Deal were not accepted from European farmers resulting in a series of strong protests during the first months of 2024 across all European Countries filling headlines with images of tractors blocking motorways and city centres, slurry dumped at supermarkets, police being sprayed with manure and pelted with eggs. Nevertheless, what is the most important is that European Commission President announced that she will withdraw the sustainable use regulation, which sought to halve pesticide use by 2030.

However, responding with row-backs on environmental standards is not the answer to farmers unwillingness to adopt Green Deals' vision and goals (Hilmi & Frison, 2024). Farmers really know the critical importance of tackling the climate and nature crisis since agriculture production is highly exposed to the increasingly severe impacts of climate change, like drought and flooding and biodiversity loss. In their majority European farmers believe the ecological transition is a necessity. This is also the case for the Greek farmers that participated in this survey.

Towards a successful implementation of European union's environmental policy, a 'sustainable' use of pesticides should be supported. In this way, there are two main pillars to reduce farmers' dependency on agrochemicals. The first one is with financial and structural support to adopt alternative pesticide solutions like biopesticides. The second pillar that should be enforced is research on alternative pesticides so that to increase these products effectiveness. Both these points were mentioned by the participants as the main disadvantages of biopesticide products. Another point of this research that should be mentioned is that farmers could increase their use of biopesticide products if they increase their awareness of the climate change. Even if in Greece phenomena of the climate change are becoming more and more frequent like drought periods and severe floodings in the main agricultural areas (i.e. Thessaly in Central Greece during the autumn of 2023) there is an intense need to rise environmental knowledge and awareness of Greek Farmers. Even if this survey is based on a small sample of farmers its results indicate a series of actions that could help Greek farmers to adapt to this new reality shaped by natural and political parameters.

To sum up biopesticides could offer numerous benefits that can help achieve the European Green Deal's objectives, including environmental sustainability, public health, and economic viability. However, their adoption should be facilitated through supportive policies, financial incentives, and ongoing research and development. On the other hand, addressing challenges related to efficacy and farmer acceptance is critical for their successful integration into sustainable farming practices.

Acknowledgements—Funding Funding: The project entitled "Development of Bio-Pesticides and -Herbicides for Sustainable Agricultural Crop Production", Acronym "BIOPESTICIDES" is funded by the Federal Ministry of Education and Research, Germany (No. 01DH21010A), General Direction of Scientific Research and Technological Development (DGRSDT-Algeria), the General Secretariat for Research and Innovation of the Ministry of Development and Investments of Greece (GGPRM-0357185 and GGPRM-0357186), the Scientific and Technological Research Council of Turkey (TÜB˙ITAK) (121N251 and 121N259) under the PRIMA Programme. PRIMA is an Art.185 initiative supported and co-funded under Horizon 2020, the European Union's Programme for Research, and Innovation.

References

Ayilara, M. S., Adeleke, B. S., Akinola, S. A., Fayose, C. A., Adeyemi, U. T., Gbadegesin, L. A., Omole, R. K., Johnson, R. M., Uthman, Q. O., & Babalola, O. O. (2023). Biopesticides as a promising alternative to synthetic pesticides: A case for microbial pesticides, phytopesticides, and nanobiopesticides. *Frontiers in Microbiology, 16*(14), 1040901. https://doi.org/10.3389/fmicb.2023.1040901. Erratum in: Front Microbiol. 2024 Jan 03;14:1258968. PMID: 36876068; PMCID: PMC9978502.

Bogoslov, I. A., Lungu, A. E., Stoica, E. A., & Georgescu, M. R. (2022). European green deal impact on entrepreneurship and competition: A free market approach. *Sustainability, 14*(19), 12335. https://doi.org/10.3390/su141912335

Breidert, C., Hahsler. M., & Reutterer, T. (2006). A review of methods for measuring willingness-to-pay. *Innovative Marketing, 2*(4).

Burton, R. J. F. (2014). The influence of farmer demographic characteristics on environmental behaviour: A review. *Journal of Environmental Management, 135*, 19–26.

Copping, L. G., & Menn, J. J. (2000). Biopesticides: A review of their action, applications and efficacy. *Pest Management Science, 56*(8), 651–676. https://doi.org/10.1002/1526-4998(200008)56:8%3c651::AID-PS201%3e3.0.CO;2-U

Doehlert, D. H. (1965). Balanced sets of balanced incomplete block designs of block size three. *Technometrics, 7*(4), 561–577. https://doi.org/10.2307/1266396

Essiedu, J. A., Adepoju, F. O., & Ivantsova, M. N. (2020). Benefits and limitations in using biopesticides: A review. *AIP Conference Proceedings*. https://doi.org/10.1063/5.0032223

European Commission. (2020). *A farm to fork strategy for a fair, healthy and environmentally-friendly food system*. COM(2020) 381 Final. Brussels: European Commission. https://eur-lex.europa.eu/legal-content/EN/TXT/?uri=CELEX%3A52020DC0381

Fenibo, E. O., Ijoma, G. N., & Tonderayi, A. M. (2021). Biopesticides in sustainable agriculture: A critical sustainable development. *Frontiers in Sustainable Food Systems, 5*.https://doi.org/10.3389/fsufs.2021.619058

Field, A. (2005). *Discovering statistics using SPSS*. Sage.

Flynn, T. N., & Marley, A. A. J. (2014). Best-worst scaling: theory and methods. In *Handbook of choice modelling*. Edward Elgar Publishing. https://doi.org/10.4337/9781781003152.00014

Hilmi, A., & Frison, E. (2024, March 25). Farmer protests: The wrong U-Turn. *Green European Journal*. https://www.greeneuropeanjournal.eu/farmer-protests-the-wrong-u-turn/

Kanatas, P., Travlos, I., Gazoulis, I., Antonopoulos, N., Tataridas, A., Mpechliouli, N., & Petraki, D. (2022). Biostimulants and herbicides: A promising approach towards green deal implementation. *Agronomy, 12*(12), 3205. https://doi.org/10.3390/agronomy12123205

Kontogeorgos, A., Tsampra, M., & Chatzitheodoridis, F. (2015). Agricultural policy and environment protection through the eyes of new farmers: Evidence from a country of Southeast Europe. *Procedia Economics and Finance, 19*, 296–303.

Kumar, J., Ramlal, A., Mallick, D., & Mishra, V. (2021). An overview of some biopesticides and their importance in plant protection for commercial acceptance. *Plants*. https://doi.org/10.3390/plants10061185

Lee, J. A., Soutar, G., & Louviere, J. (2008). The best-worst scaling approach: An alternative to Schwartz's values survey. *Journal of Personality Assessment, 90*(4), 335–347. https://doi.org/10.1080/00223890802107925

Lengai, G., & Muthomi, J. (2018). Biopesticides and their role in sustainable agricultural production. *Journal of Biosciences and Medicines, 6*, 7–41. https://doi.org/10.4236/jbm.2018.66002

Ortega, P., Salcedo, R., Sánchez, E., & Gil, E. (2023). Biopesticides as alternatives to reduce the use of copper in Spanish and Portuguese viticulture: Maintrends in adoption. *European Journal of Agronomy, 151*, Article 126996. https://doi.org/10.1016/j.eja.2023.126996

Refaat. (2021). The European Green Deal—An analysis of key aspects. *International Law & Environment*. https://www.eiir.eu/publications/strategic-affairs-publications/the-european-green-deal-an-analysis-of-key-aspects/

Siddi, M. (2020). *The European Green Deal: Assessing its current state and future implementation* (FIIA Working Paper No. 114). https://iris.unica.it/retrieve/handle/11584/313484/457281/WP114European%20Green%20Deal.pdf

Soutar, G. N., Sweeney, J. C., McColl-Kennedy, J. R., Louviere, J. J., Flynn, T. N., & Marley, A. A. J. (2015). Best-worst scaling: an alternative to ratings data. In *Best-worst scaling: Theory, methods and applications* (pp. 177–188). Cambridge University Press.

Wesseler, J. (2022). The EU farm to fork strategy: An assessment from an agricultural economics perspective. *Applied Economic Perspectives and Policy, 44*(4), 1826–1843. https://doi.org/10.1002/aepp.13239

Beyond Numbers: Listening to Patient Voices in Tuscany with Prems

Chiara Barchielli, Paolo Zoppi, Marzia Paffetti, and Marco Alaimo

Abstract Delivering high-quality, patient-centered care that aligns with individual needs and expectations is a key objective for healthcare systems worldwide. Traditionally, clinician-reported measures have been the primary benchmarks for assessing patient experience, yet they often fail to capture the nuances and diverse perspectives of the patients themselves. To address this gap, Patient-Reported Experience Measures (PREMs) have emerged as powerful tools that transform our understanding and response to patient experiences. This study aimed to analyze PREMs collected from patients discharged from ordinary hospitalization in the Central Tuscany Health Authority (USL Toscana Centro) in 2023. Data were collected via a web-based survey administered post-discharge, incorporating both closed-ended and open-ended questions about patient experiences and suggestions for improvement. Key dimensions analyzed included hospital reception and stay, staff interactions, ward conditions, and the recognition of the positive impact of staff on the patient's experience. A total of 12,670 open-ended responses were qualitatively analyzed using MAXQDA software. Out of 10,273 patients who responded to the survey, most expressed satisfaction with their care, particularly regarding kindness, respect, and overall quality. However, areas for improvement were noted, including waiting times, access to information, and care coordination. This study offers valuable insights into patient experiences within the Tuscany Central Health Authority, providing a foundation for enhancing patient-centered care.

Keyword Patient-Reported Experience Measures · Quality improvement · Patient satisfaction · Healthcare

JEL Classification Code I100

C. Barchielli (✉)
Institute of Management, Sant'Anna School of Advanced Studies, Pisa, Italy
e-mail: barchiellichiara@gmail.com

C. Barchielli · P. Zoppi · M. Paffetti · M. Alaimo
Azienda USL Toscana Centro, Florence, Italy

I. Bartuseviciene et al. (eds.), *Building Resilience Through Digital Transformation and Sustainable Innovation*, Springer Proceedings in Business and Economics,
https://doi.org/10.1007/978-3-031-90054-9_14

1 Introduction

The concept of patient-centred care has gained significant traction in recent years, driven by the recognition that a one-size-fits-all approach to healthcare is no longer sufficient. This philosophy emphasizes building a partnership between patients and clinicians, where patients are actively involved in decision-making processes concerning their care (Manalili, Santana and Group, 2021).

Traditionally, clinician-reported measures have been the mainstay for assessing patient experience. These measures, however, often focus on objective factors such as mortality rates and hospital readmission rates. While valuable, they fail to capture the subjective experiences of patients, such as satisfaction with communication, respect, and overall well-being during their healthcare journey (De Rosis et al., 2022). PREMs have emerged as a powerful tool for addressing this gap in understanding. Defined by the International Society for Quality in Health Care "ISQua", PREMs are "any set of outcome measures that are formulated to be completed directly by patients" (Shaw, 1995). PREMs encompass a broad range of domains, including patient-physician communication, care coordination, pain management, and overall satisfaction with care. The integration of PREMs into healthcare evaluation offers several advantages. Firstly, PREMs provide valuable insights into aspects of care that may not be readily apparent through traditional clinician-reported measures. Secondly, PREMs empower patients by giving them a voice in shaping and improving their healthcare experiences. Finally, the use of PREMs can foster a culture of accountability within healthcare systems, prompting continuous improvement efforts based on patient feedback (Shunmuga Sundaram et al., 2022).

Several studies have demonstrated the positive impact of PREMs on healthcare delivery. A systematic review by Coulter et al. (2009) found that PREMs can lead to improvements in patient communication, pain management, and overall satisfaction with care. Additionally, recent studies showed that using PREMs can improve patient-provider communication and collaboration in decision-making (Knapp et al., 2021; Scheibler et al., 2024; Wood et al., 2022). The decision to adopt pre-emptive measures to enhance assistance and the emphasis on utilizing open-ended questions stem from a fundamental understanding of human interaction and the intricacies of effective communication. In a world where information is abundant but often overwhelming (Yardley et al., 2010), and where individual needs and contexts vary widely, the approach of pre-emptive assistance coupled with open-ended questioning serves as a beacon of clarity and efficacy (Shunmuga Sundaram et al., 2022). At the heart of pre-emptive measures lies the recognition that proactive support yields superior outcomes compared to reactive responses (Joseph & Pojednic, 2023). By anticipating potential challenges, needs, and inquiries, assistance can be offered before they even arise, pre-empting frustration and confusion. This approach is particularly vital in fields where timely and accurate information is crucial, such as healthcare. Furthermore, open-ended questions can serve as catalysts for innovation and continuous improvement (De Rosis et al., 2020). By inviting diverse perspectives and encouraging curiosity, these questions stimulate creativity, exploration, and discovery. They challenge conventional wisdom, spark new ideas, and pave the way for breakthrough solutions to complex problems.

The aim of this study was to analyze PREMs from patients discharged from ordinary hospitalization within the USL Toscana Centro in 2023. By focusing on patient perspectives, the study sought to uncover key insights into their experiences, satisfaction levels, and areas needing improvement. The added value of this study lies in its ability to provide a more nuanced understanding of patient experiences, going beyond traditional clinician-reported measures. This patient-centered approach allows healthcare providers to better align services with patient needs and expectations, ultimately fostering a more responsive and effective healthcare system.

2 Matherials and Methods

This study employed a retrospective analysis of PREMs data collected from patients discharged from ordinary hospitalization in the USL Toscana Centro (from here, it will be referred to as USLTC) during 2023. The data were gathered through a web-based survey administered to patients after discharge. The survey included a combination of closed-ended questions to gather quantitative data and open-ended questions to elicit qualitative feedback from patients.

The open-ended questions focused on the following dimensions of patient experience:

- Hospital reception and stay: this section aimed to capture patients' experiences with the admissions process, room accommodations, and overall satisfaction with the hospital environment.
- Interaction with staff: this section explored patients' interactions with physicians, nurses, and other healthcare providers, assessing aspects such as communication, respect, and empathy.
- Ward environment: this section delved into patients' perceptions of the ward environment, including cleanliness, noise levels, and overall comfort.
- Recognition of positive staff impact: this section aimed to identify instances where staff members had a particularly positive impact on the patient's experience.

A total of 12,670 open-ended responses were collected from the survey. These responses were subjected to qualitative analysis using MAXQDA software, a tool specifically designed for analysing large volumes of textual data. The analysis involved a systematic process of coding, categorizing, and interpreting the data to identify recurring themes and patterns.

The qualitative analysis process commenced with coding, the cornerstone of transforming raw text into meaningful categories. This systematic approach involved meticulously assigning codes to segments of the open-ended responses. These codes served as labels that captured the essence of the patients' experiences. For instance, a patient expressing appreciation for a nurse's kindness might be coded with "empathy", "availability", or "a heart full of love".

Following the initial coding stage, a process of categorization begun. Coded segments were grouped together based on shared characteristics, forming broader categories. By iteratively reviewing and refining the categorized data, the researchers moved to the interpretation. This involved delving deeper into the categorized responses to identify recurring themes and patterns. Themes emerged as the unifying threads woven throughout the patients' narratives. For instance, a theme of "importance of clear communication" might be identified if a significant number of responses emphasized the value of receiving timely updates and having questions answered clearly.

3 Results

A total of 10,273 patients responded to the survey, providing a comprehensive overview of patient experiences within the USLTC. Overall, the findings indicated that patients were generally satisfied with their care, with positive ratings for aspects such as kindness, respect, and overall quality of care.

In Table 1, the main results are summarized:

As not all patients responded to all questions in the questionnaire regarding the different dimensions, the number of observations and the number of comments is reported next to each one of them. We now detail the data point by point before presenting the overall data.

Hospital reception: 3620 observations, 2907 comments. Respondents were not very adherent to the question, tending to write everything that characterized the entire hospitalization experience. It is interesting to provide some words frequencies, that refers to the number of times a word occurs within a specific dataset. This is a measure that is often used in linguistics and text analysis to understand the prominence or importance of words within a given context (Agarwal & Mittal, 2016). By analysing word frequency, it is possible to gain insights into patterns, trends, and characteristics of language usage in written communication as reported in Table 2. In this analysis, as in the others, stories about one's own illnesses and their progression have been excluded. The phrase 'professionalism and kindness' is the most frequently used word combination.

Department: 577 observations, 1634 comments. Exploring this dimension involves considering various aspects related to the physical space where patients are receiving care, in Table 3 we provide a short breakdown of the most used terms. The term "cleanliness" refers to the overall hygiene and tidiness of the ward. It involves cleaning of surfaces, linens, and equipment. Other sources of discontent concern structural elements, such as very old buildings that give the impression of dilapidation. Poor hygiene in bathrooms and old hospitals are the most frequently emphasized negative aspects. It is important to explore noise levels, which emerge as an issue from patient's narrative. Hospitals can be noisy environments due to various activities such as patient care, medical equipment, staff conversations, and visitors. Maintaining appropriate noise levels is crucial for patients' rest and recovery. The

Table 1 Main results of the 2023 PREMs analysis in USLTC

Dimension	Number of observations	Number of comments	Positive	Negative	Notes
Hospital Reception	3620	2907	1290 (Kindness, Satisfaction, Humanity)	424 (Dissatisfaction, Disorganization)	Many respondents wrote about their entire hospitalization experience
Department	577	1634	238 (Comfort, Cleanliness)	368 (Noise, Crowding, Cleanliness)	
Appreciation of professional skills	3010	3506	3506 (Physicians, Nurses, Osteopathic Physicians, Midwives)	0	Only positive comments included
Comments on hospital stay	2069	2489	1428	639 (Food, Discharge timing, Communication)	Similar to comments on reception but focused on stay experience
Relationship with staff	2026	-	800 (Positive: Nurses, Doctors, Staff)	137 (Negative: Nurses, Doctors, Staff)	Mentions of specific staff types (nurses, doctors) and general staff

comfort encompasses a range of factors that contribute to patients' comfort during their stay in the ward. It includes factors like bedding quality, room temperature, lighting, seating arrangements, and access to amenities like bathrooms and common areas.

Appreciation of professional skills: 3010 observations, 3506 comments. In this dimension there are just positive comments. This fact suggests a high level of satisfaction and appreciation for the professional skills of the staff. Here's the number of mentions: (i) Physicians (774 comments); the substantial number of positive mentions regarding physicians underscores the recognition and appreciation for their expertise, (ii) Nurses (1446 comments); the abundance of positive mentions about nurses highlights the invaluable role they play in patient care and support, and the constant presence at their bedside, (iii) Healthcare Assistants (HCAs) (811 comments); the numerous positive mentions regarding healthcare assistants reflect the appreciation for their essential contributions to patient care and comfort, (iv) Midwives (475 comments); the numerous positive mentions regarding midwives emphasize the esteem for their supportive and empowering approach to childbirth. The profound emotional intensity inherent in this momentous occasion often finds

Table 2 Words frequencies on the "Hospital reception" topic

Word	Number of observations	Notes
Kindness	1092	
Rudeness	83	
Thank you	208	
Felt safe, feeling safe, feeling in good hands	116	
Manners	27	
Satisfaction	961	Here we included the exact word and the expression "I felt good"
Dissatisfaction	236	
Professionalism	649	Professionalism is also counted along with the sinonyms "competence" and "preparation"; they have all been counted as the same occurrence
Overworked staff	55	
Humanity	123	Here, and throughout the discussion, we included terms such as "empathy", "availability", "feeling welcomed", "a heart full of love"
Disorganization/Chaos	28	
Little communication with family members	26	
Bad food	16	

Table 3 Words frequencies on the "Department" topic

Word	Number of Observations	Notes
Noise	101	Here we included "unable to rest due to noise" also
Unacceptable crowding	22	
Comfort	88	Includes expressions like "I felt comfortable", "I rested in comfort"
Adequate cleanliness	150	
Inadequate cleanliness	27	

expression in the candid and heartfelt comments provided. These comments not only underscore the deep connection and trust between midwives and the women they care for but also serve as a testament to the profound impact midwives have in shaping the childbirth experience positively.

Comments on hospital stay: 2069 observations, 2489 comments. This item was compiled in a very similar way to the "Hospital reception" dimension, as many respondents refer to the comments they made previously. However, the present comments are very long, and all of them have distinguished between "positive experience" and "negative experience". The individual contributions were counted exactly as just positive and negative as follows: (i) 1428 positive comments: patients highlight aspects related to kindness and availability of the staff, (ii) and 639 negative comments mainly concern the quality of food, perceived premature discharges, and the lack of communication between doctors and patients. Patients often voice their dissatisfaction with what they perceive as premature discharges, feeling that they were discharged from the hospital before they were adequately ready to leave. This premature discharge may lead to concerns about the continuity and effectiveness of their care, as well as anxiety about their recovery process. Patients may feel rushed or overlooked, with their medical needs not being fully addressed before being sent home. Additionally, they may worry about the potential consequences of leaving the hospital prematurely, such as experiencing complications or exacerbations of their condition. Before hospital stays were longer, patients had more time to recover fully and address any lingering concerns before being discharged. However, in recent times, there has been a noticeable shift towards shorter hospital stays as healthcare systems strive to optimize resources and reduce costs. While this approach may have its benefits in terms of efficiency and resource allocation, it has also led to an increase in concerns regarding perceived premature discharges among patients.

Relationship with staff: a total of 2026 records were analysed. Both positive and negative mentions were considered in the analysis to provide a comprehensive understanding of patients' perceptions. The breakdown of positive and negative mentions for each staff category is as follows:

- Positive Nurses: There were 219 records expressing positive sentiments towards nurses, acknowledging their dedication, competence, and compassion in patient care.
- Negative Nurses: Conversely, 56 records conveyed negative sentiments towards nurses, suggesting dissatisfaction or concerns regarding aspects of nursing care.
- Positive Doctors: a total of 156 records reflected positive feedback towards doctors, recognizing their expertise, professionalism, and effectiveness in medical treatment.
- Negative Doctors: in contrast, 57 records contained negative feedback towards doctors, indicating issues with communication, bedside manner, or treatment outcomes.
- Positive Healthcare Assistants: positive sentiments towards healthcare assistants were observed in 94 records, highlighting their valuable contributions to patient support and comfort.
- Negative Healthcare Assistants: however, 52 records expressed negative sentiments towards healthcare assistants, implying areas of improvement in their care delivery or interactions with patients.
- Positive Midwives: midwives received positive feedback in 52 records, indicating appreciation for their specialized care during childbirth and support for expectant mothers.

- Negative Midwives: only 6 records contained negative feedback towards midwives, suggesting relatively fewer concerns or issues raised in comparison to other staff categories.
- Positive Staff (in general): there were 220 records expressing positive sentiments towards staff in general, encompassing various healthcare professionals and support staff.
- Negative Staff (in general): conversely, only 17 records conveyed negative sentiments towards staff in general.

The open-ended responses revealed several areas where patients had particularly positive experiences. These included:

- Kindness and compassion of staff: patients consistently praised the kindness, compassion, and empathy demonstrated by healthcare providers. They expressed appreciation for the care and attention they received, particularly during difficult or vulnerable moments.
- Effective communication: patients highlighted the importance of clear and effective communication with staff. They appreciated being kept informed about their care plans, having their questions answered promptly, and feeling listened to and respected.
- Competent and professional care: patients expressed confidence in the competence and professionalism of the healthcare providers they encountered. They valued the expertise and skill demonstrated by staff in managing their medical conditions.

Despite the overall positive feedback, the analysis also identified areas where patient experiences could be enhanced. These included:

- Wait times: patients reported experiencing lengthy wait times for various aspects of care, such as appointments, procedures, and test results. These delays were often a source of frustration and anxiety.
- Access to information: some patients expressed difficulty obtaining clear and timely information about their care plans, treatment options, and discharge procedures. This lack of information could lead to uncertainty and confusion.
- Care coordination: patients sometimes experienced challenges with care coordination, particularly when transitioning between different services or healthcare providers. This lack of coordination could lead to fragmented care and missed opportunities for optimal treatment.
- Recognition of positive staff impact

The open-ended responses provided an opportunity for patients to recognize individual staff members who had a particularly positive impact on their experience. These instances highlighted the profound impact that individual acts of kindness, compassion, and professionalism can have on patient well-being.

This study provides valuable insights into patient experiences within the USLTC. The findings underscore the importance of listening to the patient voice and incorporating PREMs into healthcare evaluation processes. By understanding the

Table 4 Key findings of the analysis

Patients were generally satisfied with their care, highlighting the kindness, compassion, and competence of staff
Areas for improvement include wait times, access to information, care coordination, and food quality
Positive aspects of the department include comfort and cleanliness. Noise and inadequate cleanliness were noted as concerns
Patients appreciate the professional skills of physicians, nurses, osteopathic physicians, and midwives
Feeling safe and communication with staff were important aspects of a positive hospital stay
Long wait times, early arrival times for procedures, and outdated facilities were sources of dissatisfaction

perspectives and priorities of patients, healthcare providers can identify areas for improvement and work towards delivering more patient-centered care.

The positive feedback regarding the kindness, compassion, and competence of staff highlights the strengths of the healthcare system in Tuscany. These qualities are essential for building trust and rapport with patients, fostering a positive patient experience, and ultimately contributing to better health outcomes.

The identified areas for improvement, such as wait times, access to information, and care coordination, offer clear directions for future improvement efforts. By addressing these challenges, the USLTC can further enhance the quality of patient care and strengthen its reputation as a patient-centred healthcare provider.

The recognition of individual staff members who made a positive impact on patient experiences serves as a reminder of the profound impact that healthcare providers can have on the lives of their patients. Celebrating these successes can foster a culture of appreciation and encourage continued excellence in patient care. Table 4 reports a summary of the key findings:

4 Conclusion

The primary constraint of this study pertains to the analysis being confined to data from a single Local Health Authority. While this focused approach allows for a detailed examination of specific factors within the context of a particular region, it inherently limits the generalizability of the findings. However, it's crucial to note that this limitation does not diminish the significance of the study's implications. Moving forward, there exists considerable potential for scalability. By expanding the scope of analysis to include multiple Local Health Authorities across Italy, as well as extending the study to encompass other European or global regions, a more comprehensive understanding of the subject matter can be attained. This broader perspective not only enhances the robustness of the research but also facilitates comparative analyses, enabling insights to be gleaned from diverse healthcare systems, cultural contexts, and socio-economic environments. The scalability of the study offers an opportunity to uncover patterns, trends, and best practices that transcend geographical boundaries. By examining variations and similarities across different regions, valuable insights can emerge regarding the effectiveness of interventions, the impact of policy decisions, and the resilience of healthcare systems in addressing common challenges. Moreover, the ability to compare results at national, continental, and global levels holds immense potential for informing evidence-based policymaking and fostering international collaboration. By identifying successful strategies and innovative approaches from various contexts, policymakers can gain valuable insights into how to optimize healthcare delivery, resource allocation, and public health initiatives on a global scale.

Another limitation evident in this study concerns the incomplete response rates among patients to the questions posed. While every effort was made to gather comprehensive data, it is recognized that not all participants provided responses to every inquiry presented to them. This variability in response rates introduces a degree of uncertainty and potential bias into the analysis, as the data may not fully capture the perspectives or experiences of all individuals involved. This limitation underscores the inherent challenge of conducting research in real-world settings, where factors such as time constraints, respondent fatigue, and individual preferences can influence participation levels. Despite diligent efforts to encourage engagement and ensure clarity in survey instruments, it is not uncommon for some questions to receive lower response rates than others. It is important to acknowledge that the non-response phenomenon is multifaceted and may stem from various factors, including the complexity of the questions, the sensitivity of the topics addressed, and logistical barriers to participation (digital illiteracy, inadequate digital supports, etc.). Additionally, demographic characteristics, such as age, gender, and socioeconomic status, may also play a role in shaping individuals' willingness or ability to provide complete responses. While the presence of incomplete data poses challenges to the interpretability and generalizability of the findings, it also presents an opportunity for methodological refinement and future research directions.

It must be said that open-ended questions can really unveil the patient narrative (Dohan et al., 2016), as they empower patients to share their unique perspectives and experiences, providing a more comprehensive understanding of their care beyond numerical ratings. Hidden issues turn into visible ones. For instance, a patient might describe feeling rushed during a doctor's visit, a concern not readily captured by a simple satisfaction rating. Gaining context and understanding is invaluable to delve into the reasons behind patients' perceptions. And, of course, patient narrative can help healthcare providers to identify and improve specific areas of patient experiences.

The aim of this study was to analyze Patient-Reported Experience Measures (PREMs) from patients discharged from the Tuscany Central Health Authority in 2023. The study's added value is in highlighting patient perspectives to identify areas of satisfaction and improvement, providing a foundation for enhancing patient-centered care.

References

Agarwal, B., & Mittal, N. (2016). *Prominent feature extraction for sentiment analysis*. Springer.

Coulter, A., Fitzpatrick, R., & Cornwell, J. (2009). *Measures of patients' experience in hospital: Purpose, methods and uses*. King's Fund London.

Dohan, D., et al. (2016). The importance of integrating narrative into health care decision making. *Health Affairs, 35*(4), 720–725.

Joseph, R. J., & Pojednic, R. M. (2023). Performance medicine: A novel and needed paradigm for proactive health care. *Frontiers in Sports and Active Living*. Frontiers Media SA, 5.

Knapp, A., et al. (2021). Use of patient-reported outcome measures and patient-reported experience measures within evaluation studies of telemedicine applications: Systematic review. *Journal of Medical Internet Research, 23*(11), Article e30042. JMIR Publications Toronto, Canada.

Manalili, K., Santana, M. J., & Group, I. Prom. in C. P. I. S. W. (2021). Using implementation science to inform the integration of electronic patient-reported experience measures (ePREMs) into healthcare quality improvement: Description of a theory-based application in primary care. *Quality of Life Research, 30*, 3073–3084. Springer.

De Rosis, S., Cerasuolo, D., & Nuti, S. (2020). Using patient-reported measures to drive change in healthcare: The experience of the digital, continuous and systematic PREMs observatory in Italy. *BMC Health Services Research, 20*, 1–17. Springer.

De Rosis, S., Ferrè, F., & Pennucci, F. (2022). Including patient-reported measures in performance evaluation systems: Patient contribution in assessing and improving the healthcare systems. *The International Journal of Health Planning and Management*. Wiley Online Library.

Scheibler, F., et al. (2024). Patient-reported effects of hospital-wide implementation of shared decision-making at a university medical centre in Germany: A pre–post trial. *BMJ Evidence-Based Medicine, 29*(2), 87–95. Royal Society of Medicine.

Shaw, C. (1995). The International Society for Quality in Health Care (ISQua). *Audit Trends, 3*, 145–146. Leicester University.

Shunmuga Sundaram, C., et al. (2022). Patient and healthcare provider perceptions on using patient-reported experience measures (PREMs) in routine clinical care: A systematic review of qualitative studies. *Journal of Patient-Reported Outcomes, 6*(1), 1–16. Springeropen.

Wood, M. D., et al. (2022). Identifying risk factors, patient-reported experience and outcome measures, and data capture tools for an individualized pain prediction tool in pediatrics: Focus group study. *JMIR Perioperative Medicine, 5*(1), Article e42341. JMIR Publications Toronto, Canada.

Yardley, L., et al. (2010). Understanding reactions to an internet delivered health care intervention: Accommodating user preferences for information provision. *BMC Medical Informatics and Decision Making, 10*, 1–10. Springer.

Digital Transformation and Consumer Behavior

Artificial Intelligence-Powered Tools for Personalized Product Recommendations in E-Commerce: The Role of User Satisfaction on Online Purchase Decisions

Julia Mischin, Georgios A. Deirmentzoglou, Sofia Daskou, and Eirini Vlassi

Abstract Since their inception, e-commerce platforms have been continuously innovating to enhance the user experience. The application of artificial intelligence (AI) in various areas of digital marketing, especially in personalization tactics, is a key part of online businesses digital transformation. The growing use of AI-powered tools has had a significant effect on consumer behavior and is therefore becoming an emerging area that merits empirical and theoretical exploration. AI-powered personalization influences consumer experiences and decision-making. However, as the use of AI tools in e-commerce has grown rapidly in recent years, more research is needed in this area. This study, is a quantitative online survey of 182 German e-commerce users, investigating the role of user satisfaction on online purchase decisions. The data analysis shows that satisfaction in using AI-powered tools has a significant positive impact on online purchase decisions. This finding highlights the importance of implementing AI-powered chatbots and product recommendation systems in online stores.

Keywords Artificial intelligence · Personalized product recommendations · User satisfaction · Online purchase decision · e-commerce · Digital marketing

JEL Classification Codes L81 · M31 · M37

J. Mischin · G. A. Deirmentzoglou (✉) · S. Daskou · E. Vlassi
Neapolis University Pafos, Paphos, Cyprus
e-mail: g.deirmentzoglou@nup.ac.cy

J. Mischin
e-mail: j.mischin.1@nup.ac.cy

S. Daskou
e-mail: s.daskou@nup.ac.cy

E. Vlassi
e-mail: e.vlassi.2@nup.ac.cy

I. Bartuseviciene et al. (eds.), *Building Resilience Through Digital Transformation and Sustainable Innovation*, Springer Proceedings in Business and Economics,
https://doi.org/10.1007/978-3-031-90054-9_15

1 Introduction

The introduction of personalized and artificial intelligence-based recommendation systems has transformed the digital marketing industry, impacting both business strategy and consumer buying behavior in online commerce (Pereira et al., 2023). These technologies go beyond simple audience segmentation and targeting by using large-scale data and advanced analytical techniques to gain a more detailed insight into customer preferences and actions. According to Markellou et al. (2005), personalized suggestions on e-commerce platforms have the dual effect of increasing user engagement and sales conversions, while fostering long-term customer relationships.

Moreover, the machine learning algorithms embedded in these systems play a crucial role in changing consumers' purchase intentions and behaviors, as highlighted by Liu (2022). Namjun et al. (2019) found that AI-based suggestions influence customer decisions by directing buyers toward specific product categories, and buying behaviors. Although intelligent systems have a significant impact on encouraging impulsive purchases, they can also damage the reputation and user loyalty of platforms, as demonstrated by Huang and Wang (2021). In addition, customized recommendation systems help customers easily navigate through extensive product data, thereby improving the accuracy and speed of their decision-making processes (Lou, 2022).

As the use of AI tools in e-commerce has grown rapidly in recent years, more research is needed in this area. As satisfaction plays a crucial role in user's experience (Deirmentzoglou et al., 2022), the aim of this study is to analyze the factors that influence online purchase decisions based on AI recommendations and the role of user satisfaction in this relationship. In order to achieve this, field research on e-commerce users was conducted.

2 Literature Review

Innovation plays a critical role in today's business landscape (Agoraki et al., 2024a; Deirmentzoglou et al., 2024a; Pistikou et al., 2023). The evolution of digital marketing has profoundly influenced consumer behavior and their engagement with brands and products. This evolution is attributed to the enhanced utilization of online data, the proliferation of social media platforms, and diverse digital technologies. These factors have significantly impacted how consumers discover, choose, and purchase products and services, prompting the development of omni-channel marketing approaches (Ovodenko et al., 2020). A key element of this shift is the role of digital technologies like social media, mobile devices, artificial intelligence, and big data. These tools are not just reshaping consumer preferences, but are also influencing buyers' online purchasing behaviors (Singh & Thirumoorthi, 2019). The extensive adoption of digital media has led to the emergence of four main types of consumer power: demand-driven, information-driven, network-driven, and crowd-driven power. This shift has transferred substantial power from marketers to consumers, thereby altering the conventional market dynamics (Labrecque et al., 2013).

Furthermore, the advent of digital technology, including smartphones and social media, has precipitated alterations in social domains, interpersonal connections, power structures, and user inclinations. These changes have a direct impact on consumer behavior, influencing how customers interact with firms and make purchasing decisions (Gupta, 2021). The interactive nature of digital marketing expands the range of strategies for promoting products and brands, enabling a more relationship-oriented marketing approach that utilizes data collection to understand and predict customer behavior (Cairns, 2013). E-commerce customization is a rapidly growing industry that leverages data, technology, and knowledge of consumer psychology, to enhance the online purchasing experience (Deirmentzoglou & Deirmentzoglou, 2022). The approach is becoming increasingly sophisticated, with current trends emphasizing the use of tailored user experiences through the integration of modern technology and innovative tactics.

Contemporary e-commerce personalization approaches rely on the strategic utilization of client data to customize the online purchasing experience. Goy et al. (2007) emphasize the essential need of incorporating customer information into e-commerce platforms, to enhance the overall user-experience. Adolphs and Winkelmann (2010) state that recommendation engines and price comparison tools are used to provide customized offers that specifically cater to individual tastes. The fundamental objective of these customization initiatives is to align goods with customers' specific needs and preferences. This entails the creation of a structure that ensures constant content quality and delivers quantifiable results to enhance the adoption of technology (Kaptein & Parvinen, 2015). Moreover, personalization aims to enhance the provision of services and foster customer loyalty. This is frequently accomplished through recommendation systems that employ demographic, collaborative filtering, association, and content-based methodologies to accurately propose products that are tailored to the specific needs of each individual user (Wei et al., 2002).

The advent of artificial intelligence has significantly transformed the efficacy of advertising strategies. Kuang (2022) asserts that AI plays a crucial role in improving conversion rates for targeted ads by promoting innovation in content and effectively aligning advertisements with user consumption patterns. This method not only enhances the efficiency of advertisements, but also tailors them to individual requirements. Moreover, AI fosters more profound emotional bonds between businesses and consumers. As Timokhovich and Bulycheva (2021) posit, AI's capacity to examine personal data enables the development of marketing messages that are adapted to the emotional and mood states of customers, which is crucial for fostering enduring partnerships. Moreover, the significance of AI in forecasting customer behavior is essential. Bhatt (2021) asserts that the deployment of artificial intelligence (AI) in real-time data analytics empowers marketers to accurately identify and engage with the most appropriate target audiences at the optimal moments. Kaponis and Maragoudakis (2022) highlight the capacity of AI to forecast upcoming customer demands, thereby ensuring that marketing endeavors are pertinent and forward-thinking. Moreover, chatbots have become indispensable in digital marketing efforts. These programs, which are known as human interaction simulators, play a pivotal role in enhancing the quality of interaction between businesses and their digital customers, thereby improving the overall consumer engagement experience.

Kaczorowska-Spychalska (2019) posits that chatbots enhance the user-experience by fostering dynamic and engaging interactions, thereby enabling advertisers to engage in conversational communication with their audience. This heightened level of engagement frequently strengthens the connection between customers and companies. Additionally, chatbots are advantageous in digital sales because they may employ data mining and forecast customer behavior, thereby improving the customization of marketing efforts, as explained by Kaponis and Maragoudakis (2022). The predictive ability of chatbots assists to tailoring marketing strategies to align with customers' individual wants and preferences. Moreover, chatbots help archive new customer acquisition. *ManyChat* and similar platforms exemplify the effectiveness of chatbots in gathering potential customers and streamlining the sales process for enterprises (Illescas-Manzano et al., 2021). Chatbots demonstrate exceptional performance in several phases of the B2B sales funnel, frequently outperforming conventional sales techniques in terms of efficiency and effectiveness in comprehending consumer preferences (Fauser et al., 2022). This demonstrates their adaptability in various company environments.

In addition to performing practical activities, chatbots enhance relationship marketing by maximizing the utilization of social networks and establishing a competitive edge in the digital marketplace (Araujo & Casais, 2020). The first encounter a consumer has with a brand, might potentially be through a chatbot, thereby pointing out the importance of the quality of this encounter. A well-designed and amiable chatbot welcome has the potential to greatly improve the level of customer interaction with a company (Kull et al., 2021). Chatbots have a sound influence on several important aspects of digital marketing, particularly in managing extensive client bases. They imitate human interactions to provide relevant messages, hence improving customer service and response rates. Efficient communication is crucial for maintaining high levels of customer satisfaction (Nuameesri & Poomhiran, 2019). Establishing trust facilitates productive interactions between humans and chatbots. Chatbots that provide customized and dependable services play a crucial role in building the trust required for effective interactions in the field of digital marketing (Przegalinska et al., 2019).

Chatbot marketing has a significant influence on the way customers and companies connect. Factors such as interactivity, accessibility, amusement, and customization are crucial in this process (Cheng & Jiang, 2022). As Jansom et al. (2022) posit, chatbot e-services that prioritize genuine communication and effective problem-solving abilities, tend to elicit higher levels of consumer satisfaction, in specific industries such as fashion Recent studies indicate that artificial intelligence (AI) and customization have a substantial impact on customer behavior in the field of e-commerce (Khrais, 2020). AI-powered picture recognition technologies facilitate the provision of customized experiences, thereby enhancing client happiness. The process of personalization has a significant impact on the choices people make when purchasing products or services, with convenience playing a crucial role. Individualized evaluations can expedite decision-making, enhance the user experience, and influence purchasing behavior.

Li et al. (2022) employed artificial intelligence (AI) to examine the facial expressions of customers in order to customize product recommendations in the field of electronic commerce. Their results indicated that 93.2% of consumers expressed pleasure, suggesting that AI is highly effective in providing personalized experiences that are highly valued by users. Additionally, Sakina and Ali (2021) examined the impact of the customization of e-commerce platforms, on Indonesian customers. Their findings indicated that customization enhances purchase intentions, by improving perceived ease-of-use, enjoyment, and trust. Additionally, the authors observed that the practical advantages of customization outweigh the enjoyment, emphasizing the significance of tailored experiences in making purchase choices.

Balan and Mathew (2021) investigated the impact of rating-based personalization on consumer decision-making in e-commerce. Their findings indicated that personalized assessments based on ratings, facilitate the purchase process and enhance decision efficiency. Jain et al. (2018) explored the influence of hyper-customization in the fashion industry. Their findings demonstrated a significant correlation between the perceived value of customized content and the intention to make a purchase. This highlights the importance of offering meaningful personalization fashion e-commerce buyers.

Finally, Cheng et al. (2021) conducted an analysis on the elements that affect customer trust in text-based chatbots in the context of e-commerce. Their study revealed that buyer confidence in chatbots increases when they demonstrate empathy and warmth, but decreases as the tasks become more sophisticated and the bot's identity becomes more obvious.

Based on the above literature review, the following hypotheses are developed (Fig. 1):

- H1: Online Shopping Frequency (FRQ) has a positive impact on Recommendation-Based Purchase Decisions (RPD).
- H2: Trust in Online Shopping Recommendations (TRS) has a positive impact on Recommendation-Based Purchase Decisions (RPD)
- H3: Attention Response to AI-driven Personalized Marketing (ATR) has a positive impact on Recommendation-Based Purchase Decisions (RPD)
- H4: Satisfaction with AI-Powered Tools (SAT) mediates the relationship between Trust in Online Shopping Recommendations (TRS) and Recommendation-Based Purchase Decisions (RPD)
- H5: Satisfaction with AI-Powered Tools (SAT) mediates the relationship between Attention Response to AI-driven Personalized Marketing (ATR) and Recommendation-Based Purchase Decisions (RPD)

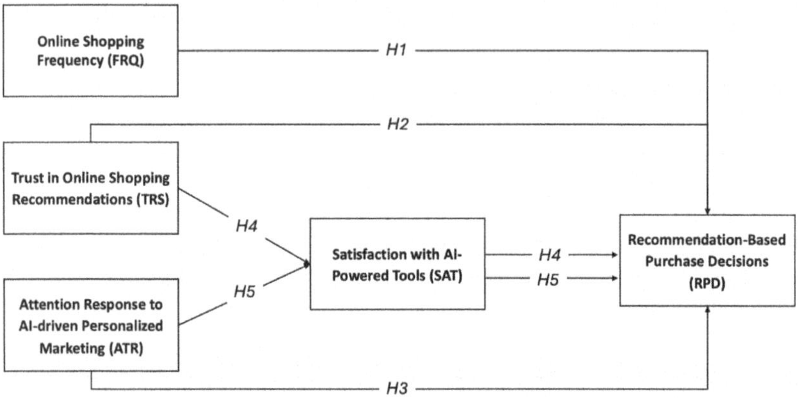

Fig. 1 Conceptual framework. *Source* Authors' construct

3 Methodology

To test the proposed hypotheses, a survey research method was employed. A questionnaire was distributed to German e-commerce users by Google Forms. A total of 182 individuals participated in the study, which employed a convenience-sampling and online-distribution method. This approach was selected for its simplicity, ease of access, and effectiveness in safeguarding the anonymity of respondents, and the speed in generating research results.

The two measurement items of the Recommendation-Based Purchase Decisions (RPD) were based on the work of Adwan and Aladwan (2022), while Satisfaction with AI-Powered Tools (SAT) was measured with three items based on Cheng and Jiang (2020) and LoPinto and Ragsdale (2010). Attention Response to AI-driven Personalized Marketing (ATR) was measured with two items based on Shrirame et al. (2020). Finally, Trust in Online Shopping Recommendations (TRS) was measured with one item based on Pavlou (2003), while Online Shopping Frequency (FRQ) is also an one-item variable. The survey items were designed on the basis of a 5-point Likert scale from 1(strongly disagree) to 5 (strongly agree) (Appendix A).

4 Findings

The study included a total of 182 participants, predominantly composed of young adults between the ages of 18 and 26 residing in Germany. The participants represented a demographic group that often engages with e-commerce platforms. Most participants were female, while there was a sizeable number of male participants, however some participants chose not to disclose their gender. The respondents had a diverse range of educational levels, ranging from high school diplomas, to master's degrees. The diversity of educational backgrounds among the participants provided an understanding of the ways in which education may impact e-commerce usage.

Relevant reliability and validity tests were conducted, such as the composite reliability (CR), average variance extracted (AVE) and Cronbach's alpha (a) of the constructs were above the thresholds (Table 1). Moreover, the square roots of the AVE (Table 1) meet the Fornell and Larcker (1981) criteria, as the square roots are greater than correlations between the variables, as shown in Table 2.

Regarding correlations, Recommendation-Based Purchase Decisions (RPD) which is the dependent variable of this study, has a significant positive correlation with FRQ ($r = 0.34, p < 0.001$), TRS ($r = 0.41, p < 0.001$), ATR ($r = 0.39, p < 0.001$) and SAT ($r = 0.45$, $p < 0.001$). Moreover, the mediator of the study, Satisfaction with AI-Powered Tools (SAT), has a significant positive correlation with TRS ($r = 0.46, p < 0.001$), PRF ($r = 0.62, p < 0.001$) and RPD ($r = 0.45, p < 0.001$) (Table 2).

In order to test the hypotheses, multiple linear regressions were conducted. First, Model 1 shows that FRQ ($\beta = 0.23, p < 0.001$), TRS (($\beta = 0.23, p < 0.01$) and ATR

Table 1 Factor loadings, CR, AVE and Cronbach's alpha

Variables		λ	CR	AVE	Cronbach a	SQRT(AVE)
TRS	–	–	–	–	–	–
FRQ	–	–	–	–	–	–
ATR	ATR1	0.86	0.85	0.74	0.65	0.86
	ATR2	0.86				
SAT	SAT1	0.78	0.84	0.64	0.72	0.80
	SAT2	0.76				
	SAT3	0.86				
RPD	RPD1	0.87	0.86	0.76	0.66	0.87
	RPD2	0.87				

Source Authors' calculation

Table 2 Correlation matrix

	FRQ	**TRS**	**ATR**	**SAT**	**RPD**	**AGE**	**Education**	**Gender**
FRQ	–							
TRS	0.30***	–						
ATR	0.14	0.41***	–					
SAT	0.14	0.46***	0.62***	–				
RPD	0.34***	0.41***	0.39***	0.45***	–			
AGE	0.10	0.02	−0.11	−0.09	0.03	–		
EDUCATION	0.10	0.17*	0.24***	0.09	0.12	−0.01	–	
GENDER	0.12	−0.04	−0.01	0.06	0.09	−0.09	0.06	–

Note * $p < 0.05$, ** $p < 0.01$, *** $p < 0.001$
Source Authors' calculation

Table 3 Multiple regression analyses

	Model 1 (RPD)	Model 2 (SAT)	Model 3 (RPD)
FRQ	0.23***	–	0.23***
TRS	0.23**	0.24***	0.17*
ATR	0.26***	0.52***	0.12
SAT	–	–	0.26**
R^2	*0.27*	*0.44*	*0.31*
F	*22.33*	*70.17*	*20.03*

Note * $p < 0.05$, ** $p < 0.01$, *** $p < 0.001$
Source Authors' calculation

($\beta = 0.26, p < 0.001$) have a significant impact on RPD; therefore, H1, H2 and H3 are supported. To test H4 and H5, the Baron and Kenny's (1986) test for mediation was used. TRS ($\beta = 0.24$, $p < 0.001$) and ATR ($\beta = 0.52$, $p < 0.001$) have a significant positive impact on SAT, confirming the first condition of the test. In addition, Model 1 shows that TRS ($\beta = 0.23$, $p < 0.01$) and PRF ($\beta = 0.26$, $p < 0.001$) have also a significant positive impact on RPD supporting test's second condition. Finally, in Model 3, SAT ($\beta = 0.26$, $p < 0.01$) has a significant positive impact on RPD, confirming the third condition. The TRS ($\beta = 0.17$, $p < 0.05$) has a reduced effect on RPD, while the effect of ATR ($\beta = 0.12, p > 0.05$) on RPD disappears (Table 3). Based on the above, H4 and H5 are confirmed.

5 Discussion and Conclusion

The purpose of this study is to analyze the factors that influence AI recommendation-based purchase decisions. Our results show that *online shopping frequency*, *trust* in online shopping recommendations, and *attention response to AI-driven personalized marketing*, have a significant positive impact on recommendation-based purchase decisions. Furthermore, the results show that *satisfaction* with AI-powered tools mediates the relationships between preference for AI-driven personalized marketing, and trust in online shopping recommendations with recommendation-based purchase decisions.

Individuals who frequently shop online, trust the AI recommendations they receive while shopping online, and notice the AI-driven personalized marketing tends to have higher recommendation-based purchase decisions than traditional marketing. However, satisfaction with the AI-driven tools plays a significant role in this relationship. Specifically, users whose attention is captured by AI personalized marketing messages tend to purchase the recommended products, but this effect is explained by the mediating influence of satisfaction with the accuracy and support provided by the AI tools.

Based on current literature, our findings align with a more comprehensive understanding of AI's impact on e-commerce. Research indicates that the use of artificial intelligence to personalize products or services has a significant impact on the preferences and decision-making of customers. AI recommendation systems, such as those mentioned by Namjun et al. (2019), have demonstrated the ability to modify client preference frameworks and change the way platform suggestions function. Moreover, the impact of artificial intelligence on forecasting consumer behaviors and tailoring the shopping experience greatly improves conversion rates and customer contentment. These discoveries offer valuable insights that have both theoretical and practical advantages. They greatly enhance e-commerce methods, especially by using advanced AI techniques to create a more customized purchasing experience. This integration offers increased customer happiness, enhances brand loyalty, and has the potential to boost revenue.

E-commerce platforms may enhance their AI strategy by examining the relationship between AI technology and critical consumer behaviors, such as product suggestions and purchasing decisions. This upgrade aims to increase client loyalty and engagement, thereby establishing a competitive position in the digital market. Furthermore, the study provides practical and implementable knowledge for focused marketing and branding efforts, allowing online shopping platforms to develop plans that are not only guided by artificial intelligence but also focused on customer requirements, highlighting personalization and contentment. This emphasis is expected to result in improved precision in reaching potential consumers and the establishment of a robust brand image that aligns with consumer needs and preferences.

This study offers a comprehensive analysis of the relationship between AI-driven customization and consumer behavior in the digital marketplace. It reveals the necessity for companies to embrace and incorporate advanced AI tools, to enhance the shopping experience and strengthen consumer engagement. This finding has a significant impact on both the theoretical and practical aspects of digital marketing and e-commerce strategies.

The primary limitation of the study is its exclusive focus on German users. By examining cross-cultural research, it is possible to gain a more comprehensive understanding of the effectiveness of AI-driven personalization, considering the significant role of cultural values in human decision-making and behavior (Agoraki et al., 2024b; Deirmentzoglou et al., 2024b). Subsequent research might investigate the influence of advanced artificial intelligence technologies, such as intricate machine learning algorithms and resilient predictive analytics, on customer choice behavior in the realm of digital marketing. Furthermore, it is crucial to consider privacy concerns and the ethical aspects of AI-powered personalization, analyzing the impact of these issues on customer trust and engagement.

Appendix

Scale Items.

Variables	Items
Trust in Online Shopping Recommendations (TRS)	TRS1—I trust the recommendations provided to me during online shopping
Online Shopping Frequency (FRQ)	FRQ1—I frequently shop online
Attention Response to AI-driven Personalized Marketing (ATR)	ATR1—Personalized marketing messages and offers catch my attention more than generic ones
	ATR2—I am more likely to notice and engage with AI marketing messages
Satisfaction with AI-Powered Tools (SAT)	SAT1—I am satisfied with the responses and assistance provided by the chatbot
	SAT2—The accuracy of personalized product recommendations is reflecting my actual preferences
	SAT3—Overall, I feel that AI-driven tools (like chatbots and product recommendations) make my online shopping more efficient
Recommendation-Based Purchase Decisions (RPD)	RPD1—I have already made a purchase based on a personalized product recommendation
	RPD2—I would make a purchase based on the product recommendations provided to me

Source Authors' own adaptation from Adwan and Aladwan (2022), Cheng and Jiang (2020), LoPinto and Ragsdale (2010), Shrirame et al. (2020), and Pavlou (2003)

References

Adolphs, C., & Winkelmann, A. (2010). Personalization research in e-commerce-A state of the art review (2000–2008). *Journal of Electronic Commerce Research, 11*(4), 326.

Adwan, A., & Aladwan, R. (2022). Use of artificial intelligence system to predict consumers' behaviors. *International Journal of Data and Network Science, 6*(4), 1223–1232.

Agoraki, K. K., Deirmentzoglou, G. A., Psychalis, M., & Apostolopoulos, S. (2024). Types of innovation and sustainable development: Evidence from medium-and large-sized firms. *International Journal of Innovation and Technology Management, 21*, 2450013.

Agoraki, K. K., Deirmentzoglou, G. A., & Triantopoulos, C. (2024b). Cultural values as catalysts of technological innovation for a sustainable future. *Sustainability, 16*(5), 2064.

Araújo, T., & Casais, B. (2020). Customer acceptance of shopping-assistant chatbots. In *Marketing and smart technologies: Proceedings of ICMarkTech 2019* (pp. 278–287). Springer.

Balan, U. M., & Mathew, S. K. (2021). Personalize, summarize or let them read? A study on online word of mouth strategies and consumer decision process. *Information Systems Frontiers, 23*, 627–647.

Baron, R. M., & Kenny, D. A. (1986). The moderator–mediator variable distinction in social psychological research: Conceptual, strategic, and statistical considerations. *Journal of Personality and Social Psychology, 51*(6), 1173.

Bhatt, V. K. (2021, November). Assessing the significance and impact of artificial intelligence and machine learning in placement of advertisements. In *2021 IEEE International Conference on Technology Management, Operations and Decisions (ICTMOD)* (pp. 1–6). IEEE.

Cairns, G. (2013). Evolutions in food marketing, quantifying the impact, and policy implications. *Appetite, 62*, 194–197.

Cheng, X., Bao, Y., Zarifis, A., Gong, W., & Mou, J. (2021). Exploring consumers' response to text-based chatbots in e-commerce: The moderating role of task complexity and chatbot disclosure. *Internet Research, 32*(2), 496–517.

Cheng, Y., & Jiang, H. (2022). Customer–brand relationship in the era of artificial intelligence: Understanding the role of chatbot marketing efforts. *Journal of Product & Brand Management, 31*(2), 252–264.

Cheng, Y., & Jiang, H. (2020). How do AI-driven chatbots impact user experience? Examining gratifications, perceived privacy risk, satisfaction, loyalty, and continued use. *Journal of Broadcasting & Electronic Media, 64*(4), 592–614.

Deirmentzoglou, G. A., Vlassi, E., & Anastasopoulou, E. (2024). DDMMO website quality, destination image and intention to use metaverse platforms. *Platforms, 2*, 180–192.

Deirmentzoglou, G. A., Agoraki, K. K., & Patsoulis, P. (2024b). The nexus between cultural values and perceptions of corporate sustainable development. *Social Responsibility Journal, 20*(2), 224–242.

Deirmentzoglou, G. A., & Deirmentzoglou, E. A. (2022, September). Pest analysis of the e-commerce industry: The case of Greece. In *Business development and economic governance in Southeastern Europe: 13th International conference on the economies of the Balkan and Eastern European Countries (EBEEC), Pafos, Cyprus, 2021* (pp. 315–323). Springer International Publishing.

Deirmentzoglou, G. A., Vlassi, E., & Agoraki, K. K. (2022, May). The effect of the hotel attributes on guest satisfaction due to the covid-19 pandemic crisis: The case of the Greek tourism and hospitality sector. In *International conference economies of the Balkan and Eastern European Countries* (pp. 283–297). Springer Nature Switzerland.

Fauser, S., Schmäh, M., Tran, L. C., Le, H. M., Bumiller, J., & Hiller, A. (2022). Will chatbots play a significant role for B2B marketingin the future? Chatbots in B2B businesses. *International Journal of Business and Applied Social Science, 8*(12), 6–12.

Fornell, C., & Larcker, D. F. (1981). Evaluating structural equation models with unobservable variables and measurement error. *Journal of Marketing Research, 18*(1), 39–50.

Goy, A., Ardissono, L., & Petrone, G. (2007). Personalization in e-commerce applications. In *The adaptive web: Methods and strategies of web personalization* (pp. 485–520). Springer.

Gupta, D. G. (2021). Book review: Consumer behavior: A digital native. *Journal of Macromarketing, 41*(3), 506–508.

Huang, Y., & Wang, X. (2021, August). Research on the influence of intelligent recommendation function on user behavior in highly digitized network platforms. In *2021 IEEE international conference on electronic technology, communication and information (ICETCI)* (pp. 250–254). IEEE.

Illescas-Manzano, M. D., Vicente López, N., Afonso González, N., & Cristofol Rodríguez, C. (2021). Implementation of chatbot in online commerce, and open innovation. *Journal of Open Innovation: Technology, Market, and Complexity, 7*(2), 125.

Jain, G., Rakesh, S., Nabi, M. K., & Chaturvedi, K. R. (2018). Hyper-personalization–fashion sustainability through digital clienteling. *Research Journal of Textile and Apparel, 22*(4), 320–334.

Jansom, A., Srisangkhajorn, T., & Limarunothai, W. (2022). How chatbot e-services motivate communication credibility and lead to customer satisfaction: The perspective of Thai consumers in the apparel retailing context. *Innovative Marketing, 18*(3), 13.

Kaczorowska-Spychalska, D. (2019). How Chatbots Influence Marketing. *Management, 23*(1), 251–270.

Kaponis, A., & Maragoudakis, M. (2022, September). Data analysis in digital marketing using machine learning and artificial intelligence techniques, ethical and legal dimensions, state of the art. In *Proceedings of the 12th Hellenic conference on artificial intelligence* (pp. 1–9).

Kaptein, M., & Parvinen, P. (2015). Advancing e-commerce personalization: Process framework and case study. *International Journal of Electronic Commerce, 19*(3), 7–33.

Khrais, L. T. (2020). Role of artificial intelligence in shaping consumer demand in E-commerce. *Future Internet, 12*(12), 226.

Kuang, A. (2022, July). Construction of personalized advertising accuracy model based on artificial intelligence. In *2022 International conference on artificial intelligence and autonomous robot systems (AIARS)* (pp. 395–398). IEEE.

Kull, A. J., Romero, M., & Monahan, L. (2021). How may I help you? Driving brand engagement through the warmth of an initial chatbot message. *Journal of Business Research, 135*, 840–850.

Labrecque, L. I., Vor Dem Esche, J., Mathwick, C., Novak, T. P., & Hofacker, C. F. (2013). Consumer power: Evolution in the digital age. *Journal of Interactive Marketing, 27*(4), 257–269.

Li, Y., Zhong, Z., Zhang, F., & Zhao, X. (2022). Artificial intelligence-based human–computer interaction technology applied in consumer behavior analysis and experiential education. *Frontiers in Psychology, 13*, Article 784311.

Liu, L. (2022). e-commerce personalized recommendation based on machine learning technology. *Mobile Information Systems, 2022*, 1–11.

LoPinto, F. A., & Ragsdale, C. T. (2010). Efficient modelling of individual consumer preferences: Facilitating agent-based online markets. *International Journal of Electronic Marketing and Retailing, 3*(1), 66–81.

Lou, F. (2022). E-commerce recommendation technology based on collaborative filtering algorithm and mobile cloud computing. *Wireless Communications and Mobile Computing, 2022.*

Markellou, P., Mousourouli, I., Sirmakessis, S., & Tsakalidis, A. (2005, October). Personalized e-commerce recommendations. In *IEEE international conference on e-business engineering (ICEBE'05)* (pp. 245–252). IEEE.

Namjun, C. H. A., Hosoo, C. H. O., Sangman, L. E. E., & Hwang, J. (2019, February). Effect of AI recommendation system on the consumer preference structure in e-commerce: Based on two types of preference. In *2019 21st international conference on advanced communication technology (ICACT)* (pp. 77–80). IEEE.

Nuameesri, S., & Poomhiran, L. (2019). Improving responsiveness conversation of Thai chatbot through sentiment analysis classification techniques. *International Journal of Engineering and Advanced Technology, 9*(2), 3733–3737.

Ovodenko, A. A., Peshkova, G. Y., & Zlobina, O. V. (2020, December). Digital evolution of consumer behavior and its impact on digital transformation of small and medium business sustained development strategy. In *2nd international scientific and practical conference on digital economy (ISCDE 2020)* (pp. 424–428). Atlantis Press.

Pavlou, P. A. (2003). Consumer acceptance of electronic commerce: Integrating trust and risk with the technology acceptance model. *International Journal of Electronic Commerce, 7*(3), 101–134.

Pereira, L., Tomás, D., Dias, Á., Costa, R. L. D., & Gonçalves, R. (2023). How artificial intelligence can improve digital marketing. *International Journal of Business Information Systems, 44*(4), 581–624.

Pistikou, V., Flouros, F., Deirmentzoglou, G. A., & Agoraki, K. K. (2023). Sustainability reporting: Examining the community impact of the S&P500 companies. *Sustainability, 15*(18), 13681.

Przegalinska, A., Ciechanowski, L., Stroz, A., Gloor, P., & Mazurek, G. (2019). In bot we trust: A new methodology of chatbot performance measures. *Business Horizons, 62*(6), 785–797.

Sakina, M., & Ali, S. (2021). Determining factors of purchase intention in personalized website context for indonesian consumers. *Journal of Economics, Business, & Accountancy Ventura, 24*(1), 139–155.

Shrirame, V., Sabade, J., Soneta, H., & Vijayalakshmi, M. (2020, July). Consumer behavior analytics using machine learning algorithms. In *2020 IEEE international conference on electronics, computing and communication technologies (CONECCT)* (pp. 1–6). IEEE.

Singh, A. K., & Thirumoorthi, P. (2019). The impact of digital disruption technologies on customer preferences: The case of retail commerce. *International Journal of Recent Technology and Engineering, 8*(3), 1255–1261.

Timokhovich, A. N., & Bulycheva, O. S. (2021). Technologies for personalization of brand marketing communications using artificial intelligence. *Digital Sociology, 3*(4), 19–24.

Wei, C. P., Easley, R. F., & Shaw, M. J. (2002). Web-based recommendation systems for personalized e-commerce shopping. In *E-Business management: Integration of web technologies with business models* (pp. 249–276). Springer.

What Stops Consumers from Purchasing Refurbished Smartphones?

Mehmet Cem Bölen, Embiya Çelik, and Erol Kılıç

Abstract Smartphones have a short lifespan and are often replaced in today's fast-paced market. As a result, refurbishment has become an essential method for extracting values from devices. Therefore, people worldwide are increasingly turning to digital device recycling platforms to sell, trade in, or recycle smartphones, highlighting their growing significance. However, several challenges may hinder the widespread adoption of refurbished smartphones among consumers. While previous studies have primarily focused on the general factors and individual differences that affect the decision-making process for buying refurbished products, research on resistance towards refurbished products is still in the early stages and seems to be quite limited. Therefore, it is essential to comprehend consumers' decision-making processes to boost their intention to purchase refurbished smartphones. To fill this gap, the main objective of this study was to identify and analyze the factors that act as barriers to consumers when purchasing a refurbished smartphone. Drawing on the innovation resistance theory, we developed a research model to explore the relationship between theory-driven adoption barriers (specifically, usage, value, risk, tradition, and image) and consumer resistance. To test the proposed model, data were collected through a cross-sectional online survey of 430 individuals who neither owned nor expressed a desire to purchase a refurbished smartphone. The collected data were analyzed using partial least-squares structural equation modeling. The results show that value, tradition, and image barriers positively influence consumer resistance to refurbished smartphones, whereas the role of usage and risk barriers received no empirical support. The proposed model explains 61% of the variance in

M. C. Bölen (✉) · E. Çelik
Open and Distance Education Faculty, Ataturk University, Erzurum, Turkey
e-mail: mehmetcem.bolen@atauni.edu.tr

E. Çelik
e-mail: embiya@atauni.edu.tr

E. Kılıç
Department of Management Information Systems, Ataturk University, Erzurum, Turkey
e-mail: 69erolkilic@gmail.com

I. Bartuseviciene et al. (eds.), *Building Resilience Through Digital Transformation and Sustainable Innovation*, Springer Proceedings in Business and Economics,
https://doi.org/10.1007/978-3-031-90054-9_16

resistance intention, which indicates a significant explanation for consumers' resistance to refurbished smartphones. This study contributes to the theoretical understanding by elucidating how usage, value, risk, tradition, and image barriers interact with consumer resistance in the context of refurbished smartphones.

Keywords Refurbishing · Circular economy · Consumer behavior · Smartphones

JEL Classification Codes O30 · O39 · Q56

1 Introduction

Recycling electronic components is an effective strategy for reducing e-waste and production costs while achieving sustainability goals. In this regard, closed loop production methods have gained attention to extract value from electronic waste and has become popular to focus on the "circular economy" (Sharifi & Shokouhyar, 2021; Zink et al., 2014). The circular economy boosts resource efficiency. It does this by maximizing transformation efficiencies keeping resources in use and prolonging next-use chains. Strategies like refurbishing and recycling achieve this (Arbabi et al., 2020). Refurbished smartphones significantly promote a circular economy. They also benefit the environment. Refurbishing smartphones can save critical raw materials and energy. It reduces emissions such as CO2 too thereby contributing to circular economy principles (Mugge et al., 2017)! The refurbishment process aligns with circular economy strategies. These strategies aim to close product cycles. They also maintain materials and resources within the product cycle for as long as possible (Pamminger et al., 2021; Škare et al., 2024). This highlights the urgent need for improved recycling initiatives and awareness programs to address the growing e-waste crisis and its environmental implications as it is possible to decrease the environmental impact of many electronic products. For instance, refurbishing a smartphone slashes its carbon footprint by a whopping 87%, and its water footprint plummets by 76% compared to cranking out a brand-new device (Zumegen, 2020).

Harms and Linton (2015) argues that consumers aren't too keen on paying for refurbished products. This reluctance to invest in refurbished smartphones may stem from concerns regarding the reliability of such devices. Hazelwood and Pecht (2021) revealed refurbished electronics may not be as dependable as brand new products which can scare consumers away from picking them. Therefore, the aim of this study is to shed light on the drivers of consumer resistance to refurbished smartphones. To the best of our knowledge, this study is one of the first to identify the reasons for consumers' resistance to refurbished smartphones from the perspective of innovation resistance.

2 Literature Review

High-tech goods such as smartphones have limited lifetimes owing to their short usage periods (Zhou & Gupta, 2020). Manufacturers prioritize rapid technological advancements and trendy aesthetics in design (Aytac & Wu, 2013), leading to the frequent release of new models. However, this contributes significantly to the growing problem of electronic waste. The refurbished product industry is growing quickly because of the availability of new and secondhand products from different models and brands. Hence, it is important to gain a comprehensive understanding of the factors that influence consumers' decisions to purchase refurbished products (Neto & Dutordoir, 2020). To date, a few studies have attempted to understand consumer purchasing behavior towards refurbished products from various perspectives (Bigliardi et al., 2022). For example, Mugget et al. (2018) found that consumers tend to consider some attributes such as price, brand value, seller identity, and refurbishing certification, when considering to purchase refurbished products. The literature also notes that perceived benefits and risks play a significant role in consumers' decisions to purchase refurbished products (Weelden et al., 2016). In addition, perceived product attributes including credibility, review, refurbishment, and ecological attributes have been found to affect young consumers willingness to purchase for refurbished products (Kurdhi et al., 2022).

Consumer attitudes toward refurbished smartphones depend on factors such as perceived risks, product knowledge, and financial rewards. For example, Onurlubas and Gumus (2023) noted that consumers in the Generation Z hold significant risk concern related to buying refurbished products. Using refurbished smartphones instead of purchasing a new smartphone contributes to lowering the global warming potential and mitigates the effects of resource extraction (Wiche et al., 2022). Regional and demographic classifications of consumers' purchasing behavior for refurbished smartphones are different. This recalls that there has to be more niche marketing for refurbished smartphones. It should be focused on the individual motivational and perceptual consumer segments' needs (Tunn et al., 2019).

Previous studies drew from theories and models to broadly explain what shapes consumers intend to buy refurbished goods but this does not give actionable insights on reducing resistance to refurbished smartphones specifically. Comprehending the precise factors capable of swaying consumer resistance is crucial to advance theoretical understanding of opposition to refurbished smartphones. Demonstrating the effect matters however it falls short of providing tangible ways to decrease resistance to refurbished smartphones. To further build theoretical knowledge of consumers' resistance to refurbished smartphones, we aim to to understand the specific factors that can influence consumer resistance in this study.

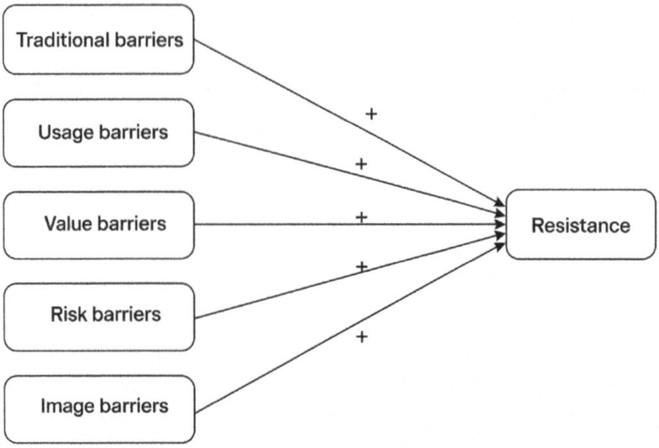

Fig. 1 Research model

3 Data and Methodology

3.1 Research Model and Hypotheses

The theory of innovation resistance (IRT) established by Ram and Sheth (1989) was used as the basis of this study. The IRT has been employed to explore the obstacles and resistance to different user innovations, such as voice assistant (Hong & Cho, 2023), m-payment (Ghosh, 2024), m-banking (Gupta & Arora, 2017), m-commerce (Hew et al., 2017), mobile services (Joachim et al., 2018), and food delivery applications (Verma et al., 2023). To the best of our knowledge, no previous attempts have been made to examine the association between different functional and psychological barriers from the IRT perspective. The proposed model is illustrated in Fig. 1.

3.2 Sample and Data Collection

Since the main purpose of this study was to explore the determinants of consumers' behavioral intentions to resist refurbished smartphones, the data gathered from smartphone owners have not owned a refurbished smartphone. In the Information System domain, the survey method is typically preferred by researchers as a leading approach for exploring human behavior and the interaction with information systems (Li & Liu, 2014). Consistent with this idea, an online survey was conducted to collect data from consumers who had never owned refurbished smartphones. Participants were selected based on non-probability sampling, and a convenience sample of male and

Table 1 Demographic characteristics of the respondents ($N = 430$)

Item	Category	Frequency	Percentage
Gender	Male	296	68.83
	Female	134	31.16
Age	18–24	95	22.09
	25–34	191	44.41
	35–44	109	25.34
	45–54	27	6.27
	54 and more	8	1.86
Income	<8500 Liras	112	26.04
	8500–15,000	203	47.02
	15,000–25,000	94	21.86
	>25,000 Liras	21	4.88

female undergraduate students was used in this study. Research findings have shown that college students' beliefs and attitudes are not significantly different from those of typical consumers (Durvasula et al., 1997). To ensure a homogenous sample of university students, participants were recruited exclusively from Ataturk University in Turkey. Participation was voluntary and anonymous. However, all participants were required to be at least 18 years of age. Following Wang and Hazen (2016), a random sample of 40 students and 40 non-student consumers in Turkey was used to assess the validity of the sample. The results of the pilot test indicated that students did not differ significantly from non-student consumers in their intent to purchase refurbished smartphones. This indicates that the selected sample serves as an appropriate representation of the target consumer's demographics. Data collection started in January 2023 and lasted for a month. After deleting 12 insincere responses (e.g. answering "Strongly Disagree" or "Strongly Agree"), a total of 430 valid responses were obtained. Table 1 presents the demographic statistics of all the respondents.

3.3 Data Analysis

The research model was tested using partial least squares structural equation modeling (PLS-SEM) via Smart PLS3.0 (Hair et al., 2011). Following the two-step approach recommended by Chin (2010), we initially evaluated the measurement framework by analyzing the reliability and validity, including both convergent and discriminant validity, of the constructs involved. In the second stage, the structural model was estimated by testing the significance of the relationships between the constructs.

The measurement model was evaluated using the reliability, convergent validity, and discriminant validity criteria of the construct measures. (Fornell & Larcker, 1981). For reliability, composite reliability (CR) and Cronbach's alpha values were examined. Cronbach's alpha scores over 0.6 are acceptable in exploratory studies

Table 2 Indicators loading

Construct	Item codes	Loadings	AVE	CR	Cronbach's alpha
Value Barriers	VB1	0.751	0.708	0.906	0.861
	VB3	0.829			
	VB4	0.898			
	VB5	0.881			
Image Barriers	IB1	0.894	0.761	0.927	0.896
	IB2	0.851			
	IB3	0.892			
	IB4	0.853			
Traditional Barriers	TB1	0.833	0.764	0.906	0.845
	TB2	0.875			
	TB3	0.911			
Usage Barriers	UB1	0.827	0.699	0.874	0.784
	UB2	0.789			
	UB3	0.889			
Risk Barriers	RB1	0.797	0.715	0.926	0.900
	RB2	0.886			
	RB3	0.819			
	RB4	0.877			
	RB5	0.845			
Resistance Intention	RI1	0.936	0.855	0.967	0.957
	RI2	0.935			
	RI3	0.937			
	RI4	0.889			
	RI5	0.926			

(Nunnally & Bernstein, 1994), while the CR values of all constructs should exceed the benchmark 0.7 (Barclay et al., 1995). As shown in Table 2, both Cronbach's alpha and CR of each construct were higher than the recommended cutoff value, indicating measurement reliability. Convergent validity was assessed using indicator loadings and average variance extracted (AVE) following the criterion proposed by Fornell and Larcker (1981). Table 2 also shows that all indicators were above the desired threshold (>0.7 for item loadings and >0.5 for AVE), which demonstrated good convergent validity (Fornell & Larcker, 1981).

Table 3 Discriminant validity

	RI	VB	TB	IB	UB	RB
RI	0.925					
VB	0.661	0.842				
TB	0.801	0.560	0.874			
IB	0.829	0.627	0.800	0.873		
UB	0.668	0.622	0.637	0.638	0.836	
RB	0.703	0.781	0.656	0.723	0.670	0.846

Three procedures were used to assess discriminant validity. First, following Fornell and Larcker (1981) recommendations, AVE is used to calculate the average variance extracted by a construct from all its measures. Fornell and Larcker (1981) suggested that the square root of the AVE value of each construct should be higher than the value of the correlation between the constructs in the research model. As shown in Table 3, the square roots of all AVE values were higher than the inter-construct correlations, indicating good discriminant validity. Second, cross-loadings were examined to check whether the measurement items loaded higher on their own constructs than on other constructs. As shown in Table 4, the cross-loadings are within the tolerance level of more than 0.1 difference between each measurement item that loads on its assigned latent variable and is loading on the other construct. (Ayanso et al., 2015; Gefen & Straub, 2005).

The results of the structural model assessment are presented in Table 5, confirming that three of the five proposed hypotheses are supported. Accordingly, the constructs of traditional barriers, value barriers, and image barriers were shown to have strong effects on the resistance to purchasing refurbished smartphones, thus supporting H1, H2, and H3. However, the usage barriers and risk barriers did not significantly affect resistance. Hence, H4 and H5 are not supported.

Table 4 Indicator item cross loading

	RI	VB	TB	IB	UB	RB
RI1	**0.936**	0.592	0.761	0.782	0.633	0.668
RI2	**0.935**	0.588	0.735	0.765	0.664	0.644
RI3	**0.937**	0.609	0.769	0.781	0.618	0.668
RI4	**0.889**	0.668	0.705	0.759	0.573	0.647
RI5	**0.926**	0.599	0.728	0.745	0.600	0.620
VB1	0.505	**0.751**	0.467	0.451	0.484	0.507
VB3	0.521	**0.829**	0.390	0.469	0.486	0.579
VB4	0.599	**0.898**	0.516	0.591	0.563	0.758
VB5	0.593	**0.881**	0.504	0.586	0.556	0.758
TB1	0.595	0.461	**0.833**	0.630	0.487	0.521
TB2	0.740	0.494	**0.875**	0.700	0.602	0.559
TB3	0.748	0.510	**0.911**	0.757	0.570	0.634
IB1	0.755	0.601	0.771	**0.894**	0.567	0.656
IB2	0.760	0.544	0.684	**0.851**	0.635	0.592
IB3	0.712	0.527	0.692	**0.892**	0.526	0.657
IB4	0.658	0.513	0.636	**0.853**	0.488	0.619
UB1	0.511	0.431	0.487	0.471	**0.827**	0.501
UB2	0.523	0.550	0.527	0.532	**0.789**	0.555
UB3	0.632	0.571	0.577	0.589	**0.889**	0.616
RB1	0.563	0.585	0.518	0.560	0.542	**0.797**
RB2	0.634	0.670	0.593	0.656	0.622	**0.886**
RB3	0.588	0.652	0.543	0.605	0.591	**0.819**
RB4	0.614	0.658	0.595	0.653	0.557	**0.877**
RB5	0.566	0.740	0.518	0.578	0.516	**0.845**

Table 5 Structural model path analysis

Hypotheses	Structural paths	Original sample (O)	Standard deviation (STDEV)	T statistics (|O/STDEV|)	P values
H1	Value Barriers (VB)→Resistance (R)	0.254	0.100	2.542	*
H2	Traditional Barriers (TB)→Resistance (R)	0.372	0.155	2.392	*
H3	Image Barriers (IB)→Resistance (R)	0.451	0.156	2.890	**
H4	Usage Barriers (UB)→Resistance (R)	0.090	0.091	0.985	0.324
H5	Risk Barriers (RB)→Resistance (R)	−0.178	0.121	1.474	0.141

4 Conclusion

This research evidences that traditional barriers are key determinant of resistance to refurbished smartphones. Previous studies have shown that traditional barriers can significantly influence users' resistance to technology adoption (Musyaffi et al., 2022). These barriers arise from conflicts between existing values and beliefs, which hinder the acceptance of new technologies (Kushwah et al., 2019). This study is consistent with previous studies which relates to established norms or practices, can also play a crucial role in shaping resistance intentions (Kumari & Kumar, 2023). This finding indicates that understanding and addressing these traditional barriers are essential for promoting the adoption of refurbished smartphones. Previous studies have also emphasized that the market for refurbished smartphones has grown significantly, yet many consumers remain unaware of the benefits and environmental advantages associated with these products (Timoumi et al., 2021). This lack of knowledge can result in a general aversion to purchasing refurbished products as consumers may prefer the perceived safety and assurance of new devices.

The results suggest that the image barrier related to people's perceptions of reputation, trustworthiness or customer service may significantly affect their willingness to use or adopt refurbished smartphones. Ignorance and misperception about the refurbishment process give a negative perception about these products therefore reduces their chances of being chosen (Mugge et al., 2017; Weelden et al., 2016). For example, misconceptions about the service that refurbishment involves makes many customers come with doubts when they are purchasing refurbished phones, specifically refurbished smartphones. To tackle these barriers, firms should incorporate ways on how consumers can gain more information and trust on the refurbished products including information regarding refurbishment process and the company's quality standards (Mugge et al., 2018).

It has been discovered that the value barriers are not so pronounced as the traditional and image barriers in shaping resistance to consumption. This finding is contrary to Sajid and Zakkariya's study (2022), which stated that value barrier was found to be the most influential as regards acting as an avenue to resistance in the e-waste recycling environment. However, traditional and image barriers which falls under psychological barriers has been seen to have a stronger indirect effect on intensity to use than usage barriers.

Although there are factors that cause resistance to purchase refurbished smartphones, usage barriers do not affect the resistance much. In this regard, this finding can be explained from several perspectives. Today's consumers are increasingly aware that smartphones that have been restored can have similar performance to brand new smartphones, particularly if firms build in a cycle of reconditioning that involves replacing specific parts and improving the quality of the reconditioning (Onurlubaş & Gumus, 2023). Thus, informing consumers about the refurbishment process and measures to ensure product quality results in the reduction of resistance (Mugge et al., 2018).

Finally, image barriers hold a major contribution to consumer resistance during innovation situations, especially in the age of IoT (Mani & Chouk, 2018). This highlights the need to understand how image barriers influence resistance intention, which is essential for developing strategies to address consumer concerns and promote the adoption of refurbished smartphones. One of the most important findings is the role of risk barriers in resistance. Accordingly, consumers regard risk barriers as insignificant barriers to purchasing refurbished smartphones. This can be caused by detailed obligations to authorized sellers, collectors, and refurbishment centers for refurbishment procedures and resale of used goods in Turkey.

Though Botetzagias et al. (2015) asserts that there is no clear relationship between socio-demographic variables and recycling, it is possible that consumers' demographic characteristics affect their ability to resist the purchase of refurbished smartphones. Age stands as one of the most important demographic variables that influence the buying behaviour. The studies also show that among the young consumers, especially the Gen Y, they are more inclined to own and use smartphones, thus implying their willingness to spend on purchasing refurbished products (Othman & Amin, 2022). On the other hand, there could be a kind of skepticism among older generations regarding refurbished goods because of the potential threats which are related to quality and reliability of such products (Moon-Koo et al., 2013). This generational gap can increase young customers' openness to the potential monetary value of the refurbished smartphones because elders may reject the concept due to the perceived psychological concepts associated with its durability and functionality (Mugge et al., 2017). Another element of the LP can be demographic characteristics and, in particular, education, which can also affect consumer's perceptions of reconditioned smartphones. More educated consumers may have more knowledge on environmental advantages of buying refurbished products, thus, may offer lower resistance (Liu & Tsaur, 2020). However, if these consumers feel that there is no noticeable improvement in wireless technology or brand image of some refurbished smartphones then the consumer resistance will not change (Kiran et al., 2019).

This study has a number of limitations, which are open to future research. First, since college students were chosen as a convenience sample, the findings of this research cannot be applied to other consumer demographics. Second, future studies on refurbished products should include other high-tech products such as tablets, smartwatches, or laptops.

References

Arbabi, H., Punzo, G., Meyers, G., Tan, L., Li, Q., & Tingley, D. (2020). Random graphs were used to analyze resource utilization in urban systems. *Royal Society Open Science, 7*(4), Article 200087. https://doi.org/10.1098/rsos.200087

Ayanso, A., Herath, T. C., & O'Brien, N. (2015). Understanding continuance intentions of physicians with electronic medical records (EMR): An expectancy-confirmation perspective. *Decision Support Systems, 77*, 112–122.

Aytac, B., & Wu, S. D. (2013). Characterization of the demand for short-life-cycle technology products. *Annals of Operations Research, 203*(1), 255–277.

Barclay, D., Higgins, C., & Thompson, R. (1995). The partial least squares (PLS) approach to casual modeling: Personal computer adoption ans use as an Illustration. *Technology Studies, 2*(2), 285–309.

Bigliardi, B., Filippelli, S., & Quinto, I. (2022). Environmentally-conscious behaviours in the circular economy. An analysis of consumers' green purchase intentions for refurbished smartphones. *Journal of Cleaner production, 378*, 134379.

Botetzagias, I., Dima, A. F., & Malesios, C. (2015). Extending the theory of planned behavior in the context of recycling: The role of moral norms and of demographic predictors. *Resources, Conservation and Recycling, 95*, 58–67.

Chin, W. W. (2010). How to write up and report PLS analyses. In V. Esposito Vinzi, W. Chin J. Henseler, & H. Wang (Eds.), *Handbook of partial least squares: Springer handbooks of computational statistics*. Springer. https://doi.org/10.1007/978-3-540-32827-8_29

Durvasula, S., Mehta, S., Andrews, J., & Lysonski, S. (1997). Advertising beliefs and attitudes: Are students and general consumers indeed different? *Journal of Asian Business, 13*(1), 71–84.

Fornell, C., & Larcker, D. F. (1981). Evaluating structural equation models with unobservable variables and measurement error. *Journal of Marketing Research, 18*(1), 39–50

Gefen, D., & Straub, D. (2005). A practical guide to factorial validity using PLS-Graph: Tutorial and annotated example. *Communications of the Association for Information systems, 16*(1), 5.

Ghosh, M. (2024). Empirical study on consumers' reluctance to mobile payments in a developing economy. *Journal of Science and Technology Policy Management, 15*(1), 67–92.

Gupta, A., & Arora, N. (2017). Understanding determinants and barriers of mobile shopping adoption using behavioral reasoning theory. *Journal of Retailing and Consumer Services, 36*, 1–7.

Hair, J. F., Ringle, C. M., & Sarstedt, M. (2011). PLS-SEM: Indeed a silver bullet. *Journal of Marketing Theory and Practice, 19*(2), 139–152.

Harms, R., & Linton, J. D. (2015). Willingness to pay for eco-certified refurbished products: The effects of environmental attitudes and knowledge. *Journal of Industrial Ecology, 20*(4), 893–904. https://doi.org/10.1111/jiec.12301

Hazelwood, D. A., & Pecht, M. (2021). Life extension of electronic products: A case study of smartphones. *IEEE Access, 9*, 144726–144739. https://doi.org/10.1109/access.2021.3121733

Hew, J. J., Badaruddin, M. N. B. A., & Moorthy, M. K. (2017). Crafting a smartphone repurchase decision making process: Do brand attachment and gender matter? *Telematics and Informatics, 34*(4), 34–56.

Hong, D., & Cho, C. H. (2023). Factors affecting innovation resistance of smartphone AI voice assistants. *International Journal of Human-Computer Interaction, 39*(13), 2557–2572.

Joachim, V., Spieth, P., & Heidenreich, S. (2018). Active innovation resistance: An empirical study on functional and psychological barriers to innovation adoption in different contexts. *Industrial Marketing Management, 71*, 95–107.

Kiran, P., Thomas, T., Johny, J., & Jose, D. (2019). Understanding the influence of utilitarian and hedonic factors on buying behaviour of gen y while purchasing smartphones. *Ushus—Journal of Business Management, 18*(4), 55–69. https://doi.org/10.12725/ujbm.49.5

Kumari, P., & Kumar, A. (2023). Investigating the dark side of mobile bookkeeping applications: A moderated-mediation approach. *VINE Journal of Information and Knowledge Management Systems, 53*(5), 985–1004.

Kurdhi, N. A., Dabadghao, S., & Fransoo, J. J. (2022). Revenue management in a refurbishing duopoly with cannibalization. *Journal of Operations Management, 69*(2), 246–260. https://doi.org/10.1002/joom.1208

Kushwah, S., Dhir, A., & Sagar, M. (2019). Understanding consumer resistance to the consumption of organic food. A study of ethical consumption, purchasing, and choice behaviour. *Food Quality and Preference, 77*, 1–14.

Li, H., & Liu, Y. (2014). Understanding post-adoption behaviors of e-service users in the context of online travel services. *Information & Management, 51*(8), 1043–1052.

Liu, H. T., & Tsaur, R. (2020). The theory of reasoned action applied to green smartphones: Moderating effect of government subsidies. *Sustainability, 12*(15), 5979. https://doi.org/10.3390/su12155979

Neto, J. Q. F., & Dutordoir, M. (2020). Mapping the market for remanufacturing: An application of "Big Data" analytics. *International Journal of Production Economics, 230*, Article 107807.

Mani, Z., & Chouk, I. (2018). Consumer resistance to innovation in services: Challenges and barriers in the internet of things era. *Journal of Product Innovation Management, 35*(5), 780–807.

Moon-Koo, K., Chang, Y., Wong, S. F., & Park, M. (2013). The effect of perceived risks and switching barriers on the intention to use smartphones among non-adopters in Korea. *Information Development, 31*(3), 258–269. https://doi.org/10.1177/0266666913513279

Mugge, R., Jockin, B., & Bocken, N. (2017). How to sell refurbished smartphones? An investigation of different customer groups and appropriate incentives. *Journal of Cleaner Production, 147*, 284–296. https://doi.org/10.1016/j.jclepro.2017.01.111

Mugge, R., Jong, W. D., Person, O., & Hultink, E. J. (2018). 'if it ain't broke, don't explain it': The influence of visual and verbal information about prior use on consumers' evaluations of refurbished electronics. *The Design Journal, 21*(4), 499–520. https://doi.org/10.1080/14606925.2018.1472856

Musyaffi, A. M., Gurendrawati, E., Afriadi, B., Oli, M. C., Widawati, Y., & Oktavia, R. (2022). Resistance of traditional SMEs in using digital payments: Development of innovation resistance theory. *Human Behavior and Emerging Technologies, 2022*, 1–10.

Nunnally, J. C., & Bernstein, I. H. (1994). *Psychometric theory* (3rd ed.). McGraw-Hill.

Onurlubas, E., & Niyazi Gumus, N. G. (2023). Investigation of the effect of risk perceptions of the generation z consumers' against refurbished products on their purchase intention. *Marketing and Management of Innovations, 14*(3), 109–124. https://doi.org/10.21272/mmi.2023.3-10

Othman, M. K., & Amin, M. Y. M. (2022). A cross-generational comparison of smartphone addiction among gen x and gen y smartphone users in Malaysia. *International Journal of Public Health Science (IJPHS), 11*(1), 320. https://doi.org/10.11591/ijphs.v11i1.21240

Pamminger, R., Glaser, S., & Wimmer, W. (2021). Modelling of different circular end-of-use scenarios for smartphones. *The International Journal of Life Cycle Assessment, 26*(3), 470–482. https://doi.org/10.1007/s11367-021-01869-2

Ram, S., & Sheth, J. N. (1989). Consumer resistance to innovations: The marketing problem and its solutions. *Journal of Consumer Marketing, 6*(2), 5–14.

Sajid, M., & Zakkariya, K. A. (2022). Factors affecting ridesharing intention in the context of COVID-19. *International Journal of E-Adoption (IJEA), 14*(1), 1–14.

Sharifi, Z., & Shokouhyar, S. (2021). Promoting consumer's attitude toward refurbished mobile phones: A social media analytics approach. *Resources, Conservation and Recycling, 167*, Article 105398.

Škare, M., Gavurova, B., & Porada-Rochon, M. (2024). Digitalization and carbon footprint: Building a path to a sustainable economic growth. *Technological Forecasting and Social Change, 199*, 123045.

Timoumi, A., Singh, N., & Kumar, S. (2021). Is your retailer a friend or foe: When should the manufacturer allow its retailer to refurbish? *Production and Operations Management, 30*(9), 2814–2839. https://doi.org/10.1111/poms.13548

Tunn, V., Bocken, N., van den Hende, E. A., & Schoormans, J. (2019). Business models for sustainable consumption in the circular economy: An expert study. *Journal of Cleaner Production, 212*, 324–333. https://doi.org/10.1016/j.jclepro.2018.11.290

Verma, A., Chakraborty, D., & Verma, M. (2023). Barriers of food delivery applications: A perspective from innovation resistance theory using mixed method. *Journal of Retailing and Consumer Services, 73*, Article 103369.

Wang, Y., & Hazen, B. T. (2016). Consumer product knowledge and intention to purchase remanufactured products. *International Journal of Production Economics, 181*, 460–469.

Weelden, E., Mugge, R., & Bakker, C. (2016). Paving the way towards circular consumption: Exploring consumer acceptance of refurbished mobile phones in the dutch market. *Journal of Cleaner Production, 113*, 743–754. https://doi.org/10.1016/j.jclepro.2015.11.065

Wiche, P., Pequeño, F., & Granato, D. (2022). Life cycle analysis of a refurbished smartphone in Chile. *E3S Web of Conferences, 349*, 01011. https://doi.org/10.1051/e3sconf/202234901011

Zhou, L., & Gupta, S. M. (2020). Value depreciation factors for new and remanufactured high-technology products: A case study on iPhones and iPads. *International Journal of Production Research, 58*(23), 7218–7249.

Zink, T., Maker, F., Geyer, R., Amirtharajah, R., & Akella, V. (2014). Comparative life cycle assessment of smartphone reuse: Repurposing vs. refurbishment. *The International Journal of Life Cycle Assessment, 19*, 1099–1109.

Zumegen, A. (2020). *Environmental impacts of a local circular economy business model: A carbon and water footprint analysis for smartphone refurbishment.* Jyväskylä University.

Technology Acceptance Model for Metaverse Applications in the Tourism and Hospitality Industry

Georgios A. Deirmentzoglou, Konstantina K. Agoraki, Sotirios Varelas, Ioannis Anastasopoulos, and Eleni E. Anastasopoulou

Abstract Metaverse has gained a lot of attention in recent years for its potential in the tourism and hospitality industry. As a disruptive technology, Metaverse offers an immersive experience that takes advantage of the virtual and physical worlds. Although this technology can bring about fundamental changes, the intention to use it by stakeholders in the tourism and hospitality industry is still not clear. This study employs the Technology Acceptance Model (TAM) to investigate the influence of perceived usefulness and perceived ease of use of metaverse applications in the tourism and hospitality industry on tourists' intention to use these applications. A survey was conducted among Greek tourists, and the findings indicate that both variables exert a significant positive impact on the intention to use metaverse applications for tourism experiences. This research fills an important gap in the existing literature on the Metaverse in the tourism and hospitality sector, while the results have significant implications for both academic and business communities.

Keywords Metaverse · Technology acceptance model · Metaverse applications · Intention to use · Tourism industry · Hospitality industry

G. A. Deirmentzoglou (✉) · E. E. Anastasopoulou
Neapolis University Pafos, Pafos, Cyprus
e-mail: g.deirmentzoglou@nup.ac.cy

E. E. Anastasopoulou
e-mail: e.anastasopoulou.1@nup.ac.cy

K. K. Agoraki · S. Varelas · I. Anastasopoulos
University of Piraeus, Piraeus, Greece
e-mail: kagoraki@unipi.gr

S. Varelas
e-mail: svarelas@unipi.gr

I. Anastasopoulos
e-mail: ganast@unipi.gr

E. E. Anastasopoulou
University of Peloponnese, Kalamata, Greece

I. Bartuseviciene et al. (eds.), *Building Resilience Through Digital Transformation and Sustainable Innovation*, Springer Proceedings in Business and Economics,
https://doi.org/10.1007/978-3-031-90054-9_17

JEL Classification Codes O33 · O39 · L83

1 Introduction

The emergence of the Metaverse signifies a critical turning point in the development of digital technologies, representing a new phase in the digital revolution (Gauttier et al., 2024). This evolving digital landscape is set to surpass conventional digital engagements, creating a new era where virtual and real-world realms merge into a unified experience. The Metaverse is indeed poised to be viewed as a groundbreaking technology that may profoundly affect society in numerous aspects over the coming decades (Buhalis et al., 2023a, 2023b). It embodies a significant shift in human interaction with technology, combining the physical and digital worlds into a seamless, immersive digital universe.

As a convergence of virtual and augmented reality, metaverse promises to enable immersive experiences and become a focal point of modern technological development and societal change (Dincelli & Yayla, 2022; Kraus et al., 2022). The term "Metaverse" was first applied by Neal Stephenson in his 1992 novel "Snow Crash" (Go & Kang, 2023). It becomes clear that this term comes from science fiction, envisioning a future where virtual and physical realities are intertwined, allowing people to interact with each other as well as with digital objects, across various platforms and environments (Buhalis et al., 2023a, 2023b). In their work, Wong et al. (2023) define metaverse as *"a convergence of multiple technologies to offer a fully rendering of visually pleasing aesthetics for simultaneous users across distances"*.

According to Yang and Wang (2023) Metaverse is expected to change the paradigms, norms and rules, creating the conditions for both threats and opportunities. The metaverse, characterized by its immersive virtual settings, holds the promise to transform the tourism and hospitality industry in various significant ways (Varelas, 2022). Notably, the metaverse can improve accessibility, promote sustainable tourism practices and provide a critical role in securing a sustainable competitive advantage.

Within the rapidly changing context of the tourism and hospitality sector (Deirmentzoglou et al., 2022; Varelas et al., 2021; Vlassi et al., 2023), embracing technology is fundamental to fostering innovation, maintaining competitive advantage, and ensuring sustainability. The tourism and hospitality industry has experienced significant transformations in recent decades, contending with both foundational and societal shifts alongside technological progress. In the aftermath of the pandemic, the critical role and urgency of integrating technology in the tourism and hospitality sector have reached unprecedented levels (Chen et al., 2022).

Technology adoption has been transformed from optional to a necessity for success in the tourism and hospitality industry. Technology improvements have various implications for both businesses and consumers, such as offering a broader range of facilities and providing personalized customer service. By embracing innovative solutions, businesses in the tourism industry can improve efficiency and sustainable development, reduce costs, enhance customer experiences, and meet the evolving expectations and current needs of travelers creating intriguing avenues for research (Koo et al., 2023; Wei, 2024).

As innovation is vital to most industries (Agoraki et al., 2024a; Pistikou et al., 2023), this study seeks to highlight the critical role of technological innovation adoption in the tourism and hospitality sector. By using the TAM, this study delves into understanding the inclination of tourists towards utilizing metaverse applications and assesses the transformative impact such applications could have on enhancing customer experiences, refining operational procedures, and altering the competitive framework. The TAM aims to investigate the elements that affect the adoption and application of Metaverse technologies among enterprises and consumers within the tourism and hospitality industry (Hasni et al., 2021; El Archi & Benbba, 2023). Therefore, the research question of this study is:

Do perceived ease of use and perceived usefulness influence the intention to use metaverse applications about tourism experiences?

The following section of this paper presents a review of the TAM and previous studies on the use of immersive tools in the tourism and hospitality industry. Section 3 outlines the methodology employed in the present study, while Sect. 4 outlines the key findings of our analysis. Finally, Sect. 5 discusses the implications of the study and proposes avenues for future research.

2 Literature Review

Davis (1989) developed the Technology Acceptance Model (TAM) as a tool that is "*used to predict as well as to explain the behavior of users about the adoption of technology*". According to the TAM, the key drivers of adoption intention are the degree to which a technology is perceived to be useful and how easy it is perceived to be to use. In fact, as far as the role of TAM in technology adoption is concerned, it sets a solid foundation to grasp the users' acquisition process, which serves as a primary notion in the successful execution of novel technologies. The TAM indicates the determinations of technology acceptance to be the guideline for the development and design of technology products to meet the needs of the users (Venkatesh & Davis, 2000).

Considering the case of the Metaverse as the enabling disruptive technology to revolutionize the business world, TAM becomes critical in this regard. The Metaverse, an environment that combines physical and virtual realities, changes the rules of technology acceptance theories. The TAM theory allows researchers and practitioners to learn how the perceived usefulness and ease of use of the metaverse affects customers' intention to use the principle in industries such as tourism and hospitality (Bhattacherjee, 2001). It is evident that TAM plays an enormous role in tourism and hospitality, as technology is the main factor that the sector relies on to increase user satisfaction. The metaverse could be assessed through TAM, as knowledge of this model would be key to designing and redesigning business operations and increasing service offerings (Buhalis et al., 2024).

TAM in hospitality and tourism has been taken up for adaptation due to the fact that disruptive technologies such as virtual and augmented reality are increasingly accepted by both customers and companies (Buhalis & Law, 2008; El Archi & Benbba, 2023b). In the early 2000s, studies showed that the Internet and mobile technologies really do transcend the travel planning and booking processes, where it is recognized that ease of use is very influential in the travel sub-processes (Werthner, 2003). Garau's (2014) research has shown how the virtual tour affects the future directions of tourists, which ultimately only focuses on the perceived usefulness in the adoption of these technologies. The expansion of the metaverse opens the way for scholars to conduct studies that explore its ability to stimulate immersive experiences of high quality. Lee and Lehto (2013) have shown that virtual reality applications (or prototypes of the Metaverse we have today) are the basis of their research, and they concluded that the level of VR could bring a tremendous increase in tourist satisfaction and attention to VR.

One of the most recent studies on this topic was conducted by Zhang and Wang (2023), who investigated how storytelling in the metaverse world can influence tourists' intentions to visit a physical destination. In addition, Deirmentzoglou et al. (2024b) investigated the intention to use metaverse platforms of a destination and revealed the significant role of the website of the destination management organization (DMO) and the image of the destination, while Shin and Kang (2024) demonstrated that the experience of metaverse travel had a significant influence on the intention to physically travel.

It is important to emphasize that while these studies clearly show that TAM still has great strength in its ability to determine how people accept the use of technology in tourism and hospitality, they also confirm the fact that technologies are constantly evolving, as are customer expectations. Thus, research continues and the focus is on the problems faced by a new platform such as the metaverse (Gretzel et al., 2015).

Usability of metaverse platforms plays a crucial role in overcoming adoption barriers among Web 3.0 visitors. If VR is to be used to simulate authentic experiences and provide a psychological presence for tourists, it must be defensibly usable. Similarly, according to Kouroupi and Metaxas (2023), the experience of the metaverse in tourism applications is highly dependent on these intelligent interfaces. Users will be more inclined to use these technologies if the interface is user-friendly and responsive in terms of navigation and interaction.

Moreover, the research conducted by Buhalis et al. (2023a, 2023b) revealed that the use of VR tours in destination marketing is an effective strategy for creating immersive experiences that influence the decision-making process of tourists. The other element associated with the positive impact of social networks is attributed to the work of Tussyadiah and Inversini (2015), who presented an example of the implementation of AR in hotel services. This technology is characterized by the provision of information relevant to the customer, which increases the quality of service and customer satisfaction. Moreover, the proliferation of applications within the industry serves to underscore the fundamental relevance of TAM. Marriott's selection of VR for destination previews (Bharwani & Mathews, 2021) and Hilton's deployment of AR-based navigation systems (Kaushal & Yadav, 2021) serve to illustrate the adaptability of these technologies with respect to ease of use and perceived usefulness, a conclusion that aligns with the findings of previous research.

Based on the above, we propose the following hypotheses (Fig. 1):

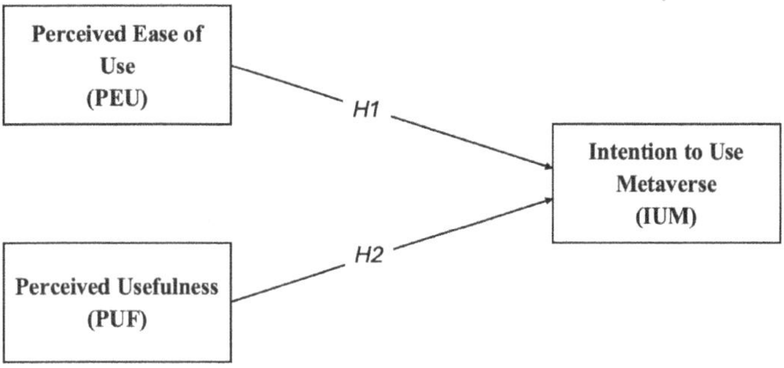

Fig. 1 Conceptual framework. *Source* Authors' construct

H1: Perceived ease of use (PEU) has a significant positive effect on the intention to use metaverse applications about tourism experiences (IUM).

H2: Perceived usefulness (PUF) has a significant positive effect on the intention to use metaverse applications about tourism experiences (IUM).

3 Methodology

In order to get insights regarding the intention to use metaverse applications in the tourism and hospitality industry, the target population of this study was travelers. Using a convenience sampling method, an online questionnaire was sent to Greek travelers through the authors' network. A screening question was used in order to ensure that the participant has travelled in the last 12 months. Moreover, in the beginning of the questionnaire a definition of Metaverse was provided along with some examples so it would be clear for the participants to complete the questionnaire.

Among the 166 participants, 50 (43%) were male and 66 (57%) were female. Moreover, 45 (39%) belonged to Generation Z, 55 (47%) to Generation Y, 12 (10%) belonged to Generation X and 4 (3%) were baby boomers. Regarding their education 29 (25%) of the respondents had a high school diploma, 36 (31%) had a bachelor's degree, 38 (33%) had a master's degree while 13 (11%) had a PhD. As for the frequency of their travels, 6 (5%) responded that they travel less than one time per year, 22 (19%) travel once a year, 58 (50%) travel 2–3 times per year, 17 (15%) travel 4–5 times and 13 (11%) respondents travel more than 5 times per year.

The main variables of the questionnaire were perceived ease of use (PEU), perceived usefulness (PUF) and intention to use metaverse (IUM). PEU was measured with four items, while PUF and IUM were measured with three items, all adapted from Ozturk (2023) and Kaushik et al. (2015). These items used a 5-point Likert scale from 1 = totally disagree to 5 = totally agree.

4 Findings

First, the required reliability and validity tests were conducted. As seen in Table 1, the composite reliability (CR), the average variance extracted (AVE) and the Cronbach's alpha (a) have sufficiently high values, much above the thresholds. Moreover, the square roots (SQRT) of AVE (Table 1) are in line with the criteria of Fornell and Larcker (1981) as the values are greater than the correlation values between the variables in Table 2.

The correlation matrix shows a significant correlation between the independent variables with the dependent variable. In particular, PEU ($r = 0.59$, $p < 0.001$) and PUF ($r = 0.70$, $p < 0.001$) are positively correlated with IUM. On the contrary, the demographic variables do not show any significant correlation with the IUM (Table 2).

Finally, in order to test the hypotheses, a multiple linear regression was conducted. The model shows that both PEU ($\beta = 0.27, p < 0.001$) and PUF ($\beta = 0.57, p < 0.001$) have a significant effect on IUM (Table 3); therefore, H1 and H2 are supported.

Table 1 Factor loadings, CR, AVE and Cronbach's alpha

Variables	Items	FL	CR	AVE	SQRT(AVE)	a
Perceived Ease of Use (PEU)	PEU1	0.90	0.94	0.80	0.89	0.91
	PEU2	0.92				
	PEU3	0.86				
	PEU4	0.89				
Perceived Usefulness (PUF)	PUF1	0.93	0.93	0.82	0.90	0.89
	PUF2	0.93				
	PUF3	0.85				
Intention to Use Metaverse (IUM)	IUM1	0.94	0.93	0.81	0.90	0.88
	IUM2	0.86				
	IUM3	0.90				

Source Authors' calculation

Table 2 Correlation matrix

	PEU	PUF	IUM	Frequency	Age	Education	Gender
PEU	–						
PUF	0.56***	–					
IUM	0.59***	0.70***	–				
Frequency	−0.07 (n.s.)	−0.05 (n.s.)	−0.03 (n.s.)	-			
Age	0.04 (n.s.)	0.11 (n.s.)	0.12 (n.s.)	0.17 (n.s.)	–		
Education	0.10 (n.s.)	0.14 (n.s.)	0.13 (n.s.)	0.26**	0.56***	–	
Gender	−0.13 (n.s.)	0.00 (n.s.)	0.01 (n.s.)	−0.07 (n.s.)	−0.21*	−0.18 (n.s.)	–

Note *p<0.05, **p< 0.01, ***p<0.001
Source Authors' calculation

Table 3 Linear regression for IUM

Predictor	B	SE B	β	t	p
Intercept	0.38	0.27	–	1.39	0.167
PEU	0.27	0.08	0.27	3.46	<0.001
PUF	0.62	0.08	0.57	7.48	<0.001

$R^2 = 0.59$, $F = 80.92$, $p =$ <0.001
Source Authors' calculation

5 Discussion and Conclusion

The objective of this study is to examine the influence of the primary variables from the TAM, specifically perceived ease of use and perceived usefulness, on tourists' intentions to use metaverse applications within the tourism and hospitality industry. The results reveal that both variables significantly impact tourists' intentions, underscoring their crucial role in technology adoption within this sector. Specifically, the findings suggest that when tourists perceive metaverse applications as easy to use, they are more inclined to integrate these tools into their travel experiences. Moreover, the perceived usefulness of these applications—such as the ability to acquire information, or receive personalized services—further motivates tourists to adopt them. The results are consistent with Davis' (1989) theory of TAM.

The findings of this study have significant academic and practical implications for the tourism and hospitality industry. Firstly, the confirmation of the significant influence of perceived ease of use and perceived usefulness on tourists' intentions to use metaverse applications underscores the importance of user experience design in shaping consumer behavior. Practically, businesses operating in the tourism and hospitality sector can leverage these insights to optimize the design and functionality of their metaverse applications, ensuring they are intuitive and provide tangible value to users. By prioritizing user-centric design principles and focusing on enhancing ease of use and usefulness, companies can increase the rate of adoption and improve overall customer satisfaction within the virtual tourism landscape. Furthermore, these findings indicate that policymakers and industry leaders should consider integrating guidelines that promote the development of metaverse applications with high usability and practical benefits.

However, this study has some limitations. First, the population of this study was only Greek tourists, a country that comparing to other EU countries has low levels of digital skills (Deirmentzoglou & Deirmentzoglou, 2022). Future research should include individuals from other countries in order to compare the results. exploring cross-cultural differences (Agoraki et al., 2024b; Deirmentzoglou et al., 2024a) in metaverse adoption and usage patterns could provide valuable insights for businesses operating in diverse global markets. Moreover, investigating the role of additional factors beyond the TAM framework, such as hedonic values, privacy concerns, and social influence, could provide a more comprehensive understanding of tourists' decision-making processes regarding metaverse applications.

Appendix

Scale items.

Variables	Items
Perceived Ease of Use (PEU)	PEU1—It will be easy for me to use metaverse applications about tourism experiences
	PEU2—It will be easy for me to learn how to use metaverse applications about tourism experiences
	PEU3—It will be easy for me to become an expert in the use of metaverse applications about tourism experiences
	PEU4—Using metaverse applications about tourism experiences will be clear and understandable for me
Perceived Usefulness (PUF)	PUF1—Using metaverse applications about tourism experiences enables me to enhance my effectiveness (e.g. acquire information, personalise experiences)
	PUF2—Using metaverse applications about tourism experiences makes it easier to manage my travel
	PUF3—Overall, I believe using metaverse applications about tourism experiences is useful
Intention to Use Metaverse (IUM)	IUM1—I am interested in using metaverse applications about tourism experiences
	IUM2—I predict that I should use metaverse applications about tourism experiences

(continued)

(continued)

Variables	Items
	IUM3—Overall, I intend to use metaverse applications about tourism experiences

Source Authors' own adaptation from Ozturk (2023), and Kaushik et al. (2015)

References

Agoraki, K. K., Deirmentzoglou, G. A., Psychalis, M., & Apostolopoulos, S. (2024). Types of innovation and sustainable development: Evidence from medium-and large-sized firms. *International Journal of Innovation and Technology Management*, 2450013.

Agoraki, K. K., Deirmentzoglou, G. A., & Triantopoulos, C. (2024b). Cultural values as catalysts of technological innovation for a sustainable future. *Sustainability, 16*(5), 2064.

Bharwani, S., & Mathews, D. (2021). Techno-business strategies for enhancing guest experience in luxury hotels: A managerial perspective. *Worldwide Hospitality and Tourism Themes, 13*(2), 168–185.

Bhattacherjee, A. (2001). Understanding information systems continuance: An expectation-confirmation model. *MIS Quarterly*, 351–370.

Buhalis, D., Efthymiou, L., Uzunboylu, N., & Thrassou, A. (2024). Charting the progress of technology adoption in tourism and hospitality in the era of industry 4.0. *EuroMed Journal of Business*.

Buhalis, D., & Law, R. (2008). Progress in information technology and tourism management: 20 years on and 10 years after the Internet—The state of eTourism research. *Tourism Management, 29*(4), 609–623.

Buhalis, D., Leung, D., & Lin, M. (2023a). Metaverse as a disruptive technology revolutionising tourism management and marketing. *Tourism Management, 97*, Article 104724.

Buhalis, D., O'Connor, P., & Leung, R. (2023b). Smart hospitality: From smart cities and smart tourism towards agile business ecosystems in networked destinations. *International Journal of Contemporary Hospitality Management, 35*(1), 369–393.

Chen, S., Tian, D., Law, R., & Zhang, M. (2022). Bibliometric and visualized review of smart tourism research. *International Journal of Tourism Research, 24*(2), 298–307.

Davis, F. D. (1989). Perceived usefulness, perceived ease of use, and user acceptance of information technology. *MIS Quarterly*, 319–340.

Deirmentzoglou, G. A., Agoraki, K. K., & Patsoulis, P. (2024a). The nexus between cultural values and perceptions of corporate sustainable development. *Social Responsibility Journal, 20*(2), 224–242.

Deirmentzoglou, G. A., Vlassi, E., & Anastasopoulou, E. (2024b). DDMMO website quality, destination image and intention to use metaverse platforms. *Platforms, 2*, 180–192.

Deirmentzoglou, G. A., & Deirmentzoglou, E. A. (2022, September). Pest analysis of the e-commerce industry: The case of Greece. In *Business development and economic governance in Southeastern Europe: 13th International Conference on the Economies of the Balkan and Eastern European Countries (EBEEC), Pafos, Cyprus, 2021* (pp. 315–323). Springer International Publishing.

Deirmentzoglou, G. A., Vlassi, E., & Agoraki, K. K. (2022, May). The Effect of the hotel attributes on guest satisfaction due to the Covid-19 pandemic Crisis: The case of the Greek tourism and hospitality sector. In *International conference economies of the Balkan and eastern European countries* (pp. 283–297). Springer Nature Switzerland.

Dincelli, E., & Yayla, A. (2022). Immersive virtual reality in the age of the Metaverse: A hybrid-narrative review based on the technology affordance perspective. *The Journal of Strategic Information Systems, 31*(2), Article 101717.

El Archi, Y., & Benbba, B. (2023). The applications of technology acceptance models in tourism and hospitality research: A systematic literature review. *Journal of Environmental Management & Tourism, 14*(2), 379–391.

Fornell, C., & Larcker, D. F. (1981). Evaluating structural equation models with unobservable variables and measurement error. *Journal of marketing research, 18*(1), 39–50.

Garau, C. (2014). From territory to smartphone: Smart fruition of cultural heritage for dynamic tourism development. *Planning Practice and Research, 29*(3), 238–255.

Gauttier, S., Simouri, W., & Milliat, A. (2024). When to enter the metaverse: Business leaders offer perspectives. *Journal of Business Strategy, 45*(1), 2–9.

Gretzel, U., Sigala, M., Xiang, Z., & Koo, C. (2015). Smart tourism: Foundations and developments. *Electronic Markets, 25*, 179–188.

Go, H., & Kang, M. (2023). Metaverse tourism for sustainable tourism development: Tourism agenda 2030. *Tourism Review, 78*(2), 381–394.

Hasni, M. J. S., Farah, M. F., & Adeel, I. (2021). The technology acceptance model revisited: empirical evidence from the tourism industry in Pakistan. *Journal of Tourism Futures.*

Kaushal, V., & Yadav, R. (2021). Delivering superior customer experience through new-age technologies. In *Industry 4.0 technologies for business excellence* (pp. 47–60). CRC Press.

Kaushik, A. K., Agrawal, A. K., & Rahman, Z. (2015). Tourist behaviour towards self-service hotel technology adoption: Trust and subjective norm as key antecedents. *Tourism Management Perspectives, 16*, 278–289.

Koo, C., Kwon, J., Chung, N., & Kim, J. (2023). Metaverse tourism: Conceptual framework and research propositions. *Current Issues in Tourism, 26*(20), 3268–3274.

Kouroupi, N., & Metaxas, T. (2023). Can the Metaverse and its Associated Digital Tools and Technologies provide an opportunity for destinations to address the vulnerability of Overtourism? *Tourism and Hospitality, 4*(2), 355–373.

Kraus, S., Kanbach, D. K., Krysta, P. M., Steinhoff, M. M., & Tomini, N. (2022). Facebook and the creation of the metaverse: Radical business model innovation or incremental transformation? *International Journal of Entrepreneurial Behavior & Research, 28*(9), 52–77.

Lee, D. Y., & Lehto, M. R. (2013). User acceptance of YouTube for procedural learning: An extension of the technology acceptance model. *Computers & Education, 61*, 193–208.

Ozturk, A. B., Pizam, A., Hacikara, A., An, Q., Chaulagain, S., Balderas-Cejudo, A., ... & Shen, Y. (2023). Hotel customers' behavioral intentions toward service robots: The role of utilitarian and hedonic values. *Journal of Hospitality and Tourism Technology, 14*(5), 780–801.

Pistikou, V., Flouros, F., Deirmentzoglou, G. A., & Agoraki, K. K. (2023). Sustainability reporting: Examining the community impact of the S&P500 companies. *Sustainability, 15*(18), 13681.

Shin, H., & Kang, J. (2024). How does the metaverse travel experience influence virtual and actual travel behaviors? Focusing on the role of telepresence and avatar identification. *Journal of Hospitality and Tourism Management, 58*, 174–183.

Tussyadiah, I., & Inversini, A. (2015). Information and communication technologies in tourism 2015. In *Proceedings of the international conference in Lugano, Switzerland* (pp. 3–6).

Varelas, S. (2022). Virtual immersive platforms as a strategic innovative destination marketing tool in the COVID-19 era. *Sustainability, 14*(19), 12867.

Varelas, S., Karvela, P., & Georgopoulos, N. (2021). The impact of information technology and sustainable strategies in hotel branding. *Evidence from the Greek Environment. Sustainability, 13*(15), 8543.

Venkatesh, V., & Davis, F. D. (2000). A theoretical extension of the technology acceptance model: Four longitudinal field studies. *Management Science, 46*(2), 186–204.

Vlassi, E., Deirmentzoglou, G. A., Agoraki, K. K., & Papatheodorou, A. (2023). When tourism and fashion cocreate: Narratives from Greece. In *Fashion and tourism: Parallel stories* (pp. 93–106). Emerald Publishing Limited.

Wei, W. (2024). A buzzword, a phase or the next chapter for the Internet? The status and possibilities of the metaverse for tourism. *Journal of Hospitality and Tourism Insights, 7*(1), 602–625.

Werthner, H. (2003). Intelligent systems in travel and tourism. *IJCAI, 3*, 1620–1625.

Wong, L. W., Tan, G. W. H., Ooi, K. B., & Dwivedi, Y. K. (2023). Metaverse in hospitality and tourism: A critical reflection. *International Journal of Contemporary Hospitality Management*. https://doi.org/10.1108/IJCHM-05-2023-0586

Yang, F. X., & Wang, Y. (2023). Rethinking metaverse tourism: A taxonomy and an agenda for future research. *Journal of Hospitality & Tourism Research*, 10963480231163509.

Zhang, W., & Wang, Y. (2023). An empirical study of the impact of metaverse storytelling on intentions to visit. *Information Technology & Tourism, 25*(3), 411–432.

Digital Disruption in Promoting and Advertising

Stavros Valsamidis, Aikaterini Tsisinou, Giannoula Florou, and Elias Gounopoulos

Abstract Online marketing plays a crucial role in the promotion and advertising of products, especially in recent years as technology has developed and new media and technological tools have emerged. The purpose of this research is to investigate the role of digital marketing and to examine product promotion and advertising. The survey involved 177 people from different cities in Greece who were approached using convenience sampling. According to the results of the survey, respondents use the Internet mainly to search for information. They are most motivated to make an online purchase by discounts and offers on products. Digital advertising has a moderate impact on respondents, while the best way to promote and advertise a product is through an e-shop. Digital marketing has significantly changed the way products are promoted and advertised, and there are many opportunities for further development.

Keywords Digital disruption · Digital marketing · Promotion and advertising · Factor analysis

---

S. Valsamidis (✉) · A. Tsisinou · G. Florou
Department of Accounting and Finance, Campus of Kavala, Democritus University of Thrace, Kavala, Greece
e-mail: svalsam@af.duth.gr

A. Tsisinou
e-mail: tsisinou@af.duth.gr

G. Florou
e-mail: gflorou@af.duth.gr

E. Gounopoulos
Department of Business Administration, University of Western Macedonia, Grevena, Greece
e-mail: egounopoulos@uowm.gr

I. Bartuseviciene et al. (eds.), *Building Resilience Through Digital Transformation and Sustainable Innovation*, Springer Proceedings in Business and Economics,
https://doi.org/10.1007/978-3-031-90054-9_18

1 Introduction

Advertising has concerned both advertisers and consumers for many years, since advertising methods and tools change as society and technology evolve. However, the purpose they serve remains the same (Baek & Morimoto, 2012). Advertising is effective when it succeeds in reaching new consumers and when it can contribute to the retention of existing consumers. The purpose of advertising is to influence one or more consumers and, to some extent, determine their behaviour (Darley et al., 2010).

The power of advertising comes from its ability to influence the consumers' mood, create positive feelings and make them react positively to the advertised products or services (Burns & Lutz, 2006). In general, the aim of advertising is to improve a company's position in the market by enhancing the company's reputation and sales.

An advertisement is intended to provide the public with information about the specific product or service (Coppola, 2021). This information is important because it reminds consumers of the existence of specific products or services, and informs a new audience of what is new on the market (Edwards et al., 2002). A new advertisement can attract the attention of consumers and promote a product/service in the market, or its newer version with more added value (Kyriazopoulos & Samanda, 2014).

However, if a consumer who has made an online purchase is dissatisfied, he/she will express his/her dissatisfaction online and negatively influence the opinion of other consumers (Vakalopoulos & Blatsouka, 2020). Consumers' attitudes are determined by many parameters and are largely related to their beliefs about online shopping (Hongjun & Aiwu, 2014).

Trust is an important factor of the consumer's attitude towards e-shoping, while the perceived security of electronic transactions, privacy and quality of service, play an equally important role (Cho et al., 2007; Hongjun & Aiwu, 2014). A consumer who believes that a person from his or her immediate environment can easily make an online purchase, he/she may change his/her opinion and adopt a positive attitude about the Internet and online shopping, suppressing his/her negative feelings towards online shopping, such as fear and apprehension (Peiris et al., 2015).

Digital marketing is a broad term that refers to the application of various advertising and promotional techniques for products and services, designed to reach consumers with the use of information and communication technologies (Desai, 2019).

With social media, the messages conveyed to consumers are more interactive and not passive or one-dimensional as in the past (Triantafilidi, 2020).The consumer can be informed by other consumers about the characteristics of a product or service, such as the price, and he/she can search for the product that best meets his/her needs, with an interface that is easy to use and interact with (Triantafillidou & Siomkos, 2018).

The dynamics of marketing in the digital age refer to the constantly evolving strategies, techniques and approaches that companies must adopt to effectively engage with customers and promote their products or services in the digital realm (Masliardi et al.,

2023). Digital marketing is a useful tool for businesses. By using digital marketing, the companies can sell their products and services more easily, improve their brand image and generate revenue through new digital channels (Dwivedi & Nath, 2020).

The advent of the digital age has brought about a phenomenon known as 'digital disruption', i.e. a transformative force that has upended traditional marketing practices and created a sense of urgency for organisations to adapt to new marketing dynamics (Olson et al., 2021). The introduction of digital technology into the broader marketing and advertising landscape has brought many changes to the marketing and advertising functions. Organisations need to rethink their business models and invest in new technological tools (Mokoena & Prinsloo, 2021). Companies can no longer afford to rely solely on traditional marketing methods. The advent of digital disruption has necessitated a shift towards more agile and responsive approaches (Kabha et al., 2023).

The purpose of this study is to examine consumers' opinions on the promotion and advertising of products through digital marketing channels. The research focuses on specific parameters related to this issue and attempts to examine each parameter separately. The parameters in question are: (a) consumers' use of the Internet, (b) factors affecting online shopping and (c) the importance of digital marketing for consumers and companies.

2 Methodology

2.1 Research Questions

The purpose of the research is inextricably linked to the research questions. Therefore, the research questions are as follows: (1) What are the reasons for using the Internet?, (2) What do consumers choose to purchase?, (3) Which factors influence online shopping?, (4) How does an online advertisement influence the consumer's decision to make an online purchase?, (5) Does the site design influence the consumer's decision to make an online purchase?, (6) What are the most important components of an online advertisement, (7) What is the best way to promote a product/service using the Internet?, (8) What are the benefits of online shopping for consumers? and (9) What are the benefits of online shopping for businesses?

2.2 Description of the Sample

A total of 177 people took part in the survey. They are consumers of different ages who were invited to take part in the survey regardless of their income or education, whether they are men or women, married or single. They do not come from any particular geographical region or city. They are citizens living in different regions of Greece.

2.3 Methodological and Sampling Framework

The research applied is quantitative. A questionnaire was used to explore and statistically evaluate the opinions of the participants. Quantitative research was chosen because it allows opinions to be recorded and evidence to be presented. Another reason is that the questionnaire is a tool that can be easily completed by the participants. The data can be processed using statistical packages and the conclusions can be interpreted objectively. The results of the study can be presented in different types of graphs and compared with the results of other surveys.

Qualitative research was not used because the results cannot be presented as in quantitative research. The use of interviews inevitably contributes to the collection of primary data but is open to subjective interpretation. In addition, quantitative research can be more time consuming and can affect the outcome of the research.

A literature review was conducted to search for sampling methods, their characteristics were examined, and finally convenience sampling was selected. This method does not achieve homogeneity in the responses to the categories of questions (e.g. gender: male, female), but it does achieve direct data collection, which was the original purpose of this research.

2.4 Data Collection and Analysis

The work began in March of 2023 and was completed in June of the same year. During all this time, the procedures carried out can be classified into two categories. The first category relates to data collection and the second to data processing. The first step was a literature review. This step was crucial for the selection of the research topic. The research questionnaire was based on questionnaires from other studies (Dwivedi & Nath, 2020; Kabha et al., 2023; Komodromos et al., 2024). The questionnaire used in this study is structured according to the parameters that are to be evaluated. Firstly, the questionnaire introduces the reader to the aim of the research. Information is given about the anonymity of responses and the possibility of withdrawing from the research if desired. After the introductory text, there are six questions regarding the demographic data of the participants (gender, age, educational level, possession of a master's/doctoral degree, marital status, income).

The following four questions assess Internet use. In two of these questions, a 5-point Likert scale was used to measure respondents' responses (1 = to a very low extent, 2 = to a low extent, 3 = to a moderate extent, 4 = to a high extent, 5 = to a very high extent). No scale was used for the remaining three questions. The next five questions examine the factors that influence online shopping. Three of them measure respondents' answers using the same scale as above. In the final section, which examines the role of digital marketing, two questions assess respondents' opinions using the Likert scale.

The questionnaire described above is the main tool used to collect the data. The research data was processed using Excel and SPSS. A total of 250 questionnaires were distributed, and 177 were filled in and processed.

2.5 Reliability and Validity

It is common to test reliability using Cronbach's test, which checks whether an instrument can make effective measurements. The purpose of the test is to examine whether the questions are related to each other, and whether they practically contribute to the measurement of the same subject. The test was carried out using statistical software and the result obtained is 0.942 (Table 1). The resulting value is very high and close to 1, where there is absolute relevance. Therefore, the questions in the questionnaire are well formulated and measure the same subject. A value of 0.7 is often used by analysts as a reference value for test. Typically, values close to 0.7 are just acceptable but not ideal, while values above the reference point provide significant evidence of reliability. Given this, a value of 0.942 indicates that the instrument is reliable (Hair et al., 2019).

The validity of the questionnaire measures its accuracy. The questionnaire survey has content validity because it contains items that cover all aspects of the construct being measured. According to Zikmund et al. (2013), the content validity test should include a literature review on the topic being researched and a pilot test with a small sample of people (e.g. professionals and academics). In the current research, content validity was also ensured by conducting a pilot survey with six different respondents than those used in the main survey.

3 Results

3.1 Demographics

Based on the data in Table 2, the demographic profile of the respondents can be outlined. 15.8% of the sample are men and 84.2% are women. In terms of age, 17.5% are up to 24 years old. 28.2% are between 25 and 34 years old and 33.9% are between 35 and 44 years old. A smaller percentage (15.8%) are aged 45 to 54, and an even smaller percentage (4.5%) are aged 55 to 64. No one over the age of 65 participated in the research.

In terms of education, the largest percentage (68.4%) has tertiary education, while a smaller percentage, 25.4%, has secondary education. Only 6.2% of the sample

Table 1 Reliability test results

Cronbach's Alpha					*N* of Items	
0.942					61	
Item-total statistics						
Item (question no)	Item mean	Item variance	Scale mean if item deleted	Scale variance if item deleted	Corrected item-total correlation	Cronbach's alpha if item deleted
7.1	4.00	1.02	217.38	958.237	0.465	0.941
7.2	4.32	0.86	217.06	956.456	0.589	0.940
7.3	3.79	1.13	217.59	954.210	0.475	0.941
7.4	4.25	0.99	217.13	955.057	0.530	0.940
7.5	3.02	1.42	218.36	957.278	0.334	0.942
7.6	3.76	1.16	217.62	943.442	0.615	0.940
7.7	3.21	1.42	218.17	948.710	0.430	0.941
8	4.12	1.12	217.26	1005.216	−0.253	0.944
9.1	2.89	1.34	218.49	947.433	0.477	0.941
9.2	2.56	1.41	218.82	953.603	0.377	0.941
9.3	3.34	1.27	218.03	944.237	0.549	0.940
9.4	2.14	1.35	219.24	961.526	0.300	0.942
9.5	2.01	1.25	219.37	959.167	0.357	0.941
9.6	3.05	1.49	218.33	958.144	0.305	0.942
9.7	3.57	1.34	217.81	955.133	0.381	0.941
9.8	3.00	1.34	218.38	947.225	0.479	0.941
9.9	2.73	1.38	218.64	943.606	0.506	0.940
10	4.40	0.73	216.98	976.454	0.252	0.942
11.1	3.23	1.14	218.15	945.921	0.588	0.940
11.2	3.84	0.99	217.54	945.966	0.680	0.940
11.3	3.07	1.12	218.31	946.761	0.590	0.940
11.4	3.53	1.08	217.85	951.387	0.539	0.940
11.5	3.81	1.12	217.56	949.634	0.548	0.940
11.6	3.75	1.11	217.63	939.438	0.705	0.939
11.7	4.19	0.97	217.19	945.247	0.707	0.939
11.8	3.97	1.14	217.41	943.596	0.624	0.940
11.9	4.14	1.08	217.24	945.151	0.633	0.940
11.10	3.37	1.42	218.01	962.437	0.274	0.942
12	2.77	0.89	218.60	970.502	0.311	0.941
13	4.57	0.74	216.81	975.747	0.266	0.941
14.1	4.19	0.94	217.19	966.190	0.368	0.941
14.2	2.47	1.17	218.91	968.537	0.255	0.942

(continued)

Table 1 (continued)

Cronbach's Alpha					*N* of Items	
0.942					61	
Item-total statistics						
Item (question no)	Item mean	Item variance	Scale mean if item deleted	Scale variance if item deleted	Corrected item-total correlation	Cronbach's alpha if item deleted
14.3	2.55	1.15	218.82	966.304	0.292	0.942
14.4	2.47	1.20	218.90	970.269	0.225	0.942
14.5	2.63	1.31	218.75	962.676	0.296	0.942
15.1	2.86	1.21	218.51	964.194	0.305	0.942
15.2	4.08	0.99	217.29	956.561	0.507	0.940
15.3	3.93	1.05	217.45	958.589	0.442	0.941
15.4	3.01	1.32	218.37	956.326	0.374	0.941
15.5	2.76	1.33	218.62	957.350	0.358	0.941
16.1	4.27	0.89	217.11	961.453	0.478	0.941
16.2	4.37	0.86	217.01	955.250	0.610	0.940
16.3	4.07	0.94	217.31	958.761	0.497	0.941
16.4	4.13	0.97	217.25	957.290	0.507	0.940
16.5	4.23	0.91	217.15	955.035	0.581	0.940
16.6	4.11	0.91	217.27	959.676	0.498	0.941
16.7	4.36	0.83	217.02	962.113	0.497	0.941
16.8	4.29	0.87	217.09	958.912	0.537	0.940
16.9	4.46	0.78	216.92	963.328	0.505	0.941
17.1	3.97	0.92	217.41	959.926	0.489	0.941
17.2	3.71	1.02	217.67	948.017	0.625	0.940
17.3	3.94	0.99	217.44	953.804	0.550	0.940
17.4	3.84	1.00	217.54	955.159	0.524	0.940
17.5	4.24	0.87	217.14	956.020	0.588	0.940
17.6	4.21	0.86	217.17	956.926	0.577	0.940
17.7	4.23	0.88	217.15	957.626	0.555	0.940
17.8	3.73	0.96	217.65	959.899	0.468	0.941
17.9	4.20	0.90	217.18	958.304	0.528	0.940
17.10	4.02	0.99	217.36	953.242	0.559	0.940
17.11	4.02	0.98	217.36	953.891	0.556	0.940
18	3.66	0.78	217.72	977.113	0.221	0.942

Table 2 Respondents' demographic data (percentage %)

Variable	Value	Percentage
Sex	Male	15.8
	Female	84.2
Age (years)	<24	17.5
	25–34	28.2
	35–44	33.9
	45–54	15.8
	55–64	4.5
	65+	0
Education	Primary	6.2
	Secondary	25.4
	Tertiary	68.4
Master's/Ph.D. holder	Yes	19.2
	No	80.8
Marital status	Married	44.6
	No Married	55.4
Income (monthly individual)	<700	51.4
	701–1000	26.6
	1001–1500	14.1
	1501–2000	4.5
	2000+	3.4

have primary education. Regarding the level of education, 19.2% have a Master's or Doctorate degree, while the remaining 80.8% do not. In terms of marital status, 44.6% of respondents were married while 55.4% were single. Finally, the largest percentage of respondents (51.4%) receive a monthly income of up to 700 euros. The income is partly higher (701–1000 euros) for 26.6% of the respondents, and even higher (1001–1500 euros) for the remaining 14.1%. Only 7.9% of the respondents receive a monthly salary of more than 1500 euros, of which 3.4% receive a salary of 2000 euros.

3.2 Use of Internet

The first research question is 'What are the reasons for using the Internet?'. Table 3 and Fig. 1 show the motives for using the Internet. The largest percentage of respondents use the Internet to search for information (83%) and to communicate (79.9%). Almost 72.4% of the respondents use the Internet to read news. 64.4% use the Internet often or very often for e-banking and online shopping, while 62.1% use it for entertainment. Almost one in three (34.5%) rarely use the Internet for downloading, while 39.5% often or very often download music, films or software.

Only 2.3% of the respondents purchase online every day, while 4% and 10.7% purchase online once or twice a week respectively. Most respondents (46.3%) purchase from an e-shop once a month, while 29.4% and 7.3% purchase online once every six months and once a year respectively (Fig. 2).

The second research question examines the types of products that consumers purchase online. According to the results presented in Table 4 and Fig. 3, 35.7% of respondents purchase technology products frequently or very frequently. Respondents prefer to purchase online travel services (61%), clothes (46.3%) and event tickets (42.4%), while they do not frequently purchase online food and dietary supplements.

Table 3 Reasons for using the Internet (percentage %)

Type of Internet use	Very rarely	Rarely	Medium	Frequently	Very frequently
News	3.4	3.4	20.9	34.5	37.9
Search for information	1.1	1.7	14.1	30.5	52.5
Entertainment	5.1	6.2	26.6	28.8	33.3
Communication	2.3	4	14.1	26	53.7
Download software, music, movies	22.6	11.9	26	20.3	19.2
E-banking, e-shop	6.2	7.3	22	32.8	31.6
Other reason	18.6	11.3	26	18.6	25.4

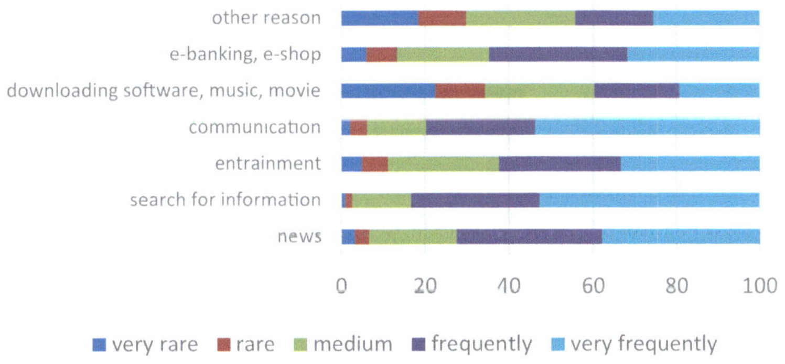

Fig. 1 Reasons for using the Internet (percentage %)

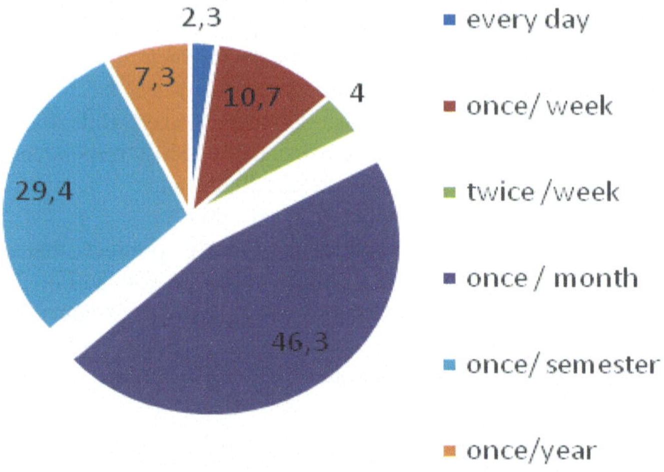

Fig. 2 Frequency of online shopping (percentage %)

Table 4 Types of products that consumers purchase online (percentage %)

Type of products	Very rarely	Rarely	Medium	Frequently	Very frequently
Technology	22	15.8	27.1	21.5	13.6
Books	32.8	19.8	19.2	15.3	13
Clothes	11.3	11.9	30.5	23.7	22.6
Foods	49.7	13.6	19.2	8.5	9
Nutritional supplements	52	15.8	17.5	9	5.6
Events' tickets	25.4	9.6	22.6	19.8	22.6
Travel services	12.4	9.6	16.9	30.5	30.5
House equipment	18.1	18.6	24.9	22	16.4
Other	28.2	11.9	33.3	11.3	15.3

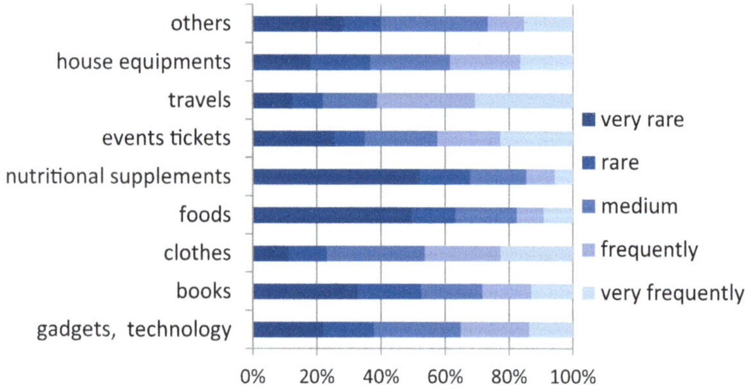

Fig. 3 Products purchased online (percentage %)

3.3 Factors Affecting e-shopping

The third research question examines the reasons for purchasing online. The most important factors for e-shopping (Table 5) are discounts, reviews and the security of the e-shop. Offers, recommendations from friends, no delivery charges and availability of products are important factors. Advertising and theft of personal data are considered as less important factors.

The fourth research question evaluated the influence of an online advertisement to the decision for an online purchase. More than 50% of the respondents (53.7%) are not actually influenced by online advertisements (Table 6), while more than 1 out of 7 (16.4%) are influenced significantly.

The fifth research question examined whether site design influences the consumer's decision to purchase online. Site design is considered a very important factor by respondents. Almost two out of three respondents (67.8%) strongly agree (Table 7) that a well-designed site makes it easier to order online, while 24.3% agree.

Table 5 Reasons for purchasing online (percentage %)

Reason for purchasing online	Not significant	Rather significant	Neutral	Significant	Very significant
Image	9	14.1	36.2	26	14.7
Offers	2.8	6.2	22.6	40.7	27.7
Advertisement	10.7	16.4	38.4	24.3	10.2
Friends' recommendation	5.1	10.2	32.2	32.2	20.3
No delivery cost	5.1	6.2	23.7	32.2	32.8
Product availability	4	10.2	22.6	33.9	29.4
Good discounts	2.8	2.8	14.1	33.3	46.9
Reviews	4	9.6	13.6	31.6	41.2
Secure site	4.5	4.5	11.9	31.1	48
Fear of personal data theft	15.8	11.3	22	21.5	29.4

Table 6 Online purchase after viewing an online advertisement (percentage %)

	%
Not at all	10.7
A little	19.2
Not much	53.7
Much	14.7
Very much	1.7

Table 7 The impact of a well-designed e-shop on the decision to make an online purchase (percentage %)

	%
Strongly disagree	1.1
Disagree	0.6
Neither agree nor disagree	6.2
Agree	24.3
Strongly agree	67.8

Table 8 Components of online advertising. (percentage %)

Component	Lower	Low	Neutral	High	Higher
Product	3.4	2.3	9.0	42.9	42.4
Person	26	23.7	35	7.9	7.3
Slogan	23.2	22	37.9	10.2	6.8
Music	27.1	23.7	30.5	11.9	6.8
Other	27.7	16.9	31.6	12.4	11.3

In conclusion, 92.1% of respondents prefer to purchase online from well-designed e-shops.

The sixth research question assessed the components of online advertising. Respondents were asked whether when watching an advertisement, they paid particular attention to the product, the person, the slogan, the music or any other component. Most respondents (85.3%) look at the product (Table 8), while only 15.2% look at the people. Almost 17% and 18.7% pay particular attention to the slogan or the music of the advertisement respectively.

The seventh research question evaluated the best digital marketing techniques, (i.e. the best ways for a company to promote their products or services online), such as the email, an e-shop, social media, search engine advertisement or any other ways. A 78% of the respondents consider that an e-shop is the most appropriate way (Table 9), while 69.5% and 38.4% think that social media and search engine marketing are effective ways. On the contrary, 37.8% of respondents believe that email is not a good way for a company to promote its products/services.

3.4 The Role of Digital Marketing

The eighth question examined the benefits of online shopping for consumers. Almost 83.1% of respondents (Table 10) stated that shopping online is much better than shopping in a physical store in terms of ease of access, while only 4.5% had a negative opinion. Almost 72.9% of respondents stated that an online shop sells products at lower prices, while 78% of respondents found a wide range of products. In addition, 80.2% believe that online shopping is more effective because the consumer can

Table 9 Best digital marketing techniques (percentage %)

Digital marketing technique	Strongly disagree	Disagree	Neither agree or disagree	Agree	Strongly agree
Email	15.8	22	32.8	18.6	10.7
E-shop	2.3	5.6	14.1	37.3	40.7
Social media	3.4	5.6	21,5	33.3	36.2
Search engine marketing	18.6	15.3	27.7	23.7	14.7
Other	27.7	7.9	37.3	15.3	11.9

compare products. The 24-h service is also seen as an important advantage by 83.6% of respondents, while 89.8% stated that online shopping offers better delivery of products.

The ninth question examined the benefits of online shopping for companies. Almost 76.9% of respondents (Table 11) agreed that e-commerce improves the image of the company, while only 8.4% disagreed. Most of the respondents (60.5%) believe that e-commerce helps companies to have loyal customers, while only 10.7% disagreed. A 70.9% of respondents believe that companies could improve their external and internal network, while only 8.5% disagreed. A 62.7% of respondents believe that e-commerce can minimize promotional costs, while 80.8% believe that the Internet will help companies assess new markets. Most respondents (84.1%)

Table 10 Benefits of online shopping for consumers (percentage %)

Benefit for consumers	Strongly disagree	Disagree	Neither agree or disagree	Agree	Strongly agree
Ease of access	1.1	3.4	12.4	33.9	49.2
Save time	1.7	2.8	6.8	34.5	54.2
Better prices	1.1	4.0	22.0	32.8	40.1
Variety of products	1.7	5.1	15.3	34.5	43.5
Ability to compare products	1.1	3.4	15.3	31.6	48.6
Better deals	1.1	3.4	19.2	36.2	40.1
24 h service	0	3.4	13.0	28.2	55.4
Ability to access a non-domestic market	0.6	2.3	16.9	28.2	52.0
Better delivery of products	1.1	1.1	7.9	29.9	59.9

Table 11 E-commerce benefits for businesses (percentage %)

Benefit for companies	Strongly disagree	Disagree	Neither agree or disagree	Agree	Strongly agree
Improve the company's image	1.1	7.3	14.7	47.5	29.4
Maintain consumer's loyalty	3.4	7.3	28.8	36.2	24.3
Improve the external and internal network	1.7	6.8	21.5	35.6	34.5
Minimize display costs	1.1	7.9	28.2	31.1	31.6
Access to new markets	0.6	3.4	15.3	33.3	47.5
Increase sales	0.6	5.1	10.2	41.2	42.9
Increase competitiveness	0.6	4.5	12.4	36.2	46.3
Reduce ties in the supply chain	1.1	7.3	33.9	32.8	24.9
Continuous operation	0.6	4.5	15.3	33.3	46.3
Better communication policy and promotion	2.3	5.1	19.2	35.0	38.4
Optimal product and order management	2.3	5.1	18.1	37.9	36.7

believe that e-commerce will increase sales, while 82.5% say it could also increase competitiveness.

In addition, more than one in two respondents (57.7%) consider e-commerce to be a way of reducing supply chain ties, while 73.4% state that companies can improve their communication policies. In addition, 74.6% believe that e-commerce will help companies improve product and order management.

3.5 *Factor Analysis*

Factor analysis was carried out in order to find data trends and correlations between the questions. The results of the factor analysis are presented in Tables 12, 13, Table 14 respectively.

Table 12 KMO and Bartlett's Test

Kaiser–Meyer–Olkin Measure of Sampling Adequacy		0.872
Bartlett's Test of Sphericity	Approx. Chi-Square	6467.43
	df	1596
	Sig	0.000

Table 13 Total variance explained

Component	Total	% of variance	Cumulative %
1	15.655	27.464	27.464
2	4.812	8.443	35.907
3	3.489	6.121	42.028
4	2.569	4.508	46.535
5	2.185	3.834	50.369
6	1.943	3.409	53.779
7	1.598	2.804	56.583
8	1.503	2.637	59.220
9	1.403	2.461	61.681
10	1.253	2.199	63.880
11	1.160	2.035	65.915

The KMO value is 0.872 > 0.7 (Table 12), so the research data is suitable for factor analysis.

The variance explained by the first factor is 27.46%, while the variance explained by the second factor is 8.44% (Table 13). These two factors explain almost 36% of the total variance of the data. The scree plot is shown in Fig. 4.

According to the results of the factor analysis, two important factors have been identified (Table 13). The first factor correlates with e-commerce economic benefits for consumers (searching for information, offers and discounts, save time, compare products, better communication) and for enterprises (access to new markets, increase sales and competitiveness, better communication policy and promotion, optimal product and order management). The second factor is correlated with questions about the facility benefits of e-commerce for consumers (entertainment, communication, downloads, e-banking, e-shop, purchasing food and dietary supplements) and companies (access to new markets, increase sales and competitiveness, better communication policy and promotion, optimal product and order management). The third axis is not related to any question.

Table 14 shows the questions that are correlated with the three main axes. Factor 1 is correlated with questions about the use of the Internet for finding information, offers and discounts. It is also correlated with respondents who believe that the Internet helps them save time, compare prices and communicate better. The second axis is opposite to the first (negative correlations) and it is correlated with respondents who

Table 14 Component matrix

Question	Factor 1	Factor 3	Factor 3
Search for information	**0.611**	0.290	−0.162
Entrainment	0.462	**0.392**	−0.076
Communication	0.536	**0.358**	−0.126
Downloading software, music, movie	0.272	**0.464**	0.034
e-banking, e-shop	0.603	**0.375**	−0.094
Foods	0.259	**0.434**	0.091
Nutritional supplements	0.319	**0.354**	0.007
Offers	**0.701**	0.209	−0.005
Product availability	**0.730**	0.228	−0.039
Good discounts	**0.737**	0.248	−0.063
Reviews	**0.670**	0.248	−0.093
Security site	**0.686**	0.200	−0.197
Save time	**0.724**	−0.335	−0.118
A variety of products	**0.602**	−0.232	0.006
Ability to compare offered products	**0.656**	−0.212	−0.020
Access to new markets	**0.687**	**−0.473**	−0.088
Sales increase	**0.669**	**−0.459**	−0.067
Increasing competitiveness	**0.629**	**−0.424**	−0.058
Better communication policy and promotion	**0.644**	**−0.450**	−0.054
Optimal product and order management	**0.653**	**−0.407**	−0.081

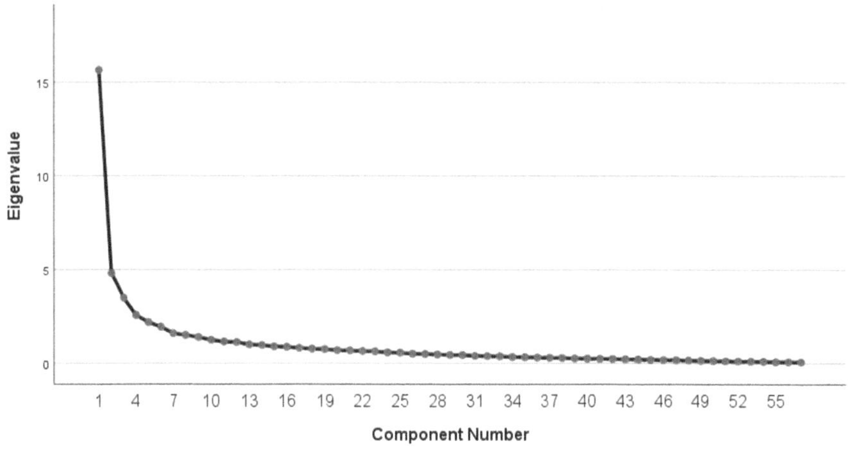

Fig. 4 Scree plot

use the Internet for entertainment, communication, downloading software, music, movies, e-banking, e-shop, food and food supplements. The third axis is not strongly correlated with any question, except "security site" and "saving time".

Monthly income, age and sex with correlated factors 1, 2 and 3 are shown in Figs. 5, 6 and 7 respectively. Positive values of factor 1 (economic benefits) are presented for those with monthly income 700–1500 euros per month and negative values of factor 1, are presented for those with monthly income greater than 1500 euros per month, which do not care mainly for economic benefits. More important negative values of factor 2, are presented for those with monthly income greater than 2000 euros per month, which are not mainly think the facility benefits using internet. They are correlated with factor 3, which is correlated with variables saving time and security site (Fig. 6). Age and gender of consumer are not correlated with factors 1, 2 or 3 as is portrayed in Figs. 6 and 7.

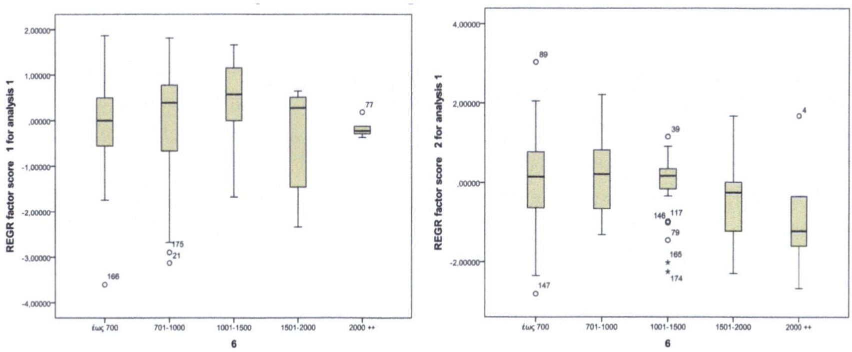

Fig. 5 Income per month and factor 1 and 2

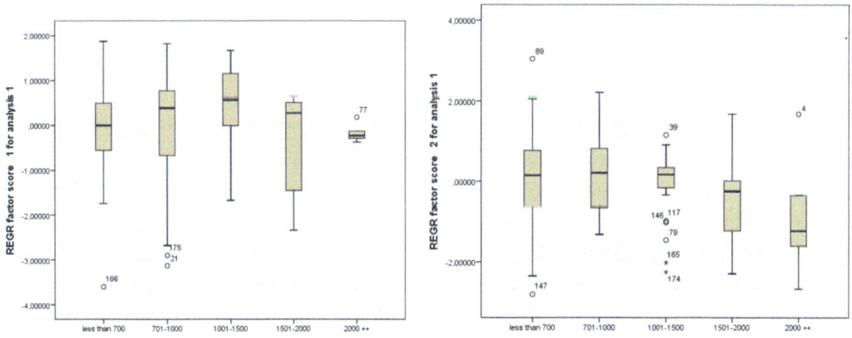

Fig. 6 Age and factor 2 and 3

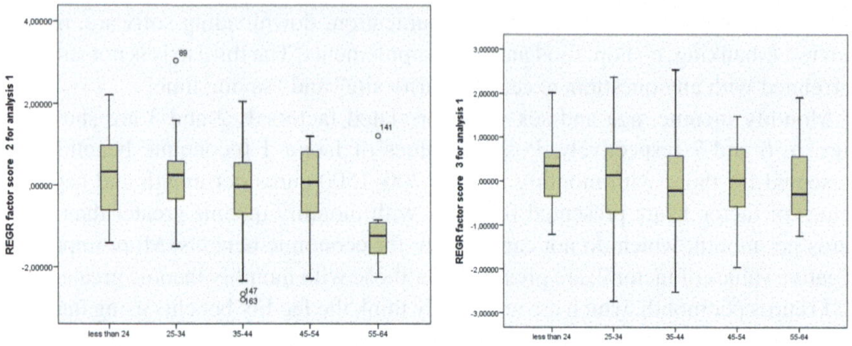

Fig. 7 Gender and factor 1, 2 and 3

4 Discussion

According to the research, consumers use the Internet mainly to search for information rather than to download software, music or films. Consumers are more likely to purchase travel services (e.g. booking hotels), clothes and event tickets online, and less likely to purchase food or dietary supplements. These findings are consistent with older studies in Greece (Gounopoulos et al., 2018). Consumers are motivated by financial incentives, such as product sales or price discounts. They take into account the recommendations of their friends and consider product availability and free delivery of products as important reasons to purchase online. However, they are reluctant to engage with online ads.

Consumers also want to use websites that are well designed and structured. They respond to advertising by focusing more on the product and less on other factors such as the slogan or music of the advertisement. They consider the presence of an online shop and social media page to be important factors in promoting a product online. Many respondents consider email and search engine marketing to be less effective digital marketing techniques.

According to the research, consumers prefer to shop online to save time. They believe that online shopping can benefit them for many reasons, such as better price, variety of products, ability to compare products, better deals, 24-h service, access to foreign e-shops and better delivery of products. The results are in line with the study of Panagiotounis (2024) who researched the relationship between consumers and the online market in Greece.

Consumers believe that the digital presence is also beneficial for companies for many reasons such as improving customer loyalty, access to new markets, increasing sales, increasing competitiveness, etc. The results of the research are also in line with the view of entrepreneurs or business managers, according to the research of Velentza and Metaxas (2023), who studied the use of digital marketing tools by tourism companies. Directors or managers of tourism companies considered the use of digital marketing tools, such as social media, to be beneficial for the company's image and for building stronger relationships with customers.

Companies should promote their products not only through traditional marketing channels, but also through digital marketing. The study found that there are several prerequisites for effective digital marketing. For example, a well-designed online store and a well-organised social media presence can help promote products more effectively. As consumers are concerned about the protection of their personal data, companies should also have a clear policy on the management of personal data in accordance with existing legislation. Companies should also offer discount incentives to their consumers, as offers are the main driver for consumers to purchase online. Finally, online advertising should include an offer and focus on the product to motivate consumers.

5 Conclusions

The research examined the relationship between consumers and the Internet, focusing on online shopping behaviour and the influence of digital marketing. It revealed that consumers primarily use the Internet to search for information rather than to download content, while key motivators for online shopping include financial incentives, product availability and free delivery.

Advertising plays a vital role in promoting products and services through both traditional and digital marketing techniques. The Internet has become the main communication and transaction channel for every consumer. It is used by companies to promote and advertise their products and services. However, there are many consumers who are reluctant to shop online and use the Internet. They are wary of technology and are concerned about the security of their personal data.

The growth of online shopping in Greece during and after the Covid pandemic represents a significant opportunity for the domestic market. This research provides valuable insights for business managers, helping them to understand customer preferences and highlighting the key aspects of digital marketing.

The study also highlighted the importance of a digital presence for businesses, noting that it can increase customer loyalty and expand market reach. A well-designed website and strong social media presence are essential for effective digital marketing, as consumers are more likely to focus on the product itself in advertisements. Companies are advised to combine traditional and digital marketing strategies, emphasing clear privacy policies and offering discounts to attract consumers. Overall, a focus on product-centric online advertising and a well-organised digital presence are key to successful online marketing.

This research highlighted the importance of e-commerce and digital marketing for both consumers and businesses. However, it has a few limitations. The survey sample is small and not representative of the general population. The analysis is primarily descriptive and more advanced statistical techniques were not fully utilized. A survey of a larger sample across the country would give a better picture of consumer preferences. A further comparison with the results of similar surveys in Greece would also help to generalise the results of the survey. In addition, a survey with different target groups (e.g. young consumers) may clarify which key elements are most important for each focus group.

References

Baek, T. H., & Morimoto, M. (2012). Stay away from me. *Journal of Advertising, 41*(1), 59–76.

Burns, K. S., & Lutz, R. J. (2006). The function of format: Consumer responses to six on-line advertising formats. *Journal of Advertising, 35*(1), 53–63.

Cho D. Y., Kwon H. J., & Lee H. Y. (2007) *Analysis of trust in internet and mobile commerce adoption.* Proceedings of the 40th Hawaii International Conference on System Science, USA.

Coppola, D. (2021). *Global number of digital buyers 2014–2021.* Accessed 15 May 2024 from https://www.statista.com/statistics/251666/number-of-digital-buyers-worldwide/

Darley, W., Blankson, C., & Luethge, D. (2010). Toward an integrated framework for online consumer behavior and decision making process: A review. *Psychology & Marketing, 27*(2), 94–116.

Desai, Dr. (2019). Digital marketing: A review. *International Journal of Trend in Scientific Research and Development.* Special Issue, 196–200.

Dwivedi, R., & Nath, P. (2020). Digital marketing: Disruption, expansion and its impact on businesses. *Parikalpana: KIIT Journal of Management, 16*(1and2), 25–43.

Edwards, S. M., Li, H., & Lee, J. H. (2002). Forced exposure and psychological reactance: Antecedents and consequences of the perceived intrusiveness of pop-up ads. *Journal of Advertising, 31*(3), 83–95.

Gounopoulos, E., Kokkonis, G., Valsamidis, S., & Kontogiannis, S. (2018). Digital divide in Greece-a quantitative examination of internet Nonuse. In A. Karasavvoglou, S. Goić, P. Polychronidou, & P. Delias (Eds.), *Economy, finance and business in Southeastern and Central Europe* (pp. 889–903). Springer. https://doi.org/10.1007/978-3-319-70377-0_61

Hair Jr, J. F., LDS Gabriel, M., Silva, D. D., & Braga, S. (2019). Development and validation of attitudes measurement scales: fundamental and practical aspects. *RAUSP Management Journal, 54*(4), 490–507.

Hongjun, G., & Aiwu, Z. (2014). Effect of e-commerce sellers' evaluation on consumers' perceived trust-Case of taobao.com. *Journal of Chemical and Pharmaceutical Research, 6*(7), 695–699.

Kabha, R., Kelkar, A. S., & Kamel, A. M. (2023). Digital disruptions and its impact on traditional marketing practices. *Educational Research (IJMCER), 5*(5), 128–137.

Komodromos, M., Harkiolakis, T., Khoshtaria, T., & Vassiliou, M. (2024). Adoption of digital technology and investigation of the impact in the marketing industry for marketing communication professionals: The case study of Cyprus and Greece. *International Journal of Technology Enhanced Learning, 16*(2), 173–191.

Kyriazopoulos, P., & Samanta, E. (2014). *Introduction to marketing—Yesterday ... today ... tomorrow.* Modern Publishing (in Greek).

Masliardi, A., Effendi, M., Ningrum, P. A., Hasnidar, H., & Mala, I. K. (2023). Digital disruption: Exploring the dynamics of marketing in the digital age. *SEIKO: Journal of Management & Business, 6*(2), 421–430.

Mokoena, A. G., & Prinsloo, J. J. (2021). *The impact of digital disruption on the marketing and advertising functions.* IBC.

Olson, E. M., Olson, K. M., Czaplewski, A. J., & Key, T. M. (2021). Business strategy and the management of digital marketing. *Business Horizons, 64*(2), 285–293. https://doi.org/10.1016/j.bushor.2020.12.004

Panagiotounis, L. (2024). *E-commerce changes in SMEs' marketing and consumer behavior: The Case of Greece.*

Peiris, P., Kulkarni, D., & Mawatha, C. (2015). An empirical study of customer adoption of e-commerce: A customer trust model to support the adoption of ecommerce among small- and medium-sized enterprises in Sri Lanka. *International Journal of Business and Information, 10*(4), 491–518.

Triantafilidi, S. (2020). *The behaviour of the Greek consumer in the modern online environment.* https://medianalysis.net/2020/11/21/i-symperifora-tou-ellina-katanaloti-sto-sygchrono-diadiktyako-perivallon/ (in Greek).

Triantafillidou, A., & Siomkos, G. (2018). The impact of Facebook experience on consumers' behavioral Brand engagement. *Journal of Research in Interactive Marketing, 12*(2), 164–192.

Vakalopoulos, K., & Blatsouka, G. (2020). Product promotion via the internet. (In Greek).

Velentza, A., & Metaxas, T. (2023). The role of digital marketing in tourism businesses: An empirical investigation in Greece. *Businesses, 3*(2), 272–292.

Zikmund, W. G., Babin, B. J., Carr, J. C., & Griffin, M. (2013). *Business research methods.* Cengage Learning Custom Publishing.

The Attitudes of Civil Servants Towards E-Gov Apps

Lambros Tsourgiannis, Stavros Valsamidis, Foteini Perdiki, and Polina Karagianni

Abstract Electronic government (e-gov) applications have been adopted by the public sector due to the recent COVID-19 pandemic. Managers in the civil sector use them as problem-solving tools, while citizens utilize them to facilitate transactions with the civil sector. Stakeholders also employ these applications to monitor civil servants. E-gov applications such as telework, remote work, distance learning, and online transactions have become part of everyday life in society. This study aims to explore the attitudes of Greek civil servants towards the use of e-government applications. A primary survey was conducted in the autumn of 2023 on a random sample of Greek civil servants. Principal component analysis (PCA) was used to identify the main attitudes of Greek civil servants towards the use of e-government applications. Cluster analysis was performed to classify them into groups based on their attitudes toward the use of e-government applications, while non-parametric tests, including chi-square, were conducted to develop the demographic profile of each identified group of civil servants.

Keywords E-Government · Digital Marketing · Public Sector · Internet · Citizens' Attitudes

1 Introduction

The lack of ICT and e-government adoption by various user groups has been The lack of ICT and e-government adoption by various user groups has been studied from multiple angles. Al-Shafi and Weerakkody (2007) explored the challenges of e-government implementation in Qatar and found that government employees often

L. Tsourgiannis (✉)
General Directorate of Internal Operation, Komotini, Greece
e-mail: ltsourgiannis@gmail.com

L. Tsourgiannis · S. Valsamidis · F. Perdiki · P. Karagianni
Department of Accounting and Finance, IDemocritus University of Thrace, Campus of Kavala, Kavala, Greece

I. Bartuseviciene et al. (eds.), *Building Resilience Through Digital Transformation and Sustainable Innovation*, Springer Proceedings in Business and Economics,
https://doi.org/10.1007/978-3-031-90054-9_19

resisted change, especially with the introduction of new services. Al-Busaidy and Weerakkody (2011) reviewed e-government practices in Oman, finding that 77% of respondents had a positive attitude toward accessibility, 85% toward efficiency, and 80% toward the availability of e-services. Baldwin et al. (2012) revealed that public servants in New Zealand held nuanced views on e-government, expressing skepticism about its role in flexible work, "joining-up" government, and enhancing citizen participation in policymaking. Saleh and Tarhini (2013) studied public sector employees' readiness for e-government in Lebanon, finding that respondents were motivated to use e-government applications and recognized their importance. Gökçeoğlu and Yavuz (2013) aimed to understand Turkish public employees' views on and usage of e-government initiatives.

Historically, governments have driven their development agendas and investments in e-government based on their own understanding (Mofleh & Wanous, 2008). A user-centered e-government strategy is essential for success (Schedler & Summermatter, 2007). By prioritizing people, governments can improve service quality, making services more usable and useful. The lack of demand for e-government services and underestimated adoption rates highlight the need to understand the factors influencing e-government adoption (Dwivedi et al., 2019). Despite the increasing number of e-government studies, most models in the academic literature are conceptual, with empirical studies largely overlooked (Ahmed et al., 2013). Factors influencing e-government adoption and diffusion vary globally (Heeks & Bailur, 2007), and although these factors are explored, the use of existing theories and models in e-government adoption research remains to be fully investigated (Rana et al., 2017). Public servants, often forgotten as potential users of e-government, are simply expected to adopt it (Baldwin et al., 2012).

While many researchers have focused on supply-side e-government adoption, relatively few have examined why citizens adopt e-government services (Gauld et al., 2010; Reddick, 2005). To understand or predict users' adoption and acceptance of technologies, many researchers have adopted the Technology Acceptance Model (TAM) (Davis, 1993), Theory of Reasoned Action (TRA) (Fishbein & Ajzen, 1975), and Theory of Planned Behavior (TPB) (Ajzen, 1985). Specifically, TAM, an adaptation of TRA from psychology, models user acceptance of Information Technology (IT) by examining how two belief factors—perceived usefulness and perceived ease of use—affect behavioral intentions. However, TAM does not consider social and human factors (Al-Hujran et al., 2015). Gilbert et al. (2004) identified that citizens' willingness to use e-government services is influenced by time and money savings, as well as improvements in the accessibility and convenience of government services and information (Al-Hujran, 2009). Trust is also a key factor in e-governance application acceptance. Venkatesh et al. (2003) developed the Unified Theory of Acceptance and Use of Technology (UTAUT), which includes performance expectancy, effort expectancy, social influence, facilitating conditions, and behavioral intention, while also considering factors such as gender, age, experience, and voluntariness of use.

AlAwadhi and Morris (2009) used the UTAUT model to study e-government service adoption in Kuwait, identifying performance expectancy, effort expectancy, peer influence, and facilitating conditions as significant determinants. These findings, though derived from a developing country, were consistent with studies in developed countries, suggesting that the factors determining e-government adoption could be universally applicable. Despite the potential limitation of using civil servants as subjects, the research offers insights into the motivations behind e-government adoption in developing countries.

Citizens' attitudes toward e-commerce, digital marketing, and e-government applications are influenced by demographic characteristics such as age, education, occupation, and income, as well as their previous internet experience (Karavasilis, 2012; Valili, 2007; Venkatesh et al., 2003). Factors like relative advantage, compatibility, ease of use, image, perceived usefulness, trustworthiness, cultural considerations, and demographics significantly impact e-government service usage (Akman et al., 2005; Al Awadhi & Morris, 2009; Carter & Belanger, 2004, 2005; Dimitrova & Chen, 2006; Hung et al., 2006). Olatobusun and Madhava Rao (2012) identified several barriers to civil servants using e-government tools, including a lack of tutor training, technology unreliability, lack of support, difficulties using online systems, time constraints, and the unavailability of additional resources needed for IT tool use.

In 2020, Greece focused on enhancing its public administration's efficiency and effectiveness through e-government applications. Reconnecting citizens with the public sector was a key strategic goal of Greece's e-government strategy from 2014 to 2020 (Gounopoulos et al., 2019). Despite these efforts, Greece lags behind other EU countries in the adoption of e-government services (Gounopoulos et al., 2019).

This study investigates the attitudes of Greek civil servants toward using e-government applications. The subsequent sections are organized as follows: The second section outlines the research methodology, the third section presents the results and discusses the findings, and the fourth section examines the implications of these results for public administration. Specifically, the researchers developed a questionnaire based on the one used by Al Awadhi and Morris (2009). The variables in the questionnaire were drawn from the UTAUT model, which has been validated for studying technology adoption across different contexts (Anderson & Schwager, 2004; Al Awadhi & Morris, 2009; Lin et al., 2004; Venkatesh et al., 2012), and tailored to explore the adoption of e-government applications within the Greek state. More specifically, this work aims to investigate the following null research hypotheses:

Ho1: "Greek civil servants cannot be classified into similar groups according to their attitudes towards the use of e-government applications"

Ho2: "The demographic and personal characteristics of Greek civil servants are not significantly related to their attitudes towards the use of e-government applications"

Ho3: "The satisfaction of the Greek civil servants from the use of e-government applications are not significantly related to main reasons they use these applications

2 Methodology

In autumn of 2023, the researchers conducted a primary survey with a random representative sample of 427 individuals, utilizing the methodologies of Tsourgiannis et al. (2023) and Oppenheim (2000). To ensure a geographically representative sample of Greece, seven regions were randomly selected from a total of thirteen. Subsequently, two prefectures were randomly chosen from each selected region. In the final stage, questionnaires were distributed to public administration services in the selected prefectures to be completed by their staff.

Initially, a preliminary survey was carried out with 30 civil servants in the Regional District of Xanthi. A pilot survey followed in May 2023 to determine if the questionnaire met the research objectives. The pilot survey results confirmed that the questionnaire was adequate for the final survey without further modifications.

Using Siardos's (1997) methodology, the researchers compared the proportion of sample members who reported using e-government applications at work with those from the pilot survey to assess the sample's representativeness. This approach was necessary because the exact number of respondents from each region was unknown, which is a limitation of the study. In the pilot survey, 68% of civil servants indicated using e-government applications for transparency purposes. Given Greece's total population of 10,816,286 (according to the Greek Census data, ELSTAT, 2020), a sample size of at least 350 was needed to achieve representativeness (with $z = 3$ and $d = 5\%$). The final sample size of 427 was deemed reasonably representative according to Siardos (1997) (with $z = 1.96$ and $d = 5\%$). Additionally, a power analysis ($\beta = 0.95$) conducted using G*POWER 3.1.9.2 software (Faul et al., 2009; Tsourgiannis et al., 2015) indicated a minimum sample size of 111 for a medium effect size (Cohen, 1988). Thus, the sample size of 427 was considered fully representative of the Greek population.

Moreover, the researchers employed statistical methodologies from Tsourgiannis et al. (2023). They conducted factor analysis to identify the main attitudes of Greek civil servants towards e-government applications and k-means cluster analysis to categorize employees based on their attitudes toward these applications. Nonparametric tests, including the chi-square and Friedman nonparametric tests, were performed to profile these civil servants regarding their demographic characteristics and reasons for using e-government applications.

3 Results and Discussion

Researchers employed Principal Component Analysis (PCA) to identify the key variables that describe the attitudes of Greek civil servants towards the use of e-government applications. To determine the number of factors, they used both the latent root criterion (eigenvalue = 1) and the percentage of variance (as shown in Table 1). They conducted several different trial rotations to compare factor interpretability, following the methodology of Hair et al. (1998).

The analysis revealed that two key factors account for 63.3% of the total variance. By interpreting the loading scores for each factor, the researchers identified the two factors (as shown in Table 2) as: (a) Improvement of public sector operations and (b) Better quality services.

Cluster analysis classified the Greek civil servants into three groups based on their attitudes towards e-government applications, as shown in Table 3: (a) those who believe e-government applications contribute to better quality services, (b) those who believe these applications contribute to the improvement of public sector operations, and (c) those who are indifferent.

More specifically, those who believe that e-government applications contribute to better quality service mainly believe that their e-governance will make their daily routine easier by solving issues regarding the:

- lack of trust for the safety of personal data
- lack of efficient free training of the public relative to the use of E-Government applications
- incomplete interoperability of the operating systems among the public authorities
- provision of incomplete services by public authorities
- use of old information systems by the public authorities
- lack of public awareness regarding the E-government applications and websites

Table 1 Results of principal component analysis

Component	Initial eigenvalues			Extraction sums of squared loadings		
	Total	% of variance	Cumulative %	Total	% of variance	Cumulative %
1	**7.388**	**45.550**	**45.550**	**7.388**	**45.550**	**45.550**
2	**2.845**	**17.783**	**63.333**	**2.845**	**17.783**	**63.333**
3	0.807	5.046	68.379			
4	0.695	4.347	72.726			
5	0.579	3.621	76.347			
6	0.492	3.076	79.424			
7	0.468	2.925	82.348			
8	0.412	2.573	84.921			
9	0.400	2.497	87.418			
10	0.381	2.382	89.800			
11	0.330	2.060	91.860			
12	0.301	1.884	93.744			
13	0.279	1.746	95.490			
14	0.274	1.710	97.200			
15	0.237	1.480	98.680			
16	0.211	1.320	100.00			

Table 2 The main factors affecting attitudes of the Greek civil servants towards the use of e-government applications

	Component	
	1	2
To which extend the benefits of the E-governance contribute to possible development of isolated and degraded areas	**0.803**	0.188
To which extend the benefits of the E-governance contribute to the control and apportion responsibilities in Public Administration	**0.772**	0.213
To which extend the benefits of the E-governance contribute to the quality improvement of the provided services	**0.768**	0.194
To which extend the benefits of the E-governance contribute to less bureaucracy	**0.765**	0.182
To which extend the benefits of the E-governance contribute to time reduction	**0.764**	0.205
To which extend the benefits of the E-governance contribute to the reduction of corruption and misgovernment	**0.759**	0.233
To which extend the benefits of the E-governance contribute to the promotion of electronic democracy and transparency with electronic vote	**0.746**	0.195
To which extend the benefits of the E-governance contribute to the cost reduction of provided services	**0.742**	0.189
To which extend the benefits of the E-governance contribute to the participation of the society to the formulation of the public policies	**0.720**	0.229
To which extend E-governance will make your daily routine easier by solving issues regarding the lack of trust for the safety of personal data	0.165	**0.813**
To which extend E-governance will make your daily routine easier by solving issues regarding the lack of efficient free training of the public relative to the use of E-Government applications	0.203	**0.805**
To which extend E-governance will make your daily routine easier by solving issues regarding the incomplete interoperability of the operating systems among the public authorities	0.252	**0.797**
To which extend E-governance will make your daily routine easier by solving issues regarding the provision of incomplete services by public authorities	0.184	**0.794**
To which extend E-governance will make your daily routine easier by solving issues regarding the use of old information systems by the public authorities	0.223	**0.774**
To which extend E-governance will make your daily routine easier by solving issues regarding the lack of public awareness regarding the E-government applications and websites	0.199	**0.779**
To which extend E-governance will make your daily routine easier by solving issues regarding the long waiting time in the web, phone and the misunderstanding instructions	0.225	**0.759**

KMO MSA = 0.922 Bartlett test of Sphericity = 4284.344 $P < 0.001$

Table 3 Classification of the Greek civil servants regarding their attitudes towards E-Government applications

Factors affecting Greek civil servants regarding their attitudes towards E-Government applications	Cluster			
	Those who believe that e-government applications contribute to better quality services	Those who believe that e-gov application contribute to the improvement of the public sector operation	Indifferent	P
Improvement of civil sector operation	0.26755	1.16368	-1.05603	0.001
Better quality of services	0.60789	-1.28373	-0.42053	0.001
N = 427	230	66	131	

- long waiting time in the web, phone and the misunderstanding instructions

On the other hand, most of the civil servants who believe tha e-gov applications contribute to the improvement of the public sector operation mainly believe that E-governance contribute to:

- the possible development of isolated and degraded areas
- the control and apportion responsibilities in Public Administration
- the quality improvement of the provided services
- less bureaucracy
- time reduction
- the reduction of corruption and misgovernment
- the promotion of electronic democracy and transparency with electronic vote.
- the cost reduction of provided services
- the participation of the society to the formulation of the public policies.

Besides the third group, the indifferent citizens, do not pay attention to any of the identified factors.

Thus, *Ho1: "Greek civil servants cannot be classified into similar groups according to their attitudes towards the use of e-government applications"* can be rejected.

The researchers conducted a chi square analysis to develop the demographic profile of each identified group. As shown in Table 4, they found that both groups: (a) "those who believe that e-government applications contribute to better quality services" and (b) "those who believe that e-government applications contribute to the improvement of public sector operations" are primarily female and hold a bachelor's degree. However, the civil servants in the first group are mostly from Generation Y, while those in the second group are from Generation X. Additionally, most of the "indifferent" group hold a bachelor's degree and are millennials (Gen Y).

Table 4 Profiling each group according to their demographics

Demographic Characteristics		Those who believe that e-government applications contribute to better quality services		Those who believe that e-gov application contribute to the improvement of the public sector operation		Indifferent	
Gender	Male	$x^2 = 9.200$ ($P < 0.01$)	40%	$x^2 = 3.879$ ($P < 0.05$)	37.9%	n.s	49.6%
	Female		60%		62.1%		50.4%
Education	Primary School	$x^2 =$ 95.043 ($P < 0.001$)	3.5%	$x^2 =$ 24.061 ($P < 0.001$)	6.1%	$x^2 =$ 53.580 ($P < 0.001$)	12.2%
	High School		27.8%		34.8%		22.1%
	University Degree		48.3%		43.9%		51.9%
	Postgraduate Degree		3.5%		15.2%		13.7%
Generation	Gen Z	$x^2 =$ 34.730 ($P < 0.001$)	6.5%	$x^2 =$ 10.970 ($P < 0.05$)	6.1%	n.s	7.6%
	Gen Y		43.5%		37.9%		43.5%
	Gen X		38.7%		45.5%		29.8%
	BabyBoomers		11,3%		10.6%		19.1%

Therefore, the research hypothesis Ho2: "*The demographic and personal characteristics of Greek civil servants are not significantly related to their attitudes towards the use of e-government applications*" can be rejected.

Furthermore, the chi-square analysis revealed (Fig. 1) that most civil servants who believe e-government applications contribute to better quality services are primarily satisfied with applications used by the public for general purposes (www.gov.gr), followed by those for tax issues and issuing certificates. Conversely, the majority of civil servants who believe e-government applications improve public sector operations are mainly satisfied with applications used for general purposes, tax issues, and social insurance. Additionally, most indifferent civil servants are more satisfied with e-government applications used for general purposes, tax issues, and general information systems.

Hence, the research hypothesis Ho3: "*The satisfaction of the Greek civil servants from the use of e-government applications are not significantly related to main reasons they use these ap-plications*" can be rejected.

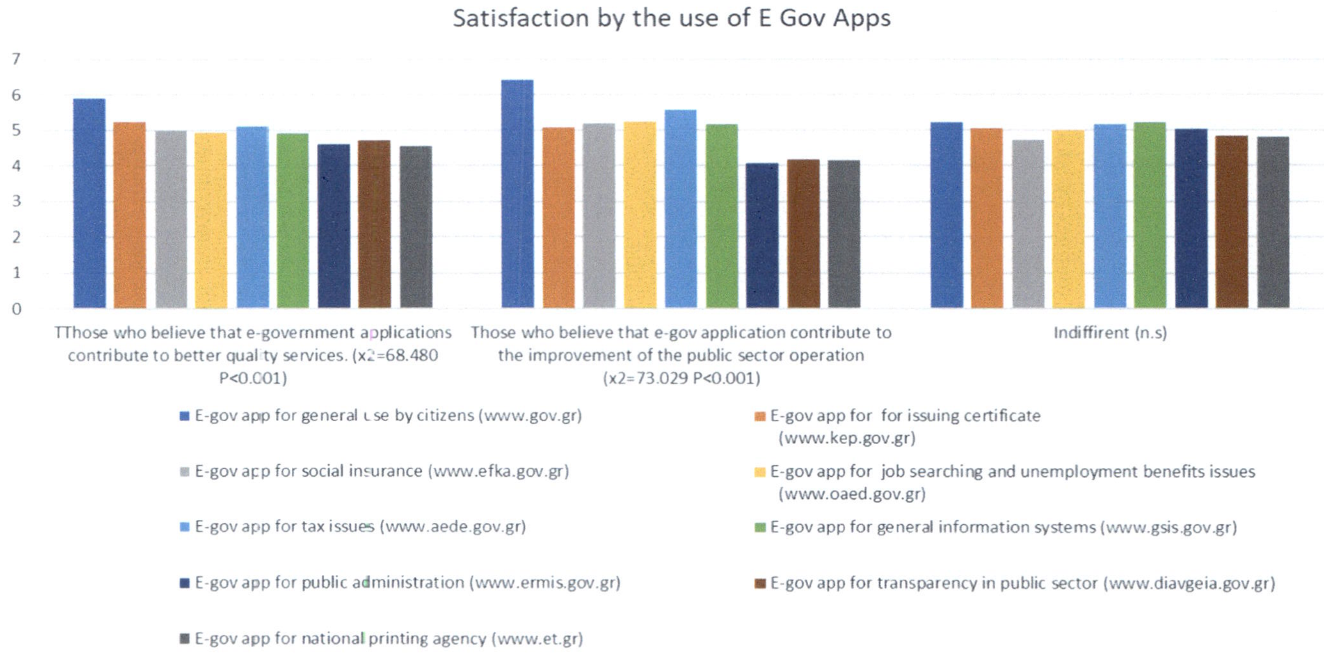

Fig. 1 Profiling each group of Greek citizens according to their preferences about the use of E Gov applications

4 Conclusions

This study provides a comprehensive understanding of Greek civil servants' attitudes towards e-government applications, revealing two main factors accounting for 63.3% of the total variance: improvement of public sector operations and better quality services. The cluster analysis classified civil servants into three distinct groups based on these attitudes.

The first group consist of those who believe that e-government applications contribute to better quality services Civil servants in this group believe that e-government applications will enhance their daily routines by addressing issues such as:

Lack of trust in the safety of personal data
Insufficient free training on e-government applications
Incomplete interoperability among public authorities' systems
Provision of incomplete services by public authorities
Use of outdated information systems
Lack of public awareness about e-government applications
Long waiting times and misunderstood instructions

Civil servants who believe that e-gov application contribute to the improvement of the public sector operation see e-government applications as contributing to:

Development of isolated and degraded areas
Control and responsibility in Public Administration
Quality improvement of services provided
Reduction of bureaucracy
Time savings
Reduction of corruption and mismanagement
Promotion of electronic democracy and transparency through electronic voting
Cost reduction of services provided
Public participation in the formulation of policies

Civil servants who consist of the group named "indifferent" do not prioritize any of the identified factors and exhibit a lack of interest in the potential benefits of e-government applications.

The demographic analysis via chi-square tests showed that gender, education and generational cohort are associated with attitudes of civil servants towards e gov apps. This study also highlighted the specific e-government applications that satisfy each group. In particular those who believe that e-government applications contribute to better quality services are predominantly female, hold a bachelor's degree are mainly millennials and are most satisfied with applications for general public use (www.gov.gr), tax issues, and issuing certificates. Those who believe that e-gov application contribute to the improvement of the public sector operation are also female and hold a bachelor's degree. This group is primarily composed of Generation X members and are most satisfied with applications for general public use, tax issues, and social insurance.. The indifferent group also holds a bachelor's degree and comprises mainly millennials and are mostly satisfied with applications for general public use, tax issues, and general information systems.

When compared to previous research, these findings resonate with those of Al-Busaidy and Weerakkody (2011) in Oman, where respondents also expressed strong positive attitudes towards e-government's efficiency and accessibility. Similarly, Saleh and Tarhini (2013) found that public sector employees in Lebanon were motivated to adopt e-government applications due to their perceived utility. However, the Greek civil servants placed a higher emphasis on reducing bureaucracy and corruption, which aligns with findings by Gökçeoğlu and Yavuz (2013) in Turkey, where transparency and accountability were major concerns. This suggests that while motivations for adopting e-government are globally influenced by efficiency and service quality, in Greece, additional factors such as bureaucracy reduction and public sector accountability play a significant role. Moreover, the findings of this study supports the arguments of other researchers that factors including relative advantage, compatibility, ease of use, perceived usefulness, trustworthiness, and demographic characteristics such as gender, education, and age have significant impact on the use of e-government services (Akman et al., 2005; Al Awadhi & Morris, 2009; Carter & Belanger, 2004; 2005; Dimitrova & Chen, 2006; Hung et al., 2006).

The current study also suggest that targeted improvements in e-government applications can address specific concerns of different civil servant groups. For instance, enhancing data security and providing comprehensive training could increase satisfaction among those focused on better quality services. On the other hand, streamlining bureaucratic processes and promoting transparency could appeal to those interested in improving public sector operations.

The demographic insights indicate a generational divide in attitudes towards e-government applications, suggesting the need for tailored communication and training strategies for different age groups. Engaging the indifferent group requires addressing their apathy and demonstrating the tangible benefits of e-government applications.

Future studies should further explore the specific barriers that hinder the adoption of e-government services, particularly among the indifferent group identified in this study. Expanding the sample to include civil servants from other sectors and regions could provide a broader understanding of the adoption patterns across the public sector. Longitudinal studies that track changes in attitudes and behaviors over time, especially as new technologies and policies are implemented, would also offer valuable insights into the evolution of e-government usage. Additionally, comparative studies between Greek civil servants and those from other EU countries could highlight whether the factors influencing adoption in Greece are unique or part of broader trends.

Overall, this study makes a distinct contribution to the international literature on e-government adoption by highlighting the nuanced perspectives of Greek civil servants, particularly their emphasis on reducing bureaucracy and corruption through e-government applications. While many studies focus on the citizen or supply-side adoption of e-government services, this research adds valuable insights into the attitudes of civil servants, a critical user group often overlooked in the literature. Moreover, the study provides empirical evidence supporting the applicability of the UTAUT model in the context of e-government adoption within the Greek public sector, thereby enriching the global discourse on how technology acceptance models can be adapted and applied in various cultural and governmental contexts.

References

Ahmed, A. M., Moreton, R., Mehdi, Q. H., & Elmaghraby, A. (2013). E-government services challenges and opportunities for developing countries: The case of Libya. In *2013 Second International Conference on Informatics & Applications (ICIA)* (pp. 133–137). IEEE.

Ajzen, I. (1985). From intentions to actions: A theory of planned behavior. In J. Kuhl & J. Beckmann (Eds.), *Action-control: From cognition to behavior* (pp. 11–39). Springer.

Akman, I., Yazici, A., Mishra, A., & Arifoglu, A. (2005). E-government: A global view and an empirical evaluation of some attributes of citizens. *Government Information Quarterly, 22*(2), 239–257.

AlAwadhi, S., & Morris, A. (2009). Factors influencing the adoption of e-government services'. *Journal of Software, 4*(6), 584–590.

Al-Busaidy, M., & Weerakkody, V. (2011). E-government services in Oman: An employee's perspective. *Electronic Government, an International Journal, 8*(2–3), 185–207.

Al-Hujran, O., Al-Debei, M., Chatfield, A., & Migdadi, M. (2015). The imperative of influencing citizen attitude toward e-government adoption and use. *Computers in Human Behavior, 53*, 189–203.

Al Hujran O. (2009). *Determinants of e-government services adoption in developing countries: A field survey and a case study*. PhD thesis. Australia: School of Information Systems and Technology, Faculty of Informatics, University of Wollongong.

Al-Shafi, S., & Weerakkody, V. (2007). Implementing and managing e-government in the State of Qatar: A citizens' perspective. *Electronic Government, an International Journal, 4*(4), 436–450.

Baldwin, J. N., Gauld, R., & Goldfinch, S. (2012). What public servants really think of e-government. *Public Management Review, 14*(1), 105–127.

Anderson J. E., Schwager P. H. (2004). SME adoption of wireless LAN technology: applying the UTAUT model. In *Proceedings of the 7th annual conference of the southern association for information systems, 7*, 39–43.

Carter, L., & Belanger, F. (2004). The influence of perceived characteristics of innovating on e-government adoption. *Electronic Journal of E-Government, 2*(1), 11–20.

Carter, L., & Belanger, F. (2005). The utilization of e-government services: Citizen trust, innovation and acceptance factors. *Information Systems Journal, 15*(1), 5–25.

Cohen, J. (1988). *Statistical power analysis for the behavioral sciences* (2nd ed., pp. 273–406). Erlbaum.

Davis, F. D. (1993). User Acceptance of Information Technology: System Characteristics, user perceptions and behavioral impacts. *International Journal of Man-Machine Studies, 38*, 475–487.

Dimitrova, D. V., & Chen, Y. C. (2006). Profiling the adopters of e-government information and services: The influence of psychological characteristics, civic mindedness, and information channels. *Social Science Computer Review, 24*(2), 172–188.

Dwivedi, Y. K., Rana, N. P., Jeyaraj, A., Clement, M., & Williams, M. D. (2019). Re-examining the unified theory of acceptance and use of technology (UTAUT): Towards a revised theoretical model. *Information Systems Frontiers, 21*, 719–734.

ELSTAT. (2020). https://www.statistics.gr/el/statistics/-/publication/SAM03/. Accessed 12 February 2022.

Faul, F., Erdfelder, E., Buchner, A., & Lang, A. (2009). Statistical power analyses using G*Power 3.1: Tests for correlation and regression analyses. *Behavior Research Methods, 41*(4), 1149–1160.

Fishbein, M., & Ajzen, I. (1975). *Belief, attitude, intention and behavior: An introduction to theory and research.* Addison-Wesley Publishing Company.

Gauld, R., Goldfinch, S., & Horsburgh, S. (2010). Do they want it? Do they use it? The 'Demand-Side' of e-Government in Australia and New Zealand. *Government Information Quarterly, 27*(2), 177–186.

Gilbert, D., Balestrini, P., & Littleboy, D. (2004). Barriers and benefits in the adoption of e-government. *International Journal of Public Sector Management, 17*(4), 286–301.

Gökçeoğlu, E. E., & Yavuz, N. (2013, October). Evaluating e-government initiatives in Turkey from the perspective of public employees: a case study and preliminary findings. In *2nd International Conference on Internet, E-Learning & Education Technologies (ICIEET 2013).*

Gounopoulos, E., Kontogiannis, S., Kazanidis, I., & Valsamidis, S. (2019). The impact of the digital divide on the adoption of e-Government in Greece. *KnE Social Sciences*, 401–411.

Hair, J. F., Anderson, R. E., Tatham, R. L., & Black, W. C. (1998). *Multivariate data analysis.* Prentice Hall Inc.

Heeks, R., & Bailur, S. (2007). Analyzing E-government research: Perspective, Philosophies, theories, methods, and practice. *Government Information Quarterly, 24*(2), 243–265.

Hung, S. Y., Chang, C. M., & Yu, T. J. (2006). Determinants of user acceptance of the e-government services: The case of online tax filing and payment system. *Government Information Quarterly, 23*(1), 97–122.

Karavasilis, I. (2012). *The electronic governance in Public Organizations' Management. The case of Greece within the framework of European Union.* PhD Thesis, Department of International and European Studies, School of Economic Studies, University of Macedonia.

Lin, J., Chan, H., & Jin, Y. (2004). *Instant messaging acceptance and use among college students.* PACIS 2004 Proceedings, 15.

Mofleh, S. I., & Wanous, M. (2008). Understanding factors influencing citizens' adoption of e-government services in the developing world: Jordan as a case study. *INFOCOMP Journal of Computer Science, 7*(2), 1–11.

Olatubosun, O., & Madhava Rao, K. S. (2012). Empirical study of the readiness of public servants on the adoption of e-government. *International Journal of Information Systems and Change Management, 6*(1), 17–37.

Oppenheim, A. N. (2000). *Questionnaire design, interviewing and attitude measurement.* Bloomsbury Publishing.

Rana, N. P., Dwivedi, Y. K., Lal, B., Williams, M. D., & Clement, M. (2017). Citizens' adoption of an electronic government system: Towards a Unified View. *Information Systems Frontiers, 19*(3), 549–568.

Reddick, C. (2005). Citizen interaction with e-government: From the streets to servers? *Government Information Quarterly, 22*(1), 38–57.

Saleh, H. A., & Tarhini, A. (2013). Public sector employees' readiness toward e-government in Lebanon: An empirical study. *Sawt Al-Jamiaa, 4*, 79–104.

Schedler, K., & Summermatter, L. (2007). Customer orientation in electronic government: Motives and effects. *Government Information Quarterly, 24*(2), 291–311.

Siardos, G. (1997). *Methodology of agricultural sociological research* (p. 367). Ziti Publications.

Tsourgiannis, L., Valsamidis, S., Karagianni, P., & Tassos, K. (2023). The use of internet and social networks during covid-19 in Greece in Economies of the Balkan and Eastern European Countries. *KnE Social Sciences*, 360–374.

Tsourgiannis, L., Delias, P., Polychronidou, P., Karasavvoglou, A., & Valsamidis, S. (2015). Profiling tourists who have holidays in the region of eastern Macedonia and Thrace in Greece. *Procedia Economics and Finance, 33*, 450–460.

Valili, A. (2007). *The attitudes of employees of citizens service centers towards computers.* Master Thesis, Panteio University.

Venkatesh, V., Morris, M. G., Davis, G. B., & Davis, F. D. (2003). User acceptance of information technology: Toward a unified view. *MIS Quarterly, 27*(3), 425–478.

Venkatesh, V., Thong, J.Y., & Xu, X. (2012). Consumer acceptance and use of information technology: Extending the unified theory of acceptance and use of technology. *MIS Quarterly*, 157–178.

The Buying Behaviour of Greek Consumers Towards Different Classes of Olive Oil

Lambros Tsourgiannis, Vasileios Zoumpoulidis, Sotirios Papadopoulos, Giannoula Florou, and Theodoros Markopoulos

Abstract Even many researchers examined product segmentation and consumer behavior in agrifood sector and mainly in wine and olive oil industry there is not an extensive examination of consumers' attitudes towards different quality olive oils. This study aims to examine the factors that affect the buying behavior of Greek consumers towards different quality olive oils and classify them into groups according to their purchasing behavior as well as to develop the demographic profile of those groups of consumers. The researchers conducted a primary survey to a random sample of Greek consumers. Principal Component Analysis, Cluster Analysis, Discriminant Analysis and non-parametric test including chi-square and Friedman test performed by the researchers.

Keywords Consumer behaviour · Olive Oil · Consumer preferences

L. Tsourgiannis (✉)
General Directorate of Internal Operation, Region of Eastern Macedonia and Thrace, Komotini, Greece
e-mail: ltsourgiannis@gmail.com

V. Zoumpoulidis · G. Florou
Department of Accounting and Finance, Campus of Kavala, Democritus University of Thrace, Kavala, Greece

S. Papadopoulos
General Directorate of Agricultural Economy, Region of Eastern Macedonia and Thrace, Komotini, Greece

T. Markopoulos
Regional District of Kavala, Region of Eastern Macedonia and Thrace, Kavala, Greece

Department of Chemistry, Campus of Kavala, Democritus University of Thrace, Kavala, Greece

I. Bartuseviciene et al. (eds.), *Building Resilience Through Digital Transformation and Sustainable Innovation*, Springer Proceedings in Business and Economics,
https://doi.org/10.1007/978-3-031-90054-9_20

1 Introduction

Product segmentation has been widely explored in marketing research, with major companies frequently categorizing their products under separate brands to address the preferences of consumers from diverse socio-economic backgrounds (Desai, 2001; Onwezen & Bartels, 2011; Salazar-Ordóñez et al., 2018a, 2018b). Numerous studies have concentrated on product differentiation, considering various food products distinguished by many factors related to price, product (James et al., 2009; Wirthgen, 2005) and health attributes (Lombardi et al., 2021; Roselli et al., 2017). Moreover, multiple authors have examined how consumers perceive food choices that vary based on country and region of origin, as well as on organic labeling (Cicia et al., 2006; Insch & Jackson, 2014; Thøgersen et al., 2017).

Consumers form numerous assessments about the foods and drinks they select each day, influenced by both deliberate reflection and automatic, habitual, or subconscious choices. Central to these reflections and choices are the quality evaluations consumers make, relying on both intrinsic and extrinsic product characteristics. Intrinsic indicators pertain to the product's own physical attributes, such as its color and flavor. In contrast, extrinsic characteristics are related but external to the product itself, including factors like brand and country of origin (Grunert, 2002). The Total Food Quality Model by Grunert (2002) offers a framework for understanding how intrinsic and extrinsic product attributes affect consumer quality perception. This model separates quality perception into stages before and after purchasing a product. Before making a purchase, consumers evaluate quality by considering various intrinsic and extrinsic attributes, shaped by their knowledge, experience, and beliefs about quality. Grunert (2002) also suggests that for most food purchases, key quality elements, such as taste, are not discernible before buying, so consumers rely on forming quality expectations. After purchase, the product then delivers a particular quality experience.

Greece is one of the top three olive oil producers in the EU, alongside Spain and Italy (Vossen, 2007; European Commission, 2024; Sandalidou et al., 2002), and holds one of the highest per capita olive oil consumption rates worldwide. Around one-third of Greece's rural population has been reported to engage in olive cultivation, with many urban households also maintaining olive groves (Sandalidou et al., 2002; Vlontzos & Duquenne, 2014). On a global scale, the olive oil market has transitioned from bulk production to a more specialized market, where olive oil is considered a high-quality product, providing insights into consumer preferences (Carzedda et al., 2021). There is no single leading factor influencing consumer preferences for olive oil (Bernabéu et al., 2020). For example, Krystallis and Ness (2005) found that Greek consumers place high value on attributes like geographic origin and organic certification, while price is among the least important factors. Italian consumers, meanwhile, also favor geographic origin, though organic attributes are less influential for them (Carzedda et al., 2021). Other factors, such as oil color, low acidity, popular brand names, sustainability, and ethical sourcing, have also been identified as key olive oil preferences (Dekhili et al., 2011; Ribeiro & Santos, 2005). In Greece, however, many households still prefer unbranded bulk olive oil sourced from friends, family, or their own production over branded alternatives (Kountouri & Prodromidis, 2017; Matsatsinis et al., 2007).

Intrinsic attributes are essential for a product's functionality and pertain to its physical characteristics. Based on prior research, this section will focus on two intrinsic qualities of olive oil: color and flavor. The color of olive oil can range from deep green to golden, primarily influenced by the levels of chlorophyll and carotenoid dyes present in the oil. These dye levels vary due to several factors, including the olive cultivar, ripeness, production region, processing methods, and storage conditions. Consequently, the color of olive oil can serve as an indicator of quality (Moyano et al., 2010).

The flavor profile of olive oil is notably distinct from that of other vegetable oils. The primary components contributing to its flavor are volatile and phenolic compounds (Aparicio & Luna, 2002). Specifically, phenolic compounds play a significant role in creating the bitter, pungent, and astringent characteristics typical of high-quality extra virgin and virgin olive oils (Boskou et al., 2006a, 2006b).

In contrast to intrinsic characteristics, extrinsic attributes do not form part of the physical product but are related to the external aspects and information associated with it. Based on previous studies, the extrinsic attributes to be examined concerning olive oil include label information, packaging, perceived health benefits, and price.

A substantial body of research has concentrated on high-quality categories, such as geographical indications (GIs) and organic olive oil. Several authors have explored the segmentation of extra-virgin olive oil categories (Dekhili et al., 2011; Roselli et al., 2017; Scarpa & Del Giudice, 2004), yet many aspects concerning hierarchically differentiated olive oil categories remain under-researched or entirely unexamined. For instance, there has been limited focus on the consumption of medium or low-end olive oils specifically. Consequently, it would be worthwhile to broaden the analysis to include olive oil, emphasizing different quality level categories and comparing the primary factors that influence consumer preferences for olive oil.

In the past few decades, various theories and models of consumer behavior have been developed. One such model, referred to as the food-related lifestyle (FRL), acts as an intermediary between values—like shopping habits, quality considerations, cooking methods, consumption contexts, and purchasing motivations such as self-fulfillment, security, and social interactions—and consumer behavior (Brunso & Grunert, 1995; Brunso et al., 2004a; 2004b; Grunert et al., 1997; Scholderer et al., 2002).

A significant amount of research on attitudes and decision-making has centered around what are known as the "cold" dimensions of consumer behavior (Simonson et al., 2001). These dimensions include the influence of beliefs on attitude formation, along with factors such as attention, perception, information gathering, learning, expertise, attribution, and decision-making rules. In contrast, the "hot" dimensions focus on the impact of emotions and mood, arousal, feelings of regret, low-involvement peripheral persuasion, hedonic consumption, conflict, and self-expressive reasons for brand preference.

Studies in social cognition and Behavioral Decision Theory (BDT) have emerged from different models of buyer behavior and communication processes (Simonson et al., 2001). Social consumer research has emphasized the communication model, which involves stages like exposure and attention, reception and encoding, cognitive response, attitude formation, intention, and behavior, investigating how judgments and attitudes are created. Meanwhile, BDT consumer research has concentrated on the decision-making model (the purchasing process), which includes stages such as problem recognition, information search, evaluation of alternatives, the purchase decision or choice, and post-purchase evaluation, with a specific focus on the factors that influence choice (Simonson et al., 2001).

The Theory of Reasoned Action (TRA) suggests that individuals weigh the consequences of their actions prior to engaging in a behavior (Ajzen & Fishbein, 1980). According to Papista and Krystallis (2012), people develop intentions to act based on their attitudes toward that behavior and the influence of social norms. However, critiques pointing out that this model did not adequately link intention to behavior (Gupta & Ogden, 2009) prompted Ajzen (1991) to create the Theory of Planned Behavior (TPB). This theory asserts that a person's intention to carry out an action is the primary immediate factor determining that action. TPB comprises three elements: (a) attitude toward the behavior, which reflects the individual's positive or negative assessment of the action; (b) subjective norm, which denotes the perceived social pressure to engage in the behavior; and (c) perceived behavioral control, referring to the individual's sense of self-efficacy or belief in their ability to perform the behavior (Papista & Krystallis, 2012). This theory has been utilized to analyze consumer decision-making processes and purchasing behaviors related to sustainable food consumption (Aetsens et al., 2009; Arvola et al., 2008; Tolouse et al., 2006; Vermeir & Verbeke, 2008).

However, the aforementioned consumer behavioral theories and models do not comprehensively address all intrinsic and extrinsic characteristics, values, marketing mix factors (including product, price, promotion, and distribution issues), and demographic aspects when examining the elements that impact consumer purchasing behavior. Instead, each theory or model focuses on only a subset of these factors.

As a result, the researchers have adapted and modified the conceptual model developed by Tsourgiannis et al. (2015) to create a recognizable framework that incorporates the intrinsic and extrinsic characteristics, values, marketing mix factors (such as product, pricing, promotional, and distribution issues), and demographic characteristics identified in the literature (see Fig. 1).

The null research hypotheses that this study examine are:

Ho1: "Greek consumers cannot be classified into similar groups according to their buying behaviour towards different categories of olive oil"

Ho2: "The attitudes of the Greek consumers towards olive oil characteristics are not significantly related to their buying behaviour towards different categories of olive oil"

Ho3: "The marketing outlet utilisation and the different olive oil categories consumers prefer are not related to any particular identified buying behaviour"

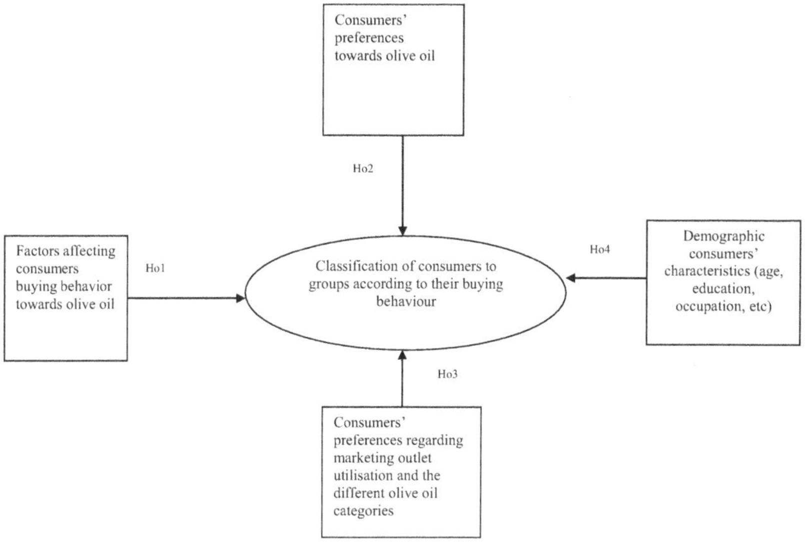

Fig. 1 The conceptual model

Ho4: "The demographic and personal characteristics of Greek consumers are not significantly related to their buying behaviour towards different categories of olive oil"

2 Applied Methodology

2.1 Survey Procedure

The survey aimed to gather data to identify the factors influencing consumer buying behavior towards olive oil in the Greek region of East Macedonia and Thrace. The focus was on Greek consumers who purchase olive oil. Data was collected through an interview survey, as consumers in this region are familiar with this research method and their educational level supports its use (Oppenheim, 2000). This method is also widely used in studying consumer buying behavior (Arvanitoyiannis & Krystallis, 2005; Fotopoulos & Krystallis, 2002). High costs ruled out large postal or telephone surveys, and since many consumers lack internet access, online surveys were unsuitable for obtaining a representative sample of the general population.

To capture consumers' true preferences, the survey was conducted at locations where purchase decisions are made, such as supermarkets. Interviews were held throughout the day to minimize shopping time-related bias (Krystallis & Chryssohoidis, 2005). Specifically, 25% of interviews took place between 9:00–15:00 on weekdays (Monday–Friday), another 25% between 15:00–21:00 on weekdays, and

50% on Saturdays (9:00–19:00). This schedule was developed based on a pilot survey indicating respondents' shopping days and times.

A systematic stratified sampling method was employed to ensure that the findings could be generalized beyond the surveyed sample. As Errington (1985) noted, random selection from the larger population is essential for making valid generalizations. Therefore, consumers were randomly selected, with interviewers approaching every sixth customer over 20 years old entering the survey area. The sample comprised 460 consumers, a size deemed reasonable relative to the area's total population and consistent with sample sizes used in similar Greek studies on consumer behavior towards food purchases (Botonaki & Tsakiridou, 2004; Tsakiridou et al., 2008; Tzimitra-Kalogianni et al., 1999).

The sample's representativeness was validated by comparing the proportion of consumers who reported buying extra virgin olive oil with those from the pilot survey, following Siardos' (1997) methodology. In the pilot survey, 92% of consumers indicated they bought extra virgin olive oil at least once. To ensure representativeness, the sample size needed was 265 consumers (with $z = 3$ and $d = 5\%$). The researchers chose a sample size of 520 consumers, twice what was needed, to align with other studies. As the proportion of consumers buying extra virgin olive oil in this sample remained about 92%, the sample was considered representative.

2.2 Questionnaire Design

Researchers identified the factors influencing consumer behavior towards olive oil through a literature review. They then designed a questionnaire tailored to meet the research objectives, which was pre-tested by academics, food marketing experts, and consumers. Subsequently, a pilot survey was conducted in January 2023 with 50 consumers. The pilot survey indicated that no modifications were necessary, allowing the main survey to proceed in the spring of 2023 as planned.

2.3 Statistical Methodology

Multivariate analysis techniques were applied to the data from 460 consumers who purchase olive oil to extract key information from their responses. This analysis was conducted in three stages. First, principal component analysis (PCA) was used to identify the variables that accounted for the maximum variance in the data, reducing it to a smaller number of uncorrelated variables (components). The appropriateness of the data for subsequent factor analysis was checked using the anti-image correlation matrix, Bartlett's test of sphericity, and the measure of sampling adequacy (MSA). Variables with a high proportion of large absolute values of anti-image correlations and MSA less than 0.5 were removed before analysis conducted. PCA condensed the key attitude variables related to various aspects of consumer behavior towards olive oil into a smaller set of underlying factors (or consumption dimensions). An orthogonal rotation (varimax method) was performed, and the factors were determined using the standard criteria of eigenvalue = 1, scree test, and percentage of variance (Hair et al., 2010). Different trial rotations were conducted to compare factor interpretability.

The factor scores were subsequently analyzed through cluster analysis to categorize consumers with similar score patterns into distinct clusters based on their purchasing behavior. Both hierarchical and non-hierarchical methods were employed, in accordance with the guidelines established by Hair et al. (2010) and Karelakis et al. (2011), to create a typology of consumer buying behavior. A non-parametric Kruskal–Wallis one-way ANOVA was conducted to validate the cluster solutions by assessing whether variables not included in the cluster analysis showed significant differences among the identified clusters. Additionally, quadratic discriminant analysis was utilized to evaluate how accurately the primary consumption dimensions derived from factor analysis could predict and differentiate cluster membership. Statistical tests, grounded in the results of the multivariate statistical techniques (including factor, cluster, and discriminant analysis), were employed to test the five hypotheses outlined in the earlier section.

3 Results

3.1 Consumers' Buying Behaviour and Attitudes Towards Different Categories of Olive Oil

Principal component and factor analyses with varimax rotation were conducted to identify key consumption preference variables. The number of factors was determined using the latent root criterion (eigenvalue = 1), the scree plot test, and the percentage of variance explained (refer to Table 1). To enhance factor interpretability, multiple trial rotations were performed, guided by the recommendations of Tabachnick and Fidell (1989) and Hair et al. (1998).

PCA identified three factors that affect consumers' preferences towards different categories of olive oil (Table 2).

In the next stage, hierarchical and non-hierarchical clustering methods were employed to develop a typology of consumer buying behavior in the Region of East Macedonia and Thrace, following the methodologies of Helsen and Green (1991) and Hair et al. (2010). The cluster analysis was performed on 460 observations, as no outliers were identified.

It identified three groups of consumers that were named according to their buying behaviour patterns towards different categories of olive oil (Table 3). These are: (a) the "product orientated" consumers, (b) indifferent and (c) the "marketing orientated" consumers.

Table 1 Results of principal component analysis regarding consumers buying attitudes

Component	Eigenvalues	% of Variance	Cumulative %
1	**7.688**	**42.711**	**42.711**
2	**2.515**	**13.970**	**56.681**
3	**2.043**	**11.350**	**68.031**
4	0.995	5.530	73.561
5	0.875	4.859	78.420
6	0.706	3.925	82.344
7	0.585	3.248	85.593
8	0.510	2.833	88.426
9	0.420	2.332	90.758
10	0.396	2.203	92.961
11	0.275	1.530	94.490
12	0.258	1.433	95.924
13	0.196	1.091	97.015
14	0.165	0.918	97.933
15	0.154	0.857	98.790
16	0.103	0.574	99.363
17	0.075	0.415	99.778
18	0.040	0.222	100.000

KMO MSA = 0.737
Bartlett test of Sphericity = 3519.330, $P < 0.001$.

In particular, the "product orientated" consumers comprise 33% of the sample. These consumers mainly are influenced in their buying behaviour towards olive oil by taste (rich, spicy, bitter of fruity), green colour, Greek origin, nutrition value, extra virgin certification, certification of PDO,GIs or organic product, smell, organoleptic characteristics, and acidity.

On the other hand, the "indifferent consists of the 19% of the sample. These consumers although they purchase olive oil they are not influenced by any particular factor.

The "marketing orientated" consumers comprise the 48% of the sample and are influenced in their buying decisions towards olive oil by are mainly influenced by attractive packaging, advertisement, standardized product, promotion and branding of the product. They also pay attention to product orientated issues including rich taste, Greek origin, Nutrition value, Extra virgin certification, certification of PDO or GIs, green colour, certification of organic product, smell, organoleptic characteristics.

Furthermore, discriminant analysis was performed to assess the prediction of group membership using the predictors derived from the factor analysis. Initially, the normality of the key strategic dimensions was examined. The Box's M test statistic (Box $M = 95.053$, approx $F = 15.730$, $P < 0.001$) revealed that the variance–covariance matrices were violated.

Table 2 Main factors affecting consumers preferences towards olive oil

Key consumption dimensions	Factor loadings
Product characteristics	
Rich taste	0.868
Greek origin	0.852
Nutrition value	0.815
Extra virgin certification	0.74
Certification of PDO or GIs	0.693
Green colour	0.681
Certification of organic product	0.564
Smell	0.563
Organoleptic characteristics	0.506
Marketing issues	
Attractive packaging	0.885
Advertisement	0.858
Standardized product	0.838
Promotion	0.774
Branding	0.716
Taste	
Spicy taste	0.917
Bitter taste	0.846
Acidity	0.8
Fruity Taste	0.584

Table 3 Characteristics of the three consumers' groups

Key consumption dimensions	Product orientated	Indifferent	Marketing orientated	P
Product characteristics	0.23920	−1.59589	0.48978	0.0001
Marketing issues	−1.00304	−0.04431	0.70202	0.0001
Taste	0.44211	−0.32401	−0.16889	0.0001
Number of consumers (n = 460)	150	90	220	

The summary of the cross validation classification derived by the quadratic discriminant analysis is shown in Table 4

Thus, the three consumption dimensions could accurately predict and discriminate consumers' into group membership.

Therefore, the hypothesis *Ho1: "Greek consumers cannot be classified into similar groups according to their buying behaviour towards different categories of olive oil* may be rejected.

Table 4 Summary of classification with cross-validation

Actual classification	Predicted classification		
	Product orientated	Indifferent	Marketing orientated
Product orientated	148	0	0
Indifferent	0	90	0
Marketing orientated	2	0	218
Total N	150	90	220
N correct	148	90	220
Proportion of Correct Classification	98.6%	100%	99%
N = 460	N correct = 458	Proportion Correct = 99.5%	

3.2 Consumers Attiutudes Towards Different Categories of Olive Oil

In the next stage, chi-square analysis performed to identify the attitudes of each group of consumers towards olive oil. In particular, the analysis indicated (Table 4) that "product orientated" consumers mainly buy the common category of olive oil (extra virgin of known brand or private labelled). The vast majority do not buy plastic packages of 4 or 5 lt, do not prefer organic, PDO of GIs or ultra premium olive oil. Most of the indifferent consumers prefer to buy the basic category of olive oil and mainly in cans of 20lt whilst the vast majority of the consumers who prefer, organic, PDO/GIs or ultra premium category of extra virgin olive oil are mainly marketing orientated.

Thus hypothesis, *Ho2: The attitudes of the Greek consumers towards olive oil are not significantly related to their buying behaviour towards different categories of olive oil"* maybe rejected.

3.3 Marketing Outlet Utilisation and Different Olive Oil Categories Consumers Prefer

In their effort to identify which marketing outlet and category of olive oil each consumer group prefers, the researchers conducted a chi-square analysis. The results (Table 6) revealed that most product-oriented and marketing-oriented consumers do not produce their own olive oil, with the marketing-oriented group preferring to buy their olive oil from supermarkets. Conversely, the majority of indifferent consumers obtain their olive oil directly from producers.

Furthermore, as shown in Table 7, the vast majority of consumers who prefer organic, PDO/GIs, or ultra-premium categories of extra virgin olive oil are predominantly marketing-oriented.

Table 5 Consumers' attitudes towards different categories of olive oil

Consumer's preferences		Product orientated		Indifferent		Marketing orientated	
Buy labeled extra virgin olive oil in glass bottle	NO	n.s	100%	× 2 = 5.000 (P < 0.05)	**67%**	× 2 = 14.545 (P < 0.001)	68%
	YES		0%		33%		27%
Buy labeled extra virgin olive oil in plastic bottle of 1 or 2 lt	NO	n.s	53%	n.s	44%	× 2 = 8.182 (P < 0.01)	64%
	YES		47%		56%		36%
Buy labeled extra virgin olive oil in package of 4 or 5 lt	NO	× 2 = 16.333 (P < 0.001)	**73%**	n.s	44%	× 2 = 22.727 (P < 0.001)	27%
	YES		27%		56%		**73%**
Buy basic category olive oil (not labelled, direct from producer) in 20lt cans	NO	n.s	53%	× 2 = 5.000 (P < 0.05)	33%	× 2 = 8.182 (P < 0.01)	64%
	YES		47%		**67%**		36%
Buy common category of extra virgin olive oil	NO	× 2 = 27.000 (P < 0.001)	20%	× 2 = 5.000 (P < 0.05)	67%	× 2 = 8.182 (P < 0.01)	64%
	YES		**80%**		33%		36%
Buy organic extra virgin olive oil	NO	n.s	53%	× 2 = 5.000 (P < 0.05)	67%	× 2 = 8.182 (P < 0.01)	36%
	YES		47%		33%		64%
Buy extra virgin olive oil PDO / GI	NO	× 2 = 8.333 (P < 0.001)	67%	n.s	56%	× 2 = 22.727 (P < 0.001)	27%
	YES		33%		44%		**73%**
Buy ultra premium olive oil	NO	× 2 = 27.000 (P < 0.001)	80%	n.s	44%	× 2 = 8.182 (P < 0.01)	64%
	YES		20%		56%		36%
Replace oilive oil with seed oil	NO	n.s	53%	n.s	56%	× 2 = 8.182 (P < 0.01)	64%
	YES		47%		44%		36%

Hence the hypotheses *H3: "The marketing outlet utilisation and the different olive oil categories consumers prefer are not related to any particular identified buying behaviour"* maybe accepted.

Table 6 Marketing outlet utilisation

		Product orientated		Indifferent		Marketing orientated	
Direct from farmers/ producers	NO	n.s	60%	× 2 = 5.000 (P < 0.05)	33%	n.s	59%
	YES		40%		**67%**		41%
Supermarkets	NO	n.s	47%	n.s	56%	× 2 = 8.112 (P < 0.05	36%
	YES		53%		44%		**64%**
Own production	NO	× 2 = 27.000 (P < 0.001)	**80%**	n.s	56%	× 2 = 32.725 (P < 0.001)	**77%**
	YES		20%		44%		32%

Table 7 The different olive oil categories consumers prefer

Preferred categories of olive oil			Product orientated	Indifferent	Marketing orientated
Buy basic category olive oil	NO	n.s	33,30%	23,80%	42,90%
	YES		32%	16%	52%
Buy common category of extra virgin olive oil	NO	n.s	34,40%	15,60%	50%
	YES		28,60%	28,60%	42,90%
Buy organic extra virgin olive oil	NO	× 2 = 11.233 (P < 0.01)	37,5%	25,00%	37,50%
	YES		27%	14%	**59%**
Buy extra virgin olive oil PDO / GI	NO	× 2 = 30.105 (P < 0.001)	47,60%	23,80%	28,60%
	YES		20%	16%	**64%**
Buy ultra premium olive oil	NO	× 2 = 15.906 (P < 0.001)	40%	13,30%	46,70%
	YES		19%	31%	**50%**

3.4 Profiling Each Consumer Group According to Consumers' Characteristics.

A one-sample chi-square test was conducted for each consumer group to develop profiles based on their personal characteristics and buying behavior towards olive oil. These profiles are detailed in Table 8. According to Table 8, product-oriented consumers are primarily female, high school graduates, and private employees. Indifferent consumers are also mainly female, high school graduates, members of Generation Y, and private employees. In contrast, the majority of marketing-oriented consumers are mostly female, university graduates, belong to Generation Y, and are self-employed or business owners.

Therefore the hypothesis *H4: The demographic and personal characteristics of Greek consumers are not significantly related to their buying behaviour towards different categories of olive oil* maybe accepted.

Table 8 Profile of each consumer group regarding consumers' personal characteristics

Demographic characteristics		Product orientated		Indifirent		Marketing orientated	
Gender	Male	× 2 = 40.333 (P < 0.001)	13%	× 2 = 13.889 (P < 0.001)	22%	× 2 = 90.909 (P < 0.001)	23%
	Female		**87%**		**78%**		**73%**
Education	High School	× 2 = 51,667 (P < 0.001)	**53%**	× 2 = 13.333 (P < 0.001)	**44%**	× 2 = 37.273 (P < 0.001)	18%
	Job Trainning		7%		11%		18%
	University Degree		7%		33%		**50%**
	Postgraduate Degree		33%		11%		14%
Generation	Gen Z	n.S	20%	× 2 = 15.000 (P < 0.001)	11%	× 2 = 19.091 (P < 0.001)	27%
	Gen Y		**60%**		33%		**41%**
	Gen X		13%		**44%**		18%
	BabyBoomers		7%		11%		14%
Occupation	Private Employees	× 2 = 46.333 (P < 0.001)	**40%**	× 2 = 23.889 (P < 0.001)	**56%**	× 2 = 10.455 (P < 0.05)	32%
	Civil Servants		33%		18%		18%
	Free Lincenced / Businessmen		13%		11%		**36%**
	Students		11%		11%		9%
	Retired		3%		4%		5%

4 Discussion—Conclusions

This study provides evidence on the factors determining the intention to purchase different categories of olive oil and offers useful insights for local policymakers to promote the demand for organic wine in the South E.U. Region, particularly in the Region of Eastern Macedonia and Thrace in Greece. The results show a significant association between buying behavior and the factors, attitudes, marketing outlets utilization, and personal characteristics that influence the choice of various olive oil categories.

Three distinct consumer groups were identified based on their buying behavior towards organic wine: "product-oriented," "indifferent," and "marketing-oriented" consumers. Each group exhibits unique preferences and characteristics, which were analyzed using chi-square tests to understand their attitudes and behaviors towards olive oil. Product-oriented consumers prioritize intrinsic characteristics of olive oil, such as taste, color, origin, nutritional value, certifications (extra virgin, PDO, GIs, organic), smell, organoleptic characteristics, and acidity. They mainly purchase extra virgin olive oil from known brands or private labels and generally avoid plastic packaging and higher-end products like ultra-premium or organic olive oil. These consumers are primarily female, high school graduates, and private employees. Indifferent consumers do not exhibit strong preferences or influences in their olive oil purchasing decisions and tend to buy basic categories of olive oil in large quantities, such as 20-L cans. This group is also predominantly female, high school graduates, members of Generation Y, and private employees. Marketing-oriented consumers respond strongly to attractive packaging, advertising, standardization, promotions, and branding, while also valuing product-oriented characteristics. They mainly purchase from supermarkets and are primarily female, university graduates, members of Generation Y, and self-employed or business owners.

The findings from the study on consumer preferences for olive oil reveal distinct segments: product-oriented, indifferent, and marketing-oriented consumers. These segments align well with existing marketing and consumer behavior theories, providing a nuanced understanding of how different factors influence consumer decisions.

Product-oriented consumers prioritize intrinsic chacteristics of olive oil. They predominantly purchase extra virgin olive oil from known brands or private labels. Indifferent consumers' lack of strong preferences suggests a minimal influence of attitude and social norms, indicating low involvement and limited perceived behavioral control in their decision-making process. Furthermore, their focus on practical aspects like quantity and convenience aligns with the cold aspects of consumer behavior, which include attention to utilitarian factors and decision rules. Marketing-oriented consumers' behavior reflects the communications model stages, such as exposure/attention and cognitive response. Their responsiveness to marketing efforts highlights the importance of effective communication in influencing their attitudes and intentions. Moreover, their sensitivity to marketing aspects and social influences aligns with the role of subjective norms and perceived behavioral control in shaping their purchasing intentions. Besides, the influence of affect, mood, and self-expressive motives in marketing-oriented consumers' decisions reflects the hot aspects of consumer behavior, indicating the role of emotions and hedonic consumption in their preferences.

This study supports the findings of Grunert (2005), Brunsø and Grunert (1995), Simonson et al. (2001), Ajzen and Fishbein (1980), Ajzen (1991), Desai (2001), Onwezen and Bartels (2011), Salazar-Ordóñez et al. (2018a, 2018b), Wirthgen (2005), James et al. (2009), Roselli et al., (2017), Lombardi et al. (2021), Insch and Jackson (2014), and Thøgersen et al. (2017).

The segmentation of consumers based on their preferences provides valuable insights for developing targeted marketing strategies. Specifically, for product-oriented consumers, marketers should emphasize intrinsic characteristics such as taste, nutritional value, and certifications in marketing campaigns and highlight the origin and organoleptic properties of olive oil to cater to their detailed evaluation criteria. Marketing strategies for indifferent consumers should focus on practical aspects such as price, convenience, and bulk purchasing options, and offer promotions that emphasize value for money to appeal to their utilitarian approach. For marketing-oriented consumers, strategies should leverage attractive packaging, compelling advertisements, and strong brand presence, as well as integrate both intrinsic qualities and marketing tactics to appeal to their comprehensive preference profile.

The study's findings, viewed through the lens of various consumer behavior theories, provide a deeper understanding of the distinct segments within the olive oil market.

By aligning marketing strategies with the specific preferences and decision-making processes of each segment, marketers can more effectively meet consumer needs and drive market success. Further research could explore under-investigated areas, such as medium or low-end olive oil consumption, to enhance the comprehensive understanding of consumer behavior across different quality levels.

References

Aetsens, J., Verbeke, W., Mondelaers, K., & Van Huylenbroeck, G. (2009). Personal determinants of organic food consumption: A review. *British Food Journal, 111*(10), 1140–1167.

Ajzen, I. (1991). The theory of planned behaviour. *Organizational Behavior and Human Decision Processes, 50*, 179–211.

Ajzen, I., & Fishbein, M. (1980). Understanding attitudes and predicting social behaviour, Prentice Hall, N.J. *Englewood Cliffs*.

Aparicio, R., & Luna, G. (2002). Characterisation of monovarietal virgin olive oils. *European Journal of Lipid Science and Technology, 104*(9–10), 614–627.

Arvanitoyiannis, I., & Krystallis, A. (2005). Consumers' beliefs, attitudes and intentions towards GM foods, from the "Perceived Safety vs Benefits" point of view. *Applied Biotechnology Food Science and Policy, 40*, 343–360.

Arvola, A., Vassalo, M., Dean, M., & Lampila, P. (2008). Predicting intentions to purchase organic food: The role of affective and moral attitudes in the theory of planned behaviour. *Appetite, 50*, 443–454.

Bernabéu, R., Oliveira, F., Rabadán, A., & Díaz, M. (2020). Influence of ethnocentrism on consumer preference patterns: The case of olive oil in Portugal. *New Medit, 19*, 55–68.

Boskou, D., Blekas, G., & Tsimidou, M. (2006a). Olive oil composition. In D. Boskou (Ed.), *Olive oil chemistry and technology* (pp. 41–72). AOCS Press.

Boskou, D., Tsimidou, M., & Blekas, G. (2006b). Polar phenolic compounds. In D. Boskou (Ed.), *Olive oil chemistry and technology* (pp. 73–92). AOCS Press.

Botonaki, A., & Tsakiridou, E. (2004). Consumers response evaluation of a Greek quality wine. *Food Economics—Acta Agriculturae Scandinavica, Section C, 1*(2), 91–98.

Brunso, K., & Grunert, K. G. (1995). Development and testing of a cross-culturally valid instrument: Food-related life style. *Advances in Consumer Research, 22*, 475–480.

Brunso, K., Scholderer, J., & Grunert, K. G. (2004a). Clossing the gap between values and behaviour—A means—End theory of lifestyle. *Journal of Business Research, 57*, 665–670.

Brunso, K., Scholderer, J., & Grunert, K. G. (2004b). Testing relationships between values and food related lifestyle: Results from two European countries. *Appetite, 43*, 195–205.

Carzedda, M., Gallenti, G., Troiano, S., Cosmina, M., Marangon, F., de Luca, P., Pegan, G., & Nassivera, F. (2021). Consumer preferences for origin and organic attributes of extra virgin olive oil: A choice experiment in the Italian market. *Foods, 10*(994).

Cicia, G., Del Giudice, T., Ramunno, I., & Tagliafiero, C. (2006, June 29–July 2). Splitting consumer's willingness to pay premium price for organic products over the main purchase motivations. In *98th EAAE Seminar "Marketing Dynamics within the Global Trading system: New Perspectives'"*. Chania, Crete, Greece.

Chousou, C., Tsakiridou, E., & Mattas, K. (2017). Valuing consumer perceptions of olive oil authenticity. *Journal of International Food and Agribusiness Marketing, 30*, 1–16.
Dekhili, S., Sirieix, L., & Cohen, E. (2011). How consumers choose olive oil: The importance of origin cues. *Food Quality and Preference, 22*(8), 757–762.
Desai, P. S. (2001). Quality segmentation in spatial markets: When does cannibalization affect product line design? *Marketing Science, 20*(3), 265–283.
Errington, A. (1985). *Delegation on farms: An examination of organisation structure and managerial control on farms in the vale of the white horse.* PhD Thesis University of Reading.
European Commission. (2024). *Market situation in the olive oil and table olives sectors.* https://ec.europa.eu/info/sites/info/files/food-farming-fisheries/plants_and_plant_products/documents/market-situation-olive-oil-table-olives_en.pdf. Accessed on 17 April 2024.
Fotopoulos, C., & Krystallis, A. (2002). *Historical evolution of consumer's behaviour and qualitive marketing studies.* Stamulis Edition.
Grunert, K., Brunso, K., & Bisp, S. (1997). Food-related lifestyle: Development of a cross-culturally valid instrument for market surveillance. In L.R. Kahle & L. Chiagouris (Eds.), *Values, Lifestyles, and Psychographics* (pp. 337–354). Mahwah, NJ: Lawrence Erlbaum.
Grunert, K. G. (2002). Current issues in the understanding of consumer food choice. *Trends in Food Science and Technology, 13*, 275–285.
Gupta, S., & Ogden, D. T. (2009). To buy or not to buy? A social dilemma perspective on green buying. *Journal of Consumer Marketing, 26*, 376–391.
Hair, J., Anderson, R. E., Tatham, L. R., & Black, C. W. (2010). *Multivariate data analysis* (7th ed.). Pearson Prentice Hall.
Hair, J. F., Anderson, R. E., Tatham, R. L. & Black, W. C. (1998). *Multivariate data analysis.* Prentice Hall Inc, New Jersey.
Helsen, K. & Green, P. E. (1991). A computational study of replicated clustering with an application to market segmentation. *Decision Sciences, 22*, 1124–1141.
Insch, A., & Jackson, E. (2014). Consumer understanding and use of country-of-origin in food choice. *British Food Journal, 116*(1), 62–79.
James, J. S., Rickard, B. J., & Rossman, W. J. (2009). *Product differentiation and market segmentation in applesauce: Using a choice experiment to assess the value of organic, local and nutrition attributes* (Working Paper). Department of Applied Economics and Management, Cornell University, Ithaca, New York, NY.
Karelakis, C., Polymeros, K., & Kaimakoudi, E. (2011). Analyzing managerial perceptions towards the performance determinants in the fisheries sector. *Fisheries Research, 110*(2), 244–251.
Kountouri, I., & Prodromidis, P. (2017). Estimating household demand for olive oil in Greece. *South Eastern European Journal of Economics, 15*, 33–45.
Krystallis, A., & Chryssohoidis, G. (2005). Consumers willingness to pay (WTP) for organic food: Factors that affect it and variation per organic product type. *British Food Journal, 107*(5), 320–343.
Krystallis, A., & Ness, M. (2005). Consumer preferences for quality foods from a south European perspective: A conjoint analysis implementation on Greek olive oil. *International Food and Agribusiness Management Review, 8*(2), 62–91.
Lombardi, A., Carlucci, D., Cavallo, C., De Gennaro, B., Del Giudice, T., Giannoccaro, G., Paparella, A., Roselli, L., Vecchio, R., & Cicia, G. (2021). Do consumers understand health claims on extra-virgin olive oil? *Food Research International, 143*, 110267.
Matsatsinis, N. F., Grigoroudis, E., & Samaras, A. P. (2007). Comparing distributors' judgments to buyers' preferences: A consumer value analysis in the Greek olive oil market. *International Journal of Retail and Distribution Management, 35*, 342–362.
Meerza, S. I. A., & Gustafson, C. R. (2019). Does prior knowledge of food fraud affect consumer behavior? Evidence from an incentivized economic experiment. *PLoS ONE, 14*, Article e0225113.

Moyano, M. J., & Heredia, F. J. (2010). Meléndez-Martínez AJ (2010) The color of olive oils: The pigments and their likely health benefits and visual and instrumental methods of analysis. *Comprehensive Reviews in Food Science and Food Safety, 9*(3), 278–291.

Onwezen, M. C., & Bartels, J. (2011). Which perceived characteristics make product innovations appealing to the consumer? A study on the acceptance of fruit innovations using cross-cultural consumer segmentation. *Appetite, 57*(1), 50–58.

Oppenheim, A. N. (2000). *Questionnaire design, interviewing and attitude measurement.* Continuum.

Papista, E., & Krystallis A. (2012). Investigating the types of value and cost of green brands: Proposition of a conceptual framework. *Journal of Business Ethics*, June 2013, 1–18.

Ribeiro, J. C., & Santos, J. F. (2005). Portuguese olive oil and the price of regional products: Does designation of origin really matter? *Tékhne Polytechnical Studies Review, 2*, 61–76.

Roselli, L., Clodoveo, M. L., Corbo, F., & De Gennaro, B. (2017). Are health claims a useful tool to segment the category of extra-virgin olive oil? Threats and opportunities for the Italian olive oil supply chain. *Trends in Food Science and Technology, 68*, 176–181.

Salazar-Ordóñez, M., Rodríguez-Entrena, M., Cabrera, E. R., & Henseler, J. (2018a). Survey data on consumer behaviour in olive oil markets: The role of product knowledge and brand credence. *Data in Brief, 18*, 1750–1757.

Salazar-Ordóñez, M., Rodríguez-Entrena, M., Cabrera, E. R., & Henseler, J. (2018b). Understanding product differentiation failures: The role of product knowledge and brand credence in olive oil markets. *Food Quality and Preference, 68*, 146–155.

Sandalidou, E., Baourakis, G., & Siskos, Y. (2002). Customers' perspectives on the quality of organic olive oil in Greece. *British Food Journal, 104*, 391–406.

Santosa, M., Clow, E. J., Sturzenberger, N. D., & Guinard, J. X. (2013). Knowledge, beliefs, habits and attitudes of California consumers regarding extra virgin olive oil. *Food Research International, 54*(2), 2104–2111.

Scholderer, J., Brunso, K., & Grunert, K. G. (2002). Means—end chain theory of, lifestyle—A replication in the U.K. *Advances in Consumer Research, 29*, 551–557.

Scarpa, R., & Del Giudice, T. (2004). Market segmentation via mixed logit: Extra-virgin olive oil in urban Italy. *Journal of Agricultural and Food Industrial Organization, 2*(1), 1–20.

Siardos, G. (1997). *Methodology of agricultural sociological research.* Ziti Publications.

Simonson, I., Carmon, Z., Dhar, R., Drolet, A., & Nowlis, S. (2001). Consumer research: In search of identity. *Annual Review of Psychology, 52*, 249–275.

Tabachnick, B. G., & Fidell, L. S. (1989). *Using multivariate statistics.* HarperCollins.

Thøgersen, J., Pedersen, S., Paternoga, M., Schwendel, E., & Aschemann-Witzel, J. (2017). How important is country-of-origin for organic food consumers? A review of the literature and suggestions for future research. *British Food Journal, 119*(3), 542–557.

Thompson, G. D., & Kidwell, J. (1998). Explaining the choice of organic produce: Cosmetic defects, prices, and consumer preferences. *American Journal of Agricultural Economics, 80*, 277–287.

Tolouse, N. O., Shiu, E., & Shaw, D. (2006). In search of fair trade: Ethical consumer decision making in France. *International Journal of Consumer Studies, 30*, 502–514.

Tsakiridou, E., Boutsouki, C., Zotos, Y., & Mattas, K. (2008). Attitudes and behaviour towards organic products: An exploratory study. *International Journal of Retail and Distribution Management, 36*(2), 158–175.

Tsourgiannis, L., Loizou, E., Karasavoglou, A., Tsourgiannis, C. A., & Valsamidis, S. (2015). Consumers' buying behaviour towards local food in Greece during economic depression period. *International Journal of Strategic Innovative Marketing, 2*, 32–48.

Tzimitra-Kalogianni, I., Papadaki-Klavdianou, A., Alexani, A., & Tsakiridou, E. (1999). Wine routes in Northern Greece: Consumer perceptions. *British Food Journal, 101*(11), 884–892.

Vermeir, I., & Verbeke, W. (2008). Sustainable food consumption among young adults in Belgium: Theory of planned behaviour and the role of confidence and values. *Ecological Economics, 64*, 542–553.

Vlontzos, G., & Duquenne, M. N. (2014). Assess the impact of subjective norms of consumers' behaviour in the Greek olive oil market. *Journal of Retailing and Consumer Services, 21*, 148–157.

Vossen, P. (2007). (2007) Olive oil: History, production, and characteristics of the world's classic oils. *HortScience, 42*, 1093–1100.

Wirthgen, A. (2005). Consumer, retailer, and producer assessments of product differentiation according to regional origin and process quality. *Agribusiness, 21*(2), 191–211.

The manufacturer's authorised representative in the EU is Springer Nature Customer Service Centre GmbH, Europaplatz 3, 69115 Heidelberg, Germany. If you have any concerns regarding our products, please contact ProductSafety@springernature.com

Printed and bound by CPI Group (UK) Ltd, Croydon, CR0 4YY
01/10/2026
02225922-0010